The German Enlightenment
and the Rise
of Historicism

The German Enlightenment and the Rise of Historicism

By

Peter Hanns Reill

University of California Press
Berkeley · Los Angeles · London
1975

University of California Press
Berkeley and Los Angeles, California

University of California Press, Ltd.
London, England

To my mother and in memory of my father

Contents

Preface   ix

Introduction   1

I   The Crisis of Historical Consciousness at the Dawn of the Aufklärung   9

II   Form and Goal of the Aufklärung's Idea of History   31

III   The Aufklärung's Image of the Future and Its Concept of Historical Development   48

IV   Human Origins and Historical Development   75

V   Historical Causation   100

VI   Categories of Causal Explanation I: Climate, Geography, and Political, Social, and Economic Structure   127

VII   Categories of Causal Explanation II: Spirit, Customs, Values, and Ideas   161

VIII   Structure of Development and Appreciation of the Unique   190

Conclusion   214

Notes   221

Bibliography   277

Index   297

Preface

An anonymous wit once described intellectual history as the study of first-rate minds by second-rate minds. A kernel of truth is buried beneath the witticism's obvious exaggeration. Intellectual history has often been the last stronghold of history written on a heroic scale. In this form it provides us with heady stuff; it jumps from mountain peak to mountain peak without pausing to inhale the air the rest of us mortals consume. These wanderings along the heights, as Friedrich Meinecke described them, are exhilarating. Yet they distort as much as they reveal. Once in a while we should descend to lesser heights where the terrain is less spectacular but impressive in its own way. This study is such an attempt. I have tried to survey the broad landscape of eighteenth-century German intellectual history from the perspective of its developing historical consciousness. In so doing, I have turned to a group of thinkers either neglected or maligned and have tried to show how their combined efforts enabled later and more famous German thinkers to soar to the heights for which they are justly remembered. As such, this study will probably annoy those who prefer the peaks or those who wish to concentrate solely upon the base. My only hope is that I have made a case for taking the efforts of these thinkers seriously. My attempted reinterpretation of the German Enlightenment questions those who see the Enlightenment as essentially cosmopolitan, those who demean the contributions made to it by the Germans, or those who oppose its German form to superior national traditions of thought.

Throughout the book, for the sake of convenience, I have taken the liberty of treating *Aufklärung* and *Aufklärer* as English words. When I use them, I refer exclusively to the German phase of the Enlightenment. When I employ the term "Enlightenment," I mean the total movement. And when I use the words "western" or "western Enlightenment," I mean the Franco-British phase of the Enlightenment.

I have received invaluable assistance and inspiration from my teachers and colleagues. Most important has been the influence of my mentor and friend, Professor George T. Romani of Northwestern University. His vast knowledge of the field of intellectual history, his commitment to scholarly integrity, and his patient concern made my years of apprenticeship an exciting and rewarding experience. I was also fortunate to have studied with Professor Gray Cowen Boyce, who was always ready to offer valuable advice and help. Professor Dietrich Gerhard has continually provided me with insights and constructive criticism since I first met him in Göttingen. Professor Hayden V.

White of the University of California, Los Angeles, has been a constant source of inspiration. His willingness to criticize both the content and the style of my work will not be forgotten. The entire manuscript was read and criticized by Professors George Armstrong Kelly of Brandeis University, George T. Romani, and Dietrich Gerhard. Substantial portions were read by Professors Hayden V. White and Helen P. Liebel of the University of Alberta. Professor Peter Gay of Yale University read and criticized chapter iii. Their comments have been extremely helpful. Needless to say, whatever the failings of this study, they are mine alone.

The research for this volume was done primarily in Göttingen (1963-1965) and Vienna (1970-1972). I should like to thank the librarians of the Niedersächischen Staats- und Universitätsbibliothek, the Oesterreichische Nationalbibliothek, and the Universitätsbibliothek Wien for their friendly assistance. I am indebted to Professor Herwig Wolfram of the Institut für Oesterriechische Geschichtsforschung, who was extremely helpful in opening up the richness of the Viennese collections. My research was made possible by grants from the Fulbright commission and from the Regents of the University of California. Mary Millsap, who did much of the typing, rendered valuable assistance in proofreading and editing.

Some of my arguments and analyses were presented in an earlier article, "History and Hermeneutics: The Thought of Johann Christoph Gatterer," *Journal of Modern History* (March 1973). I thank the editor and publisher for allowing me to reproduce them.

P. H. R.

Introduction

1

In an important study of the German Enlightenment, Max Wundt wryly observed that the term "Enlightenment" shed very little enlightenment upon the nature of the period which bears this name.[1] He was right. Scholars continue to argue about a definition of the Enlightenment's origins, its characteristics, its extent, and its modernity. Although leading to a deeper understanding of the movement itself, this debate has been limited primarily to one realm of intellectual experience, namely, to that of the Franco-British world. Most scholars of the Enlightenment (despite notable exceptions) form their principal categories of definition from an analysis of leading French and British thinkers. These categories are then applied with little or no variation to other thinkers from Europe and the Americas. The impulse animating this mode of analysis is admirable: most historians aspire to establish a basic unity that imparts meaning to diverse strains of experience. The assumption that the essence of the Enlightenment can be uncovered by investigating the Franco-British experience is, however, fraught with danger. Such a limitation sacrifices the rich and complex diversity of the Enlightenment to an arbitrarily established unity. It has also led scholars either to demean or to overrate thinkers who do not fit into the established pattern. Both assessments are nowhere more evident than in German historiography.

The German phase of the Enlightenment – the Aufklärung – has received short shrift because of the tendency to dismiss it as a poor imitation of the Franco-British model. Only the most prominent Aufklärers, Lessing and Kant, have received extensive treatment, and usually their achievements are explained in relation to problems and traditions encountered in the Franco-British experience. On the other hand, a number of eighteenth-century German thinkers who seem to have opposed certain Franco-British attitudes have been the subject of countless studies. They have been glorified as heralds of a new Weltanschauung, as men who revolted against the superficial and moralistic Enlightenment. Accordingly, the genesis of German idealism is interpreted as a revolt against a weak and imitative Aufklärung, carried on by men who stood in radical opposition to the Enlightenment tradition. The general aim of my study is to question both these premises. It is argued that the Aufklärung was not merely a poor imitation of the western model; it had its own unique character, its own set of central issues, and its own set of conflicting solutions. In many ways these solutions were advances upon positions staked out by western thinkers. As Georg Lukács has

[1]

forcefully argued, they served as the necessary theoretical assumptions upon which later German thinkers were to build.[2] In this sense, the Aufklärung does not form the dialectical antipode either to the Sturm und Drang or to German idealism.[3] Rather, there is a strong continuity between the Aufklärung and succeeding ages. The Aufklärung is the first modern period of German intellectual history, a period in which the basic problems for succeeding generations were stated, though not resolved.

One of the central questions in the regnant discussion concerning the modernity of the Enlightenment centers on the nature of its historical consciousness and on the role the Enlightenment played in the formation of the modern paradigm of historical understanding. This is the concrete question dealt with in this study. For many scholars the recognition of the historicity of all things is the hallmark of modern thought, that which differentiates a Hegel or a Marx from a Descartes or a Hobbes. Today, after long scholarly debate, the legend about the antihistoricism of the Enlightenment has finally been laid to rest. The question of the modernity of the Enlightenment's appreciation of history has taken on a new dimension; whereas scholars recognize the fact that the Enlightenment had a historical consciousness, they do not universally agree that its historical consciouness approximates the modern historical consciousness. The problem is to show a basic theoretical and practical agreement between the Enlightenment's sense of history and the type of historical thought associated with the names of Ranke and/or Hegel. It is my belief that as long as one concentrates solely upon the Franco-British experience, such a demonstration remains open to debate.[4] A careful analysis of the German Enlightenment can help to resolve this debate.

After all, it is generally agreed that the historicist mentality reached its most extensive development in Germany. It seems only natural to look at the German intellectual tradition that preceded the triumph of historicism before one can ascertain the degree to which the Enlightenment generated this mentality. Such an analysis must, however, avoid the nationalist tradition of German historiography that envisioned the rise of historicism as an expression of the German consciousness asserting itself against French cultural domination. This stereotype can be maintained only if one sees the Enlightenment as a simple unitary movement defined by a small number of Franco-British thinkers. The unity of the Enlightenment can be found in the questions its thinkers posed, not in the answers proposed. The solutions to these problems varied according to the cultural, intellectual, and existential conditions under which they were formulated. Hence the Enlightenment is far more complex than usually conceived, a complexity brilliantly portrayed by Lionel Gossman: "The Enlightenment as we can now envisage it is more like a language than a single idea, imposing by its very nature certain modes of thought on those who use it, while remaining always at the same time the expression, in any actual usage, of particular desires and meanings and a response to particular conditions."[5] Because of unique German conditions, thinkers of the Aufklärung developed an idea of history that made a positive contribution to the evolving philosophy of the Enlightenment. It is my contention that the basic postulates of Rankean historiography were established during the Enlightenment by Enlightened thinkers in Germany and that the problems Hegel sought to resolve with the dialectical method were clearly posed, though imprecisely solved, by the scholars of the Aufklärung. In this context the following questions are investigated: How did the Aufklärers understand process, conceive of time, define human nature, explain and perceive causation, and order knowledge?

2

I have deliberately avoided concentrating on the thought and speculation of the major figures of eighteenth-century Germany. German historiography has been too much concerned with the great figures of intellectual history and too little concerned with the intellectual presuppositions from which they operated. These presuppositions were forged by a host of men now relegated to the rank of secondary thinkers. By ignoring these thinkers, we abandon the attempt to discern the internal dynamics of the age. We neglect the creativity and the complexity of the Aufklärung itself; further, we fail to grasp what many German historians claim they achieve: an intimate understanding of the Weltanschauung of the period. The tasks of the intellectual historian are to uncover the intellectual presuppositions of a given period, to chart the manner in which ideas are created and transformed, and to reflect upon the dynamics of such changes. To accomplish these objectives, it is imperative for the historian to include secondary thinkers within his purview. And, it must be remembered, these men we now label "secondary" were not considered secondary in their own lifetimes. They may not influence us now, but they certainly did influence their own generation and those that succeeded it. What I seek to do is to present the collective intellectual history of a group of important secondary thinkers who helped define the nature of the Aufklärung.

In so doing, a number of questions arise: Who were the Aufklärers and where did they work? What were their social backgrounds and which social groups did they influence? What were the internal intellectual traditions upon which they built and to which western thinkers did they turn? In short, what differentiates the Aufklärung from its cognate movements in France and Great Britain? To answer some of the questions fully would require an additional volume, one focusing more upon the sociology of knowledge than upon the elaboration of certain intellectual developments. All I can do here is make a number of suggestions in order to locate the Aufklärers in terms of time, place, social environment, and intellectual tradition.

As a starting point one thing must be made clear: to speak of a "German Enlightenment" is in itself a misnomer. The term seems to imply a unified cultural and national tradition. Eighteenth-century Germany was neither a unified nation nor a compact cultural entity. In some areas in Germany, French cultural aggrandizement predominated; in others, different groups looked to contending traditions; and still others were broadly influenced by the movement I describe. Three variables account for these differences. They are political, social, and religious.

On the political level, a conflict existed between those social groups that desired a destruction of traditional political ties in favor of a strong centralized absolute monarchy, and those that favored a reformation of the German body politic without destroying the traditions of the *Ständestaat.* [6] The former were centered in the court and looked to French intellectual traditions favorable to the establishment of "Enlightened Absolutism." The latter were found in provincial towns, especially university towns, in mercantile centers, and in bureaucracies that had won or retained a certain degree of independence from monarchial supervision. The leaders of the Aufklärung belonged to the latter group. They turned toward intellectual traditions emphasizing the necessity of maintaining a degree of historical continuity, traditions more favorable to checking the power of the monarchy through the revitalization of "constituted bodies." In a set of shorthand equations, the political conflict raged between court and country, between administrative centers and provincial towns, between "Enlightened Bureaucracy" and "Enlightened Absolutism," and between large estates of the Empire and the medium and smaller states. It must be emphasized that this conflict cannot be framed in nationalistic terms, such as anti-French chauvinism versus French domination. If the French Physiocrats exercised a strong influence upon the group centered in the court, French thinkers such as Montesquieu, Diderot, and Rousseau swayed those who were critical of an absolutism patterned after the French model. The political aversion to absolutism expressed by many German thinkers also explains their fascination with British thinkers. To many Germans, England appeared to have solved the tension between change and continuity. The English had constructed a modern state without having destroyed the traditional feudal base. My first operational definition of the Aufklärung is that it is an intellectual movement that sought to reform the German body politic without destroying the *Ständestaat* tradition. To this end the Aufklärers sought to join certain elements of French, British, and German thought favorable to the establishment of a polity harmoniously combining change and continuity.

On the social level, the Aufklärung may be characterized as a *bürgerlich* movement. Here we must be careful to avoid equating the term *bürgerlich* with the modern concept of the bourgeoisie. It does not signify a unitary economic class; rather it refers to a collection of professional, legal, and economic groups held together by a number of common attitudes. These attitudes were, in large, critical of those associated with the nobility and with court circles. Piety, respect for education, moderation in speech and dress, disdain for the extravagances of the feudal code of honor, and, sometimes, frugality were hallmarks of the *bürgerlich* mentality. At the same time, the various *bürgerlich* groups were differentiated by life-styles, group identification, and corporate rights and duties. To be *bürgerlich* meant to belong to a juridical category that contained many internal distinctions. There existed a vast chasm separating the *bürgerlich* oligarchs of Nuremberg, Zurich, and Bern from the minor bureaucrat, the local pastor, or the struggling *Privatdozent.*

The juridical nature of *bürgerlich* status permits further refinement of the social definition of the Aufklärung. Those who can be characterized roughly as *bürgerlich* belonged to the established corporate order, well defined by customary usage. Despite the fact that eighteenth-century Germany experienced a "noble reaction" similar to that of France, German *bürgerlich* groups were better able to maintain their position in society than their French counterparts. Though not "rising," they certainly were prospering.[7] The impotence experienced by French bourgeois intellectuals, an impotence that drove them to radical social, intellectual, and religious criticism, was less evident in Germany. As a whole the Aufklärers worked within the system. They decried the abuses of privilege, but they were loath to abolish privilege immediately or completely.

Because of the differentiations within the *bürgerlich* category, not all groups were receptive to reform and renovation. The traditional merchant families were closely tied to the status quo. In towns such as Nuremberg and Augsburg and in the German Swiss cantons they formed a surrogate nobility. Except possibly in Hamburg, the Aufklärung was not associated with leading mercantile groups. The most active participants in the formation of the Aufklärung were academics, lawyers, and those Protestant clergymen influenced by the recrudescence of religious feeling that began with Pietism. At times they were joined by members of the lower and upper nobility whose position had been eroded by the reforms of central monarchs. In effect, the Aufklärung was advanced by the professional groups in Germany.

All these groups consisted of university-trained members. If the salon served as the symbolic intellectual center of the western Enlightenment, the university fulfilled that function in Germany. As a result, the tone of the Aufklärung was far more pedantic than in the west. But the pedanticism was compensated for by a deeper concern for *Grundlichkeit* — for thorough, painstaking work and reflection. The German university system, in contrast with that of the west, was going through a period of reform, expansion, and reinvigoration.[8] The process, begun with the founding of the University of Halle, received added impetus from the establishment of the University of Göttingen and reached fruition with the opening of the University of Berlin. Along the way, other institutions either recast their charters to meet the demands of the times or gave up the ghost, as did Helmstedt, Altdorf, and Erfurt. Throughout the eighteenth century, and especially from mid-century on, the university became the vital center for the dissemination of knowledge and the formation of educated public opinion.

On the religious level, the distinction between Catholic and Protestant was crucial. Very generally, the major thrust of the Aufklärung can be deemed Protestant in nature. The rise and spread of Pietism at the end of the seventeenth century and the beginning of the eighteenth century had seriously challenged accepted Lutheran and Calvinist assumptions. Pietism engendered a new spirit of questioning and redefinition which touched a vital aspect of German intellectual life. It resulted in a determined revaluation of Holy Scripture, in a discussion of the relation between form (institutionalized religion) and spirit, and in an examination of the nature of religion itself. On the whole, the Aufklärers were not themselves Pietists; rather, they were activated by Pietism. They sought to resolve the contradictions between Pietism, orthodoxy, and rationalism through the use of history supported by critical reflection and philosophic inquiry. Their goal was to rescue religion, not destroy it, through a transformation of its meaning and function. In so doing, they were forced to confront an ever-widening circle of historical, psychological, and philosophical problems. As Ernst Troeltsch noted long ago, the Aufklärung marked the beginning of modern German Protestant thought.

German Catholicism did not experience a parallel intellectual development. The more hierarchic structure of Catholicism, the relative isolation of its thinkers from the mass of its believers, the class distinctions separating the higher clergy from the lower, the persistence of Catholic universities in pursuing an educational program formed during the Counter-Reformation, the increasing concern with ritual, perhaps even the mystery associated with the Mass, all tended to limit the degree of creative interpretation of theological precepts. True, there was also a rebirth of popular German Catholic religious feeling and in some respects a shift in religious sentiment during the eighteenth century. Catholicism was channeled in different directions. Instead of finding an outlet in critical reflection, the Catholic movement produced an amazing renaissance in the plastic arts, seen in the construction of the numerous pilgrimage churches that dot the Austrian, Bavarian, and Swabian countrysides.

To the general characteristics that define and limit the Aufklärung must be added a specific intellectual one: the legacy of Leibnizian philosophy. The influence of Leibnizian philosophy is pervasive but illusive: pervasive because the Aufklärers continually applied Leibnizian categories, terms, and phrases; illusive because many Aufklärers rejected Leibniz's specific solutions or sharply modified them. But whether conscious opponents of Leibniz or not, the Aufklärers buttressed their works with vocabulary and assumptions drawn from his philosophy. Leibniz had pioneered an analytics founded upon the concept of contextual harmony. It provided German thinkers with a philosophical alternative to both French Cartesianism and British empiricism. Leibniz's injunction to view the world as a harmonious conjunction of individually discrete and spontaneous elements inspired the Aufklärers to probe into the problems of being and becoming, spontaneity and necessity, and to branch out into an analysis of action and perception. As they developed their thought, the Aufklärers increasingly rejected Leibniz's fixation with the mathematical model as a universal norm for all forms of knowledge. Still the image of the monad haunted them; the impetus to investigate a given entity as though it contained logical, epistemological, and aesthetic categories that were harmoniously conjoined formed a starting point for most of their endeavors.

One more point of differentiation must be made: chronologically, the German Enlightenment followed that of the west. Too often we find thinkers such as Christian Wolff and Voltaire bracketed together. They were contemporaries, but they did not share the same set of basic experiences, nor did they attempt to answer the same set of vital questions. Voltaire and his generation were clearly Enlightenment thinkers. They were anti-Cartesian; they were wary of overspeculation, concerned with man's existence in a historically determined political and social world, and dedicated to the elimination of social abuses. Wolff and his generation were still a part of the great age of speculation that preceded the Enlightenment. They had more in common with the Cartesians than with the French and British apostles of Newtonian empiricism. Wolff was concerned with universal problems of being; his ideal was to contrive a universal language of symbols (*mathesis universalis*) which could replace the imperfect language of normal discourse. In this sense Wolff was, by inclination if not by precise method, the last of the important German neo-scholastics. Only when Wolff's immediate influence waned can we detect a dominant conjunction of intellectual forces that paralleled those of the Enlightenment. This conjunction occurred around 1740, when German thinkers rejected Wolff's philosophy or transvalued it. In so doing, they either turned to western thinkers for assistance or revived the tradition established by Christian Thomasius at the beginning of the eighteenth century.[9] The questions the Aufklärers sought to answer were posed by Leibnizian philosophy. The interaction between western ideas and Leibnizian assumptions gave the philosophy of the Aufklärung its own unique character, a philosophy that directed German thinkers to evolve a method of social analysis founded on history.

From the above, we can characterize the Aufklärung as an intellectual movement formed by the conjunction of three elements: the legacy of Leibnizian philosophy, the *Ständestaat* tradition, and the Protestant religious revival generated by the appearance of Pietism. Primarily it was bourgeois in spirit, critical of absolutism, opposed to attitudes associated with the court, but not revolutionary in nature. Its intellectual center was the university and its leading proponents were drawn primarily from the professional classes. Geographically, its strongholds were found in the southwest (the German Swiss cantons and Protestant Swabia), the north (lower Saxony and Hamburg), and the northeast (Prussia and Saxony). The most important single center of the Aufklärung was the newly founded University of Göttingen. Of course, deviations from this rough geographical pattern can be noted; two examples should suffice. The Berlin of Frederick the Great was, despite certain notable exceptions, influenced by those amenable to French absolutistic thinking. On the other hand, the University of Strasbourg, though under French jurisdiction, was an important center of the Aufklärung. It was here that later German Catholic statesmen and reformers such as Metternich and Montgelas came into intimate contact with the Protestant Aufklärung.

3

All the elements that defined the Aufklärung and differentiated it from the Franco-British Enlightenment found expression in the Aufklärung's historical consciousness. The corporate nature of the German body politic induced the Aufklärers to assume a moderate political stance. They retained a respect for "healthy" tradition and an attachment to long-constituted bodies. Theirs was a reformist mentality that in times of extreme stress, such as the French Revolution, could turn to conservatism. Their distaste for radical revolution enabled them to appreciate the slow forces of historical development. The Aufklärers' religious convictions led them to espouse an idea of history that postulated an interaction between spirit and nature. To them, the freedom of the spirit attested to the existence of God. Spirit and genius remained inexplicable qualities that defied logical analysis. Though the Aufklärers conceived of spirit as an independent force, it did not exist outside history. Each historical form contained a spiritual element and an element ascribable to material and historical factors. It was the job of the historian to explore the relation between freedom and form, between individual perception and communal being. Finally, the relative lateness of the Aufklärung allowed the Germans the luxury of picking and choosing from a number of outstanding western thinkers who had grappled with problems central to the Enlightenment as a whole.

I

The Crisis of Historical Consciousness at the Dawn of the Aufklärung

1

As Paul Hazard has shown in his brilliant study, *La crise de la conscience européene,* the period encompassing the last twenty years of the seventeenth century and the first fifteen of the eighteenth century was unusually rich in violent intellectual contradictions.[1] In every realm of thought, we encounter a bewildering combination of dogmatic assertion, skeptical cynicism, cosmic despair, aggressive optimism, energetic inquiry, and introspective spiritualism which appear as confusing as the troubled political and social picture of the times. In short, it was an era of intellectual crisis, distinguished by a loss of nerve and by startling fluctuations in intellectual assumptions. The crisis, in its broadest implications, entailed a loss of self-evidence in the traditional beliefs concerning the relation of man, nature, society, and God. Truths that once were unquestioned now were assaulted; reality as traditionally conceived proved inadequate to encompass the new world picture of seventeenth-century science and the new sets of political and social configurations that were clearly emerging at the end of the century. The crisis, though touching all disciplines of thought, was especially visible in the study of history, which had, until then, often provided a convenient means through which accepted truths were propagated.

The accepted model of historical understanding was an unstable mixture of classical, medieval, and humanist elements circumscribed by and crammed into the traditional Christian interpretation of universal history. Universal history provided both a means of interpreting and selecting facts and a convenient framework for periodizing time. In its most popular form, it presented a concrete version of Holy Scripture that utilized the prophecy of Daniel to interpret God's providential plan. Accordingly, the history of mankind was divided into four periods, each dominated by a world monarchy. The last of the monarchies was usually said to begin with Christ's crucifixion and resurrection. Although this plan had originally contained powerful chiliastic overtones, countless orthodox theologians and historians had over the centuries divested it of its message of imminent redemption and its association with the destiny of a specific visible political order (e.g., Rome). By the seventeenth century, the fourth monarchy had been successfully converted into a general period of history marked by the triumph of Christianity, though the temptation to equate the monarchy with a specific political entity lingered on.[2]

Still, the concept of a unitary period of history beginning with Christ and extending through the seventeenth century disturbed many seventeenth-century thinkers; in theory it denied the actuality of the qualitative historical change they thought they were experiencing. It implied that, despite all appearances to the contrary, no basic difference could exist between the world of the apostles and that of the seventeenth century. Whatever change had occurred was superficial, dependent upon the sinful nature of man living in the eternally unstable and unreliable earthly city. By excluding chiliastic hopes from its competence and by asserting the eternal applicability of inherited religious belief, the model of seventeenth-century universal history served as a bulwark for the moral, religious, political, and intellectual status quo. It closed the future to intellectual inquiry and eternized the present by equating contemporary religious and moral belief with that supposedly proclaimed by the church of the apostles. The only type of development provided by this framework of historical periodization was that of degeneration from an exemplary norm, a degeneration that could be reversed by recapturing the purity of the apostolic era as defined by the interpreting party.[3] Even the manner of internal periodization used by universal historians reinforced the belief in the unity of the fourth monarchy. The reliance upon the classical division into years, centuries, and regimes was justified by ease of treatment, not by qualitative differentiation.

Just as the basic periodization of universal history and the implications drawn from it were questioned, so too were its modes of specific explanation. Traditional universal history had accepted the classical and humanist injunction that history be made a pragmatic and exemplary discipline. Its function was to educate, to clarify, and to corroborate. It showed how the universal rules of religion or philosophy operated in specific instances.[4] Once the general precepts of truth were demonstrated through a series of enlightening examples, a person would be better able to apply the rules of correct behavior to his daily life. The validity of exemplar history depended, however, upon a set of self-evident transhistorical assumptions that dictated the type of events to be discussed and provided meaning for the discussion. The moment these assumptions were questioned, denied, or ignored, nothing remained but a set of historical facts that became either irrelevant or bothersome. No longer did the assumptions resolve questions within an accepted paradigm of explanation; instead, they served to direct doubt against the underlying transhistorical assumption.

Such doubts were raised at the end of the seventeenth century. Traditional universal history was deemed irrelevant because its explanatory principles were no longer considered valuable or pragmatic; they failed to explain adequately those sectors of experience considered important by seventeenth-century thinkers. The only generalizations universal history employed were moralistic ones, often derived from the practices of contemporary Christianity, and they were incapable of dealing with the intricacies and difficulties of political life or of adequately uncovering the workings of the state. Hence, traditional universal history, when applied to politics, presented a gallery of ideal moral types instead of an analysis of political action. When compared with the writings of Machiavelli and other theorists of *raison d'état,* universal history seemed disastrously incompetent. For this reason, seventeenth-century political historians had, to a large extent, abandoned moralistic criteria and replaced them with the "universal" principles of *raison d'état.* The new political history was still similar in form to traditional history. It too was exemplar and its function was pragmatic, but the judgments contained therein were in basic contradiction to the transhistorical values of traditional history. Historians of the late seventeenth century were thereby faced with the dilemma of having to choose between two distinct and irreconcilable sets of universal assumptions.

The easiest, though not the most adequate, solution to this quandary was to incorporate both genres of historical explanation in the same history. The general pattern of universal history was employed as background for the discussion of recent political events. Once the writer had safely entered the preserve of recent history, he conveniently dispensed with the background pattern and concentrated upon a history that emphasized secular political life.[5] The implicit contradiction served only to bring the whole endeavor of interpretive history into question. And the proclivity of many historians to deal primarily with recent problems demonstrates their unconscious realization that the distant past as traditionally interpreted threw little light on the problems of the present. Descartes's assertion that "a man who has too much curiosity about what happened in past centuries usually shows a great ignorance of what is happening in this one" accurately reflected the mentality of the time.[6] History had ceased to be a science that reinterprets the past in order to understand the present. In this sense, it had entered into a period of crisis.

Contemporary historians did not let the attacks on history go unanswered. At a time when many thinkers were rejecting history as a vital subject, historians were busy attempting, through hard and painstaking research, to reform their field of study within the established parameters. The fruit of this protean endeavor was the development of sophisticated methods for the analysis of literary and nonliterary evidence. Antiquarians and *érudits* created the ancillary sciences of diplomatics, heraldry, epigraphy, iconography, and numismatics and offered the learned world an impressive array of lexicons, thesauri, and collections of documents, many of them still invaluable to the modern scholar.[7] Yet the immediate results of these endeavors served only to sharpen the existent crisis. The reason is simple. Antiquarians and *érudits* erroneously thought they could save history by purely methodological means.

They believed that once historical studies had been purged of the mythical and the fabulous, the purified tradition would be safe from the attacks of wholesale doubt. What they refused to realize was that the entire structure of assumptions and generalizations within which they operated was tottering. Without a firm base, without a general reshaping of the paradigm of historical explanation, it did not matter how many "purified facts" were uncovered, since the facts could always be used to prove an opposite point. The *érudits* and antiquarians soon discovered that a group of skeptical critics – called historical Pyrrhonists – used the very methods they themselves had developed to call traditional historical interpretation into doubt.

The Jesuit Jean Hardouin offers the most striking, though extreme, example of historical Pyrrhonism at work. Père Hardouin, after finding a contradiction between inscriptions on coins and literary tradition, "discovered" that virtually the whole corpus of the classical and early medieval literary tradition (with the exception of Virgil's *Georgics,* the *Letters* of Pliny the Elder, Cicero's works, and Horace's *Satires* and *Epistles*) was a forgery that had been perpetrated by a band of late fourteenth-century Italian humanists.[8] Hardouin carried historical Pyrrhonism to its logical conclusion: he resolved the contradictions found in tradition by radically rejecting all tradition. The methods of historical research had been used to destroy the competency of history.

The dissatisfaction with traditional modes of historical interpretation was exacerbated by the accepted belief that history could be intrinsically objective. The only obstacles thought to hinder the discovery of truth were the personality and the prejudices of the investigator. If one used strict self-discipline and a correct method, then truth could be unearthed. The historian was to purge himself of all sectarian interests. Pierre Bayle summed up this belief when he said that the historian was to be "neither a Frenchman nor a German, neither an Englishman nor a Spaniard . . . but a citizen of the world."[9] Impartiality – that is, belonging to no party – became the stated aim of countless historians, and the word itself was used with abandon to describe the contents of numberless histories. But despite the claims of impartiality, results did not jibe with intentions. No matter how hard historians tried, agreement on the truth of interpretation could not be reached. Despite sophisticated methods of source analysis, it became increasingly obvious that the disciples of Clio could reach agreement only when uncovering facts. The moment they imparted meaning to these facts, the same disputes arose which had existed prior to the development of the improved methods. All the "impartial accounts" still reflected confessional or political interests. Given the age's concern with attaining coherent truth, these continual disputes subjected the validity of all historical explanation to doubt.

It is within this context that the antihistorical posture of seventeenth-century philosophy can be understood. Philosophers did not deny the importance of history as such; indeed, many of them, including Hobbes, Leibniz, and Spinoza, still pursued historical studies. But they all doubted the competence of historical interpretation. Their denial of scholastic philosophy and orthodox theology naturally touched history, which drew nourishment and meaning from both. Late seventeenth-century philosophers wished to establish incontrovertible truths based on the model of logical coherence. History at its best, however, could offer only correspondent truth. The philosophers agreed, despite all their differences, that the truth of history categorically differed from the necessary truths of reason. For many, this distinction implied that history was a "lesser science," limited to finding out what happened – a definition that was still propagated in eighteenth-century Germany by Christian Wolff. History, then, was a science of particulars and could not deal with relations; it "consisted in the bare knowledge of fact."[10] History could be correctly applied only to questions where accuracy, not evident truth, was desired.

The new philosophers sought to construct a coherent science of man and nature that would build a deductive ladder beginning with simple and indisputable first principles and ending in God.[11] This objective required them to exclude from their field of inquiry those sectors of experience that were not susceptible to coherent analysis, an exclusion exemplified by their radical separation of truths of fact from truths of reason, their distaste for "probable opinions," and their denial of all metaphysical (i.e., teleological) thinking. The new philosophy "entailed," in the words of Leo Strauss, "a deliberate lowering of the ultimate goal. The goal was lowered in order to increase the probability of its attainment."[12] But the restrictions of a coherent theory of truth made it difficult for historical analysts to integrate adequately the particular with the general. The material always seemed to burst the explanatory containers designed to accommodate it; the contradictions of historical life intruded into the philosophers' efforts to forge a social science posited on identity and noncontradiction. A breach increasingly appeared between the fullness of historical fact and the logically limited modes of interpretation employed by the new philosophers. And so the new philosophy proved as vulnerable to skeptical historical criticism as traditional exemplar history had.

Pierre Bayle demonstrated this fact with his tireless criticism of exaggerated reliance upon the feeble powers of reason. He used historical criticism as a destructive weapon to reveal the blindness and ignorance of all "the dogmatists . . . who have never dreaded anything but appearing ignorant" and to show "that our reason is a path that leads us astray since, when it displays itself with greatest subtlety, it plunges us into such an abyss."[13] No evident truth was safe from Bayle's devastating critique: every product of human reason lacked necessary evidence; all philosophical distinctions (e.g., the primacy of extension and motion) were based on belief, not on necessary proof; in fact, all criteria of proof were themselves open to doubt, thereby rendering any philosophical system questionable.[14]

When Bayle chose the historical method to attack systematic thought, its function was, for him, purely negative. Ideally, its rules forced the historian to tear down facade after facade until very little meaning remained in the common notions with which we operate. But history itself was unable to impart meaning to life; meaning had to be found outside history. At most, history could help us "to learn the necessity of mistrusting reason."[15] Bayle offered the intellectual an either-or solution to the problem of meaning: "If you do not want to believe anything but what is evident and in conformity with the common notions, choose philosophy and leave Christianity. If you are willing to believe the incomprehensible mysteries of religion, choose Christianity and leave philosophy. For to have together self-evidence and incomprehensibility is something that cannot be."[16] Whatever the choice, Bayle makes it clear that it was an act of belief, determined by irrational motive, not by evidence, for the weight of his unrelenting critique undermined the objective foundations of self-evident truth.[17] Absent from Bayle's proposition was a third possibility, that of seeking meaning within the framework of historical reasoning. The historical consciousness of the era made this solution impossible because the existent mode of historical thinking offered no possible alternative to evident philosophy and revealed religion.[18]

2

The problems inherent in late seventeenth-century historiography were exaggerated in Germany because of history's total dependence on either jurisprudence or theology. The role history played as an adjunct to legal-political and religious disputation intensified its internal contradictions; further, it discredited any claims history had to independent interpretive existence. Throughout the seventeenth and early eighteenth centuries, gifted and mediocre thinkers alike used history as a club to hammer home previously established ideological positions. Even the holocaust of the Thirty Years War and the resulting Peace of Westphalia did nothing to diminish the viciousness of academic debate on two major problems: the nature of the German Empire and the true religion. Two of the most capable and influential writers of the late seventeenth century to use history to such purpose were Samuel Pufendorf (1632-1694) and Gottfried Arnold (1666-1714). Their works, classics in their own right, exerted an influence on generations to come. Yet their writings also testify to the problems of seventeenth- and early eighteenth-century historical thought, which, in turn, provides us with the necessary background for understanding the direction taken by historians of the Aufklärung.

Samuel Pufendorf, one of the few seventeenth-century German thinkers with an international reputation, was a self-proclaimed disciple of the new philosophy.[19] His self-appointed task was to apply its methods to the problems of government and society and thereby forge a coherent science of politics and morality. As a follower of Descartes and Hobbes, Pufendorf was concerned primarily with restructuring experience in order to obtain certain knowledge. He relied upon the Cartesian method to accomplish this aim.[20] Simple truths, obtained by subjecting traditional knowledge to a thorough-going skepticism, were to replace the multiplicity of traditional forms of understanding. Whatever remained intact after the onslaught of doubt served as the starting point for coherent reconstruction.[21] For Pufendorf, the correct application of the Cartesian method meant limiting the competence of investigation. Following the example of seventeenth-century physical scientists, he deliberately excluded all considerations of teleology and inherent qualities because they were immune to coherent analysis. He replaced them with the more moderate, yet manageable, standards of utility and logical relation. This act alone served to relegate history to the status of an auxiliary science, for it excluded questions of quality, which had often formed the stuff of historical narrative. History's function was now corroboratory. It was to provide pragmatic examples for the truth of philosophy. Pufendorf affirmed this objective when he repeated Hobbes's distinction between historical and philosophical truth.

Pufendorf's application of the methods of coherent philosophy to the problems of politics began with an abstract analysis of individual man. Like Hobbes, he rejected the classical definition of man as a social animal: that man could achieve "the perfection of his nature in and through society and, therefore, that civil society is prior to the individual."[22] Instead of defining man as a social animal, Pufendorf referred to him as a sociable animal. Man is capable of living in society but does so only because of self-interest. Therefore, man existed prior to society. The seemingly small shift in definition from man as a social animal to man as a sociable animal heralded a radical transformation of the concept of society and of the methods used to analyze it.[23] Society is no longer the condition of man, as Grotius still defined it; now it is the creation of man. For Pufendorf this definition was vital because it allowed him to claim that society could be studied according to the rules of coherent philosophy. He justified this contention by borrowing another Hobbesian principle, namely, that we can know only that which we make. Since man made society and since knowledge was equated with coherent knowledge, it followed that society was susceptible to rational, coherent analysis.

This basic assumption directed Pufendorf's inquiry into the rules of politics, which, in turn, established the principles he used in historical generalization and explanation. Without going into the intricacies of Pufendorf's a priori assumptions, we can single out three basic ideas that were central to his theory of politics and his idea of history: the concepts of social contract, sovereignty, and *raison d'état*.

According to Pufendorf's method of individual analysis, the existence of the social contract was essential. It alone offered an explanation of how man voluntarily surrendered his individual freedom to the state. Although the existence of the social contract could never be proven by history, it had to exist because it accorded to reason. In his discussion, Pufendorf introduced a complex set of social contracts that resulted finally in the contract whereby man subjected himself to a sovereign power through an act of will that could not be rescinded. The creation of a sovereign power was simultaneous with the creation of the state. Sovereignty, which is necessary to a state's existence, was defined according to the principles established by Jean Bodin. It was unaccountable, supreme, and indivisible. Further, to be effective, it had to be exercised by one person or one authority. This strict definition of sovereignty led Pufendorf to modify and limit traditional classical and scholastic political theory. He explicitly denied the existence of "mixed forms" of authority. Only the three regular forms of democracy, aristocracy, and monarchy were valid. All other modes of authority lacked independent existence; they merely formed temporary stages in a process of degeneration. Pufendorf went so far as to call them abortions, sicknesses, and monstrosities.[24]

Just as Pufendorf limited his definition of society to the state, he mechanically equated sovereignty with the exercisers of authority. No other institution or corporation within the state, including the church, possessed sovereign powers. The power of institutions over their individual members was limited by and derived from the indivisible sovereign authority.[25] The will of the state is really the will of the ruling authority. The actions of the state, then, are best explained by analyzing the actions of the sovereign authority. Thus Pufendorf interpreted the state as a series of relations all converging at the apex of the ruling authority.

The supreme duty of the sovereign power, according to Pufendorf, was to maintain and further the interests of the state. In so doing the sovereign was to be guided by the principles of *raison d'état,* which, Pufendorf believed, provided the political scientist with a fundamental measure for judging whether an action was good or bad (i.e., whether it achieved the desired goal or not). Pufendorf carefully distinguished between what he called true and imaginary interests of the state (*verum und imaginarium*). Imaginary interests were defined as overambitious plans, such as the desire to create a world monarchy, which inevitably led to disastrous consequences. True interests were classified as being either perpetual or temporary. Geography, natural resources, and national character (*die natürliche Zuneigung des Volckes*) determine perpetual interests. Temporary interests can be traced to transitory shifts in the power alignments among one's neighbors.[26] The former presents an unchanging world of general propositions, the latter a set of changing relations belonging to the world of history.

According to Pufendorf's definitions, the state is reduced to a mutual service and protection institution.[27] Mutual service and protection postulate order, tranquillity, and harmony, qualities that Pufendorf saw as primary virtues.[28] The best state was the best-ordered state. Here Pufendorf combined origin, function, and goal; they became one and the same. A state is created to achieve order; its function is to ensure order; its goal is to preserve order. Pufendorf's vision of social life was basically static, the only possible mode of existence being an orderly one that harmonized with the objective rules of politics or a disorderly one that ignored these rules. It is also evident from this position that Pufendorf believed that an objective social science was possible, providing one used the correct categories of definition. Disagreement was not a natural state of affairs; it merely attested to confusion or ignorance.[29] By extension, Pufendorf also believed that historical objectivity was both possible and probable if one used his definitions. Yet, Pufendorf's own historical writings reveal basic contradictions that seem to mock his original claims. They serve as ample proof of the existent crisis of historical understanding.

Pufendorf wrote extensively on history throughout his life. He began his career with it, and after dealing in turn with morals, natural law, philosophy, and theology, he returned to history, devoting the last part of his life to simultaneously composing the recent histories of the houses of Sweden and Brandenburg. As a historian, he wrote three different types of history, which I choose to call theoretical history (works explicitly applying his theoretical assumptions), derivative history (works that summed up traditional historical thought), and original history (works resulting from his own extensive archival researches). Although each type of history had its own character, the one overriding element present in them all — Pufendorf's antihistorical sense of time — testifies to the seventeenth-century crisis of the historical consciousness. Recently the French sociologist Georges Gurvitch attempted to differentiate between forms of time consciousness. One of his categories, which he called an "erratic sense of time," describes Pufendorf's attitude very well. Here "the present appears to prevail over the past and the future, with which it sometimes finds it difficult to enter into relations."[30] On a simple level, Pufendorf's present-oriented sense of time can be seen in his concentration upon contemporary history. It was not merely a preference, but an epistemological choice. For him, past history was too vague, too full of question marks, to serve as a guide to action. In this stance he paraphrased Descartes, who maintained: "Those tales [histories], moreover make us imagine many events to be possible which are not so in fact; and even the most faithful record, although it may neither change the facts, nor enhance their value, in order to make them more worthy of being related, at least always omits the least dignified and the least illustrious circumstances. Thus, the rest does not appear such as it really was, and those who regulate their behavior by the examples they derive from it are prone to fall into the extravagances that afflict the Paladins of our romances, and to conceive designs that exceed their powers."[31] Pufendorf echoed this view in the preface to the first volume of his *Einleitung zu der Historie der vornehmsten Reiche und Staaten,* where he clearly distinguished between the usefulness of ancient history and that of modern history. At most, the former could provide a few helpful rules, but to acquire a detailed knowledge of ancient history was really a waste of time and effort. Contemporary history, however, offered a reliable guide for actions; it was indispensable for every *Standesperson.*[32]

An even clearer indication of Pufendorf's erratic sense of time was his eternization of the present in his transhistorical assumptions. By applying the Cartesian method to an analysis of contemporary political life, he derived political truths which he universalized and made normal for past, present, and future. Thus he resolved two contradictory triads of time consciousness: *past-memory-regret* and *future-will-desire.*[33] The first triad looked longingly to the past. It constructed a golden age from which the present had deteriorated. This was the traditional humanist position. The second triad envisioned a teleological goal toward which the present was to aspire. This pattern was most common to radical religious thinkers such as Joachim of Flora, Campanella, and in Germany the Anabaptists. Pufendorf avoided both cosmic historical regret and future teleological yearning by locating his analytics solely in the present. Thus he could side with the "Moderns" against the "Ancients" and still deny teleological thought, which the new philosophy had taught him to mistrust. An idealized present became the standard for past and future. To borrow Herbert Marcuse's term, Pufendorf's analytics was basically "one-dimensional." It solved the problem of past and future by ignoring them.

Pufendorf's position seemingly incorporated advantages from both sets of triads. He could look with regret upon any degeneration from a regular form, but he could also believe in the ability of men to compensate for that trend by an act of will. The radical individualism of his method of operation also proclaimed a radical affirmation of free will. Once the inquiring mind had defined the rules of politics, they could be applied by the sovereign power to achieve order. By excluding teleological change, Pufendorf affirmed the unchanging relation between cause and effect. All elements of doubt were eliminated by rejecting an image of the future that in any way differed qualitatively from the present.[34] This very strategy of argument, however, limited Pufendorf's ability to understand historical development. A rejection of a qualitatively differentiated future implied the rejection of a qualitatively distinct past. The only real difference between historical epochs introduced by Pufendorf was the degree of correct education each possessed. An age falls into darkness when the true principles of politics are ignored or forgotten. The Middle Ages were dark because true learning was replaced by complex and misleading scholastic distinctions.[35] The clever priests were able to deceive and manipulate the uneducated canaille who, like women (*Weibesvolck*), are naturally impressed by extravagances (*extravaganten-Sachen*), pomp, and ceremony.[36]

Pufendorf's erratic sense of time also explains why his derivative histories took the form they did. Surprisingly, Pufendorf employed the usual pattern of universal history. The four monarchies were retained; an unconnected series of rulers, battles, and treaties fleshed out the narrative. Pufendorf did occasionally punctuate his chroniclelike exposition with judgments based on his set of transhistorical assumptions. Thus he traced Athens's troubles to the failure to differentiate between true and imaginary interests of the state. The Athenians forgot that the true interests of a city-state lay in trade and peaceful coexistence with one's neighbors. Pufendorf, however, consciously introduced his ideas in more detail only at the end of each nation's history, where he attempted to sum up the permanent interests of each state. Why did Pufendorf keep a model of historical explanation which really had little relevance to his own interests? The answer probably is that he saw little value in the whole endeavor of writing universal history. Why go through the effort of changing something that was nothing more than an introductory exercise? It was merely a prolegomenon to the real thing, the present.

The eternization of the present is most obvious in Pufendorf's two theoretical histories: *The Constitution of the German Empire,* written under the pseudonym of Severinus von Monzambano (1667), and *A Historical-Political Description of the Spiritual Monarchy of Rome,* originally written under the pseudonym of Basilius Hyperta but later included in the first volume of the *Historie der vornehmsten Reiche und Staaten.* In contrast with Pufendorf's derivative history, both theoretical histories offer well-organized thematic presentations centered on his definition of sovereignty and motivated by his desire for order. Both clearly make history an auxiliary to political science and both employ appeals to reason and conjectural constructs which take precedence over historical data.

In the history of the papacy, Pufendorf attacked the idea of an independent church by appealing to his definition of sovereignty. He argued that reason shows that a separation between church and state was unnatural. Such a separation would serve only as a continual source of mistrust, jealousy, and discord. In effect, two conflicting sovereignties would be established which would negate the rational rules of politics. Pufendorf considered the Roman church as the prime example of so unnatural a state of affairs. He even went so far as to call the papacy antireligious because it contradicted the defined nature of religion in general and of Christianity in particular. That is, it violated the law that religion should not expropriate powers belonging to civil government. The Catholic church's sovereign power was a bane to orderly European life. It existed only because of the ambition of the pope and the clerics and the ignorance of its followers.[37] Starting from these defined positions, Pufendorf then composed a history that confirmed them. It was a well-ordered piece of Lutheran propaganda.

The Constitution of the German Empire was also a disquisition on Pufendorf's idea of sovereignty. The work was so controversial that Pufendorf never officially acknowledged his authorship during his lifetime. It contains his clearest definition of sovereignty and his strongest attack against irregular forms. Like the history of the papacy, it is written in the form of a history but it contains a "necessary" sequence of phenomena that did not need historical proof. According to Pufendorf's view, Germany was originally a regular monarchy under Charlemagne. Owing to ignorance and mistakes it soon disintegrated, and the various princes acquired sovereign power over their territories. But as they were all weak, they turned to the emperor for protection. This they received by making a contract with him, which Pufendorf called the *feuda oblata.* The princes agreed to become the emperor's vassals, but the enfeoffed lands belonged to them, not to the emperor. They lost nothing by taking the lands back from the emperor as fiefs. Therefore, the princes could reclaim full sovereignty whenever they felt powerful enough. The *feuda oblata,* whose existence Pufendorf could not prove historically, allowed him to argue that the empire was not a sovereign state. It actually was a latent confederation, because neither the emperor nor the princes as a unit exercised authority over the whole. The historical part of *The Constitution of the German Empire* developed these arguments in a thematic manner, showing how Germany could not exist as a unit because it failed by definition to meet the requirements of a regular form.

Both theoretical histories were directed against "irregular" institutions: Germany was neither monarchy, aristocracy, nor democracy and the papacy was a destructive sovereignty, which had violated the principles of religion by appropriating power rightfully belonging to civil regimes. The two institutions in question were denied necessary a priori existence because they failed to conform to the truths of politics; they were mere degenerations from orderly forms. They existed only because ignorance, supported by the weight of custom, existed. In both works, human history appears as a destruction of orderly patterns owing to ignorance and human weakness. In this sense, they are antihistories, indictments against historical development. To correct the burdens of the past, Pufendorf recommended an application of the rational rules of the science of politics.

Pufendorf's most extensive historical works were his original histories. They differed from both his derivative and his theoretical histories in that he consciously began with an investigation of contemporary historical fact and hoped to end with an affirmation of his theoretical assumptions. As historiographer to the Swedish and Brandenburg courts, he enjoyed free access to their archives, a privilege he made full use of in his works: *De rebus suecicis ab expeditione Gustavi Adolphi in Germaniam ad abdicationem usque Christianae; De rebus a Carolo Gustavo Sueciae rege gestis; De rebus gestis Frederici Wilhmelmi Magni electoris Brandenburgici;* and the fragment *De rebus gestis Frederici III.* These were exercises in applied *raison d'état.* Although dealing with both the perpetual and the temporary interests of state, Pufendorf's studies concentrate on the latter, which he considered the major domain of historical analysis. The narrative chronicles individual actions and reactions of sovereigns and their ministers. It is court and cabinet history, with emphasis on international relations. As in his derivative history, Pufendorf failed to tie the elements of his original history together. There is no inner coherence, no linkage of the chain of events he describes in great detail. Not only the thematic representation but also the type of judgments contained in his theoretical history are missing. Pufendorf claimed that his duty was merely to relate what had happened; he left the act of judgment to later generations. Pufendorf was not a free agent when he composed his histories but rather an official historiographer who had certain duties to his employers. Still, he had claimed that it was possible to combine the love of objective truth with duty to one's prince and *Vaterland.* The easiest way for Pufendorf to have fulfilled his function as court historian was to write a glowing history of the prince and his acts. At times he did fall into that trap. He rendered documents freely, omitted embarrassing clauses, and added others for effect. Yet, on the whole, he did a reasonably good job in detailing what he discovered had happened.[38]

Pufendorf's refusal to judge and interpret ran counter to all his formulations. Both his derivative and his theoretical histories contained judgments founded on his universal concepts of social contract, sovereignty, and *raison d'état.* His stated preference for contemporary history should have led him to write it with even greater evaluative precision. In a sense, he was a failure as an original historian because he did not substantiate his own principles. Despite his discovered truths of politics, he could only uncover historical facts. His original histories remained political chronicles, similar in all respects to the traditional political history of his times. Any one of his contemporaries possessing an equivalent mastery of Latin style (his German was atrocious), the same critical acumen, and equal access to the sources could have written them.

Pufendorf's failure to combine theoretical form with historical content in his original histories further attested to the existent crisis of the historical consciousness. His derivative and original histories did not break from the traditional model of political chronicle. They were flat, uninspired, lifeless. His theoretical history, however, demonstrated a distinct personality. Despite its ahistorical assumptions and antihistorical purpose, it presented a closely organized and developed thematic analysis. As Erich Seeberg has observed: "This method of systematization which constructs a hypothetical history with the aid of logic probably helped to overcome annalistic historical writing. . . . Everything was driven from just repetition to mastery and reshaping of the material."[39] Yet Pufendorf, like others of his generation, such as Leibniz, failed to make history an interpretive discipline. Although his "theoretical history" had a form that could lead to a transcendence of traditional historical writing, Pufendorf himself did not achieve this transcendence. Theoretical history remained hypothetical history, with historical content used only in an illustrative and exemplary manner. The validity of Pufendorf's theoretical history rested not on the material of history, but rather on the coherence of logical argument. Theory was still divorced from practice and the breach between the particular and the general had not yet been healed.

3

It would be difficult to conceive of a sharper contrast in personalities, values, and goals than that which existed between Samuel Pufendorf and Gottfried Arnold. Pufendorf represented the moderate, safe forces of accommodation in late seventeenth-century German society. His goals of order and tranquillity, his faith in the methods of coherent analysis, and his predilection to see everything from the standpoint of law and politics accurately reflect the mentality of those groups that, for want of a better term, can be called *bürgerlich*. Pufendorf was a man of discretion, a man willing to serve any monarch who both recognized and rewarded Pufendorf's merits and ruled in such a manner that peace, order, and tranquillity were preserved. Even when Pufendorf utilized modes of thought that contained, or could contain, radical implications (e.g., natural law), he always deleted the elements most likely to threaten the status quo.

Gottfried Arnold, on the other hand, was a forceful representative of the radical elements in German society, whose radicality found its most adequate expression in religion. Arnold was the heir to and the spokesman for what Lewis White Beck has called the Protestant Counter-Reformation.[40] His spiritual forebears were Sebastian Franck, Jakob Böhme, the Spanish mystics, and even the Rosicrucians. His immediate mentors were Philipp Jakob Spener and the Quedlinburg spiritualists. Unlike Pufendorf, Arnold spurned success, detested institutionalized forms of worship and learning, and rejected order and tranquillity as desirable social norms. In fact, he equated calmness, order, and tranquillity with boredom, which itself was a sign of decadence. It was alien to Arnold's nature to function well in any system smacking of cant and social pressure, a quality that explains the drastic changes in his life. Trained for the ministry, he rejected a position as a clergyman because he believed the job forced one to become a practicing hypocrite instead of a practicing Christian. He accepted what he at first thought was the lesser evil – a professorship in history at the University of Giessen. It was not long before he became disillusioned. Scholars were, he came to feel, as bad as clergymen: they were petty egotists who cared more about honors, degrees, publications, and useless disputations than about the imperatives of Christian living. In the same year that he accepted his position (1697) he resigned it, sold his library, and turned to an ascetic life of withdrawal. Although Arnold later moderated his views, returning to the milder Pietism of Spener, marrying, and even accepting a position in the clergy, it was during his period of radical spiritualism that he wrote the work that made him famous, the *Unparteyische Kirchen- und Ketzer-Historie* (2 vols.; 1699, 1700).

The *Unparteyische Kirchen- und Ketzer-Historie* brilliantly summed up the German spiritualist position, denying with vehemence the basic values of both Catholic and Protestant theology. Arnold's history attacked all dogmatic positions. It turned traditional values upside down and offered a religious critique of society which was as uncompromising as it was harsh. In the words of Erich Seeberg, Arnold's foremost commentator, he presented an *Umwertung aller Werte,* a revaluation of all values. In this quality Arnold's work was analogous to Bayle's; it called whole areas of accepted reasoning into doubt in the name of the "choice for incomprehensibility." In the Germany of Arnold's time, the *Unparteyische Kirchen- und Ketzer-Historie* had an effect upon theological circles which was comparable to Karl Barth's early writings: it "fell like a bomb on the playground of the theologians."[41] The history was an act of defiance that generated an unbelievable response. Arnold was praised — his friend Christian Thomasius called the history the best book written on religion since the Bible — and damned even more resoundingly. Yet, despite the radicality of his views, Arnold did not offer a new concept of religion, society, or history. He was successful enough in his critique to stimulate later thinkers to reinvestigate the vital area of religious history, but he did not create a new paradigm for understanding religious or historical phenomena. Though in many ways so different from Pufendorf's histories, the *Unparteyische Kirchen- und Ketzer-Historie* revealed the same faults. It thus forms an interesting companion piece to Pufendorf's work, one that also offers the reader a document of the existent crisis of historical understanding.

Pufendorf had evolved his transhistorical assumptions from an abstract analysis of the individual. From that analysis he had developed his ideas on social origins, sovereignty, and *raison d'état*, which served as his objective, ahistorical measures for historical evaluation. In form his historical thinking reveals a self-enclosed circularity of argument. The rules of politics derived from a hypothetical conception of human nature become the standards by which individual action is judged. A similar type of circularity marks Arnold's historical reasoning. He too based his narrative upon an idealized and universal definition of Christianity which he drew from an equally abstract analysis of individual Christian behavior. His conception of the character of the true church provided him with an eternal standard against which all temporal religious phenomena were measured. Anything that varied from his conception was easily adjudged antireligious and regarded as belonging to the realm of Satan and the Antichrist.

Even the manner in which Arnold reached his definition of the church is strikingly reminiscent of Pufendorf's approach. Arnold attempted a radical simplification in definition that at one blow excluded traditional concerns with dogma, ritual, and organized forms of worship from the scope of religious history. In other words, he too dismissed qualitative distinctions in the hope of arriving at clear and valid generalizations concerning religious action. He accomplished his purpose through the simple device of establishing an equation of identity between an individual's inner and outer spiritual life. Christian belief and Christian life are the same, which means that religious phenomena can be objectively evaluated by looking at individual behavior. All other features of religion are judged solely on the utilitarian basis of their effect on action, not in terms of inherent worth or truth. Through this act, Arnold accomplished what Karl Barth has called the "humanizing of Christianity."[42]

The radicality of Arnold's approach lies in his definition, in the content of his description, of the Christian religion. During the sixteenth and seventeenth centuries ecclesiastical historians had usually striven to differentiate between the true church and the fallen church according to specific objectified standards of belief and liturgy. Arnold equated all these objectifications as inherently evil. They were evil because they were inventions of human beings; they blocked man's attempt to live the simple teachings of the Bible. The true Christian was one who, through his own will, prepared his soul to receive God's gift of grace. Once the inner life had been enlightened by the Holy Spirit, the individual was reborn; his whole way of life changed, attesting to his "true union with God and His will."[43] Because this process required a direct individual act, no external aids were necessary. In fact, external factors were obstacles in the process of attaining salvation. Arnold argued that whenever a party or a sect was created, whenever dogmatic distinctions were given preference over pious living, whenever forms of worship were standardized, whenever a hierarchy appeared, then the Antichrist had established his realm.

Arnold almost proclaimed a Manichaean duality between the true church and all institutional and social forms. He saw an irresolvable conflict between reborn individuals, whom he called witnesses of truth (*Zeugen der Wahrheit*), and society. The true church was a formless, doctrineless collection of reborn individuals who carried their own church within themselves.[44] It had fewer adherents than any orthodox institution, but it was broader in distribution: "The greatest admonition of our Saviour (which is love for all men) has taught me to find the general invisible church bound not to visible society, but dispersed through the whole world and hidden in all peoples and congregations."[45] The distinguishing factor was possession of the inner light, which naturally manifested itself in a certain mode of behavior and was, by implication, antisocial. Thus the true church was also the church militant. Its militancy consisted in rejecting all normal rules and all accepted social conventions in order to live the word of Christ. According to Arnold, such behavior served as a continual affront to the fallen church, which responded by persecuting the witnesses of truth. As true Christians always formed a minority, surrounded by a host of hypocrites, it was logical for Arnold to assume that true Christianity would be continually under persecution. He even went so far as to claim that true Christianity could not really flourish unless it was under attack. A quiet, contented church was a fallen one. [46] Arnold's idea of the church militant under continual repression enabled him to recognize the reborn without having to resort to theological or doctrinal discussion. The fact of persecution sufficed, and those who were the most persecuted were the so-called heretics. [47] Hence, Arnold came to the startling conclusion that the real witnesses of truth were to be found in the ranks of those condemned as heretics.

Here Arnold effected a reversal of traditional judgments which sent orthodox theologians into paroxysms of anger. He simply exonerated heretics from the charge of heresy because the majority had deemed them guilty. The real heretics, he claimed, were the heresy hunters, the orthodox clerics of all sects. [48] Following this strategy of analyzing all religious phenomena in individual terms, he then reduced the problem of heresy to a conflict of personalities. All dogmatic differences are dismissed as empty words (Geschwätz) that veil the real battle between the powerful and the pious. A pious man is labeled a heretic because his way of life infuriates the rich and powerful clergy. [49] It is in this manner that Arnold interpreted Pelagius. Pelagius incurred the wrath of the orthodox because he asserted the simple biblical precept that one cannot serve both God and mammon. The fallen clergy, who had sacrificed Christian precepts to their desire for wealth and luxury, responded by declaring Pelagius a heretic. To do so, they used the tactic of attacking his teachings, which, Arnold admitted, might have been overdone in places, but not in the manner in which orthodox theologians had interpreted them. [50]

But what was true Christian behavior and what differentiated the true from the fallen church? How could Arnold make such a differentiation without introducing doctrinal or theological elements? He resolved the problem with a method similar to Pufendorf's, though Arnold proceeded from a totally opposite starting point. Arnold modeled his idea of the church on his appreciation of the present. If we look closely at his definition of the church of the apostles, it turns out to be a negative description of Arnold's perception of the present. Whatever existed in contemporary organized religions was the opposite of that which formed the true church. Therefore, there were no priests, no rules of observation, no Sunday sabbath, no consecrated places of worship, no hierarchy, no confessionals, no bishoprics, no political affiliations, no theologians, no theology, no concern with riches or prestige. The apostles had been shepherds, not administrators. They had sought neither honors nor privileges but had won obedience because they not only proclaimed but actually lived God's words. The first congregations had been composed of simple folk, free from the destructive influences of wealth and learning. They had come together to praise God whenever they wished, worshiped him according to their own natures, celebrated communion daily, and held love feasts. When someone strayed from the fold, they had used persuasion and prayer, not force, to bring him back. The word "heretic" was unknown.[51]

To heighten his description, Arnold portrayed the fallen church in a rich baroque language filled with forceful pejorative images. It was a deflowered virgin, a whore, a bastard, an abortion.[52] Women had turned it into a theater filled with "dumb drunks, adulterers, whores, thieves, murderers, and bandits."[53] Arnold reserved the brunt of his vituperative attacks for the clergy and the teachers who, driven by the lust for power, continually led the people astray. Here Arnold universalized the present as he conceived it. The clergy and the teachers he so thoroughly castigated were the orthodox divines and scholastic philosophers of seventeenth-century Germany; they were his former mentors at Wittenberg and his colleagues at Giessen, whose attitudes he made the norm for all time. His criticism was so intense that it surpassed anything written by the most thoroughly anticlerical eighteenth-century philosophe. The marginalia give an indication of Arnold's vehemence; he touches on such topics as evilness of the orthodox, cunning and deceit of the orthodox, corruption of the teachers, inordinate ambition of the clergy, ignorance of the priests, murders by the clergy, persecution by the clergy, bloodthirstiness of the clergy, public godlessness of the clergy.

Arnold, who proclaimed the precept of love for one's fellowman, showed no sign of compassion for the weakness of man in society. With the same assuredness as Pufendorf, he praised and condemned without compunction. Like Pufendorf, Arnold rejected anything that tended to generate dispute without offering the prospect of an ultimate judgment. Hence his denial of theological and doctrinal debate; hence his one-sided concern with action. Arnold was positive that his strategy of drastic simplification had provided him with a sure and unfailing standard of evaluation. Simplification was therefore the principle that directed his critical and hermeneutic standards.

According to Arnold, the test of a thinker's credibility was totally existential. The sole determinant was the individual's position vis-à-vis society, not his testimony of belief. For this very reason Arnold felt compelled to announce his own existential position, which he summed up by the word *unparteiisch*. As Arnold used it, *unparteiisch* described a state of being as well as a goal of research. In its primary sense it meant nonsectarian, belonging to no organized party, disassociated from normal social intercourse. Its secondary meaning carried the common connotation of the word "impartial," that is, objective. What is critical for Arnold's hermeneutics is that he considered the latter meaning to be not merely related to the former but dependent upon it. Only a man physically and spiritually free from party adherence and belief – only a witness of truth – could write an objective history. It was a hermeneutics with the faults and also the attraction of an exaggerated sociology of knowledge, reinforced by a feeling of religious certitude. By it, Arnold could reject any type of philosophical discourse as being irrelevant, since the measure of truth is determined from the simple existential question: Was the witness reborn or not?

Arnold's hermeneutics both confirms and denies the methods of his age. He announces an objective standard of evaluation and interpretation, yet he locates this standard in something other than the guiding light of rational analysis. His hermeneutics is dogmatically antirational. Arnold drew a sharp distinction between reason and wisdom (*Sophia*). *Sophia* is the knowledge granted the reborn: it is an inner light that transcends all rational exposition because it is a hypostasis in God. *Sophia* is "the power of the most holy Trinity which at once reveals, transfigures, and heralds." [54] It is an emphatic understanding of Holy Scripture that is facilitated by the action of the Holy Spirit and achieved only by those who prepare themselves to receive the inner light, that is, by those who become *unparteiisch.* [55]

If *Sophia* is a hypostasis in God, reason is, according to Arnold, a tool of the Devil and the Antichrist. It is the language of Babel. When let loose it runs amuck, piling distinction upon confusing distinction, discrediting religion whenever it touches it. Arnold considered Scholastic philosophy and theology as archetypal products of reason gone wild. They were creations of debased heathen philosophers and could be accepted only by debased Christians. The Scholastics were agents of the Devil; their unending hairsplitting served to engender controversy, support persecution, and destroy religion. In choosing Scholastic philosophy as his special bête noire, Arnold formed a strange alliance with proponents of the new philosophy. Though rejecting their concentration upon a coherent theory of truth, he shared their goal of destroying Scholastic thinking. Thus he gave a long and laudatory account of Grotius, praised Pufendorf and Herbert of Cherbury, and had the courage to interpret Spinoza in a very favorable light.

In the same way that Pufendorf's a priori definitions limited his ability to appreciate process, so did Arnold's definition of the true church negate any new or expanded idea of qualitative change through time. The description of the apostolic church was his *Bekenntniskirche* (in Lutheranism: the confessional church), which he extrapolated into the past. From this extrapolated ideal, he measured and evaluated historical change. Obviously change implied change for the worse; his only dynamic metaphor is that of degeneration. History is a tragedy; it was, as Sebastian Franck had earlier defined it, "God's carnival play, the drama of human folly in which man turns away from God and suffers damnation, or turns to God and thereby brings upon himself the sufferings of persecution from state and church." [56] The function of Arnold's history was to offer the reader examples to help him choose the right course of action.

The *Unparteyische Kirchen- und Ketzer-Historie* is divided into two major sections, each beginning with a bright period followed by a description of degeneration into ignorance, hypocrisy, and evilness. The longest and most perfect period of grace was that of the church of the apostles. As soon, however, as that church began to compromise its actions with the demands of society, it entered into a period of decline. According to Arnold, the decline began in the second century and proceeded at an accelerated rate until the real catastrophe of Christianity — the conversion of Constantine the Great — led to a tie between church and state. Constantine sought to combine "two contradictory things"; he tried to "merge the realm of God and that of the Devil. Christ and Belial were supposed to become good friends." [57] The virgin church was defiled. Arnold portrayed the history of the regular church from this moment on as an unrelieved *mala dolorosa.* The only points of light in those dark and dismal times came from the lone rebels who rejected the idolatry of the church and its clergy.

A sudden change occurred with the appearance of Luther. In his early years (1515-1521) Luther is pictured as a man with a true apostolic message, directing him to resurrect the ancient purity of the church. Arnold treats this change from darkness to temporary light as a quantum leap. From the depths of darkness Luther announces the apostolic message, and the true church appears among the people for a brief moment. But decline is inevitable. Soon the Protestants fall into error. All the evil that for a brief interlude disappeared reappears. And so the second half of Arnold's book follows the pattern of the first. A description of the degenerate church is juxtaposed with valuable accounts of the persecuted witnesses of truth. The presentation is quite detailed; the descriptions of the "spiritual theologians" of the sixteenth and seventeenth centuries are so extensive that they are still used by historians today. Arnold's portrayal of the evil entering the Protestant churches is not a bit milder than his account of the rise of Roman Catholicism. All the faults ascribed to the Catholics return to plague the Protestants. They follow false philosophers, waste time drawing up elaborate explanations for Holy Scripture, and invent silly liturgical ceremonies. Grandiose churches filled with pictures, flags, candles, and satanic musical instruments were built and directed by pastors who were ignoramuses, alcoholics, fornicators, and seekers after prestige and wealth. What emerges is a picture of a bleak and decadent world of petty men prey to all the faults of human nature. History is nothing but a tragedy of error and force. The only recompense is the fact that the true church never dies. At all times and in all confessions there are witnesses of truth.

The total impact of the work is one of a cosmic pessimism typical of many seventeenth-century German religious writers. There is a singular lack of appreciation for historical change. All events are explained by reference to single individuals; there is no hope for society as a whole, for men living together according to the rules of society will always succumb to their baser instincts. Society equals Babel. Salvation is possible only for the isolated individual. Arnold's antipathy toward society confirms the antihistorical nature and intent of his work. Instead of a history, Arnold offers an existential choice based on two ideal types drawn from the present and clothed in the form of a history.

4

The dilemma of seventeenth-century historiography arose from the inability of historians to resolve the dichotomy between the general and the particular; they failed to mediate successfully between the general pattern of universal history and the detailed description of res gestae. Their failure resulted in a history incapable of explaining process and a historical consciousness unable to appreciate historical distance and uniqueness. Hence, historical narrative tended to leap from broad statements about the course, stages, or origins of universal history to detailed descriptions of individual action. A satisfactory interpretive relation was never established. Lacking intermediate modes of generalization, seventeenth-century historians had only two types of causal principles with which to work. Either these principles were of a general, timeless nature (God's will, Divine Providence, natural law) or they were located in the conscious actions of individuals. In actual historical narrative the latter take precedence. Events occur because a ruler is clever or stupid, informed or ill advised (Pufendorf); or religious dispute occurs because of the jealousy, impiety, and cupidity of deceitful clerics (Arnold). Since the historian traces the cause of an event to individual action, it naturally follows that he writes about famous men. In one sense, at least, history remained in the classical and medieval mold: it was still a history of elites and their deeds.

When seventeenth-century historians judged individual actions or characters, they employed a set of transhistorical assumptions, which, to them, were immune to historical criticism. Whether these values were those of traditional morality, the universal principles of politics, or values determined by the eternal battle between the saved and the damned, there application reduced historical narrative to a set of case studies demonstrating ideal types or situations. Historical time and historical distance were sacrificed to the demands of exemplar exposition which in structure, if not in intent, seemed to elevate chance and accident as prime causes of historical change. The poverty of historical interpretation was apparent even to leading thinkers of the time. The numerous criticisms leveled against the competence of history by seventeenth-century philosophers revealed both the general disinclination of the age to accept anything but a coherent theory of truth and the actual state of historical writing itself. History had degenerated into either a science of corroboration or what appeared to be a mindless fascination with trivia. As an endeavor, it was limited to what it had proved it could do best — to establish facts. It became "knowledge of those things which are or occur either in the material world or in immaterial substances." [58] The task of discovering the reasons for "those things which are or occur" devolved upon deductive philosophy, which had appropriated the model of modern mathematics for its mode of reasoning. But even this specialization of labor proved inadequate. It soon became apparent to thinkers such as Pierre Bayle that philosophy, as then conceived, was equally incapable of imparting meaning to the wealth of historical fact. Therefore the seventeenth-century crisis of historical consciousness manifested itself in all three major models of historical reasoning. Traditional historiography could no longer adequately explain events with the assumptions of providential Christian universal history. The new philosophy could not incorporate large areas of history into its schema and still retain identity and noncontradiction. And historical skepticism as employed by Bayle could destroy but not rebuild: it resembled "the warriors who put the enemy's land to the fire and sword, but who are not able to defend their own frontiers."[59]

By the beginning of the eighteenth century there was an increasing demand for a reassessment of both philosophy and history. Ultimately this demand led to a shift in modes of reasoning which can be crudely characterized as a turn from Descartes to Newton. One of the major goals of the reassessment was to evolve a strategy of analysis capable of joining history and philosophy in order to open up new vistas for man's understanding of himself and his milieu. In Germany this movement became dominant with the decline of Wolffian philosophy, beginning about the fourth decade of the eighteenth century.

II
Form and Goal of the
Aufklärung's Idea
of History

1

The historians of the Enlightenment consciously attempted to create a new model of historical explanation that stood in stark contrast to the writings of the polyhistorians. The study of history had become, for them, hopelessly irrelevant, an endeavor practiced either by social misfits or by harmless and hopeless souls who had nothing to offer the world at large. Enlightened historians, to borrow a phrase from Croce, no longer desired to be "silent keepers of the abode of the dead" as they believed the polyhistorians had been.[1] Rather, they sought to make history a discipline that spoke to the problems of contemporary life. The German Aufklärers enthusiastically joined in this undertaking. Though they shared many of the basic assumptions of the movement as a whole, their efforts did not mirror exactly those of either French or English philosophes; the Aufklärung had its own unique character, determined by its position in time and by its intellectual traditions.

The factor of time is the most obvious. The Aufklärung came later than the western Enlightenment, and so it could and did borrow from its western neighbors. Nevertheless, it was not merely a derivative movement, nor were its proponents weak imitators of Voltaire, Montesquieu, Rousseau, or Hume. The Aufklärers borrowed, but selectively, in order to confront questions already regnant in German intellectual life, questions arising, for the most part, from the impact of Leibnizian philosophy. In fact, the Aufklärung's unique character can, to a large extent, be seen as a result of the interplay between Leibnizian assumptions and Enlightenment propositions, as described by Ernst Cassirer:

If one observes the variety of stimuli that German intellectual life received from the outside – if one sees the influence that Locke and Shaftesbury, Voltaire and Rousseau, the French Encyclopedists and the English psychological analysts had – one could be tempted for a while to view the development of this epoch as a mosaic composed of single elements whose origins were foreign and extrinsic. In truth, however, a strict continuity and unity rule at the inner depths of these historical manifestations. Over against the abundance of material flowing in from outside, the Aufklärung maintained an independent spiritual form. . . .

[31]

It grew out of Leibniz's general philosophical view which it, at the same
time, restructured in retrospect.[2]

As Cassirer noted, the influences of Leibnizian philosophy in the
Aufklärung were not simple or, at times, even direct. Though Leibnizian
assumptions continually appear and reappear, and Leibnizian questions form
the starting point for many of the Aufklärers' inquiries, the Aufklärers cannot
be called conscious Leibnizians. In fact, a large number of them specifically
disassociated themselves from Leibniz's philosophy as then understood. The
famous monad controversy of the 1740s in the Berlin Academy — Leibniz's
own creation — offers ample evidence for this conclusion. If the Aufklärers
had been asked which late seventeenth-century philosopher they most
admired, the vast majority would have cited Christian Thomasius. Thomasius's eclectic philosophy emphasized history and psychology and concentrated more on the act of thought than on the products of thought. This
attitude, along with his pioneering efforts to reform the German university
system, appeared to correspond more to the Aufklärers' goal of creating a
science of humanity free from the "spirit of systems" than did the work of
Leibniz.[3]

For two reasons, many Aufklärers were reluctant to declare themselves
Leibnizians. First, Leibniz's complete philosophy was not available to them
during the formative period of their intellectual development. Not only were
his views haphazardly scattered throughout works on a dizzying number of
subjects, but some of the most important works were not published until long
after his death. The *Nouveaux Essais,* one of Leibniz's most important works,
did not appear until 1765, when many of the positions formulated therein
were already present in the Aufklärers' ideas, though in embryonic form.[4]
Because of this quirk of history, there are two dictinct moments of
Leibnizian influence on the Aufklärung. Initially, Leibniz's general philosophical position served as an unconscious stimulus to investigate certain
problems. Then, with the further publication of his works beginning in the
1760s, Leibniz's own answers to the problems he posed were accepted with
increasing frequency. Prior to 1760, however, Leibniz was basically interpreted through the eyes of his supposed disciple, Christian Wolff.[5] The
linkage of Wolff with Leibniz was the second and most important reason that
the Aufklärers, especially those concerned with history, were wary of
Leibnizian philosophy.

Wolff's relation to the Aufklärung is a complex one, for his work
stimulated yet at the same time repelled the Aufklärers. On the positive side,
his efforts to create a clear and precise German philosophic vocabulary, his
desire to reeducate the Germans, and his concern with *Gründlichkeit*
("thoroughness") won the Aufklärers' respect. Wolff's achievements in all
these realms are impressive. One has only to compare his *German Logic* and
German Metaphysics with Pufendorf's German writings; the advance in clarity
of style and precision of definition is overwhelmingly apparent. Even Leibniz

failed to equal Wolff's mastery of German as a philosophic idiom. Though Leibniz pleaded for a reformation of the German language, he himself preferred to write in Latin or French.[6] Wolff was a consummate writer of compendia, whose hallmark was a clearly defined terminology and a lack of imagerial language. His text on mathematics, *Anfangs-Gründen aller mathematischen Wissenschaften* (1710), was a classic, and both the *German Logic* and the *German Metaphysics* went through many editions, even after the *Latin Logic* and *Latin Metaphysics* appeared. In autobiography after autobiography, which the Aufklärers were so fond of writing, we find that their early discovery of Wolff's German writings opened up new vistas for them; they came to realize that German was capable of achieving a clarity equal to that of Latin or French. Johann Georg Sulzer's experience is typical. In his autobiography he related how bored he was with the training he received as a young boy when he was forced to memorize "incomprehensible words devoid of any concepts." After learning a little Latin, Greek, and Hebrew and a "barren logic and metaphysics," he was sent to the gymnasium. There he discovered Wolff and read him with a passion.[7]

Nevertheless, the Aufklärers could not agree with Wolff's general epistemological goal. Wolff strove to apply mathematical and syllogistic logic to all fields of knowledge. For him, mathematics, which he equated with syllogistic reasoning, was the propaedeutic to all understanding; it was the universal *Erkenntnismethode,* the model governing all forms of knowledge. Wolff was the last major representative of Cartesian and scholastic thought in Germany. Whatever he took from Leibniz was forced into a static mold of rigorous demonstration that divested it of the same dynamic elements that made Leibniz's philosophy so appealing to later generations. The new generation of the Aufklärung, on the other hand, was fascinated by the "real sciences," not by the "imaginary world" of hypothetical speculation.[8] The Aufklärers' autobiographies reveal that the books they treasured most as young men were travel descriptions and histories, nature poetry, and literature. The autobiographies also show that the Aufklärers experienced a new feeling toward nature, a feeling that signified a religiosity missing in Wolff's writings, a feeling that made the need to explain all nature through mathematics superfluous. The Aufklärers no longer felt compelled to speculate about the origins and the final meaning of things. They accepted the miracle of creation and the impossibility of defining God. Moreover, they were convinced that an investigation of God's creations was in itself a hymn of praise to Him. Again, Sulzer is typical. He continually sings the praises of nature and glories in the beauty of the Swiss Alps, calling them "the greatest and most admirable work of nature in the world."[9] The first book he wrote was entitled *Moralische Betrachtungen über die Werke der Natur.*[10]

The increasing distrust the Aufklärers showed toward pure speculation led them to attack, or at least to redefine, Wolff's position. Their disdain, most emphatically expressed by the historians, was at first automatically transferred to Leibniz. Many Aufklärers would have agreed with Johann Köhler's mocking reference to the ivory-towered idealist who had nothing better to do than "play with monads and speculate about a preestablished harmony."[11] And few would have doubted that this reference was to both Wolff and Leibniz. Therefore, while Leibniz's inquiries had set the direction that German thought was to follow, the Aufklärers were reluctant to accept Liebniz's answers as long as they were equated with Wolff's philosophy. The Aufklärers called in French, English, classical, and other German thinkers to battle what they thought was a fatalistic and overly rational approach to understanding. Their increasing ability to reinterpret Leibnizian assumptions throughout the last half of the century not only freed many thinkers from the restrictions of Wolff's formulations but also allowed many, such as Lessing and Herder, to discover the full import of Leibniz's message. This dual dynamic of the Aufklärung's confrontation with its own past and with other Enlightenment thinkers played a major role in determining the Aufklärung's specific historical consciousness; it testifies to the unity and the diversity of the Enlightenment.

The unity and the diversity may be seen by comparing what the philosophes and the Aufklärers found most disturbing in previous historical writing. The French, and to a lesser extent the English, directed the brunt of their critique against what they considered the aimless empiricism of the polyhistorians. The reproach of the utter mindlessness ascribed to the polyhistorical endeavor resounded with fugal consistency throughout the whole century. Fontenelle derided the silly infatuation "with the spirit of wars, treaties of peace, marriage, and genealogies" that passed for history, while Montesquieu expressed his frustration with the "compilers" by cynically suggesting that "when a man has nothing to say, why is he not silent?"[12] Bolingbroke directed his scorn against those who "heap crudity upon crudity, and nourish and improve nothing but their own distemper." In a hilarious thumbnail sketch of one such "mass of learning," whom he claimed to have met, Bolingbroke summed up the philosophes' disdain for the polyhistorian: "The man was communicative enough; but nothing was distinct in his mind. How could it be otherwise? He had never spared time to think, all was employed in reading. His reason had not the merit of a common mechanism. When you press a watch or pull a clock, they answer your question with precision. . . . But when you asked this man a question, he overwhelmed you by pouring forth all that the several terms of words of your question recalled to his memory. . . . To ask him a question, was to wind up a spring in his memory, that rattled on with vast rapidity, and confused noise, till the force of it was spent: and you went away with all the noise in your ears, stunned and uninformed."[13]

In all their attacks against collectors and compilers, the philosophes demonstrated both their wit and their despair at having to leaf through "musty monkish writings to acquire instruction."[14] It is not surprising that the Aufklärers advanced similar attacks upon what August Ludwig von Schlözer called history written in the taste of "Anno Domini men." Schlözer's critique, made in 1804, repeated the philosophes' points while acknowledging his debt to them: "History is no longer just the biographies of kings, exact chronological notes of war, battles, and changes in rule, or reports of alliances and revolutions. This was the taste of almost all the Anno Domini men in the Middle Ages. And we Germans continued to write history in this poverty-stricken manner as recently as fifty years ago, until we were awakened by the better models of the French and the English."[15]

Although they shared the philosophes' distaste for nondirected empiricism, the Aufklärers were even more wary of hypothetical and polemic history. If the French had at the turn of the century a surfeit of extensive inquiries into historical fact, the Germans suffered from an overabundance of hypothetical and polemic history. Pufendorf's essay on the nature of the German Empire and Arnold's *Unparteyische Kirchen- und Ketzer-Historie* alone generated a vast number of rejoinders written for polemic purpose and composed according to a priori assumptions. In the eyes of the Aufklärers, Germany was just freeing itself from the bonds of an inordinate passion for speculative thought. They usually referred to this bent for speculation as the "new scholasticism," which, according to Johann Salomo Semler, included among its proponents "Lullists, Ramists, Cartesians, and Leibnizians."[16] To the Aufklärers, Christian Wolff embodied all the faults of the new scholasticism. And since Wolff's philosophy still held sway in many universities, they believed it posed a more serious threat to the correct understanding of history than had the works of polyhistorians. Critique after critique was directed against what Johann Jacob Schmauß called Wolff's "prolixity, boastfulness [*Großpralerey*], and demonstrative method."[17] According to Schmauß, "the Wolffians do not read other books. . . . They do not study historical literature. When one paints history before their eyes, they pay no [real] attention."[18] Even those who had sat at Wolff's feet at Halle or Marburg were voicing similar fears. Winckelmann dismissed Wolff's work as childish nonsense (*Kindereien*) destined only to provide sustenance to mice.[19] And the famous eighteenth-century jurist, Johann Stephan Pütter, despaired that "Germany was in danger of returning to a state of barbarism," for under the influence of Wolff's deductive philosophy writers "began to neglect languages, philology, antiquities, history, experience, observations, laws, and sources of all kinds whose mastery was more difficult than just considering postulated definitions and demonstrations."[20] Even those who considered themselves Wolffians realized the deficiencies of Wolff's philosophy when applied to history. The Swiss publicist, Isaak Iselin, though retaining a great deal of respect for Wolff's accomplishments, still praised later thinkers who "freed philosophy from the terrible form to which the iron scepter of the demonstrative method had led it."[21]

The Aufklärers' fear of hypothetical and polemic history was intensified by their own reaction to much that was written by the philosophes themselves. The Aufklärers saw a danger in an overextensive abuse of the polyhistorians. Distaste for the form or the formlessness of their histories could lead to a blatant disregard for the material they had uncovered and the methods they had employed. The Aufklärung, coming later in time, enjoyed the luxury of being able both to accept and to modify positions already established by western philosophes. The academic professionalism of the Aufklärers made them more reluctant to criticize painstaking research. Like Edward Gibbon, they were aware that many philosophic historians "selected what they thought the most relevant facts according to a preconceived theory."[22] The Aufklärers readily admitted their debt to the early thinkers of the Enlightenment, but they were critical of the empirical foundation of many of the philosophes' histories. They feared that a new set of hypothetical histories would replace the ones they were destroying. Their position was basically the critique of a professional historian against a more brilliant yet less thorough dilettante, colored by the recognition that many of the new hypotheses attacked religion in a manner unacceptable to the Aufklärers.

Johann Christoph Gatterer's commentary on French historiography aptly sums up the attitudes of many German historians:

> The discipline of history [Geschichtskunde] has, like all other sciences, its changes and epochs. In the seventeenth century, French historians filled folios with their narratives [Erzählungen]. Not only did they investigate the reliability of the ancient authors they were required to follow, but they also prepared [veranstaltet] vast collections of documents, chronicles, and annals with an industriousness contemptuously referred to by their successors as German industriousness [teutschen Fleiß]. At that time these collections were eagerly purchased, read, and used, despite the fact that they comprised numerous volumes. In later ages French scholars believed that the material in all the archives and libraries had been exhausted. Therefore they sought a new way to achieve prominence. They wrote shorter histories and were more concerned with felicity of expression than with correctness of the narrative. After a while, the beaux esprits [schöne Geister] began to concern themselves with history. They reworked it according to their fancy in order to introduce their pet theories and thoughts. And as often as history allowed, they would communicate wise teachings or observations. Finally, the historical writer brought his art to perfection and taught his predecessors how to invent or alter events skillfully. The taste for reliable [gründlich] histories and collections was kept alive for a much longer time in Germany and England than in France.[23]

Distrust of the flightier works of philosophic historians and guarded admiration for the energy of the polyhistorians led the Aufklärers to argue that no matter what form history was to take, it required continual critical empirical nourishment from a systematic investigation of source materials. In this sense, the Aufklärers considered themselves the successors of the polyhistorians. Their search for a new form of history would include the attempt to continually expand and refine the methodological tools of the historian.

2

Behind the impatience with extensive source analysis shown by some philosophes lay the desire to get on and implement the goal shared by all Enlightenment thinkers concerned with history. Writers in France, England, and Germany were searching for strategies of analysis that would integrate an individual occurrence within a larger matrix of relations. They rebelled against what Fueter has called the catastrophe theory of historical explanation, by which an event is explained either by sole reference to specific individual intention or by direct and total relation to an immediately preceding event. [24] Voltaire's defense of his epoch-making *Essay on Manners* summed up the new ideal: "My aim has been much less to accumulate a vast quantity of facts, which are always self-contradictory, than to select the most important and best documented facts in order to guide the reader so that he may judge for himself concerning the extinction, revival, and progress of the human spirit, and enable him to recognize peoples by their customs."[25] The Aufklärers agreed, despite their oft-expressed reservations about the specifics of Voltaire's histories. Even more influential for the Aufklärers were the views of their favorite philosophe, Montesquieu. In *Considerations on the Causes of the Greatness of the Romans and Their Decline,* Montesquieu launched a frontal attack upon the catastrophe theory to which the Aufklärers would refer throughout the century. "There are general causes, moral and physical, which act in every monarchy, elevating it, maintaining it, or hurling it to the ground. All accidents are controlled by these causes. And if the chance of one battle – that is, a particular cause – has brought a state to ruin, some general cause made it necessary for the state to perish from a single battle. In a word, the main trend draws with it all particular accidents."[26]

The Enlightenment's imperative to explore the physical and moral causes of an event forced the Aufklärers to differentiate between source analysis and historical reconstruction. Schlözer expressed this awareness while still taking his usual potshot at Voltaire: "The critic unearths the single facts from annals and memorials (the Voltaires create them themselves or at least color them). The task of the historian is to put them together [*zusammenstellen*] to form a unity [*Einheit*]."[27] Throughout the period the Aufklärers emphasized the necessity of seeing events in their relationship or connection (*Zusammenhang*) with one another. The idea had become so general by mid-century that it was used by writers of the eighteenth-century equivalent of college brochures, whose purpose was to attract students to specific universities. In a series of letters designed to encourage students to attend the newly opened university at Göttingen, Johann Claproth wrote: "One finds that history is in excellent hands here. The historian is no longer considered a walking reference work from whom one hears about battles and sieges or learns the dates of great persons' births and deaths. Instead, it is accepted that the historian must teach us about the world. He must uncover the hidden causes of an event and show us the future that already resides in the past."[28]

The task of establishing a conjunction between particulate occurrences was especially vital to the Aufklärung's historical researches, not only because of the influence of the western philosophes, but also because of the problems posed by the philosophy of Leibniz. Leibnizian philosophy had provided eighteenth-century thinkers with a powerful set of metaphors dealing with change and individuality. One of these, harmonic conjunction, expressed a major goal of Leibnizian thought, which, as Ernst Cassirer has shown, was to combine unity with diversity without submerging one in the other. Leibniz sought to overcome a mechanical mode of analysis which merely placed things next to one another by creating an analytics that emphasized the symbiotic relation of the general and the particular. Leibniz's philosophy advanced a complete denunciation of the catastrophe theory, in which "the life process is more than the sum of the changing organic structures from one point of time to another." Instead, the life process is the development of a specific something (*ein Etwas*) that while changing still remains individual and true to its nature. The present, therefore, partakes of the past and contains within itself a picture of the future.[29] From this exposition the Aufklärers drew the conclusion that there was an intimate tie among past, present, and future which science should not and could not dissolve. The extent to which Leibniz's idea of a harmonic conjunction had become part of the fabric of general German assumptions in the last half of the eighteenth century is evidenced by Claproth's blurb extolling the historians at Göttingen.[30]

It was one thing to proclaim the importance of studying historical events in their interrelation and yet another to contrive a means to implement this goal. The Aufklärers attempted to solve the concrete problems of historical analysis through the use of two related, though conflicting, strategies of social analysis. One strategy focused on temporal succession; it discussed process. The other focused on spatial relations; it presented a cross-sectional analysis where the forward movement of time was halted to allow one to perceive far-reaching contemporary relations. The distinction approximates in rough form that between diachronic and synchronic studies in contemporary social theory.[31] The philosophical underpinnings for both strategies can be traced back to the Leibnizian recognition of development and identity, though these underpinnings were equally implicit in Montesquieu's own harmonic ideal. Here the Leibnizian moment seems dominant. According to Leibniz, change was the common element of both physical and spiritual things. The change was teleological: it was development toward a specific goal that was already vaguely prefigured by the individual nature of the thing in the process of change. The change was not automatic, however, or even purely intrinsic. The manner in which the individual unit changed was influenced by the total environment in which it existed. Accordingly, the observer could look at this change from a number of vantage points. He could choose to emphasize spatial contiguity and view the individual unit in terms of its relation with other units existing at the same time, or he could concentrate upon temporal sequence and investigate the tie that links past, present, and future.

Although theoretically complementary, the two strategies of structural and developmental analysis forced the researcher to adopt contradictory tactics of investigation and modes of representation. In simple terms, they virtually required one to choose between a study of a past epoch in and for itself and an investigation of the past as a determinant of the present. The tension between these two interests forms one of the constants in the modern discussion of the form and nature of historical inquiry. Even Ranke, who is often stereotyped in English-speaking lands by his concern with portraying how it actually was (*wie es eigentlich gewesen*), realized that it is just as necessary to describe how it evolved (*wie es eigentlich geworden ist*). As he remarked: "Though each epoch has its own right and worth in itself, one cannot overlook what had evolved from it." [32] Johann Stephan Pütter voiced the Aufklärers' concern with both tasks. After announcing his intention to explain the present by finding out how it had evolved from the past, he added: "I have made the attempt to sketch the constitution of each era as it then existed [*wie sie damahls war*]." [33]

The goal of combining the two strategies was difficult not only because of a writer's personal proclivities to favor one or the other but also because of the very nature of historical representation. The Aufklärers were cognizant of this problem. By mid-century Johann Martin Chladenius had already noted that the serial representation of historical narrative made it difficult enough just to discuss "cause and effect," which by nature is a sequential representation; when one tried to combine a cross-sectional with a developmental analysis, the task became overwhelming. Some compromises had to be made. [34]

Ten years later, Johann Christoph Gatterer also described the quandary of the historian who sought to merge structure with process:

> We have two rules whose observations are of equal importance, but whose contents seem to be so contradictory that one cannot follow both at once. The first rule is that one should represent the important events of each people or state in chronological order to gain insight into the mechanism of change within the state over the course of time. The second is that one should explain the synchronic connection of all states and empires existing at a specific period. According to the first rule, one should take up the histories of the states one after the other in chronological order. If one observes the second law, then the history of

the development of the constitution of a single state will appear too disjointed and be broken into too many disparate parts. [35]

Recognition of the difficulties involved in synthesizing these two strategies of social analysis did not deter the Aufklärers from attempting to achieve some sort of resolution. It is not unusual to encounter a thinker engaged simultaneously in pursuing both strategies and in trying to synthesize them. Gottfried Achenwall attacked the problem of understanding European affairs from all three perspectives. He pioneered the study of what he called statistics (which he defined as the acquisition of an intimate knowledge of a state's constitution) and succeeded in making it a respectable university discipline. His "statistical" studies of European states sought to delineate the basic components of a state and to perceive the components' relations to one another at a specific moment in time. Statistics was primarily a synchronic study of complex societal interrelations at any given moment. In addition to his statistical studies, Achenwall composed a more traditional history that chronologically traced the histories of various European states. His attempt to combine the cross-sectional with the dynamic, or developmental, approach is found in his *Geschichte der allgemeineren europäischen Staatshändel des vorigen und jetzigen Jahrhunderts*. Here he tried to extract the workings of supranational events from the bonds of narrow national histories and to portray them in their connections through time: "It is evident that when these great events are not treated specifically and as a whole [*besonders und im ganzen abgehandelt*] but rather buried in the history of one or more nations, the insight into the present connection of European states cannot be obtained." [36]

It is within the parameters of these three interrelated activities that the form of the Aufklärers' historical thought was forged. They directed their research, writing, and teaching to probing developmental and structural relations and to synthesizing them — an endeavor that, for want of a better term, we may call the writing of *Weltgeschichte*. For *Weltgeschichte*, as J. B. Bury defined it, is a history "focusing under one point of view, and fitting into a connected narrative, the histories of various peoples who came into relations with one another, within a given range, so that they are drawn out of their isolation and recognized to have meaning, greater or less, in the common history of man." [37] The Aufklärers applied these new criteria of evaluation to specific historical problems, which, in turn, allowed them to refine and expand their original operational assumptions. Their final goal was an attempt to achieve a deeper perception of their original premise that "all the events in the world are interconnected." [38] As Gatterer proclaimed, "The highest degree of pragmatism in history would be the portrayal of the general connections of things in the world [*nexus rerum universalis*]." [39]

The Aufklärers' quest for a new form of historical evaluation also forced them to consider a set of philosophical problems that they felt both polyhistorians and rationalists had answered incorrectly. At stake was the basic problem of determining the extent to which historical knowledge could be justified as an objective form of knowledge. The polyhistorians had broached the problem in purely methodological terms: they believed it possible to achieve impartiality, which they equated with objectivity, through the use of a reliable method of source analysis. The rationalists had approached the whole problem of objectivity with the assumptions of a coherent theory of knowledge. The philosophy of the Aufklärung groped for an answer that could harmonize these two views. While realizing the inadequacies of the polyhistorical answer, the Aufklärers had taken Bayle's critique of evident truth to heart. In its denial of eternal verities, the Enlightenment had moved away from the shelter of normative thought. Instead of looking to ultimate principles, it staked its faith on the rather illusive action of the philosophical spirit, which was increasingly described in the psychological terms of eighteenth-century aesthetics. Even the supremacy of the mathematical method as the archetype of all knowledge was reinterpreted by the Enlightenment. Now it was merely defined as the most refined product of the philosophical spirit, but limited in its applicability to the "abstract sciences." This view implied that, as Johann Gottlob von Justi contended in his prize-winning treatise on monadology, geometrical propositions were invalid when directed toward the "real sciences."[40] It became increasingly clear to the Aufklärers that each science — be it history, philology, or aesthetics — required its own logic to take cognizance of the point of view from which the science approached its object.[41]

Thus the Aufklärers were confronted with the task of establishing a set of hermeneutic principles that would validate their efforts at historical construction. The hermeneutic problems that seemed especially pertinent revolved around the following questions: (1) What differentiates history from other forms of knowledge and what does it share with them? (2) To what extent can one speak of a logic of history and what are the principles of that logic? (3) What effect does the historian's own point of view have in determining the questions he poses and the answers he provides? (4) Which faculties allow us to understand the past and how is this understanding objective? (5) What function does historical representation play in historical understanding?

3

The Aufklärers employed the term "pragmatic history" to describe their endeavors and to distinguish their conception of history from that of polyhistory. This self-proclaimed metaphor has led to a misunderstanding of the Aufklärers' idea of history. The reason is simple. The term "pragmatic history" was not unique to the eighteenth century. Its roots lie deep in the classical past and the use of it generally followed the Plutarchian idea of history teaching by example. It was interpreted in this context as late as the seventeenth century, despite occasional denials such as Guicciardini's. When contemporary readers encounter the term, they are prone to understand it in its traditional meaning without asking how the term was used. The conclusion is often drawn that since the Aufklärers spoke of history as pragmatic, they thought it had an exemplar function.[42] That assumption, however, is not correct.

The fact that the Aufklärers rejected the seventeenth-century model of historical explanation alone would suggest that they did not conceive of pragmatic history as their immediate predecessors had. Confirmation of this can be gleaned from a passing remark made by Arnold Heeren in his study of Johannes von Müller. He mentioned that the word "pragmatic" forms a part of historians' "technical vocabulary [*Kunstsprache*]."[43] The need to introduce this clarification, albeit in passing, implied that the technical term signified something more or less than the usual meaning of the word. In one book review, Johann Christoph Gatterer took an author to task because he had defined pragmatic history in a sloppy manner. Gatterer reiterated that, according to common usage, a pragmatic history is one that "unearths the causes and effects of important events."[44] Elsewhere Gatterer defined the task of pragmatic history in more detail: "The chief concern of the pragmatic historian is the search for immediate inciting circumstances and causes of important events [*die Veranlassungen und Ursachen einer merkwürdigen Begebenheiten*] and to develop as well as possible the whole system of causes and effects, of means and intentions [*Mitteln und Absichten*], no matter how confused they may at first seem. Nothing should hinder him or lead him astray in this undertaking, neither the distance between areas, nor the intervals in time, nor the different types of events themselves."[45] In actuality, pragmatic history was for Gatterer the opposite of exemplar history. Pragmatic history placed particulate events into a complex system of acting and interreacting relations; it did not abstract the singular event and attempt to discern some universally valid truth or moral from that isolated occurrence. For this reason, Gatterer (in a statement quoted above) defined the highest, though unattainable, goal of pragmatic history as the portrayal of the universal connection of all things.

The specific meaning Gatterer attached to pragmatic history was one with which the majority of the Aufklärers would agree. Johann David Michaelis simply referred to pragmatic history as "a history that traces driving forces [*Triebfedern*]."[46] Johann Schmauß called a history pragmatic if it portrayed the intimate connections in the constitution of a state; he specifically differentiated this type of history from teaching by example.[47] Johann Schröck, in a popular collection of academic biographies, *Abbildungen und Lebensbeschreibungen berühmter Gelehrten*, praised the historian Johann Köhler because of his "pragmatic evaluation of the origins and conjunction of events . . . which differentiates him from the dull collectors [*Sammlern*]."[48] And Johann Stephan Pütter asserted that "he who in the study of history is concerned with the pragmatic, not just with the single event or anecdote, will find it necessary to perceive the history of the state as an integral totality."[49]

Pragmatic history, as ideally conceived of by the Aufklärers, signalized the shift from thinking in fixed categories to thinking in terms of connections, a shift that characterized the intellectual climate of the last half of the eighteenth century.[50] Though pragmatic history was not "philosophy teaching by example" in its usual stereotypic meaning, it still was considered "useful" by the Aufklärers. Leaders of Enlightenment thought throughout Europe had little patience with "impractical" studies, and their German contemporaries shared this attitude. If history was only a pleasant way to while away one's time, if it was merely an escape to bygone days, then it had, in the Aufklärers' opinion, no right to be taught at a university. Given the two facts that the Enlightenment as a whole viewed education as a vital element for the improvement of mankind and that the study of history played a critical role in the German university curriculum of the last half of the eighteenth century, one must conclude that the Aufklärers had no doubt that history was useful. The specific uses they ascribed to history varied, however, depending upon personal activities and religious commitments.

The question of the use of history for religion was still one of the most pressing problems for eighteenth-century German intellectuals. Here the contrast between German and French concerns is most obvious. While many leading French thinkers were engaged in attacking organized forms of religious worship, the majority of the Germans were either desirous of defending them or, what was more common, of reinterpreting them in the light of a revised religious consciousness. At the mid-century mark there was still a tendency among historians born before 1720 to show that history demonstrated the veracity of the Christian message. Thus, Sigmund Baumgarten, who stood halfway between Wolffian rationalism and the newly felt concern with history, could still claim that history's major use was to show man's impotence in the face of God's will.[51] Even Johann Martin Chladenius tried in one of his lesser-known writings to prove that the introduction of Christianity had led to a definite improvement of western morals.[52] And his most famous work, the *Allgemeine Geschichtswissenschaft*, sprang from a direct religious motive. According to his own testimony, it was composed to show how the historical reliability of the Bible might be defended against the attacks of rationalists.[53] By implication it offered an answer to one of the major questions posed by rationalist commentators: How does one reconcile the contradictions existing among the Gospels?

By 1760, however, a definite change had occurred. No longer did leading religious thinkers attempt to employ history to prove specific Christian truths. Instead, these thinkers (usually referred to as Neologists) sought to redefine the nature of Christian and religious belief with the aid of historical analysis. By applying the dicta of pragmatic history to religion, they thought they could reach a deeper understanding of the relation between dogmatic assertion and religion itself. In this endeavor, the Neologists tried to steer a path between orthodox, Deist, and Pietist assumptions. Unlike the Pietists, the Neologists did not deny the importance of dogma, but they refused to accord dogmatic definition a universal validity. For them dogma was a necessary, though transitory, objectification of temporal religious belief; its formulations were reflections of a specific historical milieu, of a unique Weltanschauung. Thus religion itself was something more than a closed set of doctrines or a specific form of worship. It was an elemental drive that took on an infinite number of forms. It was in this manner that Johann Salomo Semler tried to demonstrate the persistence of religion. In contrast with Gottfried Arnold, who despairingly traced the triumph of theology over religion, Semler differentiated between "local" doctrinal formulations, which satisfied man's religious needs at specific moments, and man's expansive search for a "moral" religion, which led man to transcend these momentary manifestations of belief. In a similar vein, Johann Lorenz von Mosheim, the oldest of the Neologists, investigated the history of the church, and orientalists such as Johann Ernesti and Johann David Michaelis applied all the historical and philological tools at their disposal in an effort to understand the religious and social milieu in which the Old and New Testaments were composed. In effect, the Neologists used history to create a dynamic view of religion. History's function was twofold. On the one hand, it offered an adequate solution to the problem of dogmatic disagreement by historicizing dogmatics. On the other, it allowed the Neologists to search for the vital religious element behind the historical document and thereby achieve what Semler called a living perception (*lebendige Erkenntnis*) of religion. Historical analysis became the tool that allowed the Neologists to overcome history; to resolve the estrangement between the historical and the now, and to help prepare the way for a future expansion of religious consciousness.[54] Kant succinctly summed up the Neologists' assumptions in his seemingly paradoxical statement that religion is perfectly timeless, except in the impure manifestations of ecclesiastical history.[55]

The pragmatic value of history for law also underwent a change. Instead of using history as a means to corroborate theoretical assumptions, jurists of the Aufklärung saw in history an important means to discover the original intention of a law. It became an accepted dictum, even before the appearance of the "historical school of law," that a correct interpretation of law could be won only by investigating the historical context in which it was formulated and by understanding how it developed through time. Thus an increasing concern with German *Gewohnheitsrecht* ("customary law") characterized the works of Johann Mascov, J. J. Möser, Karl Friedrich von Moser, and Johann Stephan Pütter. The concern with *Gewohnheitsrecht* itself led to a renewed interest in the German Middle Ages, which in turn resulted in a new appreciation of the German past. In a similar manner, the problems of European politics and affairs were increasingly interpreted within the context of historical development and tradition by men such as Johann Jacob Schmauß, Gottfried Achenwall, Christian Koch, August Ludwig von Schlözer, and Arnold Heeren.

Despite the specific uses of history advanced by numerous Aufklärers, they all agreed upon the general value of historical understanding. In simple terms, they viewed the study of history as a means to expand experience, as a way to broaden one's vision and thereby to prepare the way for an enhanced future. August Ludwig von Schlözer, in one of his more ecstatic moments, defined history's value thus: "It draws one away from the blind admiration of individual realms, peoples, and events. . . . One will be liberated from the taste for the stories of wars [*Mordgeschichten*] and will perceive with enlightenment that greater revolutions have often resulted from the quiet musings of the genius and the gentle virtue of the man of wisdom than from the violence of all-powerful tyrants. . . . One will awake from the slumber in which our education had steeped us to realize that the present perfection of our loaf of bread, piece of printed paper, pocket watch, bill of exchange, planet globe, and hundreds of other things has been the result of discovery after discovery over thousands and thousands of years through which the human spirit has steadily advanced."[56]

Schlözer's uncharacteristically rosy picture reiterated an idea common to most historians of the Enlightenment. History, if studied correctly, frees man from parochial sectarianism. Thinkers as diverse as Vico and Bolingbroke expressed the same conviction. Vico's attack upon the conceit of nations ignorant of history is famous.[57] And Bolingbroke discussed the use of history in the following manner: "There is scarce any folly or vice more epidemical among the sons of man, than that ridiculous and hurtful vanity, by which the people of each country are apt to prefer themselves to those of every other; and to make their own customs, and manners, and opinions, the standards of right and wrong, of true and false. . . . An early and proper application to the study of history will contribute extremely to keep our minds free from a ridiculous partiality in favor of our own country, and a vicious prejudice against others."[58] Pragmatic history in all its variations was believed to open the mind, to extend one's knowledge, to acquaint one with the world in all its dimensions, and to dampen the fires of an intolerant and dangerous parochialism. The study of history was the study of man; its final goal was seen as self-knowledge. And this knowledge, the Aufklärers believed, would make it possible to transcend the moment by mastering the past and the present. Kant's definition of pragmatic anthropology can be equally well applied to the Aufklärung's conception of pragmatic history: it studies "what man as a creature possessing liberty of action makes of himself, or what he can and ought to make of himself."

4

In all their varied inquiries, the Aufklärers proposed a far-ranging reformation in the study of history. The question remains: By what standards should we evaluate their research, writing, and reflection? If the only test of the historian is the enduring quality of the histories he writes, then the Aufklärers were, by and large, failures. While their works demonstrated a sophisticated treatment of sources and sometimes a deep awareness of the complexity of human life and development, they failed to achieve the unity of conception and implementation that is characteristic of great history. Their works remained interesting but incomplete torsos. Their failure is not surprising, for the limitations of time, place, and social position worked against them. They were hampered by their own limited participation in the historical life of the era; by the restrictions of the institutional structure in which they worked; by the duties they felt toward their students, which led them to concentrate on the writing of compendiums; by the fragmentation of German intellectual life; and, most important, by the very magnitude of the task at hand. Their failure has caused later historians to neglect them or, even worse, it has invited ridicule and stereotype.

But the majority of the Aufklärers realized they were not great historians. They conceived of their role in the expansion and reformation of the historical consciousness as preparatory. In fulfilling this role, they were mirroring the character of the Enlightenment. The Enlightenment and its German counterpart may be seen as a great pedagogic endeavor; its leading thinkers envisioned themselves as teachers of mankind, as tutors in the "education of the human race." This desire to educate could produce great works such as Lessing's Joachimite expression of faith in the future expansion of the religious consciousness and Kant's transcendental philosophy. It also animated the efforts of those who are now forgotten. The capable, though not brilliant, professors at various Protestant universities in Germany and Switzerland also shared the conviction, so forcefully expressed by Kant, that while Europe was not yet enlightened, it could become enlightened. And as pedagogues by profession, they concentrated their efforts on teaching and explicating the principles they felt were essential to historical enlightenment. They felt it their duty to point the way that would lead to a German renaissance in the writing and understanding of history.

August Ludwig von Schlözer's variegated activities are symptomatic of this educational imperative. His inexhaustible researches into a variety of subjects are explicable not only by his character but also by the ideals of his profession. He pioneered the study of Slavic history, expanded the competency of statistics, sketched out the form in which he wished to see universal history written, contributed a study on the history of commerce, called for an intensive undertaking to collect and edit medieval Russian sources, edited Nestor's chronicles, "rediscovered" the history of the

Siebenbürgen Germans, and encouraged his students to study the history of colonization. His most famous undertaking, the publication of the two journals, *Briefwechsel: Meist historischen und politischen Inhalts* (1774-1782) and *Staatsanzeigen* (1782-1793), was expressly designed to educate the German public in politics. Everything he did had a general pedagogic goal, from the education of his daughter Dorothea Schlözer (the first woman to receive a doctorate from a German university), to the writing of children's books, to the teaching of his famous "Reisecollege" (an eighteenth-century Baedeker) and "Zeitungscollege." When Herder, in a rather petulant review, rightly took Schlözer to task for not having implemented his plan for the study of universal history, Schlözer's lengthy reply summed up the consciousness of the Aufklärers. He agreed with Herder that the plan had not been completed but countered that the proposal of such a plan was prerequisite to the writing of great universal history.[59]

To be understood, the accomplishments and the failures of the Aufklärers must be studied on these terms. The Aufklärers were primarily teachers of a new idea of history, which they transmitted to hundreds upon hundreds of students who attended their lectures and colloquiums and who read their compendiums. Given this more modest framework, the Aufklärers can be called successful. Their achievement was programmatic. They were concerned with asserting the possibility of and with establishing the methods for a new approach to historical understanding. They located problems, delineated strategies for resolution of those problems, proposed institutional changes to aid historical research, and generally redefined the whole endeavor of historical inquiry. The path opened up by the Aufklärers contributed to the creation of the modern paradigm of historical understanding. In their own way, they were concerned in fathering what is usually referred to as historicism. In their hands history became the starting point for all inquiries into the science of man. Through their efforts the epicenter for historical study was transferred to the university, where it has remained, for good or ill, until the present day. And their very success helped to generate a type of "national patriotism" that stood in a state of animated tension with their own cosmopolitan principles and made the *Gelehrtenrepublik* ("republic of the learned") the ideal center for the hoped-for regeneration of the German nation. A study of the scope, content, and import of the Aufklärers' historical thinking, therefore, points to the important role they played in forging the modern historical consciousness. Their failures serve to remind us of the equally important recognition of the Aufklärung's limitations in particular and the Enlightenment's in general.

III

The Aufklärung's Image
of the Future and Its Concept
# of Historical Development

1

The Aufklärers' call to study the interrelations of past, present, and future clearly shows that they opted for an idea of history emphasizing process or social development. Since most historians agree that the idea of social development is an elemental constituent of the modern historical consciousness, it might be assumed that the Aufklärung's paradigm of historical understanding was modern. Nevertheless, one element in the above-mentioned injunction has led many commentators to deny the modernity of the Aufklärer's idea of history. That element is paradoxically their fascination with the future, a fascination that encouraged them to include a concern with the shape of the future within the competence of historical understanding. This act has served as one of the focal points in the interpretation of the Aufklärung's (and the Englightenment's) idea of history, one that makes it necessary to pose and attempt to answer the following questions: What form did the Aufklärer's future-directed time consciousness take? Was this form conducive to the creation of the modern idea of historical development? In what way did the Aufklärers' future-directed time consciousness determine their concept of change? And, finally, to what extent did the Aufklärers' view of social change influence and reflect their own political and social values?

That the first three questions are crucial at all is owing to the fact that post-Rankean historiography deliberately excluded concerns with the future from historical reasoning. Professional historians have been trained to avoid discussion of future possibility and to be wary of any thought that could be called utopian. There is a tendency to equate utopian forms of thought with either impractical dreaming, determinist speculation, or outmoded Comtian positivism, all of which are difficult to combine with the complexity of historical life. A derivative assumption is often made, namely, that a person interested in changing the present would "not ask how society had come to be what it was, but how it could be made better than it was," as though these two questions were categorically and diametrically opposed.[1] As long as these assumptions are accepted without question, the test of the Aufklärung's historical consciousness would consist in ascertaining whether the Aufklärers were concerned with the future, whether they had an image of the future differing substantially from the known present, and whether this image informed and directed their historical understanding. If the answers to these inquiries are affirmative, then the conclusion that their idea of history was premodern would appear natural.

Very few interpreters of the Enlightenment would deny that the Enlightenment was concerned with future improvement. Though such concern might be embarrassing in a time when anti-utopias are common, it was the attitude of hopeful confidence that gave the Enlightenment and the Aufklärung their unique character. As Peter Gay contends, there was a remarkable "recovery of nerve" that found expression in a desire to set the world right – to banish ignorance, to eradicate poverty and slavery, and to forge ahead into the future. It was a time when history was seen "as the result of a causal process evolving in a complicated network of forces which man can manipulate more or less according to his wishes," a feeling described by Fred Polak as influence optimism.[2] We need only recall Schlözer's effusive description of the value of history (quoted in chap. ii) to realize the truth of this statement and to agree with most of Professor Gay's characterization of the age as "a century of decline in mysticism, of growing hope for life and trust in effort, of commitment to inquiry and criticism, of interest in social reform, of increasing secularization, and of a willingness to take risks."[3]

Granted the Enlightenment's concern with the future, may we then conclude that its future time consciousness was utopian? Professor Gay thinks not. "For the first time in history," he contends, "confidence was the companion of realism rather than a symptom of the Utopian imagination."[4] It was generated by the advances made in the quality of life in the eighteenth century – advances in medicine, science, manners, food production, and industry – and by the growth of humanitarian sentiment.[5] I believe, however, that this explanation, designed to free the Enlightenment from the charge of engaging in utopian thought, is inadequate and misleading. It is inadequate because the offered causal linkage between social time consciousness and actual social improvement is too simple and too vague. Gay makes social progress both the cause and the effect of the recovery of nerve. He establishes a relation of identity between social time consciousness and social life and justifies that relation by a third and untested dynamic assumption, that eighteenth-century social life was already pregnantly and inevitably modern, where modernity is defined as being anti-Christian.[6] Gay's interpretation is radically determinist in an unsatisfactory manner. It has led him to describe the Enlightenment in terms of a conflict between the group physically embodying the pregnantly modern (the outsiders) and those representing the already doomed past (the insiders). But even if we omit Gay's operative dynamic assumption, the immediate causal linkage between actual progress and a future-directed time consciousness is inadequate. Gay states that those "placed favorably enough to profit from the currents of the age were buoyed up by pleasing and unprecedented prospects."[7] Were these prospects really so unprecedented? Did a few new streets, improved city lighting, a grudging change in agricultural practices in a few parts of Europe, inevitably offer unprecedented prospects? Or rather, did the future-directed time consciousness of the philosophes lead them to reinterpret these modest changes in a rather "unrealistic" manner? Gay is adamant in his emphasis upon the uniqueness of the Enlightenment's recovery of nerve. But certainly the improvements he mentions were not more unprecedented than those experienced by the upper social classes in the Renaissance or in the High Middle Ages. Even the novel development of science in the seventeenth century failed to generate a similar recovery of nerve. A general improvement in the quality of life is not then the answer to the problem of the recovery of nerve. In all, the issues are far too complex to validate the assertion that the recovery of nerve which Gay describes with such elegance is directly derived from existing social conditions.

I do not mean to deny that a relation between social time consciousness and social change exists; that is virtually self-evident. But, as contemporary dialectical and phenomenological sociology suggests, the ties between social life and the genesis of ideas are far more intricate than is generally supposed. Increasingly, total social life is being interpreted as a pluridimensional set of realms that dialectically react with one another. Ideas, values, and symbols do not necessarily reflect material conditions exactly, nor do they merely reaffirm given social convention on a more abstract plane; they do act and interact with other social realms. At times ideas or values are in advance of other realms; at other times they lag behind.[8] It follows then that the fact of progress, or even the recognition of progress, does not invariably lead to a recovery of nerve. It also follows that a simple linkage between both realms of social life is highly questionable.[9]

In the instance of Germany, it is even more difficult to see how advancements made in the quality of life during the first half of the eighteenth century could adequately account for the Aufklärers' specific attitudes toward the future. True, change did occur, but as most commentators would admit, the forces of tradition and continuity were far more prevalent. To cite one example, while the material and social worlds of Gottfried Arnold and Johann Salomo Semler were much the same, their respective views of religious development differed radically. Within a short period of time the tendency toward nostalgia present in Arnold's vision had been replaced by Semler's dynamic definition of religion. German thinkers had substituted a desire to forge ahead to the future for their thirst for final answers. As always, numerous reasons for this phenomenon can be offered, such as the revitalization of religious belief, the acceptance of the Newtonian world view, the apparent decrease in the frequency and intensity of war, the nascence of capitalism, the renewed trust in the Ständestaat, and the feeling that the Treaty of Westphalia would prevent a repetition of the horrors of the Thirty Years War. But all these factors are incomplete; many are intangible while others apply equally well to the periods before and after the Aufklärung and countless other factors and questions could be added. What can be said is that there was a new mood, one of whose hallmarks was that it indulged in and was fed by a future-directed time consciousness. We might even say that the mood was foreshadowed by the parents of the Aufklärers in the symbolic act of naming their children. It may be pure coincidence or a totally irrelevant fact, but the first name "Johann" was universally popular. Given the vibrant religious atmosphere of eighteenth-century Germany and the added fact that the majority of the Aufklärers' fathers either were clergymen or were closely related to clergymen, it may not be too farfetched to see the wish for a new and better world in their preference for the name of the author of Revelations of Saint John the Divine. Be that as it may, it is hard to maintain that the Aufklärers' hope for the future was a companion to realism.

Professor Gay's tying of the Enlightenment's vision to existent social reality is, above all, misleading. He minimizes the "otherness" of the Enlightenment's image of the future by bringing it back into the realm of assumed probability instead of desired possibility. According to Gay, the philosophes were men who "saw life getting better, safer, easier, healthier, more predictable — that is to say, more rational — decade by decade; and so they built their house of hope less on what had happened than on what was happening, and even more on what they had good reason to expect would happen in the future." [10] Gay makes the philosophes into early social engineers who extrapolated present trends into the future, rather than thinkers who tried to create a vision of that which is not. It seems to me that men who "found a new meaning in the grandiose myth of Prometheus" [11] were not voicing a confidence that was the companion to realism. The Enlightenment's unique concern with the future was a revolution in patterns of thought, but one that surpassed the material foundations for the revolution. It was thought ahead of time, thought that dialectically opposed the moment by maintaining that *life does not have to be like this.* In form, it was utopian thought because it implied that it had a vision of *that which is not yet.* By utopian thought, I mean thinking in future terms where some image of the future is envisioned which is opposed to the present. This image does not, however, have to be systematically defined. [12]

In virtually all the Aufklärers' writings there is the idea of a future world that could be and should be qualitatively distinct from the present. The most famous examples are Lessing's *Education of the Human Race* and Kant's *History Written from a Cosmopolitan Point of View,* but their general expectations were certainly not unique. Well before Lessing wrote his *Education,* Semler expressed an analogous view of the unfolding expansion of man's religious consciousness based on a vision of a higher, "moral" Christianity. His continual efforts to demonstrate the time-bound nature of all dogmatic positions were based on his belief that "Christ and the apostles are founders of the new teachings and basics of a spiritual religion, a religion that is in the process of continual perfection."[13] According to Semler, the Bible "is and remains the new beginning and the source of a more perfect religion for Christians. But the perfection is there only *actu primo* . . . ; it requires a certain amount of time and an elevation of the Christians themselves before the perfection of Christianity can be achieved."[14] An equally potent image of the future was that of the world living in perpetual peace. Not only Kant and the Abbé de Saint-Pierre, but hosts of other commentators attempted to realize this goal by replacing the study of national confrontation with what they thought were the arts of peace. Thus, Gottfried Achenwall promised his readers to deal "more with the *artes pacis* than with the *artes belli,* more with the conditions of tranquillity than with those of dispute."[15] In fact, the Aufklärers' concern with the *Primat der Innenpolitik* reflected their ideal that the path to peace was through internal improvement. In a more general vein, the Swiss publicist Isaak Iselin voiced an almost Kantian dedication to the possible improvement of mankind. He described the theme of his anti-Rousseauistic *Geschichte der Menschheit* as "the progress of mankind from external simplicity to an increasingly higher degree of light and well-being."[16] Johann Martin Chladenius was also convinced that "future things pertain to historical understanding"; he devoted the concluding chapter of his *Allgemeine Geschichtswissenschaft* to this very subject. Finally, in 1793 Schlözer summed up the whole mood by asserting: "Besides the two types of inquiries — What makes up a present state? How did it develop into what it is? — there is a third: What should it be and what could it be? . . . Answering this question is the end goal of our whole study."[17]

All of this leads us to affirm the content of the usual critique of the Aufklärung's historical consciousness. The Aufklärung did engage in a form of utopian thought and that thought did influence and direct their historical inquiries. Are we then to conclude that the Aufklärung's historical consciousness was premodern, that the Aufklärers were blind to the forces of continuity, or that their future-directed gaze made them insensible to their own time? I do not believe this conclusion is a necessary one. Rather, I think the Aufklärers' image of the future sharpened their historical perception and made them more aware of the inequities of their time.

At first glance, the elements in utopian thought conducive to historical thinking are not apparent. Here the specific form of utopian thought is crucial. Until the eighteenth century, utopian thought was thought out of time and familiar place, portraying "a timeless *should* that never *is*."[18] It usually described social relations according to the principles of logical deduction and placed the described utopia in some remote region or in some prehistoric golden age. The Enlightenment's rejection of a priori thinking and its concern with the "real" as opposed to the "imaginary" naturally influenced the form of its utopian thought. Even though the traditional forms of utopian criticism were still cultivated (e.g., Diderot's *Supplément au Voyage de Bougainville*), utopian thinking became increasingly defined in terms of time and known place. The utopian image was placed in future time and within the boundaries of European and German space. No longer did the Aufklärers deem it relevant to talk about ideal republics; instead, they tried to conceive of how Europe or Germany might be brought to its own form of perfection. In other words, the Aufklärers historicized the utopian ideal; the problem of utopia became a historical problem which called for a historical analysis of the relation of past, present, and future. By this act we find a decisive "turn from nostalgia to anticipation; from criticism to intimations of dynamism."[19]

Despite the real and sometimes violent differences of opinion concerning the specific outlines of the desired image of the future and the ease of its achievement, the Aufklärers assumed that qualitative change was both desirable and possible. But qualitative change was intellectually defensible only if one could point to previous qualitative change. This element in their utopian imagination encouraged the Aufklärers to investigate the past, and it was this assumption that made their utopian imagination analogous in form to historical imagination. Both the Aufklärers' utopian imagination and their historical imagination were based on the concept of process: both conceived of a set of social relations that were qualitatively different from those existing at the present; both saw the present as only a stage in the total process of social development, as a moment in the triad past-present-future which was necessarily tied to both ends of the triad. The historical and the utopian imagination mutually reinforced each other. The more historical analysis could show that the present evolved from something that was qualitatively different, the more one could believe that a new set of social relations could be forged from those in existence. And vice versa, the more fervently one believed in the possibility of the creation of the new world, the more one was compelled to search for the unique character of earlier ages. In a very important sense, modern historical imagination destroys classical utopian thought and becomes its successor, for it asserts the "otherness" of both past and future. Modern historical thought differs from classical utopianism in that it offers a more direct challenge to action. By emphasizing the tension between change and continuity, it asserts the possibility of change and also recognizes the difficulty of implementing that change. Two worlds, that of the *never-to-be* and that of the *is* are replaced by that of the *not-yet* and that of the *is that can be made the not yet*. History now had a new function, to trace how society had evolved and might evolve. And it had a new orientation – it was to be a history of humanity. In place of a *Heldenleben,* history became the story of the inconspicuous and the unnoticed carriers of history.[20] Once again Schlözer summed up the new direction of historical research: "No longer was the historian merely to follow the paths where conquerors and armies had marched to the beat of the drum. Instead, he should travel the unnoticed route followed by traders, apostles, and travelers." [21] The Aufklärers' temporally and spatially bound image of the future accounted for an interest in investigating the past with a new set of assumptions.

The dynamic ideal of creating a differentiated future from an explored past and present explains the Janus-like reaction of the Aufklärers to their own time. The steady concatenation of hope and despair, of praise and condemnation, which is evident in even the most sanguine prophets of progress, testifies to the conjunction of the utopian ideal with the realization of the complexities of historical change. The mercurial Schlözer was a sensitive register of this feeling. Just as he offered ebullient praise to man's progress, he also punctuated his works with Tacitean notes of despair at man's barbarity to his fellowman. The pages of the *Staatsanzeigen* were filled with examples of European and German backwardness; Schlözer described with statistical detail the burdens borne by Bohemian peasants, the dehumanizing effects of serfdom ("One of the most frightening results of long-term slavery is that the slave loses all feelings for his human condition"), and the easily overlooked injustices perpetrated by Swiss oligarchs. In the same vein, Isaak Iselin's *Geschichte der Menschheit,* though positing the possibility of progress, was not a paean to achieved progress. Progress occurs, but ever so slowly. If one were to look at eighteenth-century Europe carefully, one would see that it is almost as barbarous as ancient Greece and Rome, a point of view neither self-congratulatory nor nostalgic. [22] Johann Christoph Gatterer, a fervent admirer of things German and a believer in the excellence of "German liberties," offered his readers this rather dismal characterization of his age: "I live in a time when Germany, according to its laws, is supposed to be a limited monarchy, but according to custom it is a state where a powerful ruler can usurp the law when he wishes and devour a weaker state. Even a weak ruler — be he prince, duke, or nobleman — is still powerful enough to torment and expel a few hundred or a few thousand people whom he calls his subjects." [23] In all these critiques, the Aufklärers believed that a historical investigation of abuses would help lead to their abolition. The writing of history, then, was conceived of as a preparatory act to change, one that diagramed the manner in which social change occurs and the degree to which it is possible.

2

As the Aufklärers developed an attitude toward the general dynamics of change, they increasingly came to take a position that varied from that of many western philosophes. In simple terms, the Aufklärers viewed the process of change as more tortuous and complex than most of the philosophes conceived it to be. The reasons are many. On an existential level, the Aufklärers' commitment to the *Ständestaat* induced in them a cautious attitude, which was reinforced by the hierarchic traditions of the academic profession. Further, since the majority of the Aufklärers were inhabitants of small provincial towns, they were well aware of the vast number of people totally untouched by the forces of the Aufklärung. Many of these still lived and thought as their forebears had in the fifteenth and sixteenth centuries. In virtually every *Dorf* in Germany, one still encountered soothsayers, astrologers, necromancers, and alchemists. [24] The belief in ghosts and evil spirits was widespread; in fact, some Aufklärers shared this belief. [25] Roads were bad, travel was dangerous, food distribution inefficient, poverty apparent, and many towns were still in a state of decay; some of them contained not a single house with glass windows. And everywhere a confusing set of privileges and customs bothered even the most highly respected professor. When one considers the amount of time and energy some of them spent in acquiring the privilege of brewing their own beer, it is hard to see where they found the time to write all the books they did.

On an empirical level, the Aufklärers' own historical studies showed that German history offered little encouragement that change could be rapid and easy. Weren't Germans still plagued by conditions that had their origin in the distant medieval past? Hadn't it taken centuries for Germany to escape the grip of *Faustrecht* ("rule of force"), and couldn't one still observe its lingering influence in the German body politic? Hadn't the welcome religious renovations of the sixteenth century led to the bloodbath of the Thirty Years War? And wasn't the age still burdened by silly scholastic disputations on unimportant points of dogma? For many scholars the lessons of the past showed that it had taken a very long time indeed for Germany to achieve even the slight flicker of Enlightenment it now possessed.

Not only did the persistence of tradition influence the Aufklärers' vision of the mechanics of change, but also the influence of Leibniz's general philosophical assumptions induced them to investigate the problem of change in a manner differing from that of the western philosophes. Again, the Aufklärers' position reflects their ambivalent attitude toward Leibnizian propositions. They were torn between the sensationalist formulations of western thinkers and Leibniz's analogous comparison of the soul to the monad. While disregarding the geometric base of the Leibniz-Wolffian heritage, with its emphasis upon clear and distinct ideas, the Aufklärers were intrigued with the assumption that perfection was not a static quality already present in the nature of things; rather, it was seen as a possibility to be achieved by the active power of the spirit. Instead of viewing the mind as a passive reflector of sensations and impressions, the Aufklärers accorded it an inherent creative energy. Thus they wavered between what we may call a realist and a quasi-idealist conception of historical change.

Realist theorists of historical propulsion usually confine their analyses to the natural tendencies of the object. The mind's function and the function of historical consciousness are limited to perceiving the given, objective relations of the natural development. Modern idealism, on the other hand, is based on the recognition of a basic duality between mind, or spirit, and matter; the tension between the creative moral spirit and the amoral natural world becomes the motor force of historical development. The spirit or mind works upon the empirically given to fashion progressively the apprehension of the world. Here the empirical world becomes the tool of the creative spirit and its regulating force. The idealistic image of the future envisions a world where a harmony between spirit and matter is achieved, a harmony characterized by the subject's ability to transcend and dominate the empirical world.

That the Aufklärers were torn between these two models of dynamic change is evident in their attitudes toward the historical writings of Montesquieu and Hume. Their almost unbounded admiration for Montesquieu, a feeling that reflected their own cautious stance, led them to discuss the impact of the external, the empirical, upon the course of history. As we will see later, they incorporated all Montesquieu's categories of historical explanation and many of his specific observations into their own works. They agreed that "mankind are influenced by various causes: by the climate, by the religion, by the laws, by the maxims of government, by precedent, morals and customs."[26] But Montesquieu's analysis was more applicable to uncovering the static "spirit of the times" existing at a particular moment. His ideas provided the Aufklärers with invaluable aid in dealing with the element of historical space and also cautioned against overambitious plans for rapid change. They did not, however, offer the Aufklärers equivalent aid in dealing with the sphere of dynamic time.[27] This deficiency explains the Aufklärers' equal admiration for Hume's *History of Great Britain*, first published in 1754, which emphasized another dimension of historical being. Instead of dealing with the static substratum of spatial relations — the Montesquieuan categories of climate, geography, and national character were virtually ignored — Hume concentrated on the inner element of historical life. The Aufklärers found in the *History of Great Britain* a portrayal of the interaction between man's psychological character and objective societal forces. Hume described passions, emotions, rationalizations, religious commitment (he called it enthusiasm), and he attempted to trace their effect on politics. His alternative approach encouraged the Aufklärers to follow a course already pregnant in certain Leibnizian formulations. Increasingly, they located the motor element of history in the actions of man's spirit. Historical change became explicable in terms of the creative spirit acting on and from the existing societal environment. The Aufklärers accepted the Englightenment's concern with harmony and used it to define their image of the future as a transcendent harmony between spirit and nature. Historical development became the story of man's attempt to achieve this harmony.[28]

The first impulse in Germany to reexplore the relation between nature and spirit came from the anti-Wolffian camp. By the 1740s a number of Wolffian critics, who had previously been on the defensive, began to denounce what they considered an overly rationalistic approach to the science of man. Drawing intellectual nourishment from the ancients, the Pietists, the later writings of Thomasius, and especially from Shaftesbury, they attacked the seventeenth-century proclamation of the omnicompetence of the mathematical method, whose application to natural law they found particularly galling. Johann Jacob Schmauß, an extremely successful teacher of history and natural law at Göttingen and Halle, was one of those who argued along these lines.[29] His major adversaries were Pufendorf and Wolff. During the thirties and forties Schmauß evolved a concept of natural law which he offered as an alternative to the *Systemengeist* of the "new scholasticism." Schmauß attacked Pufendorf because the latter had discarded ancient concepts of natural law and had replaced them with a "universal proposition — the *Socialitaten* — from which he derived all human obligations through mere deduction based on a superficial observation of an imagined state of nature."[30] According to Schmauß, Wolff — a "spinner of philosophical webs" without the "least experience of daily life" — had carried this tendency to the point of absurdity.[31] The fatal mistake of both Pufendorf and Wolff, Schmauß declared, was that they did not present a law of nature, but rather a positive law based on some assumption of what nature should be.

Schmauß's conception of natural law emphasized the irrational; he directed the investigator to look at the totality of human nature, to uncover what was inborn in man, and to identify man's primary drives and motivations. Modern theorists of natural law erred when they sought the solution to the riddle of human nature in man's reason.[32] The key to unlocking the riddle lay in man's heart and will. "When one wishes to formulate a true idea of natural law, one must conceive of a law that is inborn in the human heart and will, a law that is profoundly felt and experienced in the heart itself, and not first derived after complicated syllogisms."[33] Schmauß agreed with Shaftesbury that "the most ingenious way of becoming foolish is by a system," and he had no desire to make himself appear foolish.[34] Therefore, he rejected any systematic attempt to define man's nature. He was confirmed in this belief by his own historical studies. When one turns to history, Schmauß contended, man can nowhere be found as described by modern natural law. And, he continued, if the historical world differed so radically from the philosophers' description, then there was something wrong with that description. Since history shows reason to be a rather rare occurrence, the possession of reason cannot form the basic operational definition of human nature. According to Schmauß, the emotions and the voluntative elements of human nature precede the rational. Reason is a product of development, not a given quality; it is a propensity man possesses which might be nourished by man's will. Here Schmauß modified the traditional concept of man's two natures by denying reason a universally fixed category of existence. Will is master and reason its handmaiden. The former is natural, the latter only possible.

With this observation, Schmauß suggests a new standard for evaluating historical action. If reason is just a weak flicker, numerous events cannot be measured in terms of the conscious actions of reasonable men. Instead, irrational motives — motives of the heart and will — loom large in the process of change. But had Schmauß stopped there, he would have been left with an explanation for change that paralleled that of extreme Pietism. Since Schmauß was not a Pietist, he introduced other dynamic elements to explain human action. Though the instinctual drives are primary, they can be redirected by tradition and developed reason. Thus Schmauß saw historical development as a complex interreaction among three levels of life: primary instinctual drives, developed reason, and the forces of tradition. He formulated this idea in his discussion of one of the Aufklärung's most vital concerns, the relation of morality, ethics, and positive law. With Shaftesbury as his guide, Schmauß discriminated between an ethics derived from positive law (reason) and one that, as Shaftesbury said, was "derived from an immediate feeling and finer internal sense." [35] The latter springs from the heart and is basic because man possesses an instinctive moral drive. This drive finds specific expressions in human society, but these expressions vary according to the nature of the society. Hence, positive ethical laws are only the concrete expressions of the *instinctibus moralibus* and are thus determined by the factors of time, place, and social environment. It follows, then, that no one system of ethics completely exhausts the ethical possibilities of man. What is forbidden by positive law may be allowed by natural law.

In Schmauß's argument the rough outlines of the Aufklärers' attitude toward historical development are perceivable. There is the assumption that man's instinctual drives are never fully encompassed by any one system of ethics. Writers like Johann David Michaelis denied such commonplace moral rationalizations as the "natural aversion" to incest and argued that the natural aversion was really the product of a positive system of ethics. Michaelis asked his readers whether they themselves felt a *horror naturalis* and, if they did, whether it was not a product of education rather than of an inborn instinct. After all, Michaelis argued, the "history of the human race contradicts the idea of a natural aversion." [36] But the important feature of Schmauß's theory of natural law for the development of an idea of dynamic change was his belief that man's nature cannot be defined in any other way than as an energy, a potential for perfection. "Potential" implies the ability to transcend the concrete now for a yet to be realized future. But the act of transcendence is immensely difficult because of the power of tradition, which "has so strong an effect that the inborn instincts can be weakened and almost completely suppressed." [37]

While presaging the route later followed by a host of thinkers, Schmauß's natural law was, in one sense, highly unsatisfactory. His almost synonymous use of the terms "heart" and "will" and his description of their actions were too illusive. If the dynamics of change were to be found in the conflict among man's irrational instincts, his developed reason, and the forces of tradition, the Aufklärers felt a further study into the nature of man's "heart and will" was necessary. And here they drew aid and assistance from eighteenth-century German aesthetics, a field developed by men schooled in Wolffian philosophy.

3

Considering the anti-Wolffian posture of Aufklärung historians, it may seem paradoxical that in their analysis of change they used assumptions evolved by self-proclaimed Wolffians. But the situation becomes less paradoxical when we remember that by mid-century Wolffians and non-Wolffians alike were concerned with a complex of problems that were extraneous to the major thrust of Wolffian thought. Wolff had virtually ignored the problem of irrationality. Though distinguishing between "higher" and "lower" cognitive faculties, he had directed his syllogistic analytics to the former. The mid-century shift in intellectual concerns allowed Wolff's admirers to open up a new field of investigation that did not overtly reject Wolff's work. Aesthetics, as seen by the Wolffians, was the "science" of experience and creation. It was a catchall for everything that did not belong to traditional logic.

Aesthetics proved so valuable to historians because the two disciplines shared a common set of problems and concerns. Unlike earlier aesthetic thought, eighteenth-century aesthetics increasingly abandoned the goal of establishing positive artistic norms. Instead, the problem of creating and appreciating beauty was defined in psychological terms. The questions of how we experience beauty and how we explain the act of creation took precedence over the question of what were the correct norms for composition. The outstanding problem for eighteenth-century aesthetics became that of irrationality. And the study of the irrational led aestheticians to explore the relation of the individual to the general, the nature of feeling and judging, the process of creation, and the phenomenology of the spirit. These were the same philosophical problems the Aufklärers considered vital for an understanding of the dynamics of process.[38]

In addition to a set of common philosophical problems, history and aesthetics used the same "documents," namely, the written word and the artistic artifact. The whole complex of issues raised by the seventeenth-century quarrel of the Ancients and the Moderns led eighteenth-century thinkers to reassess the connection between human expression and human development. Except for the most unabashed proponent of modern superiority, the problem of the excellence of ancient art, to say nothing of the meaning of Holy Scripture, called for a study of the relation of art to science, of the understanding each conveys, and of their connection with the milieu in which they were formed. This became a historical problem touching the core of the triad past-present-future. Aesthetics was forced to incorporate historical problems into its scope. If aesthetics is given its most general meaning — "that branch of the sciences of man which, through the study of various artistic forms, aims at investigating the development and the anthropological, psychological, and linguistic stages of mankind"[39] — then the affinity between history and aesthetics becomes apparent. The Aufklärers were aware of this affinity, as well as of the importance of both disciplines for the study of religion, and combined ideas drawn from all three disciplines; all three — history, aesthetics, and religion — showed a deep concern with the questions of the meaning of language, poetry, myth, metaphor, and artistic representation.

Finally, there was a strong concurrence in the goals of aesthetics and history; they held a similar image of the future. A philosophical analysis of irrationality could and should lead to a transcendent apprehension of the world, whereby reason and feeling would merge on a higher plane of understanding. Both disciplines, as practiced by eighteenth-century German thinkers, assumed the possibility of a leap onto a higher plane of understanding. Knowledge was the prerequisite and the agent of this advancement of the human spirit.[40]

The fact that the most valuable German contributions to eighteenth-century aesthetics came from the Wolffian camp may be traced to two factors. The first was programmatic rather than essential. Despite all its faults, Wolffian philosophy did proclaim the need to deal with problems systematically and thoroughly. Wolff was the apostle of German *Gründlichkeit*. Since the specific tools of Wolffian analysis were not designed to deal explicitly with the realm of the darkly conscious, the Wolffians were left with only an imperative: Approach the problem philosophically; find the logic of the soul that is the analogue of reason! The second factor was more substantial; it was Wolff's retention of Leibniz's comparison of the soul to the forward-striving monad (though the one-faculty theory of the soul caused enormous difficulties and was finally rejected). These two components enabled Wolffian aesthetics to deal in a novel manner with the questions of perfectibility, genius, and the phenomenology of the spirit; the solutions the Wolffians proposed helped historians to formulate a more comprehensive theory of historical development.[41]

The first real impetus to treat these problems philosophically came from Wolff's most brilliant disciple, Alexander Baumgarten.[42] Baumgarten was able to enter realms never touched by Wolff because he was one of the few who had fully mastered Wolffian philosophy; he became conscious of both the merits and the limitations of formal syllogistic logic. The major fault of Wolff's logic was its inability to deal with the irrational, with what he called "confused perceptions." Baumgarten sought to complement traditional Wolffian philosophy by evolving what he called a study of "sensitive

knowledge," the type of knowledge conveyed by art. He invented the word
"aesthetics" to describe this activity. Cognizant of the pitfalls of an aesthetics
founded either on universal norms or on pure effect, Baumgarten tried to
devise a method of observation which would mediate between positive and
empirical modes of apprehension. Instead of obliterating the concrete by
divesting it of its qualitative elements — the ultimate goal of Wolff's
"universal knowledge" [*mathesis universalis*] — the aesthetic method directed
the observer to dwell upon concrete phenomena while attempting, at the
same time, to understand them philosophically. As Alfred Baeumler observed,
the aesthetic method is incompatible with either normative or purely
empirical thinking because it asserts the autonomy and freedom of the
subject while seeking to measure human experiences according to something
above empiricism. "It hovers between the poles of experience and normative
thinking."[43] History and aesthetics shared the same goals. Both were
concerned primarily with the concrete, and both attempted to impart
meaning to the concrete.

Baumgarten turned to the idea of perfectibility as the philosophical
concept capable of rescuing aesthetics from abstraction or arbitrary subjec-
tivity. He argued that there must be a perfectibility of the senses analogous to
the perfectibility of reason; but this perfection did not correspond in any way
to the perfection of mathematics.[44] The artistic representation was seen as a
sensuous representation of an image of perfection. Baumgarten explained this
perfection through the act of creation. The perfection of a work of art lay in
its unique power to weld diverse impressions and confused apperceptions into
an individual whole that conjured up a pure image. Baumgarten still applied
the Wolffian term "confused" to this image, but he freed it of its pejorative
connotations. Actually, he meant "fused," incapable of being dissected or
analyzed. The artistic perfection consisted of a phenomenological conjunction that "encompasses both center and periphery in a single glance."[45]

While Baumgarten was struggling to develop his aesthetics, others — some
of them either wary of Baumgarten's work or unfamiliar with his mature
theories — were forging ahead along similar lines.[46] Even before Baumgarten
announced his aesthetic views, Johann Jacob Bodmer attacked all theories of
art that sought their justification in either positive rules or mere sense
impression. His two major targets were the Wolffian Gottsched, who
attempted to standardize poetry according to correct rules of composition,
and the Frenchman the Abbé Dubos, who traced the impact of art to sense
impression. In his own attempt at definition, Bodmer differentiated sense
impression, logical thought, and what he called artistic reflection. The first
was merely mechanical, the second purely analytic, the third a combination
of reasoning and feeling.[47] He hinted that artistic vision is a form of
revelation, whereby a new ideal of the world is proclaimed. And Bodmer
virtually made the artist a Promethean figure, a "wise creator" who through
the power of his vision forces his contemporaries to think and act in a new

mold. He is a Homer, a Dante, a Milton — a man who reflects the spirit of his times while helping to change it.[48] Here Bodmer came to a position reminiscent of Schmauß's: change occurs through the complex interreaction of will, reason, and tradition. Bodmer also introduces a teleological element missing in Schmauß. Each creation of genius results in an expansion of consciousness which can be reexperienced. In the process of reexperiencing, the path is opened to the apprehension of a better world and to the transcendence of the now. As Carlo Antoni made clear, Bodmer's gaze was directed toward the future, toward the dawning of a golden age of literature and, by implication — for Bodmer gave literature an ethical function — of life.[49]

By the 1760s the Leibnizian idea of perfectibility had become one of the central concepts of German aesthetics. In 1755, three years before the second volume of Baumgarten's *Aesthetica* appeared, Moses Mendelssohn had applied the idea of perfectibility to artistic understanding. He maintained that "the healthful, the tasteful, the beautiful, the practical, all pleasures stem from the idea of perfection."[50] Mendelssohn drew a distinction between the perfection of man's physical nature, which is generally complete, and the perfection of his inner nature, which is potential: "Alone the inner man is incomplete. . . . men have to work, to work tirelessly for improvement."[51] Even more than Baumgarten, Mendelssohn concentrated upon the dynamics of creation, upon the action of the "positive power of our soul" on the given empirical environment. All artistic creation, and by extension all historical creation, results from the inborn drive toward perfection, called by Reimarus *notio diretrix*.[52] In this formulation, the aestheticians were trying to combine the concrete with the lawlike; they sought to explain a single occurrence within the context of extended and harmonic relations. The idea of perfectibility functioned as the normative concept linking individual creations together. It was the propulsive drive behind every great work of art; it was the unmoved mover. Eighteenth-century German aestheticians defined perfection as the achievement of a harmony between inner life and outer life, a harmony that was best apprehended in the perfect sensuous presentation. Here the aesthetic and historical ideals met and mutually reinforced each other. The relativity of the ideal of perfection was justified and described through the historical concept of the individual spirit of the times, while the aesthetic use of perfectibility strengthened and clarified the historical conception of process. Binding the two ideals together was the common denominator of the image of spiritual harmony.

How is harmony to be achieved? What are the dynamics of the creative spirit? These questions animated the whole aesthetic endeavor, tying it so closely to psychology that the boundary lines between the two disciplines are hard to discern. Baumgarten had implied that the elements of perception formed an interrelated whole (referred to in eighteenth-century terminology as the *Seelenkräfte*); others tried to draw up the phenomenology of this whole. One of them was Johann Georg Sulzer, who did his most important work in the 1760s. Sulzer was a disciple of Bodmer's (Antoni called him Bodmer's "Wagner"), a friend to Mendelssohn and Nicolai, an admirer of Haller, and a translator of Hume; he applied ideas and insights drawn from them all in his attempt to chart the action of the spirit. In 1763 Sulzer offered the Berlin Academy (he was president of the Class for Speculative Philosophy) a summation of his views.[53] Adopting a popular tactic of analysis, he drew an analogy between the act of seeing and that "which goes on in the soul's inner perception."[54] The tactic's popularity stemmed from its easy application to the problem of the relation between the observer and the observed, between external and internal perception.[55] The state of the soul, Sulzer postulated, was determined by the action of two faculties, the faculty of apperception (*faculté d'apercevoir*) and the faculty of feeling (*faculté de sentir*).[56] Each of these faculties, when dominant, produces in turn a specific state in the soul, with each state embodying a diametrically opposite subject-object relation. The state of meditation (*l'état de meditation*) produced by the faculty of apperception is completely object directed. It is the state of pure cognition, where "the activity of the soul is so limited to a single object that the sensations themselves lose their strength. . . . the soul has neither feeling, nor propensity, nor will."[57] When in this state, "man becomes himself an abstract being, unattached to anything in the world. Everything he does that extends beyond the object of his meditation, he does mechanically or without knowing; he has all the symptoms of an imbecile."[58] The opposite state, the state of feeling (*l'état du sentiment*), is purely subject directed. Here "feeling is an act of the soul which has nothing in common with the object that produces it or occasions it. . . . It is not the object at all which one feels; it is one's own self."[59] It is obvious from these capsule descriptions that Sulzer considered both states inadequate. One, based solely on subjective feeling, was too vague. The other was too narrow; its very clarity distorted any true apprehension of the world in all its dimensions. In fact, Sulzer was sometimes harsher on pure cognition than on feeling; he derided the learned imbeciles and offered the following observation, with which Goethe could have agreed: "Profound meditation has the effect of a microscope, which shows us the smallest elements of an object very distinctly, but which at the same time so reduces our field of vision that it is impossible to see the entire object."[60] Therefore Sulzer introduced a third state of the soul, a conjunction of the state of meditation and the state of feeling, which he called the state of contemplation (*l'état de contemplation*). He distinguished among the three states in the following manner: "There is one state where man sees very distinctly and feels nothing; another where he feels strongly and sees nothing; a third where he sees and feels clearly enough to recognize what is outside him and what is in him."[61] The third state – a synthesis of knowing and feeling – is a form of intuitive understanding which leads to an appreciation of a totality.

Sulzer's discussion virtually called for the introduction of a third faculty of the soul to account for the state of contemplation, but he never took that step. Moses Mendelssohn and Johann Tetens did. In his early writings Mendelssohn ran into the same difficulties as Sulzer; he described three states of delight, but he traced them back to two faculties. Later, however, he added a third faculty to account for the state of "restful satisfaction," similar to Sulzer's state of contemplation, and called it the faculty of approval (*Billigungsvermögen*). Tetens also proposed a three-faculty theory, citing the faculties of feeling, understanding, and will, but he complicated the issue by sometimes adding a fourth faculty and sometimes returning to a two-faculty idea. But whether one listed two, three, or four faculties, the important thing for the historians of the Aufklärung was the concept that creation entailed a dynamic interaction between the subjective faculties and the objective world.

The Aufklärung's evolving phenomenology of the soul increasingly drew a distinction between spirit and nature (the former being active, the latter passive) and considered spirit to be multilayered. The terminology was vague and often contradictory; the number of powers of the soul the Aufklärers discerned was variously two, three, or four, with the tripartite division becoming the more popular. Usually the analysts distinguished among the power of cognition (usually called *Verstand; Vernunft* more often referred to logical constructs), the power of experience (some thinkers subdivided experience into feeling and passion), and the creative power (referred to as either the *Einbildungskraft* or the *Dichtungskraft*).[62] A work of art resulted from the harmonious action and interaction of all the faculties acting on nature; it took the form of a distinct living image that instantaneously spoke to all the *Seelenkräfte*. This emphasis upon the active role of the mind, or rather of the senses, imagination, and cognitive faculty working in harmony and creating an image from nature, offered the historians of the Aufklärung a paradigm of explanation for directional change. It seemed to provide the key to show how man attempted to reach the inborn potential for perfection which Mendelssohn and countless others had postulated and also to explain the difficulties man had in attaining it.

One more element of the new aesthetics — the aesthetic vision of the creative genius — captured the attention of historians. The concept of genius served to fill the void between the objective idea of perfectibility and the subjective tendency of aesthetic psychology. It was in the man of genius that the two spheres of the individual and the general converged. The idea had already been advanced by Bodmer, was propagated by Sulzer, who said that Bodmer had taught him "to consider the poet [*Dichter*] as a master and a prophet,"[63] and was reinforced by Mendelssohn. By 1760 thinkers in all fields were engaged in describing the nature of genius. The relatively obscure theologian Friedrich Gabriel Resewitz (1729-1806) offers a typical example. In his *Versuch über das Genie* (1760), Resewitz described genius as intuitive knowledge (*anschauende Erkenntnis*) which simultaneously grasps the general and the individual. Given the traditional Leibnizian definition of perfection as unity in diversity, Resewitz was saying in effect that genius is a form of perfect knowledge. Resewitz was even more explicit when he defined divine knowledge as intuitive knowledge of the whole world. Although he did not say so, the implication was clear: genius partakes of divine knowledge. Naturally, as a theologian Resewitz denied that man could ever aspire to total intuitive knowledge, but he did argue that it was within man's ability to incorporate past and present intuitive knowledge into his world view, an act that would expand his own consciousness by making it approach divine wisdom.[64]

For the historians of the Aufklärung, the new concept of genius had a number of implications. First, it allowed the Aufklärers to evaluate great historical figures — for example, Moses, Socrates, and sometimes even Jesus — on the basis of new standards. Their achievements could not be seen as analogous to artistic creation, as being conjunctions of the universal and the concrete expressed in a form that necessarily reflected the spiritual and social environment in which the genius lived. The idea of genius encouraged the Aufklärers to explain change in terms of spiritual change, but it also emphasized the difficulty of that change. Change was neither automatic, for genius was unpredictable, nor easy, since the acquisition of the products of genius required a restructuring of thought and action. The idea of genius also reinforced the Promethean view of human nature that distinguished the thinking of the Aufklärung. Not only that, it helped to define the Aufklärung's image of the future. The utopian imagination was seen as an active force that was itself limited in its scope of outlining fully the shape of the future. Each image of perfection was itself an incomplete one, and for that reason each implied a direction, not a closed definition of the end of all things. Art as well as history had an infinite realm of future possibility.

4

The ease with which anti-Wolffian assumptions could be joined to Wolffian aesthetics in explicating the problem of historical process is illustrated by Isaak Iselin's *Geschichte der Menschheit,* written in 1764 and revised in 1768. Iselin was neither a professional historian nor a German academic. But he was one of the many Swiss who, though having an intimate acquaintance with French and English thought, reflected the German influence.[65] Iselin's own intellectual development attested to the merging of the two German strains of Wolffian and anti-Wolffian thought. Originally a Wolffian, he fell under the sway of Schmauß while attending the University of Göttingen. From then on, he sought a middle ground where he could unite his historical interests and his bent for philosophy. He thought he had achieved such a resolution in his *Geschichte der Menschheit.*

Iselin's *Geschichte* was not an original work; rather, it was a popular summation of the modern thought of his time. Its supposed concern for the complexities of historical life is far less apparent than Iselin thought. Unlike his teachers at Göttingen, Iselin never mastered the critical apparatus of historiography. He drew the bulk of his historical material from unreliable and incomplete travel reports, which made many of his judgments stylized, naive, and superficial. Yet Iselin's lack of critical acumen was compensated for by his sensitivity to the currents of intellectual life. Catching the mood of the times, his work demonstrates how in Germany the idea of process became associated with man's spiritual struggle to overcome nature. It was an adamant denial of realist theories of historical propulsion and a fervent declaration of faith in a transcendental image of the future.

The stimulus for writing the *Geschichte der Menschheit* came from two sources. The first was Iselin's negative reaction to Rousseau's *Second Discourse* and *Social Contract,* a reaction so strong that it impelled Iselin to write a rejoinder. The second came from Lord Home, the English aesthetician, who suggested that Montesquieu had also failed to uncover some of the basic causal elements in history: "Montesquieu did not develop those causes that flow from human nature itself — from our passions and from our natural desires." [66] Stimulated by this remark, Iselin sought to write both an "anti-Rousseau" and a complement to Montesquieu which would emphasize psychological dynamics. One can sense the influence of Schmauß, Sulzer, Mendelssohn, and Baumgarten in Iselin's work. His definition of natural law parallels that of Schmauß: man is a social animal with a natural social drive, not an animal just capable of sociability. Man's unique nature cannot be defined merely by his cognitive ability but rather by something more primary, which Iselin called man's "inner feeling." It was the inner feeling that was the "focus of all the forces that set man in motion." [67] Iselin also believed that man had an inborn ethical drive, which he equated with Mendelssohn's formulation of man's propensity toward perfection. This was the quality that distinguished man from animals. Once animals reach maturity they are complete; they all possess the qualities of their species in approximately the same way. [68] Man is different. His perfection is a future possibility. "A universal law of nature seems to limit animals to the narrow confines of the senses and to the present. Another law, just as universal, apparently drives men to break out of their present boundaries and to lift themselves from one level of perfection to another." [69] This inborn drive, this basic "uneasiness" of man, is the motor force of history. It is an idea strikingly suggestive of Kant's concept of "social insociability."

Iselin used the psychology of aesthetics and supplemented it with Montesquieu's environmental categories of influence to explain the dynamics of change. In Iselin's scheme the active force of human history resulted from the action of the *Seelenkräfte*; the forces retarding and restricting history were those of the social and physical environment. Iselin divided the

Seelenkräfte into the three powers of sensation (*Empfindung*), imagination
(*Einbildung*), and cognition (*Verstand*). Though ever present in man, they are
not always found in the same proportions. This belief led Iselin to construct
three ideal types of human behavior: man ruled by his senses, man ruled by
his imagination, and man ruled by his reason. These ideal types were then
analogously applied to historical development, creating a threefold periodization of history which resembles Lessing's, as later expounded in *Education of
the Human Race* (1780). The first stage, the state of savagery, pictured man
as a victim of his senses, especially of his passions. In this stage man was in his
infancy; the Montesquieuan categories of climate and geography played an
overwhelming role because of man's basic weakness. The restlessness of the
human spirit, however, could not be contained. The uneasiness of man made
it impossible for him to live forever in the eternal present. Quickly the forces
of creative imagination were aroused; stimulated by the challenges of the
environment itself, the human spirit responded and men drew together within
tighter bonds of social existence, which in turn encouraged them to attempt
to control nature. At first a hunter, man became a cultivator. He harnessed
the power of fire and began to shape the elements of the earth. The age of
imagination had begun.

Adopting the metaphor of growth, Iselin labeled the age of imagination
the childhood of man. But it was an extended childhood. In fact, the age of
imagination, or barbarism, corresponded to virtually the whole of recorded
human history. It took a long time indeed before man was to manifest even
the first sign of puberty. In his description of this age, Iselin demonstrated
the ambivalent attitude of the Aufklärung toward imagination. The
Einbildungskraft was the faculty that grew most quickly. It elevated sensate
impressions beyond the boundaries of the present. It was for Iselin, as for
Sulzer, the creative element in man's nature: "With a magic power it extends
sensate images to boundless vistas. It calls forth the possible and the absent,
the past and the future, from dark realms. It renders the human race so many
services that it is beyond the power of language adequately to characterize
each of its specific effects. . . . Now it renews the consciousness of past
sensations in the soul; now it portrays what is not present; now it reveals
what drives or what drove others to action, assisted by language, feelings,
thoughts, and actions; now, with an even more astonishing magic, it pierces
into the secrets of the future by comparing the present with the past, opening
thereby a new field for man's spiritual activity; now it raises itself with a bold
and excessive energy above the boundaries of the actual to create new forms
[*Gestalten*] which are sometimes great, sometimes unusual, sometimes
reasonable, sometimes ridiculous."[70] The age of imagination is the age of
image creation; its language is that of poetry and metaphor. The *Einbildungskraft* offers the key to man's greatness, but it is also the source of his possible
destruction. Knowing no boundaries, obeying no rules, imagination may fall a
victim to dissolute licentiousness. Imagination, when it lacks a guide, is just as

likely to apostrophize half-baked ideas and dangerous actions as to lead to the truly great. The age of imagination is the middle realm of history – our realm – from which man will either raise himself or plunge into an abyss of barbarism unknown to man's infancy. It is a period marked by brilliant peaks and dark, forboding valleys. It was this realm with which traditional historical analysis concerned itself.

If the age of imagination were the only realm of historical life, man's prospects would appear bleak. Yet the middle realm was not one of uniformly repeating cycles. Each peak incorporated something from former ages. And with the development of the new field of spiritual activity, that of historical understanding, the contemplation of a new future was made possible. Iselin believed that the study of history, aided by philosophy, would show that an alternative to the present did exist and would help to implement that alternative. The third age was to be an age of reason; it was also a future age. Like Kant, Iselin was not naive enough to believe that his century was an enlightened age; rather, it was a time when the first tentative steps toward enlightenment were being taken. The door to the new age of freedom had cracked open a bit, but only a little bit. How could it be otherwise? Certainly great advances in thought were being made, but if one looked around, one still found barbarism everywhere. Even the most fortunate of lands – Switzerland and England – were not havens of enlightenment. To Iselin's credit, he was not one of those Swiss who were wont to see Switzerland as the homeland of freedom. Almost everywhere, people were ruled by arbitrary laws imposed by mediocre rulers. And women were even worse off than men. Iselin was one of the many eighteenth-century champions of women's rights. He firmly believed that women were more sensitive than men, that they were less often led astray by barbaric imagination, that they had a finer appreciation of the beautiful, and that the feminine (one might almost say the "eternal feminine") would be the element that could lead man away from his quixotic quest for an imagined glory.[71]

In the third age, the age of human maturity, harmony among the three faculties would be achieved. Reason, the last faculty to develop, would guide the other two by directing their energies toward understanding the nature of man. Only then can man obtain freedom. Here we encounter one of the essentials in an idealist conception of history. The attainment of freedom was postulated upon an act of knowing; the realization of the image of the future was possible only through a conscious act. Geniuses, who can discern the true relations between man and man and between man and his environment, were to be the primary agents in the attainment of the new age. The leap into the future had to be accomplished by an enormous educational effort. True freedom, which means harmony between the inner and the outer life, can never be imposed by force; it is the product of a spiritual revolution. "I differentiate between two types of *Policierung,* or of the moderation of manners. The first is imparted by the outer forms of society. It is ordered by kings, judges, and ruling bodies. Often it is the creation of a middling knowledge and a preponderance of power. It forces order on a people but is incapable of making them love it or value it. The second improves the mind and spirit [*die Geister und die Gemüther*]. It is the work of sublime reason and therefore requires infinitely more time and effort."[72] When Iselin used the term "sublime reason," he meant the intuitive knowledge of genius, not logical abstraction. Only when man achieves this conjunctive awareness provided by the three faculties working in harmony can he overcome nature; only then can he direct nature to serve his own welfare and happiness.

The stated purpose of Iselin's *Geschichte der Menschheit* was to contradict Rousseau. In content and conception the book failed to accomplish this purpose, for Iselin simply did not have the ability to demolish, or even to perceive, Rousseau's complex and sometimes contradictory vision. Iselin's work was overly abstract, an easy prey for the critical professional historians of his time. Nevertheless, despite its obvious faults, the *Geschichte der Menschheit* serves in a limited sense as a symbol of the period. It captured a mood far different from that of Rousseau, whose writings reflected a pessimistic reaction to the horrors of history.[73] The *Second Discourse,* the *Social Contract,* and even *Émile* were basically antihistories, "flinging . . . the accusation of delinquent development against virtually all governments."[74] Salvation, if possible at all, was, for Rousseau, an act against history. Rousseau was an apostle of pathos, regret, passivity; Iselin was one of hope, expectation, and activity. Rousseau's antihistories paid homage to a time that might have been. Iselin's metahistory offered hope for a time that might be. Iselin was a prophet of will who saw that the road to progress lay in mastering the past in order to overcome it. In this he was typical of the Aufklärung.

5

The activist assumption in combination with the aesthetic analysis of inner man also influenced the academic historians' conception of process. Most evident was the Promethean theme, which was accompanied by a rough idea of challenge and response. August Ludwig von Schlözer offered a glowing portrayal of how man can be a second creator, an *Untergott,* capable of transforming nature to suit his needs. He drains swamps and lakes, opens up the hinterland by building canals, turns deserts and wastelands into flowering and fruitful provinces through irrigation, and overcomes enormous obstacles in order to bring more land under the plow.[75] Man is stimulated to undertake these activities by the challenge of nature: "A thousand powers lie dormant in man and will remain dormant if they are not awakened by a challenge."[76] Johann Christoph Gatterer advanced a similar theme. He spoke of man as a *Nimmersatt,* a creature never satisfied with his lot, one that strove continually for something better: "Man has it in his power to dominate all three realms of nature; he can rule over the earth's soil, change its climate, reshape its elements, alter its boundaries, and expand internal communication. Not only does he have this power; he uses it, sometimes to advantage, sometimes to disadvantage. . . . Man has the right to improve nature because of his given sovereignty over the earth and its products. The more needs people recognize, the more enlightened they are; the more people are capable of desiring, the more they know, and therefore the more enlightened they are. *Ignoti nulla cupido.*"[77]

Gatterer's debt to Wolffian aesthetics is evident. His definition of human nature — derived from that aesthetics — determined his view of change, a view that implicitly emerges from Gatterer's work. The instability of man's nature allowed man to overcome the basic challenge of the environment by creating a new environment, the social, to protect him from the attacks of nature. The social world created by man was always limited, however; each form of social organization had a given range of possibilities. As long as these were unfulfilled or were in the process of completion, civil society flourished. Government, religion, customs, and culture were in harmony with one another. Once the boundaries of possible development within a given form were reached, then a disparity among elements of life would appear; it would lead to a historical crisis and either dissolution or new and expansive creation. It was this type of explanation, strongly reminiscent of Montesquieu, which Gatterer advanced for Rome's fall. Rome's original constitution created the conditions for its success, but that very success led to its fall. It acquired too much wealth; it absorbed too many foreign customs; it overextended its area; it restructured its whole economy. The resultant change in basic patterns of culture and thought finally undermined the older Roman idea of *virtus.* [78] The silent revolution that took place in the body politic was ignored, and a feeling of nostalgia enervated the power of the empire to respond to the new situation.

The Aufklärers' activist idea of change was tempered by their recognition of the extreme difficulty of effecting purposive change. If man could be an *Untergott,* he could also be an *Unterteufel.* The thousand powers that lie dormant in his soul could take on an infinite number of forms, ranging from enlightenment to the most despicable barbarism. Hence, man's activities could be improved only through a massive attempt at reeducation. The pedagogic element, so pronounced in German idealism, was already evident in the Aufklärers' willingness to equate progress with the task of educating the human race. For these professional schoolmasters, the school became a powerful symbol; the education of humanity was analogous to the education of the individual, and both were to be trained through historical knowledge. [79] Since the attainment of freedom was to be preceded by a spiritual change, the Aufklärers were skeptical of any immediate attempts to change the whole pattern of social life. Throughout their work they warned against abstract project making. They were derisive of the few philosophes (Turgot,

Tanucci) who were able to play a major political role and who had attempted, the Aufklärers believed, to recast society completely without paying attention to the customs, manners, and traditions of their lands.[80] The Aufklärers cautioned that "the statesman, when contemplating new creations or improvements, is better advised to be guided by experience and example than by general laws."[81] Even the art of making wise laws – a favorite eighteenth-century subject of discussion – was seen as a function of custom and tradition, not of general law.[82]

Once again we can perceive the spirit of Montesquieu hovering over the specific formulations of the Aufklärers, especially Montesquieu's pronouncements emphasizing relativity and the power of individual tradition. In his *Considerations on the Causes of the Greatness of the Romans and Their Decline,* Montesquieu clearly condemned radical change, arguing that theoretical knowledge is not sufficient to encompass the complexity of the state: "When a government's form has been established a long time and things are arranged in a certain way, it is almost always prudent to leave them alone, because the reasons for such a state having endured are often complicated and unknown, and they will cause it to maintain itself further. But when one changes the whole system, one can only remedy those difficulties that are known by theory, and one overlooks others that can only be brought to light by practice."[83] In *Spirit of the Laws,* Montesquieu emphasized that customs and manners cannot be changed by law: "We have said that the laws were the particular and precise institutions of a legislator, and manners and customs the institutions of a nation in general. Hence it follows that when these manners and customs are to be changed, it ought not to be done by laws; this would have too much the air of tyranny. . . . Nations are in general very tenacious of their customs; to take them away by violence is to render them unhappy: we should not therefore change them, but engage the people to make the change themselves."[84] Here is the program of the Aufklärers in capsule form. The process of getting the people to make changes themselves was an educational act.

The Aufklärers viewed their historical writings as a necessary prelude to reeducation. For example, Johann Stephan Pütter expended an amazing amount of time and energy in tracing the outlines of German constitutional history, becoming in his lifetime one of the most respected jurists in Germany. In this endeavor, one of his major concerns was the reception of foreign systems of law (he listed three: Roman law, canon law, and Lombardic feudal law) into Germany during the Middle Ages. Although he believed that each of these three systems was produced in a milieu alien to that of medieval Germany, he recognized that certain intellectual and religious attitudes and certain changes in the social organization of the medieval Germans had allowed them to incorporate foreign laws. (He cited, for example, the ideas of the translation theory and the theory of the two swords, the rise of cities, the increasing prosperity of the elites, the tendency to send men to Italy to be educated, and the "natural" tendency of the city dweller to prefer rational systems over age-old traditions.) These reasons were, by and large, no longer valid, though the laws still remained operative: "The binding power accorded foreign laws undoubtedly originated from historical errors which, if the situation were repeated today, would no longer have the same motivating power. . . . Could one seriously claim that Justinian, Charles V, and Joseph II stand in the same relation to one another and that a compilation made in Lombardy of the feudal law of that region actually pertains to the German Empire [teutsche Reich]?"[85] That Pütter recognized the power of tradition but also called for its transcendence is evident from an earlier book, where he expressed the hopes the Aufklärers put in their historical writings: "Unless one knows the causes and origins of a disease and uses a remedy that stops the source, it is impossible to cure the disease without causing more serious damage."[86] Pütter's answer to the problem of foreign laws was a typically German one: he sought the cure in the "healthy" traditions of Germany. Pütter called for a study of German common law (Gewohnheitsrecht) to counter the influence of the three systems of foreign law. Gewohnheitsrecht offered a tool capable of moderating the abstractions of the foreign systems: it would lead the way to a new harmony between law and custom.

The writing of history was, however, only a part of the education of humanity. The Aufklärers believed it should be accompanied by action, by a continual attempt to reform specific abuses.[87] Their vision of progress was basically reformist, and their sense of future time was regulated by their feeling for past time. Change was for them incremental. Continual concrete improvement would ultimately lead to a piecemeal restructuring of the state and to the creation of the mentality of freedom. It was a program of little steps leading to silent revolutions, which reveals the mentality of a liberal, well-educated civil servant. Progress was to be achieved through professional expertise animated by a concern for the public good. The nation's leaders were to be thinkers, poets, educators, administrators, engineers, and merchants. It was a bürgerlich ideal. In the specifics of the Aufklärers' idea of change we find a conjunction of the various levels of their social life. The revolutionary implications of their quasi-idealist position is tempered by the hierarchic structure of the Ständestaat, the conservative conventions of the academic profession, the tensions of an economic organization straddling the periods of mercantilism and nascent capitalism, and the emerging idea of the Bildungsstaat.[88]

The easiest way to explain the moderate, cautious, and pedagogic nature of the Aufklärung's political and historical ideal, as well as the Aufklärers' concern with the inner life and the spirit, is to invoke the stereotype of the unpolitical German. The usual argument runs that the classes propagating enlightened ideals were weak and ineffective. For this reason their ideals remained pious hopes with little practical effect. In search for an ersatz for active political involvement, the Germans turned to the realm of the spirit. By extension this argument seriously questions the political and practical viability of any historical theory that approaches idealism. In a very important sense, the stereotype is a correct one. The smallness of most of the German states, their limited resources and goals, the power of the *Ständestaat* tradition, the incompetence and stupidity of a number of petty princes, and the provincial character of Germany as a whole virtually excluded the type of political consciousness we would call modern. Yet, on another level, the argument concerning the political ineffectiveness of the Aufklärers could be reversed. Though constricted in their activities, the Aufklärers were not totally excluded from participation in the political life of their age, as were the majority of the French philosophes. The Aufklärers' activities had a direct influence on German administrative procedures and ideas.

It has long been recognized that the genesis of the German bureaucracy can be traced to the eighteenth century. The training of that bureaucracy was entrusted primarily to the universities, the centers of enlightened thought in Germany. The tendency to see the university as a nursery for civil servants ensured a close tie between *Katheder* ("lecture podium") and government. In fact, many professors, especially jurists, supplemented their teaching duties by advising ministers and by drawing up elaborate plans for reform, ranging from the establishment of widows' pensions and poorhouses to the restructuring of schools and courts. The titles *Hofrat* and *Geheimrat* granted to famous scholars further attests to this tie. The students of the Aufklärers, whether noble or *bürgerlich,* were the ones who manned German bureaucracies, ran German schools, and preached from German pulpits. The Aufklärers were so successful in their educational efforts that a new definition of social roles was established. Without denying the value of an aristocracy, it became a generally held view that the aristocracy was to become useful, which meant they were to become educated. The Aufklärers' cautious position can be traced to the fact that they were part of the establishment, and not, like their French counterparts, outsiders excluded by a powerful "noble reaction." Despite all the various inequities within the German states, despite a "noble renaissance" that also touched Germany, the educated classes had a better chance of finding a position than did those in France. The Aufklärers' vision of change reflected the assurance of men who expected to be able to work within the system as a whole.[89] Circumscribed, though not excluded, by the *Ständestaat,* they created an attitude described by Helen Liebel as "Enlightened Bureaucracy," which stood in stark contrast to the ideas of the politically excluded philosophes — especially the physiocrats — and which questioned the efficacy of Enlightened Absolutism. The Aufklärers' ideals were exemplified in the work of such men as Sonnenfels, Bernstorff, Montgelas, Schlosser, Hardenberg, and Stein, all of them students of the Aufklärers. But the Aufklärers' attitude toward change was also reflected in the conservative reaction to the French Revolution of men like Ernst Brandes and August Wilhelm Rehberg. Both had been trained in the Pütter school of German constitutional history well before they read Burke.

IV
Human Origins
and Historical Development

1

Had a German scholar of the mid-seventeenth century been asked to compose a history of his own state, he probably would have begun his narration with the Creation, described the expulsion of Adam and Eve from Eden, recounted the stories of the Flood and the Diaspora, the history of the Chosen People, and the birth and death of Christ. He would next have discussed the history of the Roman Empire or the Fourth Monarchy and then shown how his state had been founded either by a direct heir of Noah or, if he were clsssically minded, by a survivor of Troy. Only then would the author have felt ready to plunge into a chroniclelike recounting of the battles and changes of rule he thought necessary for an understanding of historical change. This elaborate undertaking would be cramped into the confines of traditional Christian chronology, which dated the beginning of the world about four thousand years before Christ.

At the end of the seventeenth century a conscious proponent of modernism would have responded to the same request in a different manner. Though he might have introduced the Christian scheme and the Christian chronology, the major part of his narrative would have shown how at a distant time past a group of individuals, directed by their desire for self-preservation, had agreed to join together to form a state, a union they sealed by acceding to a basic social contract. The author would then have spent considerable time describing the nature of the "necessary" social contract and used it as a measure to evaluate the events that took place in recorded time.

It is easy to see that these two approaches were implicitly, if not explicitly, in contradiction to each other. The traditional approach was postulated upon the belief that revelation, as recorded in the Old and New Testaments, provided an objective source of historical interpretation. The second approach, even when making concessions to the traditional interpretation, assumed that coherent truth founded upon the law of noncontradiction offered the correct standard for historical evaluation. Nevertheless, despite the almost dialectical confrontation between natural law and revealed religion, the two approaches had much in common. Both the concrete application of Christian mythology and the analysis of modern natural law provided the historian with a set of transhistorical symbols supported by a universal truth (revelation or coherent truth). Both of these allowed the interpreter to judge historical change according to incontrovertible standards of what was or what rationally must have been. Both obtained their standards from a "prehistorical" evaluation of human nature, that is, from a specific idea of origins; and since both proclaimed a finitely definable idea of human nature, they were in essence opposed to the idea of future qualitative change. Just as the orthodox Christian believed that there was nothing new under the sun, so too did the theorist of natural law proclaim the universality and permanence of his definitions of societal relations. Change, for both, was an ebb and flow within certain limited and known types of human behavior.

Logically, one could expect that the Aufklärers' dynamic image of the future and their rejection of logical abstraction would have abolished the need to return to either the biblical or the natural law images of social creation when explaining historical development. Yet history does not always accord with logic. Despite the Aufklärers' "opening" to the future, they only reluctantly abandoned recourse to the Christian and natural law models when discussing change. Their reluctance is not difficult to understand. No matter how unique or how modern certain areas of their perception were, the power of tradition and habit still influenced the form in which they expressed their ideas. Christian mythology and natural law had created powerful symbols of representation that had become crystallized in the thought patterns of the time. Natural law and Christian myth, as well as classical precedent, formed the commonplace of discourse. They provided the metaphors and the unconscious models with which the Aufklärers framed their arguments.

The Aufklärers' persistent use of these symbols and metaphors was reinforced by their ambivalent attitude toward the specifics of Christian interpretation and the constructions of natural law. With very few exceptions, the Aufklärers were professing Christians. But their religious consciousness was increasingly tending toward the unorthodox. As we have seen with Semler, they shied away from overly dogmatic explanations of Judeo-Christian myth. They were more prone to interpret the biblical message less as a literal truth than as a guide to moral action. As scholars they were trained in the tradition of natural law, but their professed Christianity also made them wary of purely naturalistic explanations of life. The Aufklärers did not immediately exclude a description of first beginnings from their paradigm of historical explanation. Rather, they first attempted to retain and incorporate both the Christian and the natural law models of social origins; then they sought to revise both to accord with their newly won historical consciousness. Finally, after a long struggle, the Aufklärers came to believe that the breach between a priori definitions of the beginning of history and their idea of historical development could not be healed. In their final solution, the Aufklärers chose to ignore − not to deny − both explanatory models when dealing with historical development. In effect, it was a choice that cut the bonds tying historical explanation to any and all creation myths or their substitutes. It also paved the way for extending past human time far beyond that envisioned either by explanation of social origins or by the Aufklärers themselves.

2

The most potent and deeply ingrained set of symbols for the Aufklärers was still the biblical. As sons of pastors, teachers, professors, and merchants, the Aufklärers were brought up on the Bible and on stories from it. Pastors, tutors (often imported from Switzerland because of its reputed piety), and parents regularly explained to them the significance of Christ's birth, death, and resurrection. As children, many received instruction from works such as Johann Hübner's immensely popular *Zweymahl zwey und fünffzig auser-lesene biblische Historien,* which related biblical stories and presented useful principles that could be drawn from them. Each story, told in simple German, was followed by three *Haupt-Lehren* (basic lessons) and a set of questions. Hübner informed his young readers that the Creation showed that woman should obey man and that polygamy was counter to God's design, just as the Annunciation taught one to recognize the prime virtues of chastity, humility, and resignation to God's will.[1] Whether beneficiaries of Hübner's wisdom or not, all the Aufklärers had as youths witnessed and participated in the new wave of religiosity precipitated by Pietism. The extravagances of the reborn, who spent hours diagraming and discussing the state of their souls, and the sterility of the extreme orthodox, who endlessly repeated the formulations contained in the symbolic books of Lutheranism (Act of Concord and Augsburg Confessions), sometimes threw the young men into a state of confusion. Still, very few Aufklärers lost their faith.[2] As students, the large majority of them planned to study theology, though most of them changed their minds while attending the university. But they remained professing Christians. It was not unusual for an Aufklärer to spend his first morning hours in devotion or in reading from Holy Scripture, as the capsule portrayal of Johann Christoph Gatterer, drawn by Charlotte von Einem, shows: "Piety ennobled all his feelings; every morning he held devotions with his seven children: there he stood — head uncovered, before God!"[3] Despite the Aufklärers' abhorrence of dogmatism, the Bible was still a living thing for them. As Adolf von Harnack observed, "They knew themselves to be Christians and felt bound to God."[4]

The persistence of the Aufklärers' religious belief made it difficult for them to surrender Christian historical assumptions, even if these conflicted with their conscious vision of change. Their reluctance to renounce Christian tenets was strikingly apparent in their attitude toward Christian chronology. Theoretically, the Aufklärers' image of the future, combined with their idea of incremental change, called for a chronology reaching far back into the distant past. Christian chronology, which assigned less than six thousand years to the earth's existence, was too constraining. Yet it took a while before they were able to surrender it.[5]

In 1726 the Halle-trained historian and jurist Johann David Köhler declared that "the best chronologists date the beginning of the world on the twenty-sixth of October in the year 1657 before the Flood and 3,947 years before Christ's birth. To be sure," Köhler added, "the ancient Egyptians and Chaldeans, as well as the modern Chinese, make the world many thousands of years older, but Holy Scripture is more believable than all other books of heathen fables founded on the ancients' vain search for fame."[6] More than forty years later Köhler's successor, Johann Christoph Gatterer, could still agree with Köhler's basic chronological assumption. Like Köhler, Gatterer mocked the Chinese: "They wish to appear far older than they are, even though they are one of the oldest peoples. They play with millions of years as children play with balls."[7] He maintained that only Christians and Jews could correctly ascertain the age of the world. Heathens, no matter how enlightened, were incapable of such knowledge.[8]

Gatterer offers a startling example of the thinking on various levels that characterizes any age. As we will see in later chapters, Gatterer was a leader in reforming historical methodology, in redefining the tasks of universal history, and in posing important questions in historical hermeneutics. Yet he continually clung to the belief that the Old and New Testaments offered a factual framework for evaluating the spectrum of human time. Gatterer's acceptance of the literal truth of Christian myth is most evident in his earlier works, *Handbuch der Universalhistorie* and *Einleitung in die synchronistische Universalhistorie,* which present a strange mixture of uncritical belief supported by elaborate rationalizations; Christian myth is proclaimed and then defended by pseudoscientific justifications.

Gatterer began his early histories with the Creation and then related Adam's fall and the expansion of Adam's family. Without a hint of reservation, he accepted the idea that the first inhabitants of the earth lived for hundreds of years. He even provided the reader with a handy chart showing the declining steps in man's life span. "The normal age that a person can attain today is between seventy and eighty years, only about a twelfth of what it was at the beginning of time. Man's life span, therefore, may be divided into six levels or steps:

First Step:	1	:	900-969 years. (A.M. 1656).	Until the Flood.
Second Step:	2/3	:	600 years.	Just after the Flood.
Third Step:	1/2	:	450 years.	Arphaxad, Selak.
Fourth Step:	1/4	:	239 years.	Building of the Tower of Babel; Pelag lived for 239 years.

Fifth Step: 1/8   :   120 years.   Mosaic era
                                                    (A.M. 2493).

Sixth Step: 1/12   :   70-80 years.   Since David's time.
                                (A.M. 2696).

Gatterer explained the difference in life spans by recourse to a hypothetical natural history. He maintained that the earth, being created perfect by God, took a while to reach its present stage of imperfection after Adam's original sin. The immediate post-Adamite air had been cleaner and healthier, the earth richer and more fertile, the fruits and vegetables bigger, better, and more nourishing. From the "facts" of this conception of early natural history and the extended longevity of man Gatterer concluded that the earth was far more populous before the Flood than at any time thereafter.

The problem of population perplexed those who held on to the traditional Christian chronology. Skeptics had long pointed out that repopulation after the Flood must have taken longer than envisioned in the Bible. Gatterer's rejoinder was twofold. He based his first attack on the idea of qualitative historical differentiation. He argued that modern theories of population (propounded by English proponents of political arithmetic and by Johann Süßmilch) could not be universally applied to all lands and all times. There were too many variables that either hampered or encouraged population growth. Among modern deterrents to population increase he listed the institutionalization of monasticism, the numerous fast days in Catholic lands, the growth of wealth and opulence, and the appearance of new diseases such as venereal disease. His second tactic employed an elaborate set of computations based on man's longer life span and the mathematics of progressions to show that repopulation was indeed possible within so short a time. Throughout the rest of Gatterer's earlier works, there is the same rationalization of the irrational. Unlike his treatment of later ages, Gatterer portrayed early historical development as sudden and revolutionary. Instead of a story of incremental steps, he regressed to the earlier catastrophe theory. One man or one event changes the whole of historical life. Gatterer relates how Adam invented language, as though he, Gatterer, had been present when the first grunt was uttered. Gatterer claimed that Jubal, a descendant of Cain, invented instrumental music; that Thubalcain developed the arts of metal-working; that Naema discovered the art of spinning; and that a Phoenician named Taaut invented the alphabet in A.M. 1829 (which, according to Gatterer's calculations, would have been 2154 B.C.).

In Gatterer's later works a change of attitude does occur. He increasingly moderated his precise description of prediluvial society, abandoned his naturalistic rationalizations, and minimized the Christian-centered nature of his work, though he still retained the Christian time span. While beginning with the Creation, his periodization of historical time no longer depended on the major events of Christian myth. Instead of keeping the traditional tripartite division — the Creation to the Flood, the Flood to Christ's birth, and Christ's birth to the present — Gatterer introduced a complex system of periodization. He divided historical time into three sections, determined by degrees of social organization. Within these three periods he discerned a four-part differentiation which he dated by two sets of events, those pertaining to the Christian world and those pertaining to the non-Christian world. He further characterized each of these four subperiods by the manner in which they expressed their heritage. He summed up his system in the accompanying chart, which testifies to Gatterer's attempts to incorporate the Aufklärung's cosmopolitan interests into a history founded on scriptural authority. Gatterer needed to hold on to an absolute; his form of religious belief required that something — for him, the factuality of Christian chronology — remain exempt from critical historical analysis.

GATTERER'S CHART

Social Organization	Non-Christian Events	Christian Events	Form of Knowledge
I. CREATION OF THE WORLD (A.M. 1)			
No nations and no kingdoms		Adam's fall (1) Arts (900-1000) Flood (1656)	Age of myth and revelation
II. FOUNDING OF NATIONS (1809)			
	Assyrians (1874) Persians (3425) Romans (3838-3939) Parthians (3808-3845) Persians (A.D. 226)	Idolatry Dispersal Christ's birth (3983)	Era of biblical information and classical history
Eight ruling nations or system of subjugation	**III. VÖLKERWANDERUNG (5 SAEC.)**		
	Germans and Slavs (5th cent.) Arabs (622) Mongols and Tartars (1209-1369)	Papacy (6th cent.) Crusades (1069-1291) Printing (1440) Fall of Constantinople (1453) Rebirth of learning	Era of chronicles and manuscripts
IV. DISCOVERY OF AMERICA (1492)			
System of alliances and system of subjugation		Reformation (1517) Council of Trent (1545-1563) Balance of power (16th cent.) Treaty of Westphalia (1648) New philosophy (16th-17th cent.)	Era of collectors, critics, aestheticians, and pragmatists

Even as Gatterer was struggling to fit the history of the world into the framework of traditional Christian chronology, other thinkers of the Aufklärung were reinterpreting the Bible in such a way as to make Gatterer's need to hold on to the literal truth irrelevent. The stimuli for the Aufklärers' fundamental reinterpretation came from all sides. Spinoza's biblical criticism, Bayle's skepticism, Voltaire's scorn, and Richard Simon's sympathetic reconstruction reinforced the antidogmatic tendencies generated by the clash between Pietism and orthodox Lutheranism. The supporting pillars in the biblically centered system of time consciousness were being undermined and destroyed on all fronts. Bolingbroke, greatly admired by the Aufklärers, voiced a typical critique: "The genealogies and histories of the Old Testament are in no respect sufficient foundations for a chronology from the beginning of time, nor for universal history." The systems of men such as Scaliger, Bochart, Petavius, Usher, and Marsham were "so many enchanted castles; they appear to be something, they are nothing but appearances: like them too, dissolve the charm, and they vanish from sight."[9] Bolingbroke also mocked those who purported to explain in detail the early experiences of man: "The creation of the first man is described by some, as if Preadamites, they had assisted at it. They talk of his beauty as if they had seen him, of his gigantick size as if they had measured him, and of his prodigious knowledge as if they had conversed with him. They point out the very spot where Eve laid her head the first time he enjoyed her."[10]

Such critiques were certainly not new; skeptics and critics of the seventeenth century had already voiced them. Yet they did not really bear fruit in Germany until the eighteenth century. The reason for the late development in Germany cannot be ascribed to backwardness alone. The earlier critiques were either rejected or ignored because Germans felt they were being made from a naturalistic position. Christian apologists could just as easily reverse the attack and show how natural law and natural theology were also founded on some rather undemonstrable assumptions. In a manner reminiscent of Bayle, Johann Martin Chladenius had no trouble pointing out the false premises and a priori definitions of human nature which animated the naturalist critique.[11] In fact, he argued that all the talk about a first natural religion was based on mere speculation. At least the Christians had a historical account. If the Christian historians waxed eloquent about the details of Adam's first actions, so did the proponents of natural law describe in loving detail the state of nature and the formation of the social contract. Until the eighteenth century, charge and countercharge were leveled from positions based on the assumption of absolute certainty. In a sense there was little room for discussion; either position could be easily dismissed if one simply followed Bayle's advice and chose either revelation or coherent truth.

Many Aufklärers, however, were not satisfied with either choice, for each implied the exclusion or subordination of the other. They attempted to resolve the conflict between reason and revelation by historicizing both. The goal of the movement derisively called Neology was to free the study of religion from its subservience to either dogmatics or coherent analysis. The Neologists incorporated many of the rationalist critiques without sacrificing Christianity. Encouraged by the efforts of the leading Neologists – Mosheim, Michaelis, Semler, Ernesti, Jerusalem, and Abbt – the Aufklärers felt they could surrender Christian chronology without rejecting Christianity.

Crucial to this process was a modification of the idea of divine inspiration as applied to biblical exegesis. According to the Neologists, divine inspiration had served as a major prophylactic against criticism and was the source for interminable internecine contention. Semler summed up this position: "All the numerous long-standing disputes among Christians . . . arose from explaining the Bible as though it were an integral unit and from joining all the collected descriptions into a single theory."[12] Some seventeenth-century theologians had carried the idea of divine interpretation to such absurd limits as to claim that the medieval rabbinical designations for the verbal signs of the Hebrew text were dictated by the Holy Spirit, a position promulgated by the Swiss Formula of Consensus of 1675.[13] The Neologists broke with tradition by interpreting the Bible as a collection of books written at different times in response to certain existential circumstances. They did not deny that God's commands were transmitted, but they believed that the transmission was accomplished by human agents responding to specific conditions. Each book of the Bible contained not God's words unalloyed but God's commands to Jews and Christians of specific and differentiated eras. The message always expressed a moral law, clothed in what Semler called a "local" or "provincial" dialect. Each book, therefore, was an amalgam of moral truth qualified by existential condition. Its language and mode of expression reflected the manner in which earlier peoples understood the world. It would have been silly, the Neologists argued, for God to have his message transmitted in Newtonian language at a time when that language would have been totally incomprehensible. It would be equally silly for a person of the eighteenth century to believe that the world was created in six days because this was the way a "primitive nomadic people" grasped and expressed God's majesty. Given this assumption, the Neologists asked such questions as: When were the various parts of Holy Scripture written or sung? For whom were they written and for what purpose? What did the language of that time signify and portray? In what social, cultural, intellectual, and political milieus were they composed? In a manner analogous to eighteenth-century German aesthetics (Semler even referred to hermeneutics as an aesthetics), the Neologists focused on the act of scriptural composition and the act of its original understanding.[14] By so doing, they implied that the expressions of time found in the various books of the Bible referred less to absolute time than to the time consciousness of the people who had received God's message.

Johann David Michaelis's approach to the problem of chronology was typical of the Neologists' analysis. Because his historical approach freed him from the burden of attempting to resolve all biblical contradictions, Michaelis proclaimed that the manner in which the ancient Jews had transmitted their sacred knowledge was different from that of modern Europeans. Chronology was important to eighteenth-century men, but it was relatively unimportant to Jews of the Mosaic era. Moses had never intended to offer a complete chronology of terrestrial time. Instead, he presented his people with a selective genealogy. Moses was a prophet, not a historian. He recorded only those events that had meaning in the memory of his people and revealed God's message. The rest was either unimportant or unknown to Moses. [15] Michaelis's view implied that while the Bible was not incorrect, it certainly did not present a complete factual account of man's total life span on this earth. This theme animates the whole Neological attempt at biblical exegesis. Each book of the Bible was composed by a witness who transformed God's imperative into time-influenced images. Since the Bible was a collection of books written or compiled by single individuals, obviously contradictions would occur. Even if the authors had been contemporaries, they would necessarily have seen related events from different points of view. With a bold stroke, the Neologists reversed the attack upon Holy Scripture by asserting that the contradictions in the text attested to its validity. The job of the exegete was to make the writer's point of view evident so that God's moral message could be better understood.

As a true Aufklärer, Michaelis further believed that what is unknown cannot be replaced by a priori assertion. When the historian is faced by a question mark and has no way of resolving the question, he should merely say, "I don't know." "In a situation, therefore, where our historical accounts are so contradictory," Michaelis wrote, "the safest method is to make no positive affirmation whatsoever. Arguments a priori can never decide a question which merely relates to a matter of fact."[16] This position led Michaelis to take a stand on Christian chronology which Gatterer never dared to take. In a letter to his prize student, August Ludwig Schlözer, Michaelis offered his solution to Schlözer's difficulty in drawing up a chronology for man's earliest history: "Here is my suggestion for the solution of your doubts. In simple German it says: we have no chronology from Abraham's birth till the Flood! That is not pleasant, but that's the way it often is when one deals with the ancient history of peoples. . . . No chronology is still better than a false chronology, better than a chronology that is in continual contradiction with history and makes the few fragments we do have unbelievable."[17]

Modern as this suggestion may sound, it did not mean that Michaelis abandoned all attempts to construct a universal chronology from the confusing genealogies of the Old Testament. In the same set of letters to Schlözer, Michaelis argues that the usually accepted time ascribed to the

Jews' stay in Egypt should be extended by 215 years: "Through such an extension, not only is the age of the world lengthened by 215 years, but one wins 215 years for the period between the Flood and Moses. Thus it is more comprehensible how the world at Moses' time could be so populous and so cultured."[18] In addition, Michaelis contended that the period between Moses and Solomon should be increased by 112 years. Michaelis, though expanding the spectrum of time, still unconsciously viewed distant times with standards that contradicted his own conception of the difficulty of change. For example, we can see how he conceived of change in his description of the creation of the written word: "Generally, we must consider that languages were spoken before they were written. Writing was probably a very late discovery by the human race, and it must have taken an enormously long time before it was recognized that the tones, whose beginnings appeared to encompass an immeasurable number, could be reduced to a few simple tones.... In addition, the single elements of the language, which one pronounced and from which the language was formed, were not letters but syllables, even though these could be further divided by art and reflection. It must have been a great genius indeed who first recognized that these apparently innumerable elements were composed of still smaller parts and that these parts were so limited in number that a sort of alphabet could be constructed."[19] This view is typical of the Aufklärers' concept of spiritual change. It entailed a slow process of reducing the infinite complexity of the immediate sensate world to an appreciation of unity within diversity. Michaelis's extensions of time were but a drop in the bucket and certainly not sufficient to satisfy the demands of his own idea of historical change. An outside observer could easily see that the few hundred extra years he envisioned could not account for the slow process of spiritual formation. Michaelis pointed to a path that would allow later historians of the Aufklärung gradually to escape from the problems raised by Christian chronology. Although he himself could not follow the path to its end, his student Schlözer did.

Schlözer shared the cosmopolitan and universal interests of his mentor. He was well versed in the latest theories of the natural and biological sciences; he had mastered Michaelis's philological and methodological principles; he could read a number of languages, including Latin, Greek, French, Italian, English, Russian, Swedish, Icelandic, Hebrew, Syrian, and Chaldean; and he was conversant with economic theory and statistics. In addition, he was well traveled and thoroughly knowledgeable about current affairs in Europe. All these accomplishments have led many scholars to compare Schlözer with Voltaire, though Schlözer himself would have found the comparison insulting. He was too much the Christian to feel honored by comparison with Voltaire. What they did share, however, was an expansive and cosmopolitan view of the world. Even more than Voltaire, Schlözer was fascinated by the panorama of the action and interaction of historical peoples. His broad view, supported by an uncommon knowledge of original sources, influenced him to approach the problem of historical generalization with studious care. In an early work Schlözer paraphrased Michaelis's modest expression of historical skepticism and elevated it to one of the basic laws of the historian: "Excuse me if I tear down more than I build, if I doubt more than I decide, if I eliminate myths rather than establish truths. The basic law of the historian is *ne quid fals dicat.* I would rather know nothing than be deceived." [20] Schlözer applied this dictum to Christian chronology in his proposal for the study of universal history, *Vorstellung seiner Universal-Historie,* and in his lengthy and heated rejoinder to Herder's excited and scathing review of the *Universal-Historie.*

The critical attitude to biblical chronology was apparent in Schlözer's interpretation of the earth's creation. Aware of the latest discoveries of botanists, mineralogists, and geologists, and an avid reader of Buffon and Linnaeus, Schlözer had no difficulty in accepting the fact that the earth had existed aeons before man's first appearance and that it had undergone a progressive development before reaching its present state. He made his position clear in his reply to Herder: "I hope Herr Herder doesn't seriously believe that our earth and our universe were called forth from nothing and created 144 hours before Adam's birth. If he really believes that, this is hardly the place to give him all the necessary instruction. History knows nothing about the *creation* of the earth. . . . But the earth's most recent transformation is known by tradition, recorded by Moses, Sanchuniathon, Berossus, and Orphic philosophy. It was a great revolution whereby the earth, having been submerged for a myriad of years, slowly dried up and became a fertile land, inhabitable by creatures like ourselves. . . . The remnants of petrified mussels found on the highest mountains attest to this transformation. And traces of previous transformations or revolutions of the earth through fire and water, which may have lasted even longer than the last, are being uncovered by physicists. The earth where elephants roamed the Arctic Circle in herds and where American plants grew in Lyons must have been a different place from what it was in the recent time of Adam." [21] Having accepted the implications that could be drawn from modern geological discoveries, Schlözer was forced to interpret the six days of the Creation symbolically. Each "day" represented a stage in the transformation of the world and the evolution of life. The last transformation witnessed the appearance of man. The sons of Adam, man as species, were the most recent inhabitants of a much older world. Still, though man's life on this earth was of relatively short duration, the historian had no way of discovering how long man had roamed the earth. Hence, Schlözer excluded man's earliest history from the competence of historical inquiry: "The first age of man . . . is devoid of information. No archaeological remnants, no written annals, remain. Only dark accounts about the beginning of all things." [22]

A symbolic interpretation of the Creation and a reluctance to accept biblical chronology do not necessarily mean that the Bible was to be rejected as incorrect; Schlözer merely felt that the Bible was not intended to be a complete and accurate historical account. He accepted the Neological explanation that Holy Scripture was sacred poetry. Its incontrovertible truths were moral and ethical. Its historical elements reflected the oral traditions of an ancient people. Historically, Holy Scripture was as accurate as, say, the *Edda*, the *Iliad*, or any other myth or saga. It could be evaluated only when other comparative sources were available. Schlözer's solution to the problem of biblical origins is, therefore, a modest one. He did not deny the authenticity of the Bible; he merely said much of it could not be proved or disproved. Since historical analysis must be based on evidence, and since eighteenth-century historians had very little evidence concerning early man, the problem of first origins had no place in historical writing: "The historical investigator never seeks the Ur-inhabitants of a land; he knows almost a priori that he cannot find them. But should he not seek those who were *first known?* . . . Naturally that inquiry would not bring him down to Babel or Noah, but he does not want to go that far. He stops when annals and traces stop; he names *aborigines* the people mentioned last and forgets the empty period between his *aborigines* and Noah."[23] History should ignore the question of first origins and leave it to either prehistory or metaphysics, for without "written memorials there can be no history."[24] Following this precept, Schlözer limited his own universal history to the period commencing with Moses and the foundation of the Roman Empire. He solved the problem of dating by making Christ's birth a central point from which he counted backward and forward. (Later he suggested that an even better midpoint would be the sixth century when the classical world ended and the medieval West and the Byzantine East were founded.)

Schlözer's proposal implied a basic methodological revision of the problem of chronology. Like all such changes, it entailed a shift in basic attitudes. The practical choice of accepting some moment within known history as a fixed point for purposes of calculation revealed an altered attitude toward the scriptural version of human origins. Schlözer obviously did not invent the new system. Dating from Christ's birth goes back as far as Eusebius. But Schlözer was one of those who totally discredited the lingering practice of coupling the new system with a system beginning with A.M. 1. The new method, which by 1780 had displaced the older system, opened the time scale at both ends. It attested to a willingness to accept basic alterations in man's appreciation of the scope of past historical time. As Hannah Arendt has noted, the new method allows one to look "back into an infinite past to which one can add at will and into which we can inquire further as it stretches ahead into an infinite future."[25] Of course, drastic changes did not occur at once. People attuned to thinking of man's total earthly existence in terms of a few thousand years did not immediately accept figures running into hundreds of thousands or into millions. The new system did, however, free scholars from the necessity of holding on to the Christian time span in order to save Christianity. As they applied their ideas of the process of social change to the distant past, they increasingly felt it necessary to expand the spectrum of past time. Anticipation of change combined with an analysis of the difficulty of change finally led to a revision of the deeply ingrained view of past time.

This revision was already present in the work of one of Schlözer's students and warmest admirers, Johannes von Müller. Von Müller, like Iselin, was one of those Swiss who had been energized by their studies in Germany. Escaping from the confines of a provincial Swiss town, von Müller soon expanded his intellectual horizons at Göttingen through hard study and voracious reading. The thinkers who most influenced his intellectual development were Schlözer, the Berlin theologians, Rousseau, Montesquieu, Voltaire, Mosheim, and Thomas Abbt. Though von Müller's fame as a historian rests primarily upon his *History of the Swiss Confederation* (written at Schlözer's suggestion), he also composed a short universal history, *Vier und zwanzig Bücher allgemeiner Geschichten besonders der europäischen Menschheit,* in which he dealt with the problem of chronology. In the 1786 edition, von Müller followed Schlözer and numerous other writers by giving an evolutionary account of the development of the world and of life. He also treated the scriptural account of man's early history in the Neological manner by considering it an example of sacred poetry; he referred to it as the Mosaic saga. In his chronological calculations, von Müller first admitted the difficulty of dating ancient history and then estimated the span between Christ's birth and Adam to have been about 5,722 years. Again, for the modern reader, this figure seems ludicrous, yet it marked an increase of 1,739 years over Gatterer's and 1,718 years over Usher's computations. That is, it increased the time traditionally allotted to the period between Adam and Christ by almost half. But the important point was that by 1786 even the Swiss, to whom von Müller addressed this work, were not overly distressed by the expansion of pre-Christian time. The dogmatic spirit that had animated the Swiss Formula of Consensus of 1675 was on the wane.

Another and even more important implication lay in Schlözer's refusal to integrate first origins into historical inquiry. The moment an analysis of prediluvian man was transferred to metaphysics and prehistory, the images associated with scriptural portrayals of man's first experiences lost their power to direct explanations of historical causation. The Christian creation myth was hermetically sealed off from the remainder of historical analysis. The metaphors of man's fall, of degeneration from a golden age, were deemed inapplicable to the act of historical understanding. The Aufklärers gave the word "origin" a different meaning. No longer did it signify the beginnings of all things, but rather the traceable origins of certain human institutions. Since documents and archaeological traces form the basis of understanding origins, all attempts to uncover an *Ur-Volk* or an Ur-language were deemed fruitless and highly dangerous. As Schlözer said, such concepts often served as a "fiction that provided each people with a convenient conjecture that it possessed a piece of land through the right of first settlement or that it was a *Stammvolk* in the literal sense, the first or stem of all peoples."[26]

Modern historians may wince at Schlözer's devotion to written sources as the basis of history. Schlözer, however, did not deny the importance of nonliterary evidence; no student of Michaelis's could. But he believed that nonliterary evidence alone was insufficient for the construction of an adequate historical account of change. Schlözer therefore distinguished between prehistory (which he called metahistory), based primarily on nonliterary evidence and folk tradition, and history that used written materials supplemented by other forms of evidence. Moreover, it must be remembered that in Schlözer's time the distinction had a salutary effect upon historical understanding. With one blow Schlözer attacked the fragile house built by overzealous historians who had sought the origins of their people in biblical or mythical traditions. More often than not, these writers had used a pseudoscientific etymology showing that an individual nation was named for a founding father, whom they traced to Noah or to the survivors of Troy. In his short summary of Russian history, Schlözer described this practice: "The superstition and ignorance of past centuries have spoiled the history of every nation; they have also spoiled ours. There was a time when we searched for our ancestors in the land of the Tower of Babel; the Slavs were found at the siege of Troy. . . . There was a time when it was believed that the town of *Moscow* took its name from Mosoch, grandson of Noah; that Tobolsk took its name from Toubol; that Kiev was built by Ki, descendant of Mosoch. Letters patent that Novgorod had received from Alexander the Great were produced. . . . Ignorance, I emphasize, has devised its own miseries. The miseries existed in the centuries of the barbarian, but history, directed by common sense, with the torch of criticism in hand, scorns them."[27] By rejecting mythical explanations for the origins of society, the Aufklärers opened one path for historical evaluation of societal change. Another obstacle, however, confronted those who would deal historically with a state's ancient past: the idea of natural law that was in many ways analogous to a new mythic interpretation of man's origins.

3

It may seem farfetched to discern an analogy between the formulations of modern natural law and Christian myth. As a rule, the triumph of natural law in the seventeenth century is interpreted as an example of secularization par excellence. And it was. The problem is that use of the term "secularization" does not close the discussion; it merely opens it. "Secularization" is a term historians apply with so much abandon that it has acquired the unenviable quality of appearing to explain something without saying anything concrete or definite. More often than not, it expresses a form of "quick-think" whose meaning is purely emotive, signifying the pleasing idea of a liberation from dogmatism. Without going into the myriad uses of the term, I think we can say that secularization is a process whereby particular sacred traditions and certainties lose their sacredness and self-evident certainty.[28] Here the term "sacred" is used in its broadest meaning. As Mircea Eliade has defined the term, "sacred" includes that which a society singles out as special things, places, or acts that are distinct from others. These define a "real" reality that has its own time, or rather timelessness, and its own reality that differs from everyday, profane reality.[29] To avoid undue fuzziness, the question of secularization must be related to specific religious facts; that is, the process of secularization is not a denial of religion as such, but rather a change within a given religious tradition. Further, as Professor Kees Bolle has shown, secularization is part of a dialectical process whereby the negation of certain elements makes future religious revival possible. Secularization and mythification (the creation of new religious symbols, or the defining of a new "real" reality are components of the same process).

Secularization, therefore, is nothing new. Every religious tradition undergoes a continual questioning whereby certain mythic elements are revised, reinterpreted, or rejected. In its most common form, secularization is signified by an unconscious loss of confidence in the traditional mythic portrayal. No longer is the word "mythic" accepted without question. Instead, an author feels compelled to explain it by reference to some form of rationalistic justification. An example is Gatterer's pseudoscientific attempts to defend scriptural accounts of the Creation and man's origins. In my view, however, this process of loss of mythic self-evidence is not uniform. There are critical times when contradictions between traditions and their rationalizations are consciously perceived by a number of thinkers, who then attempt to replace worn-out images with images of their own making. They try to substitute a new real reality more in tune with the intellectual currents of their time. Here image and counterimage claim the same authority and vie for the same adherence. Both attempt to occupy the same ground.

It was this form of radical secularization that animated the efforts of the creators of modern natural law. Despite its important debt to classical and scholastic theories of natural law, modern natural law is really a new creation that sprang from the unique religious problems of the seventeenth century.[30] In their formulations, modern theorists of natural law tried to stake out a realm independent of theological overlordship and social necessity. The creators of natural law battled the omnicompetence of both God and the state and sought to provide an eternal and universal basis for resolving the problem of right and might. Such diverse thinkers as Hobbes and Grotius attempted to divest natural law of its specific Christian content. They redefined the idea of nature and in so doing put forward a new explanation for the origin of things. As Cassirer has observed, "Nature . . . does not refer to the existence of things but to the origin and foundation of truths. To nature belong, irrespective of their content, all truths which are capable of a purely immanent justification, and which require no transcendent revelation but are certain and evident in themselves. Such truths are now sought not only in the physical but also in the intellectual and moral world; for it takes these two worlds together to constitute a real world, a cosmos complete in itself."[31] In its goal and in its function, natural law represents a substitute form for the traditional mythic categories of the Creation and the Fall. In their place we find the postulates of coherent analysis. Natural law was a discipline that did not depend upon experience, but upon definition, not upon facts, but upon strictly logical proof. It was ahistorical because it was timeless; it represented a new real reality because it stood outside and above experiential explanation, though it served as the core for understanding all experience. It was thought to exist even if man did not always recognize it, just as gravity existed before Newton discovered it. Natural law was interpreted as the force that arranged things: "It is 'ordering order' (*ordo ordinans*), not 'ordered order' (*ordo ordinatus*)."[32]

The central role played by the idea of the state of nature — life antedating civil society — attests to the similarity of function between modern natural law and Christian myth. As Leo Strauss has shown, such an idea was alien to both classical and scholastic theories of natural law. For classical thinkers the state of nature referred to life in a healthy civil society, whereas Christian thinkers always drew the distinction between the state of nature (which they divided into the pure state of nature and the state of fallen nature) and the state of grace. Both explanations were mainly concerned with the duties man owes to existing society. It is only with Hobbes that the state of nature antedating civil society becomes an essential part of natural law. This coincidence was no accident. Rather, concentration upon a stage preceding empirical observation was necessary to the new naturalism of the seventeenth century. Hobbes contended that empirical images could not be the source of real reality. Inspired by the advances of mathematical physics, he rightly realized than an analytics founded on empiricism could lead to the conclusion that a body's qualities were real and, therefore, irreducible. This argument ran counter to the method so forcefully championed by Galileo. Hobbes maintained that the only things men actually know are the things they make themselves. Since empiricism is merely reflection upon what is already made, it is not actual knowledge. The proper way to acquire knowledge is through extreme negation (theoretically to abolish the universe), selective abstraction, and then logical reconstruction. The philosopher was to work under the assumption that the world as constituted did not exist; then he was to create it anew through deduction, proceeding always from the simple truth to the complex. The philosopher was a demigod who created order from chaos.[33] Hobbes's state of nature was the prerequisite beginning for his further creation. In it he conceived of man isolated from all social bonds (a contradiction in terms for scholastic and classical theorists), postulated man's driving force (self-preservation), and logically showed how this force led man to form a social contract. In Hobbes's analysis, the social contract regulated all further relations; he used it as a measure for all historical events. In form, the logical analysis of presocial man served as a substitute for Christian myth. As a purely logical construction, it stood outside time, free from all the accidents of secular time, and it provided a universal measure for determining right and wrong.

The difference between modern natural law and that of its classical and scholastic predecessors lies in the conscious attempt to replace Christian mythical tradition with a logically more satisfying explanation for social origins. It is this process that gives modern natural law its unique qualities, which may be summed up in the following manner. Modern natural law is by intention opposed to traditionalism and to historicism. It is founded upon an analogy between the lawfulness of the natural world and the lawfulness of universal principles. Its principles are therefore considered eternal, independent of the whims and actions of all sovereign power, be it the power of God or of an absolute monarch. Natural law asserts and describes the existence of a state of nature and derives its principles from an analysis of individual man, endowed with specific drives or driven by objective forces prior to the creation of civil society. Finally, it posits a basic social contract (different from a governmental contract that specifies a certain form of rule) whereby man forms a society.[34]

Natural law, though analogous in function to Christian myth, must not be considered as a new mythology. Mythification is not a process of conscious creation. Just as secularization is inevitable in every living religious tradition, so too is the gradual and unnoticed process of mythification. A single person or a small group of thinkers cannot invent a religious symbol. When they try, very often the new symbol has so much in common with the one that is to be replaced that old and new can be brought together into some sort of agreement. So it happened with natural law. After the initial shock of being presented with two conflicting explanations for origins based on two different ideas of real reality (revelation and coherent truth), it did not take thinkers very long to reconcile coherent analysis with revelation. Through the efforts of men like Wolff and Pufendorf in Germany, natural law was made safe for Christianity or Christianity was made safe for natural law. This act of eclectic compromise made an outright attack on natural law more difficult for the Aufklärers than one would have assumed.

The eclectic combination of tradition and countertradition often left a rather ill-defined or vague theoretical base, surmounted by positive hopes and programs usually associated in some way with ideas drawn from modern natural law. Peter Gay makes this point clear.[35] The language of natural law contained a powerful critique of existing society. As used by the admirers of

Locke, it offered a ready vehicle for advancing programs for reform. The Aufklärers still used terms such as "contract," "state of nature," and "natural law" in their polemic writings. It was just too tempting to contrast the battle of all against all with the life in a well-ordered and well-administered state or to talk about man's inalienable rights when criticizing serfdom. When applied to specific problems, however, these terms became increasingly estranged from their original theoretical assumptions. This estrangement, I believe, can be traced to the same consciousness that allowed the Aufklärers to resolve the problem of biblical chronology. Impelled by a new religious consciousness, they came to disregard both the literal truth of the Christian explanation of origins and the necessary truth of the ersatz view proclaimed by modern natural law. Even the evolution of their attitude toward natural law paralleled that of their treatment of Christian chronology. First there was an attempt to keep natural law; then there was a transvaluation of its terms; and finally the historians of the Aufklärung chose to ignore it, relegating it to the realm of metaphysical hypothesis.

Natural law and revelation could be most easily retained by carving out hermetically distinct spheres for each, spheres that touched each other only infrequently. Thinkers could vary their emphasis by shifting back and forth from one realm to the other. At one time revelation could be viewed as a universal guide; at another it became a special case. For most early writers, the scriptural account of the Creation still sufficed to explain man's prediluvial history. After mentioning the Flood, the Diaspora, and the Confusion of Languages, writers turned to natural law to show how civil society was formed. Now the biblical account was reserved for the Chosen People alone, whose history became a unique case. This strategy allowed thinkers to deal with all peoples without having to refer constantly to Christian myth. Natural law became the basic principle governing mankind as a whole. Even a heathen was driven by the laws of nature to form a social contract.

Convenient as this solution seemed, it still raised a number of problems. One concerned the manner in which the state of nature had been defined. Theorists of natural law postulated the existence of isolated individual man in the state of nature. The scriptural account of man's origins assumed certain social ties to have existed, namely, those of the family. Most Aufklärers preferred the biblical interpretation. Gottfried Achenwall offers a case in point. In his explication of natural law he used the traditional terminology of contractual beginnings. The state was created by contract; its goal was to ensure happiness.[36] These agreements Achenwall called fundamental contracts (*Grundverträge*); the laws derived from those contracts he called fundamental laws (*Grundgesetze*). The organization of the state established by fundamental laws he termed the basic constitution (*Grundverfassung*), which shaped the nature and character (*Natur und Wesen*) of the state.[37] The critical point was the manner in which the fundamental contracts were formed. According to Achenwall, they were agreed to by a number of families who joined together to avoid the hardships of unorganized society. He deliberately omitted any explanation of how the simpler familial organization arose. Soceity existed prior to the formation of sovereign rule, which meant that the contract described was a governmental, not a social, contract.

Achenwall's friend and colleague Johann Stephan Pütter went even further. Pütter introduced other forms of social organization between the state and the family, called *Gemeinde* ("a loose grouping of people") and *Volk* ("a collection of families and/or *Gemeinde*"), which he characterized as semicorporate bodies lacking sovereignty: "A state is formed as soon as a *Volk* . . . agree to unite forever under a sovereign power."[38] Here is the kernel of a developmental approach to explain the formation of civil society. Beginning with simple relations, the more complex units of *Gemeinde* and *Volk* arise until finally the sovereign state is created. Schlözer, picking up this theme, used the moment of state formation as the point separating history from prehistory. He acknowledged that the state always grew from less complex social organizations, but he argued that only the state offered historians a proper vehicle for the application of the methodological tools of historical scholarship. "Nonhistorical peoples," that is, peoples not living in a state, should be studied "metapolitically." Metapolitics in this sense was similar to anthropology. It dealt with questions of human nature, of early social organization, and of early law.[39] As mentioned earlier, Schlözer's desire to draw so radical a distinction between history and prehistory is disturbing; still, for his time it signified a bold rejection of the literal interpretation of the Bible and of the formulations of modern natural law. History was cut free from its reliance upon any explanations of first beginnings and was charged with the task of developing its own methods to explain social change.

The increasingly adamant refusal to discuss the state of nature and the formation of the social contract signified a return to classical and Christian concepts of natural law. Man again is seen as a social animal, not merely as a man capable of sociability. The idea of sovereignty is not contained in the formation of social ties; it is interpreted as a product of advanced social development. The rights and duties of man, therefore, must be related both to the general idea of a contract and to the historical shape of that contract. The contract is a positive law establishing a form of government, but it is based on the traditions of the people who agree to the contract. From this argument, Pütter and others concluded that each state must have its own unique *Staatsrecht* ("constitutional law").[40]

It does not follow that pro forma summaries of the methods of modern natural law were immediately forgotten. Contradictions between introductions to method and method itself spiced the works of most of the Aufklärers. In a general introduction to the study of law, Pütter told his readers that a study of natural law was indispensable to the jurist. And in describing natural law he virtually repeated the Hobbesian assumptions that one must conceive of the time when no states or other social connections existed, and that one must imagine that two or more people existed without binding connections and then discuss what mutual rights and duties they must observe.[41] Yet Pütter's own work demonstrated a total disregard for this "indispensable" discipline. For him, the only valid way to discuss German law was to turn to history. In his discussion of German law and German history, Pütter was more concerned with showing the falsity of Pufendorf's interpretation of German constitutional history, which drew its principles from natural law, than with applying its methods. Each nation had its own particular law, unique to itself and nontransferable. Further, that law was not given at any one time but is in a continual process of change and adjustment to internal and external forces. Law is the reflection of the "character of the nation," which meant that the true sources for early Germanic law were the customs and traditions of the people: "In addition to written laws, many parts of German constitutional law rest only on customs or traditions. They form a type of unwritten law that is observed in one way and not in another because *one had always done it that way*. It is on this foundation that the binding power of common law, as expressed either explicitly or implicitly by the lawgiver, is based."[42] Instead of studying positive law — and natural law was a form of positive law — the legal scholar would be best advised to listen to the "voice of the people."[43] Pütter's whole method betrays a distrust of abstract speculation; in content it attests to the evolution of an epistemological ideal different from the one that directed modern natural law.

Pütter himself hinted at this ideal. The Hobbesian method was founded upon an extreme rationalism; reality was what man had created through his rational reconstruction of the world. Pütter, trained by a good Calvinist tutor, entertained sincere doubts about the competence of man's reason. For him, reason was a useful but limited tool. At most it could achieve a vague and imprecise reflection of God's truth.[44] Hence the a priori "philosophical" method must be used with care. If overdone, it "easily blinds the eyes of youth, often misleading them to a conceited position where they look down in scorn, without valid grounds, at other disciplines, especially history."[45] The empirical strain in Pütter's work is far more dominant than in the theories of Hobbes and Pufendorf; so too is his belief that Christian revelation offered the scholar a truer impression of the existential condition of man than the constructions of natural law. In this sense Pütter reflects the change of attitude stimulated by the Enlightenment's general distrust of abstract rationalism and the German Neologists' desire to rescue the content of revelation by freeing it from its dependence upon dogmatism or rationalism.

This change is significant because it marks a break with the usual attempts to reconcile revelation and natural law. In previous efforts, thinkers reluctant to admit a contradiction between revelation and natural law always reached a point where they were forced to choose one of the two sets of truths to explain the other, using one to make the other "understandable." Christian Wolff had solved the dilemma by opting for natural law. Because natural law was rational and man's perfection lay in his rationality, Wolff believed the method of natural law the best to uncover the real reality of social life. Wolff never denied the primacy of revelation; he denied its contents. He maintained that genuine revelation had to accord with reason. Things like miracles were not possible because they degraded the perfection of God. Wolff, like Hobbes, believed it possible for the rational thinker to reconstruct the whole world, to begin with simple mathematical truths and finally to build up a system that ended with God. With a mind-boggling presumptuousness, he offered his contemporaries a description of a man-centered universe, where everything is ordered according to natural law for the benefit of man. Even the sun and stars exist for man's convenience: the sun gives him the opportunity to make sundials; it allows scholars to read and write books; it enables man to determine magnetic deviation. In short, Wolff concluded, the "sun exists in order that events may take place on earth; and the earth exists in order that the existence of the sun not be purposeless."[46]

The new epistemology of the Enlightenment and the beliefs of the Neologists were directed against such overrationalist explanations of both natural law and Christian revelation. The tendency of the Aufklärers was to redefine the word "natural" to make it accord with the observable qualities of man. Their work advanced a new model of scientific inquiry for the study of man. In the process, they felt forced to revise the standard rationalist evaluation of the powers of reason. Two of Wolff's earliest critics, Johann Gottlob von Justi and Johann Jacob Schmauß, hammer away at this point. For them reason was at best a fragile tool, far overshadowed by man's passions and emotions. It was like the peak of an iceberg; it hid the real form of man's human nature. In a manner similar to Hume's, both believed reason to be the handmaiden of man's passions, which implied that any explanation founded on reason alone (including natural law) really clothed irrational motives. In his critique of the idea of the balance of power, Justi made the point clear: "A creature such as man, who possesses so many depraved predispositions and emotions and who also is endowed with the qualities of reason, is able to clothe his perverted and wrong actions in beautiful forms and masks. . . . One always shows the world the pretty side of actions that actually result from the storm of one's passions. Reason, the dangerous companion of the passions, is always ingenious enough to construct whole systems to veil injustice."[47]

One increasingly senses a feeling of distrust in the vaunted claims for the powers of man's reason. History was shown to be filled with examples of the impotence of reason.[48] It was a vain folly to stake man's salvation on abstract concepts; instead, the program of the future must be founded on a recognition of man's total nature. Schmauß's critique is based on this assumption. The fault of Wolff, Pufendorf, and the whole school of modern natural law was their attempt to equate natural law with morality, to derive man's rights and duties from an abstract definition of man. Schmauß, the cosmopolitan and experienced diplomat, lashed out at what he saw as the pedantry of the typical German *Stubengelehrte* ("professional book-worm").[49] Fascinated with their own deductions, these spinners of philo-sophical webs (*philosophische Grillenfänger*) had forgotten a point made by Paul and reemphasized by Thomasius, namely, that will and reason are not two separate categories of human nature. Instead, they are inexorably joined. In most human actions, will is the master and reason its servant, ready to accommodate itself to its master's wishes. Even when reason seems to have the upper hand, there is actually a continual interaction between reason and will.[50] Therefore, natural law is a law of inborn instinctual drives, not a law of reason, and any system of natural law derived from a long and tedious set of abstractions is a contradiction in terms. Any closed rational system of rights and duties claiming authority from natural law is a chimera; it really is nothing but an overadorned positive law.

Schmauß removed the difficulty of reconciling natural law and Christian revelation by denying that natural law provides a basis upon which a political, social, or moral ethic can be constructed and by dissolving the identity between "is" and "ought" in seventeenth-century uses of the word "law." Natural law deals with the "is" of human life, morality with the "ought." According to Schmauß, moral philosophy is a composite of three disciplines drawn from the "three ideas of *justi, honesti,* and *decori.* Natural law belongs to the discipline of *justi*; it makes up only one part of morals."[51] The discipline of natural law studied man's inborn passions only. It dealt with the possible, not with the desirable. Even then, it was a worthy study; it was a type of divine law because it investigated one of God's creations. Natural law, however, must not be confused with a positive human law (*legibus positivis humanis*), a positive divine law (*legibus positivis divinis*), or the whole of Christian revelation (*revelatione divini*).[52] The very fact that natural law examines man's given qualities negates its use as a foundation for positive moral codes. A moral code is always a limitation and a redirection of specific human drives or actions. It judges certain actions as admirable or despicable; by so doing, however, it admits that such actions are possible, that they are natural. Therefore, while morality may decry suicide, incest, gluttony, and tyranny, these actions are not *by nature* alien to man. With this device Schmauß undermines the argument that natural law cannot be contrary to morality.

Schmauß's position is at once an extension of seventeenth-century assumptions and a transvaluation of them. He consistently followed the seventeenth-century ideal that a science of nature must be value free. Like many of the Aufklärers, he saw that seventeenth-century theorists of natural law had gone too far; they had confused the declarative and normative senses of the word "law"; by combining the "is" with the "ought" they constructed a dogmatism as inflexible as that of the orthodox theologians. Hobbes, Pufendorf, and Wolff were more prone to define a doctrine than to accept man as he was. The really striking point of Schmauß's natural law, however, is his conception of nature. He was one of the many Aufklärers groping toward an idealist view of nature tinged with pantheism. Almost unnoticed, the shadow of Spinoza had crossed their thoughts, paused, and left its imprint. But it was not Spinoza unalloyed. The Stoic philosophers, Cusanus, Raymond Sabund, Paracelsus, Jakob Böhme, and Shaftesbury, all appear and are mentioned in notes and asides, sometimes in the most unexpected places. Even the Encyclopedia did not escape their pervasive influence. In his article on chemistry, Venel calls for a new Paracelsus, for a man who could overcome the mechanistic view of nature and who with "experimental instinct" would catch a glimpse of "the life of nature."[53] Schmauß acknowledged Shaftesbury's influence and, though reluctant to praise Spinoza openly (understandable when we remember that many still thought of him as the degenerate Jew of Amsterdam), implicitly recognized his debt to Spinoza in a long and sympathetic summary of the latter's views in the first section of *Recht der Natur*. By 1780 Spinoza was a household word for German thinkers even though his theories were still barely perceived; they were a source of violent contention, as evidenced by the battle between Mendelssohn and Friedrich Heinrich Jacobi over Lessing's supposed Spinozism.[54]

The Aufklärers chose bits and pieces from these thinkers and combined and recombined them to formulate an idea of nature different from that of seventeenth-century pantheism and in direct contradiction to the mechanistic idea of nature. It was an interpretation that excluded the fatalism and monism of Spinoza. The world is in God, but not identical with God. It is the creation of His thought. Nature as a whole, nature in its totality, offers a living testimony to God's majesty. To conceive of it as simply a set of mathematical relations, to reduce it to mere motion and extension, is to do violence to God. As Schmauß said, nature as created testifies to a divine law; as a creation of God it is beyond man's competence to explain how it was formed or what made it function. At most it can be studied in its variety and in its growth. The Aufklärers were ready, as Michaelis said, "to take the world as it is now."[55] It was this attitude that motivated the Swedish naturalist Linnaeus. Though sometimes stereotyped as the cold, calculating rationalist who devoted his life to counting flower petals, Linnaeus was driven to pursue his studies by the belief that he was peering into God's secret cabinet.[56] In the same manner, Albrecht von Haller's poetry of nature and his anatomical studies were suffused with a religious veneration of the wholeness and infinite variety of God's creation. The Aufklärers found it no longer necessary to calculate and reason about the unknowable. Nature was there to be observed, to be charted, to be reexperienced.

A new epistemological ideal accompanied the new idea of nature and stood in contradiction to the ideal of mechanical physics. There was a widespread attack upon the rationalistic methods of natural law, in which Lessing, Mendelssohn, Sulzer, and Abbt Jerusalem all joined. So did Diderot and Buffon; both lashed out at the inadequacies of the mechanistic approach and pleaded for an application of the biological method which, they maintained, offered direct, experiential understanding. The idea of direct understanding, called by the eighteenth-century Germans *anschauende Erkenntnis,* dominated the epistemology of the latter half of the eighteenth century. Aestheticians turned from the study of the rules of composition to look at the process of artistic creation; natural scientists became enamored of the study of growth and change; students of juridical theory abandoned the attempt to postulate an eternal law of social creation in order to focus upon a study of the development of law within society. Increasingly, the desire for direct experiential understanding led thinkers to concentrate upon history. Since man was both participant in historical development and creator of history, historical knowledge was a form of direct participation and direct understanding. Scholars accepted the Hobbesian formulation that we know only that which we make, but they transferred it to the realm that man made, the realm of history.

Nowhere is this transference more evident than in the Neologists' reinterpretation of Holy Scripture. They argued that historical understanding would again make the Word of God a living thing. Semler makes the point clear: "In the answers and defenses of the Christian religion against the attacks of naturalism, one usually resorted to inserting too much from the *theological tradition.* . . . The serious application of *history,* the investigation of what is historical and what is not, has now put us in a position where we can be conscious of *our own* perception [*Erkenntnis*]. Therefore we are capable of experiencing a moral awareness that, to our advantage, is ever expanding, is able to apply the contents of the beneficial and efficacious religion of Christ without having to fall back upon the old provincial theological language. . . . The beginning of all learning is and remains historical; but *individual* perception [*Erkenntnis*] is no longer foreign and historical; instead, our historical understanding produces a new result, individual awareness of the new powers of understanding and judging and acceptance and application of the newly perceived things. Now it becomes a *living* perception [*lebendige Erkenntnis*] . . . . This individual perception of all capable Christians is so surely their own individual, new, immanent perception that they will not find it precisely formulated either in the Bible or in any other book or dogmatic formula."[57]

By 1770 the altered conception of nature and epistemology, in combination with the new attitude toward revelation, had made the traditional approach to natural law superfluous. The primal act of social creation either was ignored or was surrounded by so many reservations that its meaning was completely changed. The intriguing problem for an analysis of law, society, and government no longer concentrated on an explanation of how society first came into being; it dealt instead with the historical problem of the evolving relation between man and society. Schlözer summed up this shift in intellectual orientation: "Man is a social animal by nature; were this not true his existence and development would be incomprehensible. But the type of society in which chance places him forms him and makes him a Newton, a cannibal, or a saint. Since the beginning of the human race, a beginning we do not know and cannot rationally reconstruct, three basic types of social organization have developed in succession: familial [*häuslichen*] organization, civil [*bürgerlichen*] groups, and state-society [*StatsGesellschaften*]."[58] The problem of social change captured the enthusiasm of the Aufklärers. How is national character formed? How can it be changed? What is the relation between law and society? These are the questions that animated their researches. And behind them all lurks the basic question: How can we make that cannibal or that saint into a Newton? Neither the formulations of modern natural law nor the literal interpretation of the Bible provided the Aufklärers with answers they could call sufficient.

V
Historical Causation

1

For the modern historian the act of explaining historical change is so intimately tied to the concept of causation that it is virtually impossible to talk about one without discussing the other. It is generally agreed that those elements a historian establishes as causal, the manner in which he derives effects from causes, and the degree of sufficiency he accords a causal conclusion are important measures of the adequacy of his historical explanation. They also reveal a closely knit cluster of intellectual, psychological, religious, and social values that ultimately reflect the historian's lived experiences and future expectations. Any attempt to unravel and explicate these values is difficult enough; but the task is further complicated by disagreements between historians and philosophers of history as to the meaning and use of causation in history.[1] Causation as a concept, as a tool of historical explanation, has itself become an object of hermeneutic discussion, the contours of which have had an enormous influence upon the evaluation of past historical thought. Though the importance of the causal principle is universally recognized, two related, yet different, strategies for its analysis have evolved. One strategy concentrates upon the epistemological question: What did a former age mean when it used the term "causation"? The other focuses upon the act of causal explanation: How did a former age explain causal change? In simple terms it is the difference between idea and practice. Both strategies are equally valid, and both are, in theory, directed toward the same goal: to grasp the reciprocal interaction between idea and practice which determines the totality of the age's appreciation of historical change. But the tactics of each strategy often lead to conflicting evaluations of the subject under consideration. One need only recall the continuing discussion of the respective merits of Herodotus and Thucydides, of Machiavelli and Guicciardini, of Hegel and Ranke, for partial confirmation of the difficulties in successfully joining the two strategies.

The problem of combining an analysis of the Aufklärers' idea of causation with their practice of causal explanation is especially difficult, for there are no outstanding historians comparable to those mentioned above or, for that matter, to Gibbon and Voltaire. Instead, we are confronted with a more or less general endeavor undertaken by a number of capable thinkers confronting a problem too large for any one of them to resolve totally. Their goal was to forge both a new idea of causation applicable to historical analysis and a new method of synthetic causal representation. As so often happens, thinkers adept in one area were not equally adept in the other; a fragmentary quality still characterized the Aufklärers' work. Sometimes we encounter a brilliant insight into the nature of historical causation or a sparkling portrayal of the complexities of historical change. Yet such manifestations do not totally satisfy. The Aufklärers were struggling to create a new paradigm of historical understanding. They posed important questions, expressed admirable intentions, and raised points that are still current, but synthesis eluded them. Their efforts were necessary to the formation of the modern paradigm of historical understanding, but once that paradigm was firmly established, once it became self-evident, their pioneering work could easily be forgotten.

In order to clarify the novelty and direction of the Aufklärers' appreciation of historical causation, I think it advantageous to deal with the two strategies of analysis in separate chapters. I discuss the hermeneutic strategy first, not for reasons of philosophical preference, but rather because previous investigations into the Aufklärung's idea of causation have greatly contributed to the conclusion that the Aufklärung was locked within the ambit of "superficial rationalism."

2

The strategy of hermeneutic analysis is most commonly found in German works of what I choose to call the neo-Rankean school.[2] Most neo-Rankeans either question the competence of causal explanation or accord it secondary importance in historical understanding. A distinction is made between nature (the realm of causation) and life (the realm of "spirit"): a world of mechanistic laws is opposed by a world of indeterminate and individual creation. The movement of history is seen as an interaction between the free and the determinate realms of life. This view implies that causal explanation alone is incapable of recapturing the essence of historical change because it excludes the ineffable quality of individualism. Any theory of history proclaiming the preeminence of causal relations is therefore adjudged antihistorical. Any theory of history that is future directed is deemed a contradiction in terms because it is impossible to foresee the form of future individuality. By far the majority of neo-Rankeans believe the Aufklärung to be ahistorical because of its expressed concern with causation, its interest in the future, and its use of mechanical metaphors. In the neo-Rankean view, the Aufklärers merely carried the injunctions of seventeenth-century physics over into the realm of history and laid the foundations for nineteenth-century positivism. This critique of the Aufklärung's sense of history is founded on two assumptions. The first involves a statement of fact: the Aufklärers accepted, unchanged, the model of causal analysis drawn from the physical sciences to explain change; the second involves an epistemological assumption: causal explanation alone is insufficient for an understanding of historical change. For this inquiry, the validity of the former assumption is vital.

At first glance, the evidence seems to support the neo-Rankean contention. Throughout the eighteenth century the Aufklärers themselves lovingly and endlessly proclaimed the need to uncover causes and describe effects. As early as 1729 Johann Jacob Schmauß called any history that failed to show cause and effect a history without soul and life.[3] In 1754 the eminent church historian Johann Lorenz von Mosheim reiterated this theme in more detail. In his remarkably long-lived *Ecclesiastical History,* Mosheim described the duty of the historian:

> It is absolutely necessary to trace the effects to their causes, and to connect events with circumstances, views, principles, and instruments that have contributed to their existence. A bare recital of facts can at best enrich the *memory,* and furnish a certain degree of amusement; but the historian who enters the secret springs that direct the course of outward events, and views things in their various relations, connexions, and tendencies, gives thus a proper exercise to the judgment of the reader, and administers, on many occasions, the most useful lessons of wisdom and prudence. It is true, a high degree of caution is to be observed here, lest in disclosing the secret springs of public events, we substitute imaginary causes in the place of real, and attribute the actions of men to principles they never professed.[4]

In 1767 Johann Christoph Gatterer put forward virtually the same theme: "The chief concern of the historian is to search for the occasions and causes of an important event [*die Veranlassungen und Ursachen einer merkwürdige Begebenheit*] and to develop as well as possible the whole system of causes and effects, of means and intentions [*Mitteln und Absichten*], no matter how confused they may seem at first."[5] Clearly, the concept of causation fascinated the Aufklärers.

Even the descriptive metaphors the Aufklärers employed seem to add support to the neo-Rankean contention that the Aufklärers thought in rationalistic mechanical terms. "Springs of action" is definitely a mechanical allusion, and so are the overworked images of the machine, the clock, and the balance. Writer after writer invoked them to explain the intricacies of political and social life. Schlözer seems to offer proof enough. In one of his earliest works he defined the state as a complex machine. A quarter of a century later, four years after the beginning of the French Revolution, he tenaciously repeated the comparison.[6] As one eminent historian has pointed out, however, "Isolated metaphors do not make historical interpretations."[7] Equally important is how such metaphors were used and what they were intended to show. Schlözer's use of the machine metaphor is an apt example.

The basic similarity between the state and a machine which Schlözer chose to emphasize was that both were created by man. This point may sound trivial to twentieth-century readers, but it certainly was not trivial to those reacting against seventeenth-century justifications for absolute rule. A machine requires constant attention, repair, adjustments, and alterations. Calling the state a machine is therefore a good metaphor to use when denying the idea of a divine and immutable order. When so used, the machine metaphor served to emphasize the Aufklärers' attitude toward origins, to proclaim the possibility of achieving future change, and to reaffirm the right of the critical mind to make the state a subject of free investigation.[8]

But what of development? Here the machine metaphor is definitely inappropriate. If the state were really like a machine, it would follow that certain rational rules allowing for its efficient operation existed. When taken to its logical conclusion, the machine metaphor would lead one to elevate mechanical causal explanations as primary to historical understanding. Schlözer confronted the problem in a description of change he wrote in 1767:

> No institution lasts forever; no decree is eternal. A certain ebb and flood reigns even for the most educated people. In this manner, too, is the state a machine. Its wheels wear down; some become useless; its driving force falters. . . . Soon new and more wheels are needed; new powers that before were not visible manifest themselves and competition arises between the new forces and the already operative ones.
>
> The larger the state, the more it is a compound machine; the more complex it is, the more frequently it requires improvements. Thousands of years may pass before the whole sum of its forces can be recognized; it may take hundreds of years before its powers become operative and still hundreds more before they operate in the best possible way. The best of plans may confront obstacles that will nip them in the bud; or, even if they become effective, they may generate a whole series of undesirable, unexpected results that would far outweigh the planned effects of the original program. For no man can totally comprehend the full chain of events that led to a state's formation.[9]

Despite all Schlözer's allusions to wheels and driving forces, the impact of his description is not precisely that of mechanical action and interaction. Powers manifest themselves after slumbering for hundreds of years; undesirable and unexpected events run counter to all rational expectations; plans are "nipped in the bud"; forces arise and come into conflict. Clearly the metaphor proved inadequate for the description, with the result that Schlözer vitalized the image of the machine – not an unusual occurrence in an age where the machine still possessed a quality of mystery. Schlözer's description of the growth of the awe-inspiring compound machine called the state evokes an impression of long, slow, and tortuous change that can never be totally encompassed by causal explanation. The machine metaphor is modified by another metaphor drawn from Leibnizian thought, the metaphor of conjunction and compound (*zusammengesetzen*); the compound unit is more than the sum of its parts, for the manner of conjunction carries with it its own force. Therefore the state, the creation of the human spirit, assumes an almost organic character in which the whole is greater than the sum of its parts.

Upon careful reading of the Aufklärers' writings, it becomes clear that they usually joined the machine metaphor to the Leibnizian metaphor in order to avoid overly mechanical explanations. One of Schlözer's teachers, Johann Stephan Pütter, defined Germany in an analogous manner. It was a *zusammengesetzte Gesellschaft* (a "compound society") that could not be classified according to any rational set of ideal types, which meant that it could be examined only in terms of growth and development. This new method of appreciation Pütter called a "higher way of classifying states."[10] By the middle of the eighteenth century mechanical allusions had already become restrictive, pro forma figures of speech, whose use could just as easily obfuscate as enlighten. It is not unusual to find an increasing tendency to mix metaphors and join images which later appear contradictory. Thus Schlözer used his mechanical image when he chose to emphasize the human origin of social institutions and often added a genetic image when he described the institution's growth and development. As he said in 1771, "The best way to periodize the history of states is, without a doubt, the genetic, which shows their step-by-step rise and fall."[11] Upon close examination, the Aufklärers' use of metaphor does not totally support the neo-Rankean contention that the Aufklärers accepted without alteration a mechanical model of cause and effect.

3

Careful evaluation of the Aufklärers' analysis of the principle of causation confirms their dissatisfaction with purely mechanical models. A sizable number of Enlightenment thinkers questioned the assumption that the physical model of causal analysis was ubiquitously applicable to all disciplines. The attack on ideas of mechanical causation came from many sides, though Hume's direct assault upon the idea of causation was the most radical expression of this developing discontent. Defenders of revealed religion, repelled by naturalistic critiques of Holy Scripture, and thinkers proclaiming an organismic and metamorphic idea of nature (e.g., Diderot) called for a different approach in evaluating the life sciences and the sciences of man. They were joined by another, forgotten group, the eighteenth-century chemists who, clinging to a jumble of alchemic ideas, Paracelsian principles, and Stoic theories, sought to discover a new method of "experimental instinct" to replace the methods of Newtonian physics. German aestheticians also called the model of deductive analysis into question in their attempt to evolve a "logic of the soul." Finally, the *Ständestaat* consciousness, so strong in German-speaking areas, stimulated a number of poets, primarily Swiss, to sing the praises of the uniqueness, beauty, and "local genius" of their homeland, qualities that defied mechanical, or causal, definition.

The general mistrust of airy speculation which suffused the natural philosophy of the Enlightenment also played its part. By elevating empiricism over mathematical deduction, natural scientists helped to sow the seeds of displeasure with deduction, even when they heartily proclaimed Newton the prime bringer of light to a world still enveloped in the shadow of scholasticism. Any scientist who ventured too far into speculative causal thinking was therefore impelled to justify his approach. Lavoisier, the very embodiment of the deductive method and almost an ideal example of the vaunted French rationalism, tendered the following justification for a method that a hundred years earlier would have been accepted as the model of advanced thinking: "Dangerous though the spirit of systems is in the physical sciences, it is equally to be feared lest piling up without any order too great a store of experiments may obscure instead of illuminating the science."[12] At the heart of the diverse presuppositions, which crossed, recrossed, and at times conflicted with each other, was the question of which models of order would be appropriate to the various sciences. The result of the debate certainly was not clear-cut, though the debate itself served to undermine the self-evident acceptance of the physical model of cause and effect and to make causation a serious problem for hermeneutic investigation. In Protestant Germany and Switzerland the problem had especial relevance because of the conjunction of the elements of a renewed religiosity, the heritage of Leibnizian thought, the *Ständestaat* tradition, and, surprisingly, the rejuvenation of the universities, where an attempt was made to combine advanced thinking with scholarly *Gründlichkeit*.

One of the first Aufklärers to raise the question of the efficacy of causal explanation in history was Johann Martin Chladenius. A theologian, his interest in history was primarily religious. Born of a family expelled from Hungary because of devotion to the Lutheran cause, he himself remained actively committed to the Lutheranism that characterized the seventeenth century. This commitment, however, did not take the form of a sterile dogmatism; instead, Chladenius tried to refurbish Lutheran belief by joining together a modified Wolffian rationalism, a Thomasiusian concern for "practical philosophy," an interest in classical rhetoric, and his awareness of historical understanding. He thought he could tread his way through the twin dangers of espousing either a natural religion or a purely subjective religion of the heart. Anticipating the Neologists, Chladenius located the fault of previous attacks on, and defenses of, the Bible in a reliance upon dogmatic and rationalistic assumptions. This reliance, he argued, was illegitimate because Holy Scripture was written in the form of history — though it was far more than a history — and should be interpreted according to the principles of historical understanding. In his first major work, *Einleitung zur richtigen Auslegung vernünfftiger Reden und Schriften* (1742), Chladenius developed the idea that there were two different kinds of understanding – historical and dogmatic – and different sets of rules for interpreting historical and dogmatic statements.[13] His second major work, the *Allgemeine Geschichtswissenschaft* (1752), defined the principles of historical interpretation. It offers a brilliant discussion, which still bears reading, of many of the problems of historical hermeneutics. Joachim Wach, an observer not prone to overstatement, called the book one of the first "critiques of historical reason" and placed Chladenius on the level of Herder, Wilhelm von Humboldt, Johann Gustav Droysen, and Wilhelm Dilthey.[14]

A discussion of the problem of causation formed only a part of the *Allgemeine Geschichtswissenschaft,* yet Chladenius raised a number of questions that have remained basic to the ongoing controversy over the appropriateness of causal analysis and explanation in history. For Chladenius, the central questions in a discussion of historical causation concerned the existence of general historical laws and asked whether historical truths could be presented in the form of sufficient and self-evident cause-and-effect relations. His point of departure, expressed in his first work, is now a familiar one. He sought to differentiate between dogmatic and historical sciences by looking at their objects of investigation. The dogmatic, or abstract, sciences dealt with a world external to man; they were descriptive and their generalizations were logical, deductive, and self-inclusive because they were pure creations of the human intellect. The historical sciences, on the other hand, investigated both the external physical world and the internal world of human values. They were intensive sciences whose objects of investigation were the real, moral bodies (*moralische Wesen*) of the state and of society.[15] Historians were delegated the task of explaining an interacting series of complex and confused (*verwirrt*) events, some of them fairly predictable – actions determined by social position, tradition, and law – and others resulting from the indeterminate effects of the action of the spirit. In an approach paralleling that of Neologists and aestheticians, Chladenius also emphasized the irrational, nonpredictable nature of man, tracing "will and individual freedom" as the sources of most actions.[16] Because the hypostatic element of historical action stemmed from man's voluntary nature, a nature defying rational definition, it was impossible to formulate general laws of history or to organize historical explanations according to the traditional model of causal analysis.[17] "Conjunctions, connections, and causes in history . . . stem from people's actions, which are conditioned by their will, their resolve, and their conceptions."[18]

Throughout his work, Chladenius spiced his exposition with a host of examples. He chose the problem of Charles V's retirement to illustrate the inadequacy of general laws in historical explanation. Chladenius first cited the popular generalization that Charles retired because of the depressing outcome of a number of his undertakings. If that were true, Chladenius observed, the following general law might be employed: "If one's fortunes drastically

change for the worse, then one will become disgusted with the whole affair
and wish to lay it aside." In form the argument came "very close to a
so-called causal conclusion [*Causalschluß*]." But was it a sufficient explanation? Chladenius doubted it: "To tell the truth, such changes in fortune alone
would not be enough to compel this great emperor to take so important and
unusual a step. Therefore, one often adds the explanation that Charles's
declining physical powers reinforced his decision to seek peace and quiet. Yet
many people are plagued by streaks of bad fortune and poor health and still
refuse to surrender their power. It follows, therefore, that the above
explanations do not exhaust all the possibilities. The remaining reasons must
stem from the individual mentality [*Gedenckenart*] of this monarch."[19]
Even in the relatively simple task of investigating the motives of a single
historical actor, the historian discovers that no single general law is sufficient
to explain the event. Had Chladenius been endowed with a better sense of
humor, he might have concluded his example in the manner of a recent
commentator who advanced a similar line of argument. The general law
illustrated by the case of Charles V is: If a monarch of the same era with
exactly the same way of thinking and the same character and personality as
Charles V encountered the same series of bad fortune at the same period in
his life and experienced the same decline in his powers, then that monarch
would retire. For Chladenius, the example was meant to demonstrate that in
complex situations (called by him confused events [*Verwirrungen*]), where
historical change is most evident, the inadequacy of causal explanation is
more apparent.[20] Each causal conclusion, instead of ending the debate, calls
forth another series of questions and explanations which tend to reduce the
so-called general law to a complex description of a single nonrepeatable event.

In this argument Chladenius introduces two determinate variables that
nullify a total reliance upon general laws in historical understanding: the
ineffable quality of human nature and the unique configurations of time and
place. Before a historian can explain an event, he must first understand not
only the characters of the historical participants but also the "unique
circumstances occasioning the event and the specific mentality of the
time."[21] The prominence Chladenius accorded these two elements strongly
suggests that he was influenced by the formulations of classical rhetoric, an
influence documented by the title of his first work. Chladenius's choice of
the "mentality of the time" as a regulator of causal analysis corresponds to
the rhetorical concern with the lived truths of a society, with *sensus
communis*. Throughout the eighteenth century a number of thinkers found in
the idea of *sensus communis* a congenial weapon to criticize rational
philosophy. Dubious about the universal application of logical demonstration
to the problems of society, they turned to "common sense," the source that
directs "us in the common affairs of life, where our reasoning faculty would
leave us in the dark."[22] The practical reason of common sense was
considered superior to pure reason because it was a rule of heart and will, a

living expression of man's instinctive moral drive. The revaluation of man's will and instinct, evident in Chladenius as well as in Vico, Shaftesbury, Hutcheson, Hume, Schmauß, and Justi, parallels the rhetorical concern with man's pathos – his passions and instincts.

The eighteenth-century return to rhetoric demonstrates the complex manner in which new ideas are generated. Thinkers of the Enlightenment, dissatisfied with the universal claims of the modern deductive method, turned to a more distant past for help in overcoming their immediate present. Since rhetoric had always formed a counterpoise to speculative philosophy, it provided thinkers with an alternative position from which they could operate. In Germany, the return to rhetoric was intensified because rhetoric proved congenial to two popular intellectual movements, movements that found institutionalized expression in the German university.

The first stimulus came from the increasing popularity of Christian Thomasius's espousal of the ideal of *Gelahrtheit* a socially directed ethic including "moral, legal and educational philosophy."[23] Chladenius had specifically referred to this ideal in the subtitle of his *Allgemeine Geschicht-swissenschaft.*[24] Thomasius drew a sharp distinction between practical philosophy (*Gelahrtheit*) and formal, scholastic, university philosophy (*Gelehrtheit*). His goal was to transform the German citizen into a *Weltbürger,* not to create another generation of pedants. He concentrated upon the prerequisites of practical life, showing little sympathy for metaphysics, formal theology, or deductive logic. To him a syllogism was "merely a fashionable way of embellishing the known, or, at best, a device for classifying knowledge."[25] The educational direction of his goal and the concern with "common sense" led him to undergird his eclectic philosophy of life with ideas and methods drawn from classical rhetoric. Important from the point of view of the development of German attitudes was that Thomasius, unlike his contemporary Leibniz, chose to proclaim his ideal from the university podium (and, for the first time, officially in the German language). This successful tactic seriously influenced German university reform for the rest of the century. The illusive goal of *Gelahrtheit* – though often redefined in its specifics – animated all the numerous attempts to recast eighteenth-century university structure.[26]

The second stimulus for a revitalization of rhetoric came from a direction seemingly opposed to Thomasius's worldly ethic, namely, from the new religiosity that colored the whole of the Aufklärung. Originated by Pietism, the recrudescence eventually touched all Protestant sects. Carried and propagated by the German *Bürgertum,* the new religiosity shared one common goal with the idea of *Gelahrtheit*: to make basic truths immediately accessible to the average German *Bürger.* The new religiosity also elevated the *vita activa* over the *vita contemplativa,* placing far less weight upon dogmatic theology and emphasizing instead the practical problems of the pastoral function. The revived interest in the edificatory duties of a prospective cleric was conducive to a renewed interest in rhetoric, which, as the theologian Chladenius defined it, was the study of how one can express a true idea in sensate forms.[27] This concern was also reflected in the university curriculum. At the major centers for the training of Protestant clergymen – at Halle, Wittenberg, Leipzig, Erlangen, and even at the more aristocratic and juridically oriented Göttingen – rhetoric, eloquence, and ecclesiastical history took precedence over dogmatics.

Both impulses, the religious and the worldly, gave the study of rhetoric and eloquence a new lease on life during the first six decades of the eighteenth century; it was only natural that Chladenius would turn to them for assistance. It must be remembered, however, that the rhetorical concerns of Chladenius and other eighteenth-century thinkers differed from those of their classical and Humanist predecessors. The difference lies in the imposing edifice of modern natural science and philosophy, which blocked any uncritical return to classical and Humanist rhetoric. Whoever in the eighteenth century turned to rhetoric did so with the conscious awareness of the hermeneutic problems posed by modern philosophy. Rhetoric was a tool, an adjunct to eighteenth-century thought, to be used when possible; thinkers of the eighteenth century had to go beyond the imperatives of rhetoric to confront the challenge posed by the proponents of coherent analysis.

Chladenius seemed to be aware of this challenge, for he did not rest his argument on the two variables of the individuality of peoples and of times. As formulated, Chladenius's position could easily have been countered by the contention that it did not deny the theoretical possibility of sufficient causal explanation; it merely emphasized the difficulty in uncovering causes. One could argue that the example of the explanations offered for Charles V's retirement merely testified to the rather poor set of generalizations historians had been satisfied to employ. All that might be needed were a few general laws of psychology to solve the problem. It could also be claimed that one might be able to derive the mentality of the time through the proper application of general laws and that, with sufficient study, a general law might be uncovered expressing the causal relation between the immediate environment and historical change. Chladenius included two points in his exposition that logically denied the possibility of ever attaining complete historical truth via the route of coherent analysis. Further, he did not hesitate to draw the conclusion to which this argument led: that history is in form, organization, and nature a different type of understanding from that of the dogmatic sciences.

Clearly, a Leibnizian assumption enabled Chladenius to take this position: he conceived of the moral world as a universal and infinite conjunction (Zusammenhang). The total conjunction influenced the individual and the individual elements were symbiotically related to one another and to the whole. Thus any attempt to isolate a limited set of historical phenomena and still retain their full complement of causal elements was impossible, for

"history in itself has no end; it is always attended with its own consequences."[28] Though choice was necessary to explain the past, the act of
considering certain events as worthy of note (*merkwürdig*) and others
unworthy was basically arbitrary, negating any possibility of arriving at
self-sufficient general historical laws. Chladenius employed a similar strategy
in his discussion of the relation between the observer and the object being
observed. He boldly expanded the Leibnizian analysis of optics into a general
theory of understanding, which in certain ways resembles Karl Mannheim's
idea of relationism. Chladenius contended that man as observer, being himself
rooted in the moral world, cannot extract himself from his milieu to survey
sufficiently the total relations of the elements of historical life. All historical
thinking is thinking in time and from a specific vantage point in time. Thus,
logically, every history is written from a specific vantage point (*Sehepunkt*).
Since the time-bound observer can never fully perceive the universal
connection, he can never fully understand the causes of events. Chladenius
concluded that there is no such thing as an "impartial," or value-free,
history.[29] In order to rescue historical understanding from dogmatic
formulations, Chladenius, like Michaelis and Schlözer, constructed his theory
of history upon the radical recognition of the insuperable limitations of
human perception: "The limitations of our perception both of the nature of
the soul [*Gemüthe*] and of external conditions make it impossible for us ever
to perceive [*einsehen*] the causes of an event, though we can acquire some
idea of them."[30]

Chladenius's root metaphors are drawn from the act of seeing, not from
cognition. At critical junctures he introduces such terms as *Sehepunkt*
("vantage point"), *Zuschauer* ("observer"), *einsehen* ("perceive"), and
anschauen ("contemplate"). To see means to experience, but not to
experience passively. Experience is not mere sense impression etching an
indelible picture upon an impassive tabula rasa, nor is it a logical category;
rather, it is a product of the interaction between sense impression and an
active *Gemüthe,* a term that is elusive because it signifies a spiritual mood.
Historical understanding is an understanding of the spirit, or *Gemüthe,* an act
of reexperiencing or seeing again, though from a different vantage point. It is
not the apprehension of a mechanical cause-and-effect relation. Chladenius
defined the difference between historical and causal comprehension: "A
history is a series of events that fit and merge together in succession. In
general laws one encounters an internal differentiation whereby certain laws
are basic premises and others are results, corollaries, and theorems; and
indeed their relation to one another is that, when one knows only the first, he
can generate the others through his own cognition. The same differentiation
is not possible for historical events. . . . Every successive event must, like the
preceding event, he perceived by an act of *intuitive judgment* [*Anschauungsurtheil*]. Therefore, historical understanding consists of a series of true
intuitive judgments that are transmitted from soul to soul through reports,

narratives, documents, testimonies, and repetition."[31] Chladenius cautioned
his readers not to make the mistake of equating the term "historical cause"
with the usual meaning of the word "cause": "If one hears of causes in
history, it is easy to assume erroneously that the events of the world follow
one another in precisely the same way a conclusion follows from a basic
premise and that history can thereby be expressed in deductions and
syllogisms. But here we encounter the greatest difference. In general laws, one
law follows the other or is already contained *in the other*. With historical
truths one cannot maintain that what follows is already subsumed in what
preceded it."[32]

Chladenius's definition of historical understanding as an intuitive judgment
(he used the terms *Anschauungsurtheil* and *iudico intuitiuo* interchangeably)
is crucial because it unites the two elements of his hermeneutics: the rational
and the intuitive. Chladenius's attack upon causal analysis was not an attack
upon rationalism, but rather an attempt to limit reason's competence. It was
this quest, a quest typical of the Aufklärung, that led Joachim Wach to
compare Chladenius with Dilthey; and there is something analogous in
Dilthey's and Chladenius's positions. Like Dilthey, Chladenius did not deny
that the same elemental logical processes inform all scientific inquiry (Dilthey
defined them as induction, analysis, construction, and comparison).[33]
Chladenius argued that since the object of historical understanding differs
from that of "dogmatic" understanding, its form must also differ.

Chladenius attempted a synthesis of rationalist and Pietist hermeneutics.
His position and that of the Aufklärers in general seemed to be formed by the
catharsis that resulted from the naked confrontation between Wolff and the
Pietist Francke. It had cleared the air, stimulating the Aufklärers to transcend
the two conflicting strains, which were, for awhile, housed at the University
of Halle. From the Pietists, Chladenius accepted the emphasis upon "inner
feelings." Yet he realized that a history drawing its principles solely from the
"inner light" could easily lead to the circular and present-minded thinking
found in Arnold's *Unparteyische Kirchen- und Ketzer-Historie*. Chladenius,
who abhorred Arnold's work, continually emphasized the importance of
rational methods in all scientific disciplines. The logical processes guide the
researcher in his attempt to understand and rediscover. Diligent research,
comparison, and imaginative reconstruction are the prerequisites to the final
apprehension of a real, individual conjunction. In the final analysis, however,
historical understanding is founded upon the ability to reexperience past life,
though that is made possible only through a methodological interpretation of
all historical sources.

Chladenius did not propose banning all the terms associated with causal
analysis, though he was reluctant to retain the word "cause" (he favored the
weaker term *Gelegenheit* — "occasion"). He suggested how causal vocabulary
could be retained: "If one wishes to establish a differentiation in historical
proof and create something similar to a principal law in a demonstration, it

has to be done in the following manner. We have already seen how a history is begun. A certain occasion [*Gelegenheit*] is chosen from which a decision or an action follows, which is then attended by many other results. The occasion is treated as though it were outside history and differentiated from it, even though the occasion is necessary to understand the causes of the following events. The *first* event in time upon which the rest of history depends is the *beginning* of the history; this we call the first premise [*Grund*] and that which evolves or flows from it, its results [*Folgen*]."[34] Accordingly, all historical thinking requires an arbitrary choice by a time-bound observer as to where to start and where to finish, a choice that negates any claim to total certainty.

4

If one measures Chladenius in terms of direct historical influence, his hermeneutics is unimportant. Chladenius was not the founder of an important school of thought, nor was he long revered as a seminal thinker, a phenomenon perhaps explicable by his early death (at the age of forty-nine), his commitment to orthodox Lutheranism, his position as a professor of theology, and the fact that he never composed a history. Even Semler, whose hermeneutic principles were similar and who spent a year teaching at Altdorf, very close to Chladenius's Erlangen, hardly mentioned Chladenius in his two-volume autobiography. The only thing Semler thought interesting about the theologian was his penchant for cooking his own food. Yet Chladenius is important in another way. We find in his theory of history the rough outlines of a cluster of arguments directed against the self-sufficiency of causal explanation which became increasingly common to historians of the Aufklärung. His thinking is worth resurrecting because it points to the direction in which the thought of the Aufklärung would travel.

This direction becomes evident when we turn to the ideas of Johann Christoph Gatterer, who presented many of the points cited by Chladenius in a clearer form. It is possible that Gatterer received his inspiration directly from Chladenius. Gatterer, seventeen years Chladenius's junior, was educated at Altdorf and taught at a nearby gymnasium while Chladenius was at Erlangen. Still, Gatterer never acknowledged Chladenius's influence and, unlike many of Gatterer's contemporaries, he usually was rather scrupulous about such matters. Suffice it to say that there is a similarity in their positions which, I believe, can be just as easily traced to the developing tendency of the Aufklärung's attitude toward history as to direct influence. As I have suggested, the sources and desires for a revaluation of causal analysis were everywhere present. Even a passing knowledge of developments in aesthetics and Neology and an acquaintance with Leibnizian thought and classical rhetoric could lead to the position advocated by Chladenius. And Gatterer had more than a passing acquaintance with the intellectual developments of his time. He was a voracious reader who was actively concerned in the problems of historical scholarship. At the height of his fame and influence — during the 1760s and 1770s — he participated in a dizzying number of scholarly activities. He founded a famous historical institute, edited and contributed heavily to two successive journals published under its auspices, and wrote extensively on the historical ancillary sciences and universal history. He taught a special course in historical methodology, the "Enzyklopädie," which set out to define the goals and limits of historical thinking. Along with his colleague and occasional opponent Schlözer, he helped to replan the German translation of the famous English cooperative world history.

Unlike Chladenius, Gatterer never attempted to present his ideas in a complete exposition of the problems of historical logic and representation. His views on the efficacy of the concept of causation are scattered throughout a number of writings and articles, making a coherent reconstruction of his theory of causation difficult. One of the most striking difficulties is Gatterer's own contradictory evaluation of causal analysis. At one time Gatterer encouraged the historian to seek the causes and effects of events: "Nothing should hinder or lead him astray in this undertaking, neither the distance between areas, nor the intervals in time, nor the different types of events themselves."[35] At another time he recognized the impossibility of achieving this goal because of the historian's inability to transcend his own historical vantage point. "Each [historian] has his own *Standort,* his own point of view, which for one event or situation under investigation makes a part of that event at one time important, at another unimportant, and at still another time it is totally disregarded."[36] Gatterer himself, however, saw no contradiction in these statements, a fact that requires some examination, even allowing for man's natural tendency to contradict himself without realizing it.

The apparent ambivalence of Gatterer's statements on causation stems from his attempt to investigate the problem of perception critically. Borrowing heavily from aesthetics, Neology, and rhetoric, and motivated by a genuine religiosity, Gatterer rejected the Cartesian and Wolffian ideal that all sciences had to employ a universal form of organization and explanation, the form of mathematical demonstration. He supported his contention by turning from an analysis of form to a consideration of the creation of form, a strategy strongly suggestive of aesthetics. According to Gatterer, scientific form and organization were products of an elemental drive, the "philosophical spirit" acting on a specific type of subject matter, impelled by a certain cluster of questions, and directed toward a definite goal. By relating all forms of knowledge back to the objective operations of the "philosophical spirit," or the impulse to analyze critically, Gatterer was able to differentiate between basic forms of knowledge without having to choose one of them as primary. Like Chladenius, Gatterer maintained that there were two basic types of knowledge — knowledge of the abstract and knowledge of the individual —

and he argued that since the goals of these two forms of scientific inquiry differed, so must their methods of organization and explanation.[37] The distinction between historical and cognitive knowledge was not new. Both Hobbes and Wolff employed it, but for a reason different from that of Gatterer and his contemporaries. For Hobbes and Wolff, the distinction served to demonstrate the inadequacies of the historical sciences, since both thinkers accepted the belief in a monolithic and ideal scientific form. For the Aufklärers, who rejected the idea of a monolithic scientific form, the distinction led to espousal of the excellencies of historical understanding. According to Gatterer, the natural sciences (a prime example of abstract knowledge) dealt with abstractions and ideal forms; their methods of operation consisted in isolating the subject of investigation from its total environment, reducing its elements to abstract or symbolic formulas, and expressing their relations in mathematical or syllogistic terms. The path to truth in these disciplines, Gatterer contended, is "marked by minor detours, sometimes by major ones, but it never follows a direct route to its goal because of the intricate [umständlich] development of its concepts from its original premise."[38]

The historical sciences, on the other hand, focused on the individual event. History dealt with life as experienced; its métier was the understanding of past experience. As the science of the real and the actual, it was the most immediate and accessible form of organized knowledge.[39] No matter how convincing and comprehensive a mathematical demonstration might be, a good history would always be more compelling. Abstract proof required long, complicated, and tedious mental operations; historical proof spoke directly to the senses, the imagination, and reason. It encompassed the full range of human experience because it employed the "three ways to arrive at visible proof," whereas abstract knowledge touched only the faculty of reason.[40] History, for Gatterer, was a prime form of anschauende Erkenntnis ("intuitive knowledge").[41] Although both Gatterer and Chladenius saw history as a form of anschauende Erkenntnis, there is a marked note of self-assurance in Gatterer's work which is absent in Chladenius's. Gatterer is no longer on the defensive; instead of arguing, he simply proclaims the superiority of historical understanding over abstract analysis in questions dealing with man and his social world. Part of his assurance stemmed from his ability to draw upon the structural analysis of the psyche proposed by eighteenth-century aesthetics. Instead of vaguely invoking the will and the soul, Gatterer could now say that the superiority of history arose from its ability to speak to all the Seelenkräfte ("faculties of the soul"). History was living truth, not sterile ratiocination.[42]

If history was, as Gatterer claimed, an individual anschauende Erkenntnis, what role did causal analysis play in historical understanding? Gatterer had no intention of denying the validity of abstract understanding; that would have been sheer madness for most eighteenth-century thinkers. Abstract reasoning

was as much a product of the "philosophical spirit" as historical understanding and, when used in the right situation, was highly valuable. Also,
while Gatterer continually cautioned historians in the use of deductive
hypotheses, he did not follow Johann Gottlob von Justi in seeing a radical
incompatibility between abstract and concrete sciences. Justi, in his prize-
winning anti-Wolffian essay on the theory of the monad, dogmatically
maintained that when "one combines a geometrical concept with a
metaphysical one, a false conclusion will invariably result. The reason is
evident. Geometry deals with abstract things while metaphysics, on the
contrary, deals with actual things."[43] Gatterer, in a slightly more guarded
tone, wrote in his *Abriß der Universalhistorie*: "The use of hypotheses is not
so effective in history as in the natural sciences; in fact, most of the time they
obstruct the path to historical truth."[44] Gatterer sought to establish an
independent region for history, but it was one that sometimes impinged on
that of the natural sciences, since both regions were expressions of the
elemental philosophical spirit. This led Gatterer to take an ambivalent
attitude toward causation; on one level of appreciation, he acknowledged the
importance of adducing causal relations, though he considered this activity as
basically heuristic. On another level, he sought to differentiate between the
final forms of historical and abstract reasoning and to redefine the idea of
historical causation so that it agreed with his distinctions.

On the heuristic level, Gatterer interpreted history as a user, not a
producer, of general causal laws. General causal laws, according to Gatterer,
proposed certain guidelines by which the historian could choose important
events from the plethora of material and organize them so that they became
manageable. As Gatterer saw it, the historian and the natural scientist shared
a common task: both were required to pose a set of intelligent questions,
search for materials pertaining to the questions, and arrange the materials so
as to make the whole comprehensible (*faßbar*). History, like every other
science, had to be based on the tactics of choice, limitation, and
interpretation within the boundaries of a specific problem. Strange as it may
sound, Gatterer used causal analysis as a heuristic to overcome the mechanical
criteria of organization employed by historians of the seventeenth and early
eighteenth centuries. Those earlier historians were content to arrange their
facts under such rubrics as wars, congresses, internal affairs, acquisitions of
territory, and commerce. They mechanically divided historical time into
uniform chunks corresponding to either years or centuries. Gatterer, however,
wanted to go beyond the artificial topical organization; to him, history had to
show natural connections.[45] We are again reminded of Gatterer's injunction,
already cited, to let nothing like arbitrary divisions of time and events hinder
the historian in his studies.

Gatterer believed he had found ample confirmation for his position in the
writings of the classical historians, especially Thucydides, Tacitus, and Livy.
He felt no compunction about using the ancients to criticize his immediate

predecessors. The vehemence originally generated by the "Quarrel of the Ancients and Moderns" had subsided, and a quickening German reinfatuation with the Ancients was already noticeable.[46] Gatterer considered the classical historians superior because they had evolved what he called a system of events (*System der Begebenheiten*), which had allowed them to perceive the "inner connection of events [*innere Verhältnis der Begebenheiten*]" and the relation between "causes and effects [*Ursachen und Wirkungen*]."[47]

When Gatterer proclaimed the need to establish a system of events, he did not use the word "system" in its seventeenth-century guise, that is, as a *pictura mundi,* but rather in its older and more general meaning of placing things together. A system of events was a method of organization that dissolved the lifeless categories set up by polyhistorians. It was an analytical construct that allowed the historian to distinguish between the important and the unimportant. It allowed him to focus upon a set of phenomena, to exclude others, and to draw connections between those that hitherto had been separated. Gatterer's usage of the word "system" was similar to Winckelmann's, who proposed to study Greek art within the system of Greek life.[48] By carefully implementing ideas and questions derived from the idea of causation, the historian created a unique construct, determined by the type of problem and the material to be studied. But, as Gatterer also emphasized, the creation of a system of events was not the end of historical inquiry; rather, it was the beginning, the preliminary to attaining what he called evident, or intuitive, historical understanding. A system of events offered a skeleton, or structure, within which the historian might work, but it remained lifeless; Gatterer likened it to the classificatory systems of contemporary biology, such as the system of Linnaeus. It allowed one to "survey the whole," to discriminate, but not to integrate.[49] It gave knowledge, not understanding.

Gatterer may well have derived this distinction between descriptive abstract knowledge and intuitive understanding from the aesthetic theories of Baumgarten, Sulzer, and Resewitz. Historical understanding, as Gatterer conceived it, was an active apprehension of the individual and the whole, made possible by the action of the *Seelenkräfte*. It was not simply a process of conscious rational thought, though rational analysis was necessary. The categories of rational and intuitive understanding were not disjunctive, but rather contingent; intuitive comprehension, offered by the historian, subsumed conceptualization and raised it to a higher order of understanding. This mode of understanding could not be taught systematically; even though method is indispensable for every historian, it had to be accompanied by "genius [*Genie*]."

By implication, Gatterer's position affirmed a substantive difference between the concept of historical causation and the concept usually associated with a coherent theory of truth. To perceive how and why an event took place, the historian had to go behind the structure and reexperience what Gatterer called the "spirit of events [*Geist der Begeben-heiten*]"; this spirit alone made it possible to see how one event led to another.[50] He had to think himself back into the past (*sich hinzudenken*)[51] and make the past present. The historian had to create what Gatterer termed the "ideal present [*idealer Gegenwart*]" in the soul of the reader.[52] The historian "produces a whole that once existed, through his . . . narrative. He makes the dead live again and turns past into present. In a certain manner he brings himself and his readers close to a divine understanding through his imitation, which while admittedly weak is nevertheless true. This under-standing sees nothing as past or future, nothing as abstract; rather everything is present and individual. It is intuitive knowledge [*anschauende Erkennt-nis*]."[53] In this statement of intention, the intellectual interests of Gatterer's generation are clearly discernible. Like Mendelssohn, Gatterer equates *anschauende Erkenntis* with a type of "divine wisdom." And, like Semler, he seeks to bridge the estrangement between past and present. The generation's fascination with the interconnection between the whole [*Ganze*] and the individual and its concern with reliving the past attest to the Aufklärung's developing belief that the act of historical understanding contained a fundamental and unavoidable irrationality. To achieve this *anschauende Erkenntnis*, the historian had to search out the "inner connection" of the parts of a nation and to discover its inherent character or spirit.[54] He had to discover not only how people thought and acted, but why they had acted as they had. The final causal explanation for any historical event was not to be found in any general rule of human behavior, but rather in an appreciation of a unique conjunction of psychological, intellectual, individual, social, and temporal contiguities that was still related to the general connection of things in the world [*nexus rerum universalis*].[55]

Given his discrimination between abstract and individual understanding, Gatterer felt compelled to demonstrate that historical proof and abstract proof, while different in form, were equally valid. It was obvious, he argued, that the historian could not begin with certain basic a priori premises [*Grundbegriffe*] and then, by following the deductive method, generate the data that he had to explain.[56] Yet he still had to adduce connections and explain synthetic units of relation. How could this be done? Historical investigation began with the establishment of the event or happening to be colligated with its contingencies. This first step required the historian to show that the event had occurred or that people at some previous time had believed that the event had occurred. The next step was to bring everything into a system of events, which required the use of the philosophical spirit to see some events as causative, others as contingent. Finally, the historian had to think himself into the past and emphatically reexperience the spirit of events. When the final synthesis seemed to answer definite questions that had originally necessitated the inquiry and when the material was firmly established, then Gatterer could say that the relations were demonstrated.

Demonstrations of this sort had, Gatterer maintained, the same degree of validity as an abstract demonstration. The reason? Because both were valid and sufficient products of the philosophical spirit: "A system of events in a history and a system of deductions in an exact science have close similarity to each other. What for the latter are the basic postulates and premises are for the former causes and occasions. The development of a concept from its premise and the development of an event from its causes and inciting events are both actions of the philosophical spirit. And in both instances . . . visible proof is attained only when they are complete and persuasive."[57]

5

The reservations Gatterer and Chladenius expressed about the applicability of traditional causal analysis to history illustrate a basic predicament in the Aufklärung's historical thought. Fascinated by the problem of man's irrationality, the Aufklärers increasingly sought to chart the irrational stimulus behind the act of cognition. The result of such inquiries led to a redefinition of the concept of reason itself. No longer was reason considered the final, irreducible substratum upon which a science of man could be constructed. Instead, it was seen as a derivative of some elemental psychic or instinctive substructure conditioned by the temporal objectifications of life. The altered concept of reason implied that the products of abstract reason no longer provided timeless universal norms for judging human action. Nevertheless, the Aufklärers had no desire to surrender the idea of historical regularity, or what they called *Gesetzmäßigkeit* or *Regelmäßigkeit*; to do so would have meant that the critical spirit was incapable of illuminating the processes of history, an admission that would have signified for them a return to dogmatic thinking and a negation of the goals of the Enlightenment.

To resolve the predicament of asserting the existence of historical regularities while doubting the competence of reason, the Aufklärers employed the following tactics: they admitted that there were causal factors in history; however, these factors were to be dealt with in conjunction and with an awareness of the elements of time and growth; finally, the causal explanation was considered as a perspective of truth, not as a closed and universally valid explanation. The Aufklärers justified the validity of a historical explanation by its ability to impart experiential or intuitive understanding, thus historicizing the concept of understanding to accord with their image of the future. There is no closed form of understanding; rather, understanding entails a continual expansion and incorporation of past and present reality with a view to overcoming them in the near or distant future. Active historical understanding, therefore, is prerequisite to the attainment of freedom, since it alone enables us to transcend the limitations of the moment.

Jacob Wegelin (1721-1791), the Swiss historian and philosopher of history, effectively employed all these themes. He offers an example of the extent to which the Aufklärers had rejected the idea of mechanical causation while attempting to formulate a system of causation applicable to historical explanation.[58] Wegelin, like his fellow countrymen Iselin, von Haller, Sulzer, von Müller, and Bodmer, had a broad and cosmopolitan education. Following the example of many well-educated Swiss, he left Switzerland after a period of intellectual apprenticeship to seek his fortune in Germany.[59] During Wegelin's stay in Switzerland as student, *Hofmeister* ("private tutor"), pastor in the French Church in Saint Gall, and professor, he was able to establish contacts with a wide range of important eighteenth-century thinkers, including Rousseau, Albrecht von Haller, Iselin, Johann Jacob Breitinger, and especially Bodmer, with whom Wegelin forged a close and lasting friendship. It was through Bodmer's good offices that Wegelin found the opportunity to leave Switzerland. Realizing that Wegelin was not duly appreciated in Saint Gall, Bodmer introduced him to Sulzer, who was so impressed by Wegelin that he convinced Frederick the Great to offer Wegelin an appointment as professor of history in Frederick's newly established *Ritterakademie*.[60] Accepting immediately, Wegelin in 1765 moved to Berlin, where he shared a house with Sulzer and where he remained for the rest of his life. Within a year Wegelin became a member of the Berlin Academy and later its archivist.

In his writings on the philosophy of history, Wegelin accurately reflects the increasingly critical posture assumed by the Aufklärers toward abstraction, the use of general law, and the analytical methods of natural law.[61] In a manner strikingly similar to that of Chladenius and Gatterer, Wegelin attempted to establish the limits and the competence of historical understanding by using the Wolffian distinction between cognitive and historical knowledge while reversing the conclusions earlier associated with this distinction.[62] History's ability to open up new worlds of experience and understanding more than compensated for the lack of logical clarity associated with deductive philosophy. Wegelin justified this contention in two ways: he first denied the possibility of applying deductive analysis to history; then he affirmed the independence and the validity of historical understanding.

Like Chladenius and Gatterer, Wegelin advanced the proposition that since the moral world differed in quality from the natural world, the respective methods of investigation and understanding in the two worlds must also differ. To support this proposition he borrowed heavily from aesthetic and psychological theory and from Leibnizian philosophy, which had received a new impetus from the publication of the *Nouveaux essais* in 1765. According to Wegelin, the natural scientist differed from the historian in that he was concerned primarily with immutable and transcendent principles governing the world of matter and motion. The historian, on the other hand, was primarily concerned with the mutable and semifree products of the human spirit, with values, morals, opinions, ideas, and social conventions, all of which found expression in uniquely individual forms of social organization.[63]

Using Leibniz's idea of infinite and universal connection, Wegelin maintained that it was impossible to isolate a set of universal causal principles that govern the moral world. The basic cause of an event remained forever concealed from the gaze of the historian, hidden within and carried by the complex conjunction of related events. Typical of the philosophy of the Aufklärung, Wegelin emphasized the futility of searching for final causes: "One merely has to think of the claims of materialism and idealism and the many hypotheses drawn from them to be convinced that one can never uncover the essence of bodies. The same holds true in the search for the first and imperceptible parts of the conjunctions in the moral and the political world. Why have so many systems of natural laws and peoples arisen if simple and correct ideas about the origins of social life and nations exist?"[64] Like Schlözer, Wegelin eliminated the question of social origins from the competence of historical investigation. The historian was best advised to ignore the attempt to uncover the prime cause of things since such an endeavor would lead only to the creation of an insubstantial historical hypothesis.[65] Instead, he should show how one mode of social organization changed into another.

So far, Wegelin's discussion of the distinction between the causal concepts of history and the natural sciences does not greatly differ from those of Chladenius and Gatterer. But Wegelin was not content to demonstrate the inapplicability of the deductive methods of causal analysis; he also attempted to construct a system of causation applicable to history which was founded upon Leibnizian philosophy and contemporary psychology. Working from these two positions, Wegelin advanced a hybrid form of an *Ideenlehre* to explain historical change.

Wegelin made ideas, opinions, and values the major objects of historical investigation, considering them primary causal factors and also objective reflections of basic social relations. In effect, he tried to stake out a middle position between a pure sociology of knowledge and an idealistic *Ideenlehre*. He offers a theory of consciousness that recognizes the causal moment of the *Ideenwirkung* ("effect of ideas") without according ideas a fully independent metaphysical existence. Ideas, therefore, are both sub- and superstructure, at times mere reflectors of social relations, at other times producers of social change. Despite the fact that some scholars referred to Wegelin as the Prussian Montesquieu, his stance reflects the Aufklärers' attempt to join Montesquieu to Hume, to merge environmental and psychological causation in order to obtain a dynamic theory of social change.[66]

Basic to Wegelin's appreciation of change was the Aufklärung's definition of man as an active creature (Gatterer called him a *Nimmersatt*) who was never content to remain locked within the bounds of a single social or value system.[67] Like Iselin, Wegelin located this impetus to change in man's psyche, in the action of what he called the *Einbildungskraft,* which "knew no limits" in its ability to transform given conditions into new, and sometimes more powerful, social and moral images. The *Einbildungskraft* is the motor of spiritual activity. Impelled by this continual restlessness (Iselin's "uneasiness"), man acted in the world, creating certain forms of social organization and value systems; both of these influenced later thought and action and served as foils against which thought and action were directed. Every historical moment, therefore, contained a complex set of competing elements, which Wegelin called at times *continuité de durée* and *continuité d'accession* and at other times the dead and living forces of a society (*die toten und die lebendigen Kräfte der Gesellschaften*). Today they would simply be called the forces of continuity and change.

For Wegelin, the objective expression of the conjunction of these forces at any moment in time was the shared values and ideas of an age and a people. Taken as a whole, these values and ideas represented the given *Volkscharakter* of a people at a certain stage of historical development: "The ruling system of public opinions, values, customs, and usages affects the soul, just as good or bad air affects the lungs."[68] This climate of opinion enveloped all social classes and was discernible in the actions of a people. But the *Volkscharakter* was not, in Wegelin's view, an eternal constant, or a racial given, or a pure derivative of such environmental factors as geography and climate. Though containing elements of each, it was also a product of historical development: "It is the steplike cultivation and development of a people's original predispositions and contains at once the sum of all these moments."[69] Given this definition, it was imperative for the historian first to acquire an *anschauende Erkenntnis* of a nation's *Volkscharakter* before attempting to discuss the causes of a historical event: "One must be able to obtain a correct and extensive idea of the ruling opinions of an era and a society because they determine, to a greater or lesser extent, specific actions."[70] Borrowing a metaphor from contemporary aesthetics, Wegelin termed this activity *Colorit* and defined it as the "art of correctly and effectively delineating the character of a whole nation and the characteristic features of the most important representatives of a people."[71]

To apprehend a people's character meant, for Wegelin, to grasp the spiritual life of the people as expressed in its language, opinions, and ideas. While admitting the importance of the *Volkscharakter,* Wegelin did not make it the sole or primary causal determinant in history. Wegelin was not a holist. In fact, holism as a theory of history ran counter to the Aufklärung's attitude toward the triad past-present-future. On the most basic level of experience, the idea of a nation so uniform in character that high and low, *Bürger* and peasant, scholar and shoemaker, would think and act alike seemed frightening, strange, and forbidding. It evoked in these advocates of the *Ständestaat* the image of a despotic *Massenstaat* ("rule of the masses") where an original thinker would be branded a heretic or executed. Believing in the excellence of the "German freedoms," which they thought ensured unity in diversity, the Aufklärers viewed homogeneity as evidence of degeneration, reminiscent of the French attempts to form a strong unitary state at the expense of the Huguenots.

On a more theoretical level, holism was unacceptable because it contradicted the Aufklärers' image of the future. As a method of analysis, holism makes the organic conjunction (the ineffable individuality that cannot be understood by a dissection of its parts) the simplest and most basic object of investigation; the parts are defined and made comprehensible by reference to the whole. Hence, whatever change the unit undergoes is explained by citing inherent, supraindividual, and often inevitable tendencies that relentlessly drive the organic unit through time. In effect, a holist theory of history negates or minimizes the element of free and conscious human action. The most an individual can do is to recognize the course of history and harmonize his actions accordingly; freedom consists only in recognizing directional change, not in being able to influence the direction of that change. But it is precisely the element of active human creation and freedom that lay at the core of the Aufklärung's vision of change. Although the Aufklärers readily admitted the limitations of individual action and the frailty of human reason, they still conceived of positive historical change as an act of human will against or in harmony with a given set of social and intellectual conditions. For them, regression or disintegration occurred when man failed to act, when with sheeplike acquiescence he allowed himself to be carried along by the forces already present in a society, that is, to be totally ruled by the national character. The Aufklärers saw the faint glimmer of enlightenment that they believed characterized their age as a hard-won product, not as an inevitable result of historical development.[72] More pessimistic than some of their French contemporaries, they were continually worried lest they fall back into the abyss of barbarism that was as historically close to them as the Thirty Years War. The Aufklärers modeled their idea of change on the process of education, positing a slow and tedious process of slight, and sometimes imperceptible, step-by-step improvement. Society did not change according to some set of all-encompassing laws, but rather from within, through conscious attempts at social improvement, called by Wegelin and his coevals *Policierung*.[73] To return to Wegelin's metaphor of *Colorit*, the *Volkscharakter* colored actions, it did not give them form. In order to perceive the form of historical change, the historian had to look into the complex reaction of the elements composing society and discern the competitive elements that drove society ever so slowly forward or backward.

Wegelin's dissection of these forces reveals a pluridimensional world of contingent yet differentiated value systems. In addition to the general *Volkscharakter*, he asserted, each class, each *Stand*, each profession, even each individual, has its own character, *Vernunftlehre* ("philosophy"), morality, and politics, all unquestionably serving as guides to action.[74] Each of these value systems forms an analogue to the national character; they contain dynamic forces and forces of stability, with the difference that some social groupings are more prone to follow traditional modes of thought while others are more likely to break with tradition. Change arises from the conflict between these sets of "dead and live forces." It sometimes takes the form of conflict between social groupings and interests. Hence, Wegelin proposes a theory of both social and ideational conflict. The conflict takes place on all levels and in complex interaction, but in each situation it can be diagramed by using the Newtonian idea of the tension between centrifugal and centripetal forces.

The centripetal forces are those of tradition and inherited custom; their carriers are those unwilling or unable to think and act beyond socially accepted opinions and values. Although Wegelin could not use the word "conservatism" — it had yet to be coined — he was describing the conservative posture. The conservative, or, as Wegelin called him, the "society man [der gesellschaftliche Mensch]," raised the given norms of society or his class to an absolute; the habitual was the prime determinant of action. Though capable of reflection, the "society man" never makes the effort to reflect on the nature and the meaning of his values; instead, he orders all his actions to conform to his inherited norms.[75] Wegelin's discussion of "society man" takes the form of a social typology. Whole groups, such as the Roman Senate or the nobility at the time of the Crusades, respond in the same manner to specific situations because they are ruled by their own Vernunft-lehre. The vast majority of men are, therefore, society men. Although society men are found in every class, the classes most prone to such an attitude are the uneducated. Incapable of perceiving distinctions, they are unable to conceive of transcendental change. They are true "outer-directed" men.[76] Wegelin located the appeal of the conservative mentality in the psychological antipode of the element of striving. If man is a Nimmersatt, he is also an Ordnungsmensch. Security, ease, and habit appeal to those who want to expend the least amount of psychic energy in coping with the problems of life. Tradition forms the vehicle for these feelings. It is the soul of the dead forces; it offers a place of refuge from the storms of change and doubt. Since Wegelin believed all forces are relative to their historical situation, he did not condemn the dead forces outright. Wegelin's Newtonian analogy makes it obvious that the centripetal forces are necessary to harmonic development, for they offer the continuity that makes peaceful change possible. It is the degree to which they predominate and the relation they have to the living forces which are important.

The living forces, or centrifugal forces, are the dynamic elements in society, the ones released by man's instinct to change. If the dead forces are founded upon unclear perception and questionless conformity, the live forces draw their power from the free actions of criticism and reconstruction. Through reflection and transcendental thinking, man lifts himself from an outer-directedness to a position of ethical self-reliance. Though no single man can ever reach this goal, Wegelin asserted the possibility of getting increasingly closer to it. True to the ideals of the Enlightenment, he cited the special realms of the living forces as art, commerce, manufactures, and "sound philosophy." In this listing, however, he differentiated between expansive forces that have their own lawlike nature and those that are products of free action. The most prominent example of the former is commerce. Expansion and activity are the governing principles of commercial enterprise, bringing in their wake change and conflict and, through conflict, possible improvement.[77] In addition to commerce, Wegelin cited ideas that had a metaphysical character; they struck a basic chord of human nature. As an example of such an idea, Wegelin listed the concept of universal justice (*allgemeine Billigkeit*), whose origins in Europe can be traced to the medieval reception of Roman law; its acceptance was a "revolution in the idea of civil justice."[78] Once formulated, the very force of such ideas made them impervious to destruction, even though their principles might momentarily be denied. They remained a constant source of action in the historical life of the community that was aware of them.

In addition to these lawlike causal elements which "already lie in the soul and need only to be awakened," Wegelin introduced the indeterminate factor of "original genius." In so doing, he mirrored the general development of eighteenth-century aesthetic and psychological theory. The original genius differed from society man in that he was able to conceive of the world in a manner that would frighten those governed by tradition, opinion, and custom.[79] The idea of the original genius provided the necessary link between the dead and live forces in Wegelin's theory of historical causation. Without it, he would have been hard put to explain slow, imperceptible change, using his chosen Newtonian concepts of centripetal and centrifugal forces. In a sense, the Newtonian theory was a theory of statics: it described the harmonic stability of the whole using the dynamic interaction of the parts. When applied to history it could adequately serve only two explanatory functions: it could explain the given national character and it could explain the character's total dissolution. But it was precisely the middle ground between static harmony and explosive disintegration which fascinated Wegelin and his reform-minded contemporaries. They needed an element to account for progressive or regressive step-by-step change. Wegelin located this element in the indeterminable actions of the original genius.

According to Wegelin, the original genius was one who forged a new synthesis between dead and living forces. Through an original rethinking and reexperiencing of the shared values of his society, he introduced standards of value and action that announced the dawn of a growing understanding of life.[80] He joined the vision of the artist to the powers of the man of the world, providing thereby both the summation of his epoch and the point of a new departure. He is both inventor and actor, man of his time and man of the future.[81] Limited by the mentality of his own time and place, the great man is nevertheless still able to force the life of his nation into a new orbit. Here, in this description, the efforts of eighteenth-century aesthetics, psychology, and Neology meet. Wegelin ascribes the effect of the original genius on his age to the genius's ability to express his newly discovered ideals in immediate, experiential terms; that is, the genius offers his age an *anschauende Erkenntnis* of a new and different world.

Wegelin excluded speculative philosophers from the category of original genius. Just as Schmauß attacked Wolff for being imprisoned in an ivory tower of his own making, Wegelin criticized scholastic philosophers because they had lost touch with the demands of their own time.[82] In this critique, Wegelin reaffirmed the Aufklärers' ideal of pragmatic knowledge: an idea, a value, is pragmatic only if it stirs something in the soul, if it leads to action, if it uses a given set of experiences to transform those very experiences. The great man is the artist who imaginatively transforms the given rules to create a new form of artistic experience. He is Bodmer's Dante or Milton, Lessing's Shakespeare, Lichtenberg's Hogarth, Mengs's Raphael, and Christian Gottlob Heyne's Homer. The original genius was the religious, or ethical, thinker who transcended the *Lokalvernunft* ("understanding indigenous to an area") of his time to forge a higher vision of the moral and ethical world. He was the imposing figure of Moses the lawgiver as described by Michaelis and seconded by Wegelin or of Jesus as envisioned by Semler and Lessing.[83] He was also the great political figure: Charlemagne, Emperor Frederick II, and for many in the eighteenth century, especially for members of the Berlin Academy, Frederick the Great.

Though emphasizing the indeterminate element of original genius, Wegelin did not let genius stand outside its time. If great men "appear to have more insight, they still cannot go further than their own horizon [*Gesichtskreis*] or beyond the intellectual material at hand."[84] The genius's horizon is also limited by specific feelings of duty and *ständesmäßige* relations.[85] For this reason, it is impossible to judge either the actions of a genius or the actions of a society according to some universal norm of right and wrong.[86] Superficial moral judgments founded on today's assumptions have no place in history.[87] Wegelin also argued that effective genius cannot appear haphazardly at any moment in historical development. The effect of genius is conditioned by the social situation itself. Only when conflicting systems of ideas become so hardened that a situation of crisis evolves can genius have an effect. If the genius is born in the wrong time or place, even the most active individual will be engulfed by his surroundings.[88] An idea or a value system can be changed only when a certain self-confidence in that system is shaken, when the psychological readiness for change is imminent. Here Wegelin verges on the brink of a theory of social determinism, but he never accepts that theory; the genius can be effective only at certain critical times, but crises in themselves do not ensure the appearance of an original genius.

Wegelin's attempt to evolve a theory of historical causation was typical of the predicament faced by the Aufklärers. On the one hand, he employed the relativistic implications of the Aufklärung's analysis of cognition to deny the use of general historical laws; on the other, he refused to surrender all sets of normative assumptions. He thus proposed a set of descriptive categories for causal development which would enable the historian to grasp the interconnection of events without falling victim to the directionless inquiries of the polyhistorians. In theory, Wegelin's evaluation of historical causation offered a sophisticated appreciation of the elements influencing change, including a recognition of the complex interaction of long-term lawlike elements, mediate and temporal conjunctions, and indeterminate "original" action. The major question that still has to be posed is how and in what manner did the Aufklärers employ their causal principles in historical writing.

VI

Categories of Causal Explanation I: Climate, Geography, and Political, Social, and Economic Structure

1

The most popular model of historical explanation at the beginning of the eighteenth century located the agent of historical change in Divine Providence. Such was the approach of Bossuet, whose magisterial work *Discours sur l'histoire universelle* stood as a continual challenge to the philosophes and the Aufklärers. This approach was also favored by mediocre, but influential, German historians of the turn of the century, such as Johann Hübner.[1] But the Aufklärers were often wary of Divine Providence as an explanatory device because it encouraged historians to accept fanciful stories that readily confirmed God's active role in history. This attitude is more than obvious in Hübner's works. In the seventh volume of his *Kurtze Fragen aus der politischen Historie* (on the history of Mainz, Trier, and Cologne), he related the famous legend of the Mouse Tower (*Mäuseturm*): Hatto, archbishop of Mainz, once had a number of beggars burned. As they screamed with pain, Hatto exclaimed: "Listen! Listen to my mice squeal!" From that moment on Hatto was pursued by swarms of mice. He finally sought refuge in a tower on an island in the middle of the Rhine, but even there he was denied safety; the mice swam across the river, climbed the tower, and ate the bishop alive. The mice then scoured the countryside, destroying all public inscriptions of the bishop's name. God's tribunal had clearly condemned the bishop. To support the authenticity of this story, Hübner employed an equally fanciful and tortuous defense. He argued that (1) a tower called the Mouse Tower does exist; (2) the story of Hatto and the mice has been recounted from time immemorial; (3) a similar event – mice eating a ruler alive – occurred in Poland (claimed Hübner) in 823, and what is possible in Poland is possible on the Rhine; (4) this story has as much validity as the biblical account of the Egyptian frogs; and (5) Hatto himself continually swore: "If I don't tell the truth, let me be eaten by mice."[2]

It is unnecessary to comment on the flaws in Hübner's logic and in his choice of historically important events; the Aufklärers were painfully aware of these faults and traced many to the habit of using Divine Providence as a causal explanatory principle. The time had come, they felt, to abandon what Schlözer described as Hübner's and Bossuet's "vacuous babble of the pulpit [*fades Kanzelgeschwätz*]."[3] More disturbing to the Aufklärers were the inherent implications of Divine Providence: to invoke Divine Providence meant that the historian abandoned the attempt to explain historical change in human terms; it also meant the historian claimed the power to perceive what God's intentions had been. The use of Divine Providence offered an explanatory model that was both too vague and too presumptuous; it contradicted the whole thrust of the Aufklärers' emerging religious and epistemological assumptions. Johann David Michaelis adequately summed up the Aufklärers' displeasure with Divine Providence as an explanatory device:

> Now this kind of reasoning, in which we argue from what, according to our opinion, Divine Providence ought to have performed or neglected, has never afforded me the smallest conviction, when the question simply related to what has or has not happened, even in cases, where I have fancied, that I could clearly perceive, why one mode of proceeding would have been more beneficial than another. Our views are too confined, and we know too little of the whole chain of causes and effects, to determine what the wisdom of the Deity should ordain: we must believe, that whatever is ordained is for the best, even though to our imperfect views it should appear otherwise. The history of mankind can furnish us with numerous examples, which we might suppose to be incompatible with the wisdom and justice of the Deity: we know that powerful combinations are frequently formed to violate and suppress the truth, and that even those warriors, whose object is tyranny and rapine, are not seldom rewarded by splended victories. We do not call in question the truth of such combinations and victories, because we cannot reconcile them with divine wisdom: but satisfied of the reality of the facts, we still confide in the Deity, and trust that the final event will not be unworthy of the Great Creator of all things.[4]

Alternative models of explanation did deal with historical development in human terms, but they also had serious defects. One model, derived from classical and humanist historians, can be called, for want of a better term, the "great man theory" of history. Towns and nations are founded by a single wise lawgiver, such as Lycurgus or Solon; language and writing are invented by a single genius; major turns in history are single-handedly effected by great warriors or monarchs. All events are pictured in terms of individual combat and intention. As employed by historians of the late seventeenth and early eighteenth centuries, this approach was a prime example of what Eduard Fueter has called the catastrophe theory. The great man theory allowed only a minimal amount of connection between events, thereby leading its practitioners onto very tenuous grounds. When individual intention became the central explanatory tool in the writing of history, historians fell into the trap of reasoning from historical results back to conscious, individual design. In other words, there existed the tendency to establish an identity between cause and effect, which readily lent itself to propaganda uses. The image of the scheming priest manipulating the ignorant canaille for his own devious purposes was the most obvious kind of short circuit in historical reasoning to arise from the great man theory. It was not only used by philosophes eager to eradicate *l'infame,* but had been so well cultivated during the seventeenth century that eighteenth-century writers could offer very little new except to distribute the attack equitably among all religious establishments.

The Aufklärers condemned this mode of reasoning on the grounds that it was too rational (it drew too tight a line between cause and effect), too misleading (it overestimated the powers of man's control of events and man's own self), and too inimical to religion. These loyal Protestants even decried its method of evaluating the medieval Roman Catholic popes, an unheard of complaint for seventeenth-century thinkers. According to the Protestant explanation, the popes initiated the Crusades because they desired to increase their power and wealth. Johann Lorenz von Mosheim devoted a long footnote in his *Ecclesiastical History* to attacking this explanation. Maintaining that this hypothesis was "devoid of any solid foundation," Mosheim continued:

> Certain it is, that the Roman pontiffs could never have either foreseen, or imagined, that so many European princes, and such prodigious multitudes of people, would take arms against the infidels and march into Palestine; nor could they be assured beforehand, that this expedition would tend to the advancement of their opulence and authority. For all the accessions of influence and wealth, which the Roman pontiffs, and the clergy in general derived from these holy wars, were of a much later date, than their first origin, and were acquired by degrees, rather by lucky hits, than by deep laid schemes; and this alone is sufficient to show that the bishops of Rome, in forming their plan, and exhorting the prosecution of these wars, had no thoughts of extending thereby the limits of their authority. We may add to this consideration, another of no less weight in the matter before us, and that is, the general opinion which prevailed at this time, both among the clergy and the people, that the conquest of *Palestine* would be finished in a short time, in a single campaigne; that the Divine Providence would interpose, in a miraculous manner, to accomplish the ruin of infidels; and that after the taking of Jerusalem, the greatest part of the European princes would return home with their troops, which last circumstance was by no means favorable to the views which the pontiffs are supposed to have formed of increasing their opulence and extending their dominion.[5]

An accompanying explanation held that the kings and princes of Europe supported the Crusades because they wished to increase their power by eliminating bothersome vassals. Mosheim rejected this view as equally groundless, even though it was "adopted by several eminent writers such as Vertot, Boulainvilliers, and others, who pretend to a superior and uncommon insight into the policy of these remote ages. The reasons, however, which these great men employed to support their opinion, may be comprehended in this simple argument, viz. 'Many kings, especially among the Franks, became more opulent and powerful by the number of vassals, who lost their lives and fortunes in this holy war; therefore, these princes not only permitted, but warmly countenanced the prosecution of this war from selfish and ambitious principles.' The weakness of this conclusion must strike everyone at first sight." Mosheim denied the whole idea of ascribing historical events to the conscious actions of single individuals: "We are wonderfully prone to attribute both to the Roman pontiffs, and the princes of this barbarous age, much more sagacity and cunning than they really possessed; and we deduce from the events, the principles and views of the actors, which is a defective and uncertain manner of reasoning."[6]

A third model of historical explanation elevates chance over design. Great events result from trivial and minute causes. In a sense, this accident theory is the negative counterpart to the great man theory. In the latter, man is the master of his fate, the conscious creator of history. In the former, man is the plaything of fickle and unpredictable forces; he is impotent to affect history in any conscious manner. Probably the most famous examples of this form of explanation are Pascal's bon mot about the length of Cleopatra's nose and Voltaire's puckish *Dialogue entre un Brachmane et un Jésuite,* where he traces the cause of Henry IV's assassination to the Brahman's stepping out of bed with his right foot instead of his left. An example much closer to us in time is the supposed effect of Richard Nixon's five o'clock shadow on the outcome of the 1960 American presidential election. Although the Aufklärers sometimes fell victim to using this form of explanation, they generally rejected it for four reasons. First, it denied the possibility of creating a science of history based on any norm for the assessment of causal connection. It denied that one type of event was more worthy of note and investigation than another, a denial that promised to make historical study more chaotic than ever. Second, the accident theory was "catastrophic" in that historical change occurred suddenly and incomprehensibly without any internal development. The Aufklärers' attraction to Montesquieu's work and their Leibnizian background made them reject this supposition. Third, the idea that man cannot influence history in any purposive manner – even though his influence be partial – ran counter to their image of the future. Fourth, the explanation conflicted with the Aufklärers' religious sensibilities. To elevate chance over design in historical analysis seemed to confirm by analogy the naturalist argument that the world was created through a chance collision of atoms. Though the Aufklärers refused to use Divine Providence as an explanatory tool, they still believed in the existence of an overall plan. The accident theory of historical explanation ultimately denied such a belief.

With the rejection of existing models of historical explanation, the Aufklärers were forced to contrive a new set of principles to explain historical change. They therefore sought to establish the categories of historical life worthy of investigation and to evolve a method whereby the factors considered important could be brought into conjunction. In attempting to combine analysis and synthesis they were guided by the idea that "of all events in organic nature, one event could be not only the cause of another but also its effect."[7] The job itself was monumental. If we return for just a moment to Hübner's work, the difficulties the Aufklärers faced in reforming the general understanding of history becomes evident. Granted, Hübner is eminently forgettable; he was a man of mediocre talents with an even more mediocre mind. Still, his writings were immensely popular at the time and they reflected certain assumptions (or a lack of assumptions) about history that were typical of a large section of the German reading public at the beginning of the eighteenth century. The most obvious difficulty was the lack of standards for choosing and evaluating historical events.

Hübner defined history as the science of noteworthy things (*merkwürdige Dinge*) that have occurred since the creation of the world. The dictum that the historian investigate things worthy of note could and should imply the operation of some sort of selective principle. Not so with Hübner, however; he took his principle to heart and found that all things were noteworthy. The only balm Hübner offered the historian who had to resolve the problem of selection was a six-part system of classification. Each of the six categories of "things" had its own type of history: (1) *Historia Politica* ("things pertaining to worldly regimes"); (2) *Historia Ecclesiastica* ("things pertaining to God's church"); (3) *Historia Philosophica* ("things of scholarship"); (4) *Historia Physica* or *Naturalis* ("things of nature"); (5) *Historia Technica* or *Artificalis* ("things pertaining to artists, artisans, and craftsmen"); (6) *Historia Mixta* or *Miscellanea* ("things pertaining to common life").[8] Hübner gave the reader an example from each category to make his divisions clear. The only clarity the examples offer the modern reader is a realization of the distance separating Hübner's assumptions from our own. At best, the examples appear as simple stories with an obvious moral; at worst, they are irrelevant anecdotes. The most incredible example illustrates category 5, *Historia Technica* or *Artificalis*. Hübner relates that a magician at the court of Emperor Wenceslas was competing with an imported Bavarian jester. The magician won by "eating the jester whole, as though he had been a piece of bratwurst." Because this outcome infuriated the Bavarian king, Emperor Wenceslas ordered the magician to bring the jester back unharmed. The magician obeyed the command by ordering a large pail of water, squatting over it, and expelling the jester *per posteriora*, unharmed, in one piece. Hübner concluded that if one still had difficulty in classifying "noteworthy things" it was because one had not mastered the system of each class ("daß man das eigentliche Systema von einer jedweden Classe noch nicht im Kopf hat").[9] Needless to say, the Aufklärers proved incapable of mastering, or unwilling to master, the secrets of Hübner's system.

Instead, they directed their efforts toward answering the following question: What is a historical fact, that is, what elements in the infinite profusion of occurrences make the past intelligible? This question was necessary if the Aufklärers hoped to evolve a method of synthetic historical explanation, for it touched at the heart of the problem of choice and interpretation. The Aufklärers sought to discover the criteria that allowed one to decide what belonged in a well-planned and well-executed history and what was superfluous and irrevelant to historical explanation. Socially significant historical categories, once established, served as regulative forces to condition the Aufklärers' causal explanations. In approaching the problem of historical explanation in this manner, the Aufklärers thought they could invest the singular occurrence with new meaning by relating it to larger configurations of social being and development. This objective required them to jettison much of what had belonged to historical analysis – a task easier said then done – and to incorporate hitherto unexplored dimensions of historical being into their historical narrative. They believed their approach would make history both richer (filled with a host of important and related events) and leaner (less cluttered with irrelevant material). The anecdotal approach so common to seventeenth-century historiography was to be replaced by a history of peoples, customs, cultures, and institutions.[10]

One strategy that helped the Aufklärers was their increasing tendency to define the state as a moral body, analogous in some respects to the individual. This was certainly not a novel idea. It had been used by a score of medieval political theorists, the foremost being John of Salisbury. In more modern times both Hooker and Pascal had employed the analogy to attack mechanical forms of thought. Its resurrection by a host of eighteenth-century thinkers again testifies to their ability to use older views of social life to combat the naturalistic doctrines of seventeenth- and early eighteenth-century political theory. The ancient analogy of the moral body proved especially useful because it offered the Aufklärers a conceptual framework for dealing with interacting historical forces. As early as 1752 Johann Martin Chladenius used the analogy to explain societal change. According to Chladenius, a moral body such as the state consisted of a unity of wills possessing a definite and unique character. Like an individual, the moral body had an outward form or constitution and an inward spirit or soul which mutually influenced each other.[11] Historical explanation had to account for the effects of the moral body's form and spirit and the dynamics of this interaction. A mere recounting of individual occurrences or a singular concentration upon individual intention failed to satisfy the requirements of historical explanation. Chladenius argued that individual actions and circumstances were worthy of note only if they exerted a discernible effect upon the moral body's constitution or spirit.[12] Supraindividual considerations of time, growth, and conjunction would have to be included within the competence of historical explanation. True, in Chladenius's formulation there lurked the danger of drawing too radical a differentiation between history and biography, of sacrificing questions of individual character and existence. If taken to its logical conclusion, Chladenius's definition of society as a moral body — a definition repeated by numerous Aufklärers — could lead to a holistic idea of history.[13] The Aufklärers, however, did not pursue the analogy to its logical conclusion. As noted above, holism stood in stark contrast to their shared hopes, experiences, and ideals. Rather, the Aufklärers used the analogy to counteract the extreme nominalism of seventeenth-century historical explanation. Nowhere did the Aufklärers abandon their belief that individuals could purposively affect history through an act of will, albeit in a circumscribed manner. What the Aufklärers did seek to understand were the supraindividual elements of societal and spiritual conditioning which limited and redirected individual action. The image of the state as a moral person allowed the Aufklärers to differentiate two interacting categories of historical influence — the external and the internal or spiritual.[14] External influence dealt primarily with the effect of structure and environment on historical life; the internal, with values, custom, "spirit," time, and ideas. In simplified terms the two categories dealt with form and freedom, determinateness and individuality. Without drawing too sharp a distinction between elements in continual interaction, I believe it easiest to discuss each category in a separate chapter.

2

The Aufklärers' evaluation of the external features of historical life — their concern with what may be called the objective categories of social, political, economic, and environmental structure — usually followed a definite pattern. Starting from the most general influence, that of the physical environment, the Aufklärers proceeded to the more limited causal moments until they arrived at the unique structure that was a conjunction of all the constituent forces. In this procedure of analysis, they derived much from the work of French and English philosophes.

The Aufklärers found Montesquieu the most congenial philosophe of the first half of the century. His moderate liberalism, his devotion to the mixed constitution, his tendency to support the *Ständestaat,* his denial of the catastrophe theory, and his advocacy of the Germanic origins of the French state struck an immediate chord of approval. Even the obvious deficiences of his great work, *The Spirit of the Laws,* failed to diminish his influence. Looking at it from the worst possible angle, *The Spirit of the Laws* could be considered a gigantic hodgepodge filled with compelling insights that were unfortunately marred by credulous observations drawn from a congeries of books, histories, and travel reports. Even to his own contemporaries, Montesquieu's book appeared highly unsystematic and at times openly bewildering, a judgment that has not been dispelled despite the herculean efforts of later commentators to discern in it some inner systematic unity.[15] The unsystematic nature of *The Spirit of the Laws* had the virtue of allowing the Aufklärers to emphasize and criticize certain observations without having to accept or reject the work in toto. The book's lack of structure seemed to embody the principle of relativity (emphasizing at various times a host of causative factors without giving any one of them total overriding precedence) while still denouncing any and all catastrophic ideas of historical change. It was a work that could challenge and confirm, that provided food for thought and invited partial refutation. Perhaps more than any other work, it laid bare the difficulties and hopes of the Enlightenment's search for a comprehensive idea of society and societal change.

In *The Spirit of the Laws*, Montesquieu listed those causal factors he thought vital to social development: "Mankind are influenced by various causes: by the climate, by the religion, by the laws, by the maxims of governments, by precedents, morals and customs: whence is formed a general spirit of nations."[16] Clearly Montesquieu believed that social phenomena were explicable only in terms of the configurations of the space, time, and tradition in which they occurred. One of his objectives in *The Spirit of the Laws* was to evaluate political and moral phenomena from the vantage point of each of these categories. The treatise implemented a method described independently four years later by Chladenius: "The word 'side' is properly associated with a body, but it has long become traditional to speak of the sides of other things, especially of the 'sides' of a moral body. One can, for example, look at the institution of matrimony, the military establishment, and maritime affairs from this side and that . . . whereby one takes many individual parts arising from singular causes into consideration and examines them as a whole."[17] Nevertheless, this strategy ran the danger of transforming each topical exposition into a self-contained unit ruled by one causal principle. It has led to a misunderstanding of Montesquieu and of those who drew intellectual nourishment from him. Especially misunderstood is Montesquieu's discussion of the element of space (particularly climate) upon customs, laws, political organization, and spirit in books XIV through XVIII. Though but a small part of the total work, these chapters left an inordinate impression of Montesquieu's contemporaries and later commentators.[18] In fact, with the possible exception of Montesquieu's "discovery" of the principle of the separation of powers, these five chapters are probably the most famous of *The Spirit of the Laws*.

Montesquieu drew a direct relation between climate and human character (colder climates produce vigorous, bold, courageous, and frank people, whereas warmer climates induce sensuality, indolence, and servility) and established a correspondence among laws, customs, and climate. Montesquieu explained the Muslim ban on wine by reference to Arabia's climate, claiming that such a prohibition would be impossible in climates where colder weather induced the drinking of strong spirits.[19] He attributed the high suicide rate in England to a climate that continually put Englishmen in states of "distemper."[20] He elucidated marriage customs by relating them to climate, maintaining that polygamy was natural to warm climates (because girls ripened early and also lost their beauty early) while monogamy was natural to temperate climates. [21] Finally, he drew a correlation between political liberty and climatic environment, arguing that "the effeminacy of the people in hot climates has almost rendered them slaves; and that the bravery of those in cold climates has enabled them to maintain their liberties." [22]

Although Montesquieu did not originate the theory of climatic causation — classical thinkers had hinted at it and in modern times it can be traced at least to Jean Bodin and was frequently used by early eighteenth-century German theorists — the Aufklärers' propensity to employ it in their historical explanations stems primarily from Montesquieu's influence. [23] This reliance is obvious in the writings of Johann David Michaelis, who made it his goal to study Mosaic law "with the eyes of a Montesquieu." [24] The resulting work, *Mosaisches Recht* (1770-1775), was a masterpiece of its time. It opened new paths to understanding the Old Testament. Michaelis attempted to sketch the milieu of the Mosaic era by combining historical, legal, sociological, political, and linguistic researches. [25] His central thesis proclaimed the relativity of all laws to the circumstances in which they had been formulated. To Michaelis, as to Montesquieu, climate was one of the factors that helped to account for the endless variety of human legal institutions. Michaelis reiterated Montesquieu's explanation for the Muslim ban on wine (1:23), his assumption of the heightened sensuality of southern peoples (6:55), his belief that polygamy was more natural to southern climates because of early puberty and stronger passions (2:181-182), and his claim that northern nations were less prone to bloody acts of revenge stemming from jealousy (5:246-247). In countless other places Michaelis employed climate to explain eating habits, dress, work habits, and the incidence of certain diseases.

Michaelis was not alone in the implementation of Montesquieu's theme of climatic causation. Johann Lorenz von Mosheim also related liberty to colder climates, claiming that "the northern nations enjoyed, in their frozen dwellings, the blessings of sacred freedom, which their government, their religion, a robust and vigorous frame of body and spirit derived from the inclemency and severity of their climate, all united to preserve and maintain." [26] Isaak Iselin adopted the most extreme form of Montesquieu's climatic assumptions in his descriptions of early peoples: men of the north were strong in body, short on imagination, unbending in spirit, not easily contented; men of the south were indolent, weak, complacent, and devoted to sensual pleasure and outward peace. Slavery and fear were the fruits of the south; unruliness and bravery were the products of the north; temperate climates generated freedom and virtue. [27]

It would be a mistake, however, to overemphasize the importance the Aufklärers attached to climatic causation. In their historical explanations they seldom accorded it primary importance. In fact, they usually hedged and qualified more than Montesquieu himself had. For them, climatic causation was a possible factor in the shaping of past experience, but it was only one of many factors. Even when the Aufklärers spoke of the influence of the purely physical environment — in the general category of spatial causation — they did not assign climate the prime position. Equally important were questions of geography and topography: What is the nature of the land? How fertile is the soil? What natural resources are readily available? What bodies of water are nearby? They well knew that ancient Egypt, though influenced by its climate, was also a child of the Nile. They believed that the scarcity or plenitude of natural resources could either stimulate or retard action. As we have already seen, it was this last assumption that supported Schlözer's rough approximation of a theory of challenge and response. This idea too could be found in Montesquieu: "Countries are not cultivated in proportion to their fertility, but to their liberty; and if we make an imaginary division of the earth, we shall be astonished to see in most ages deserts in the most fruitful parts, and great nations in those where nature seems to refuse everything." And later he concluded: "The barrenness of the earth renders men industrious, sober, inured to hardship, courageous, and fit for war, they are obliged to produce by labor what the earth refuses to bestow spontaneously."[28]

For the Aufklärers, the category of spatial causation served as a general starting point, a very rough indication of what the physical barriers and inducements to historical development might have been. They turned to it most often when discussing early societies, for they believed that simpler forms of social organization were less capable of generating artificial bulwarks to counteract the forces of the physical environment. Nevertheless, all believed that the more complex a society — that is, the more artificial — the less effect climate and geography had in shaping national character. At this point the elements of time and tradition became predominant. We may wince at some of the generalizations the Aufklärers drew from spatial causation, generalizations that reveal both their ignorance of distant cultures and their unquestioned stereotypical prejudices, but we can still appreciate the impulse that underpinned the observations. As Schlözer expressed it, they sought to transform "pure dry geographic" data into "political geography," to show how the ecological environment might affect and constrict man's existence. [29]

3

The Aufklärers' discussion of causation next focused upon the temporal political, religious, economic, and social structure of a society and tried to discern the interrelation among these external structures. This program, however, was not at first completely perceived and was never totally implemented. As with everything else, the Aufklärung's conception of causal connection entailed a developing awareness, an idea in the making, not a finished and self-contained paradigm of explanation. Initially, the Aufklärers concentrated primarily upon political structure. They clung to a habit of thought propagated by political theorists of the seventeenth and early eighteenth centuries. During the 1740s and early 1750s, the Aufklärers still made the question of constitutional form paramount to the understanding of politics, and they investigated constitutional form according to the traditional classical definitions of monarchy, aristocracy, and democracy. Their primary interest in form is easy to understand. The training the Aufklärers had received as youths reflected the traditional juridical emphasis upon constitutional form as the key to political analysis. The methods evolved by the theorists of natural law, especially by Pufendorf, added even more weight to the concern with form in sovereignty and the stability of life. Moreover, this strategy of analysis had virtually defined the contours of the compelling problem of the nature of the German polity during the seventeenth and early eighteenth centuries. Pufendorf's little essay on the German Empire had cast a long and powerful shadow. Even Montesquieu's *Spirit of the Laws* helped, at first, to direct political discussion to the question of form; one of his major theses ascribed a single energizing principle to each major constitutional form. Indeed, the concern with form was universal to all disciplines immediately prior to the Aufklärung. Aesthetics and religion provide the most obvious examples. Early Wolffian aesthetics, especially as propounded by Gottsched, consciously strove to describe the correct classical form for poetic composition. And in religion, questions of ritual and dogma occupied a position of prime importance, despite the growing influence of Pietism. It is not surprising that the Aufklärers at first considered it self-evident that "the form of a government had a tremendous effect in forming a nation's character." [30]

Nevertheless, within a relatively short space of time, a noticeable change occurred. By the end of the 1750s the question of constitutional form had lost its primary position; it was replaced by a new and critical attitude toward traditional political analysis. At the same time the Aufklärers showed an increasing concern with economic and social structure. In effect, their political and historical thought no longer tended to equate form with content. This was as true of aesthetics and religion as it was of political theory. Just as the excellence of art could no longer be comprehended by form alone and the nature of religious understanding could no longer be defined in purely ritualistic or dogmatic terms, so the understanding of political life could no longer be encompassed by a discussion of constitutional form. Without denying the importance of form (in either aesthetics, Neology, or political analysis), the Aufklärers groped for a perception of the unique conjunction of spiritual, moral, and structural elements that animated a specific historical entity at a specific time; they came to believe that the true key to political understanding lay in grasping the nature of that unique conjunction. Arnold Heeren made the position clear at the end of the period. After remarking that the illusion created by speculative political theorists, who ascribed primary importance to constitutional form, had been dispelled, he asked: "What is every constitutional form [*Staatsform*], if nothing but an empty form? What is it, if it is not a track upon which a wagon travels (to use an analogy that is applicable though a bit demeaning for such a subject)? Naturally, it is not unimportant [*gleichgültig*] how this track is constructed, . . . but no matter how excellent its construction, does it follow that the wagon will remain in the track? Can the track alone force the wagon to remain in it? That depends upon the team of horses and the driver." According to Heeren, the real driving forces of the state were the morality and enlightenment of the people and the spirit and efficiency of the administration.[31] Since these forces could be discerned only through historical analysis, the Aufklärers slowly reached the conclusion that history took precedence over theoretical politics. They had come to the realization that a new approach to the science of politics was needed before they could fully comprehend the configurations of modern life. In effectively breaking with classical political science, the Aufklärers were following a general tendency of Enlightenment thought.

The Enlightenment's transformation of classical political thought has recently been described by Franco Venturi in a stimulating series of lectures.[32] Concentrating on the evolution of the modern republican ideal, Professor Venturi shows that the growing contradiction between the reality of life in eighteenth-century republics and the republican ideal led to a new definition of that ideal. By the middle of the eighteenth century the ancient European republics no longer offered a viable alternative model to absolute monarchy as they had done in the seventeenth century. That republics sought shelter in a frozen idealized past, that they either refused to answer the needs of reform or were incapable of answering them, ensured that "not only did the ancient republics occupy a position of marginal importance compared with the absolute states, but they were on the fringes of history itself."[33] Nevertheless, though the ancient republics appeared either moribund or fossilized to many eighteenth-century observers, the republican ideal itself was far from moribund. The ideal "was separated from the historical forms it had taken in the past, and became increasingly an ideal which could exist in a monarchy such as the English one at the beginning of the eighteenth century, just as it could spread on the continent. It became an incitement to liberty beyond the historical circumstances of the past on either side of the Channel. It was the seed of an enlightened utopia."[34]

Precisely the same kind of shift in patterns of thought was later effected by the Aufklärers. It entailed a rethinking of the meaning of the terms *republic, democracy, monarchy, aristocracy*, and *despotism*, a rethinking that produced the conclusion that the reality (or spirit) of political life could contradict the form of political organization. Thus, monarchies might be able to embody the republican ideal and republics might become despotic oligarchies. Paradoxically, this rethinking rejected history in order to enrich historical understanding. By freeing the republican ideal from existing republican forms, eighteenth-century thinkers emphatically declared their independence from the postulates of classical political thought. Sometimes thinkers of the Aufklärung got carried away and totally ignored the importance of political form. Thus, one of the "fathers of cameralism," Johann Heinrich Gottlob von Justi, used Pope's famous lines, "For forms of government let fools contest / Whate'er is best administered is best," as his guiding principle. But denial of the importance of form remained a minority view. On the whole, the revaluation emphasized the need to concentrate upon the specifics of the historical community and to consider the possibilities of development within the context of that community's character. The revaluation affirmed that the spirit animating a nation was, in effect, as important as its outward form.

Certainly the Aufklärers did not cease to discuss the effect of simple, or classical, constitutional forms upon historical development, but they altered the context of the discussion. Whereas Pufendorf, for example, had placed his trust in pure forms powerful enough to ensure order, the Aufklärers were concerned about the misuse of power and the stifling effects of a form impervious to the forces of progressive change. The specter of France under Louis XIV and the claims of Enlightened Absolutism cast doubt on the flexibility of Europe's remaining republics and on the wisdom of concentrating power in the hands of one man or one group. The Aufklärers sought to discern how vulnerable each classical form was to the force of despotism. They evaluated all three classical forms from this vantage point and found all three wanting.

The Aufklärers were especially critical of absolute monarchy. They were so distrustful of human nature that they believed very few men, no matter what their stated intentions, could resist misusing unlimited power. This refrain ran through all the Aufklärers' discussions; it was adequately expressed by Johann von Justi: "Whenever I am informed of a man's great power, I immediately show him how gravely that power can be misused." [35] August Ludwig von Schlözer shared this view and supported it with firsthand observations. Between the years 1761 and 1767 Schlözer lived in Saint Petersburg, where he voraciously studied the Russian past and present. After his return from Russia he began his lifelong attack on all forms of despotism, both in his books and especially in his highly influential journals, the *Briefwechsel* and the *Staatsanzeigen.* [36] According to Schlözer, the fatal flaw of an absolute monarchy was that the operation of the state depended upon the whims, prejudices, and character of the monarch: "The state is a dead mass to which the monarch imparts life. . . . The monarch lives for the state and the state lives through him." [37] Whatever contributes to his own fame and glory, the monarch interprets as beneficial to the state. And given the weakness, pride, and egotism of most monarchs, the search for glory usually precipitates disastrous attempts at conquest.

In addition to the inordinate power of the ruler, the problems of succession and of continuation of policy reinforced the tendency of the monarchy to degenerate into despotism. The most dangerous type of succession was, Schlözer thought, the patrimonial, where the monarch chooses his successor, as did Peter the Great. According to Schlözer, such a system invariably humbles the realm. Factions vie for titles and position, advisers become hopeless sycophants, and court and nation both reveal a degrading servile mentality, more befitting dogs than men. [38] Because of constant battles between factions, radical shifts in direction, and the capriciousness of the patrimonial system, it is impossible to maintain a consistent policy and thereby to improve society: "The truth is – and one should not be surprised or hold it for a paradox or an insult – that Russia has not made a single advance in culture since Ivan's time. That Peter the Great did not do more than shave a few beards is more than a bon mot; it is a statistical [i.e., sociological] fact." [39] Other methods of transferring power, though better, were all deficient: "An elective monarchy has some good points; the mistakes of a predecessor are easier to correct. Yet who does the electing? Certainly not the people. One party appropriates this right, sells its votes to the highest bidder, and thereby slowly transforms a tolerable monarchy into the most intolerable aristocracy. . . . And who is elected? The house elects because it is either bribed or surprised and then deludes itself by claiming to have made the election according to the ability and the service of the man elected." [40] Here Schlözer sums up the feeling most Aufklärers held about their own history, about what they thought was the tragedy of the German medieval past. What of an inherited monarchy? That too is an affront to good rule: "What has been said countless times with common sense [Witz] and force against hereditary monarchies is completely true." [41] The only advantage Schlözer accorded a hereditary monarchy was that some rulers might try to conserve some of their lands for future generations.

Schlözer's critique of monarchism reflected a basic assumption of the Aufklärers. To a man, they abhorred the idea that animated all forms of monarchial rule, namely, that the monarch was the father of his people, that the holders of power alone knew what was best for their subjects. Paternalism ran counter to the ideals of the Enlightenment; it denied the independence and creativity of the individual spirit; it stood in stark contrast to the stated educational aims of the Enlightenment because it blocked attainment of the consciousness of freedom. Schlözer's political journals emphasized the idea that national character and the characteristics of classes were not inborn qualities. Rather, they were determined by social condition. If serfs are indolent, if they are incapable of winning their freedom, it is because they were reared in the most paternalistic of all systems: "Indolence, yes! Indolence and slavery are inseparable. Educate a baron of the Empire [Reichs Freiherr] as a serf and he would be as indolent as a beast of burden." [42] Later Schlözer attacked the whole concept of the dear, loving Landesvater who benevolently rules his obedient children: "A father rules his children because they are not of age, that is, they lack understanding; only the father can successfully guide them through the world. The children of the *Landesvater,* however, are not a bunch of uninformed boys. Many are more intelligent than he; and when they obey him, they obey for a totally different reason than that of heeding the authority of a father."[43] Heeren shared Schlözer's view and attacked the patent absurdity of the paternalistic justification for monarchic rule.[44]

Absolutism, the most extreme form of monarchism, was seen to be one of the basic causes for the persistence of ignorance, servility, and docility. According to the Aufklärers, Enlightened Absolutism was equally pernicious. It mattered little who held power, whether it was Louis XV, the Well-Beloved, or the Portuguese minister and philosophe, Pombal. As long as absolute rule existed, the free exchange of ideas was excluded. In fact, the Aufklärers sometimes viewed Enlightened Absolutism as more dangerous than older forms of despotism because of its decided ideological nature. Schlözer's criticism of philosophes who exercised absolute power summed up the Aufklärers' attitude: "History has shown that professional academics [*Gelehrte von Profession*] as well as clerics are the natural friends of despotism, but only when they wield power. Because they are sure of their opinions and desire to improve humanity, they try to implement every program that comes to their minds, stifling in the process all opposition or resistance. The desire to stifle resistance is a definite mark of despotism. Compare this kind of absolutism with the work of the present prime ministers (formerly professors), Marquis Tanucci in Naples and M. Turgot in Versailles."[45] Except for those directly employed by absolute monarchs, especially the Prussian and Austrian rulers, the Aufklärers expressed deep distrust of the concentration of power in a centralized state. Like the French followers of Montesquieu, they hoped that constituted bodies would shield the nation from the excesses of despotism. Partly sheltered by the corporate structure of the university, they advocated a reformed *Ständestaat* and hence defended the German Freedoms and regional autonomies against absolutist incursion.[46]

The Aufklärers were equally critical of democracy and for similar reasons. To them, as to most Enlightenment thinkers, democracy presented a negative counterpart to absolute rule. It also sacrificed individual creativity and development to arbitrary and capricious rule, which in this instance came from the masses. Democracy as a constitutional form generated mediocrity and deadening conformity. Anyone who challenged the accepted, unquestioned rules of society faced expulsion or even extermination. Democracy was, in Wegelin's terminology, the embodiment of "society man." It evoked in the Aufklärers' minds the frightening image of mob rule, an image reinforced by the popular themes of Socrates' death, Münzer's excesses, and Jesus' crucifixion at the hands of a people who only a week earlier had cheered his entrance into Jerusalem. The Aufklärers expressed a deep-seated distrust of the masses. The common folk (*Gemeine-Haufen*) were fickle; when aroused, they were ready prey for unscrupulous demagogues. In Mosheim's view, "there are no opinions, however absurd, and no stories, however idle and improbable, that a weak and ignorant multitude, who are more attentive to the pomp of *words*, then to the truth of *things*, will not easily swallow." [47] When not excited, the masses were impervious to innovation and opposed to deviations from accepted norms. Because society men were unable or unwilling to question, they opposed the unusual. The original thinker or the innovator was bound to be crushed, for who, asked Schlözer, "could stand up against the majority?" [48] Thinkers of the Enlightenment believed the democratic form viable only in a small city-state; once the state became too large (in either area or population), democracy inevitably degenerated into a democracy in appearance only (*Schein-Democratie*). The Aufklärers buttressed their arguments by reference to contemporary example. Of the eighteenth-century states calling themselves republics, almost all were ruled by a closed corporation of powerful patrician families. Certainly the democratic ideal was not regnant in political units masquerading under the name and form of a republic.

Moreover, even if all the conditions favorable to democracy existed, the Aufklärers still judged it an unstable form because of the weaknesses of human nature. Although their image of man no longer accorded with the traditional Christian evaluation (many of the Aufklärers referred to themselves as "half Pelagians"), it still contained enough pessimism to question the self-sufficiency of man as man. The Aufklärers had replaced the orthodox description of original sin with a psychological analysis emphasizing man's inherent irrationality. Swept along by his passions and his self-interest, man was incapable of living in a world free of institutional restraints. And the restraints of democracy were not considered strong enough to hold man's baser instincts in check over the long period required for his step-by-step improvement. Thus, while the Aufklärers were willing to accord democratic forms the power of generating periods of brilliance, they judged democracy incapable of achieving permanence. Sooner or later, the darker side of man's nature would triumph over the civic responsibility necessary for the functioning of democracy. Heeren gave voice to this assumption in a short essay on the rise of modern political thought (1803): "One can readily see that the republican form, in which the nation takes an active part in legislation, can, in the abstract, be admirable. But everything depends upon the character and cultivation of the nation and upon its ability to adjust to making decisions in large assemblies." With the French example fresh in his mind, Heeren emphasized the unlikelihood that such an adjustment would be made. Above all, a republic needed "peace and gravity" to achieve success. [49] Earlier, before the French Revolution had intensified the Aufklärers' distrust of democracy, Gatterer had summed up the Greek experience: "With the introduction of democracy, which was instituted almost everywhere, the Greeks slowly extended their ability to perceive [*lernte sich allmählich fühlen*].... Then the great Greek mentality [*Denkungsart*] developed; the Greeks' love of fatherland grew and that love made them heroes and victors over the Persians. Soon, however, they became effeminate [*weiblich*], arrogant, disunited. Philip appeared with his barbarian and warlike Macedonians and took away the Greeks' prized treasure, their freedom." [50] Schlözer's evaluation was harsher. In direct contradiction to Winckelmann's portrayal of the pure simplicity and quiet greatness of the ancient Greeks, Schlözer saw them as a pack of brawling, egotistical individuals lacking all sense of proportion. [51]

The Aufklärers did not so much deny the democratic ideal as attack the long-term viability of the democratic form of government. Their image of the future envisioned the education of humanity, which, if and when achieved, would discount many of their temporally conditioned criticisms of society man. These criticisms were directed against the "multitude" of eighteenth-century Germany; against the peasant, for example, who refused to improve agricultural techniques because the old methods were traditional. Whether this critique was valid or not is another question; nevertheless, it was made with the assumption that things could be changed, that with a proper education the peasant would alter his attitudes and turn to improved methods. The Aufklärers condemned the democratic form (as then conceived) because it could not ensure the peace and stability necessary for correct *Bildung* — for internal improvement. The very instability of that form would lead to a type of rule that stood in stark contradiction to the democratic ideal; despotism would parade under a democratic front. In other words, the Aufklärers rejected the classical democratic form because its weakness made it unable to guarantee freedom in the modern age. The democratic form was incapable of meeting the needs of the moment, of ensuring a society "both powerful and free," and of "creating a state that was not tyrannical and yet was efficient." [52]

Of all the Aufklärers, Schlözer was the most persistent in advancing this argument. Indeed, he did it with so much conviction that not even the sacred cows of the Enlightenment — the ancient Greeks, the American revolutionaries, the modern Swiss — were safe from attack. He warned that the American appeal to natural law made it easier for powerful individuals to obtain power because natural law dissolved the bonds of common and positive law. The result, Schlözer maintained, would be the creation of a moneyed aristocracy worse than any hereditary aristocracy because of its singular concern with the cash nexus (he saw hints of this tendency in the formation of the Society of the Cincinnati). [53] Here Schlözer's distrust of democratic forms merged with the Aufklärung's critical evaluation of natural law.

If the Americans were threatened by the specter of oligarchic rule, the Swiss, Schlözer believed, had long ago fallen prey to it. According to him, the Swiss cantons were ruled by a group of self-perpetuating oligarchies under which freedom had become merely freedom from financial burdens. To achieve this freedom, the Swiss had sacrificed freedom of thought and independent action and the right to a fair hearing. So long as the patriarchial rulers of Bern, Geneva, Fribourg, and Zurich did not plague the people with too many taxes, they could rule as a closed corporation. Even blatant perversions of justice, such as the execution of Waser in Zurich, comparable, thought Schlözer, to the Calas case, went unnoticed. Schlözer was especially hard on cantonal authorities because he held that local governments were more susceptible to the influence of powerful factions than larger units, a position that Madison later argued forcefully in *The Federalist Papers*. In the case of the Corsican rebellion, however, Schlözer fully seconded the Enlightenment's obvious sympathy for the rebels against the ancient republic of Genoa. The rebellion had captured the imagination of thinkers throughout Europe, who saw it as a revolt against both patrician oligarchy and colonialism. It "had assumed the appearance of a conflict of the pure against the corrupt, of the poor against the rich, of the people of the land against the people of the city, of an oppressed nation against those who claimed the right to govern from afar." [54] Schlözer, in a highly romanticized history of Corsica, went so far as to credit the followers of Pasquale Paoli with "reawakening the spirit of freedom" in Europe. [55] Though the Aufklärers did not always agree with Schlözer's specific judgments, and though many found his language abrasive, they did share his belief in the inherent instability of popular rule, in the danger of factions, and in the tendency of certain economic groups to assume power in democracies. [56]

The Aufklärers' evaluation of aristocratic rule was even harsher. Very few found anything good to say of it. They usually gave aristocratic rule such short shrift that reference to the Polish experience sufficed to discredit it. At best, the Aufklärers admitted that an elective aristrocracy was better than an inherited one, which "was one of the most unfortunate constitutional forms." [57] Part of their scorn reflected their interpretation of what they considered the missed opportunities, the false starts, and the tragic turns of medieval and early modern German history. Many of the Aufklärers attributed the failures to the egotism and the lack of national purpose which they believed characterized the feudal lords of the High Middle Ages. Despite a growing interest in medieval culture, the Aufklärers showed little sympathy for medieval politics. For them, the High Middle Ages was the period of *Faustrecht* par excellence, the period when, beginning with the Great Interregnum, the aristocratic element was dominant. The Aufklärers, as sons of *bürgerliche* pastors, schoolteachers, and merchants, had nothing but scorn for aristocratic deportment and the aristocratic code of honor. Writer after writer condemned the silliness of court life, the quixotic practice of the duel, and the wastefulness of court pomp. The Aufklärers, though not calling for the abolition of aristocracy, were well aware of the shortcomings of the typical German aristocrat; they desired to reeducate the aristocracy to make them useful and to create bureaucracies based on talent, not birth. [58] Very few ventured a defense of aristocracy as a desirable form of government. Since respectable defenses were lacking, extended criticisms were unnecessary. A German revival of interest in aristocracy as a desired constitutional form had to await the immediate postrevolutionary era when the political theories of Karl Ludwig von Haller (Albrecht von Haller's grandson) captured the imagination of recalcitrant East Prussian Junkers.

Behind these negative evaluations of traditional constitutional forms lay the conviction that the models of antiquity were not applicable to modern Europe. In effect, the Aufklärers rejected classical political theory because it failed to answer the basic political question of the time: How can a society be created that will be both powerful and free, that will be efficient yet not tyrannical? Unable to find the answer either in classical theory or in the theories of natural law, the Aufklärers turned to a historical analysis of a state's political development. In so doing, they reached the conclusion that the majority of European states did not conform to traditional constitutional models; instead, many states were what the Aufklärers called compound, or pluralistic, societies (*zusammengesetzte Gesellschaften*), formed through a long process of development and stamped with an individual character not definable by abstract analysis. The Aufklärers lost their interest in ideal types and concentrated on empirical observation; history took precedence over theoretical sociology and political science.

The Aufklärers' heightened awareness of historically conditioned forms of political organization stemmed in part from their reaction to the prevailing discussion over the nature of the German Empire. Ever since Pufendorf's scathing indictment of the Empire (humorously summed up by Voltaire in his famous remark that the Holy Roman Empire was neither holy, Roman, nor an empire), German theorists had sought a method to describe a polity that many believed was functional and amenable to reform. At first the solution remained locked within the parameters Pufendorf had established. Eventually, however, political commentators attempted to discern in the German Empire the outlines of a new type of political organization, that of the compound society. It became a standard tenet of political analysis to differentiate between simple constitutional forms, those capable of being subsumed under the traditional categories of monarchy, aristocracy, and democracy, and compound, or conjoined, forms, which required a new mode of analysis. [59] This differentiation paralleled the contemporary distinction being made between simple ideas capable of being reduced to a syllogism and "confused" (i.e., fused) ideas which called for a different type of understanding. If a state had a complex form, then it had to be studied by a "higher way of classification" founded on the ideas of growth, development, and conjunction.

In this revaluation of political analysis, the Aufklärers, unlike their French counterparts, were optimistic about the possibilities of slowly transforming existing social units, of building upon the already given without first destroying the heritage of the past. As I have suggested, this attitude resulted in part from the Aufklärers' sense of participation (limited though it might have been) in influencing administrative policy in many of the German *Ständestaaten.* The Aufklärers' image of the future was accompanied by a reformist mentality; in France, on the other hand, the philosophes lost faith in piecemeal reform and opted instead for radical transformation. Professor Franco Venturi makes this point clear: "We must still return to the problem of whether the delay in the transformation of France did not also derive, at least to a certain extent, from a distrust of partial reforms, from the lesser importance attributed to the problems of the penal code, from the conviction which finally prevailed among the *philosophes* that only a complete and integral transformation of society would make possible the improvements advocated by Beccaria."[60] The Aufklärers were confident of their ability to influence reform; they trusted in the function of the university as a center from which independent voices could be raised to capture the nation's imagination; and they believed in the reform capabilities of the *Ständestaat.* They never fully accepted the French philosophes' conclusion that radical change was necessary to ensure the realization of their utopian image. By clinging to a program of reform, of what they described as the making of silent revolutions, the Aufklärers reinforced the need to investigate the manner in which the state had been formed. This assumption led them to evaluate past and present in a new way; the complex state was seen as a conjunction of a number of elements welded together in varying combinations by the forces of history. Each complex state was a moral body with its own distinct character. Traditional political analysis proved too restrictive to account adequately for that body's formation, its character, and its variety. Everything was far more complicated than usually envisioned; the complexity meant that the word "constitution" no longer applied to form alone. Achenwall so testified in the preface to his *Staatsklugheit:* "Above all, it must be noted that the idea of the state as used throughout this work is not an abstract conception containing nothing more than general characteristics and their attendant features, which could appear in any and all possible states. Instead, it is an idea with more precise boundaries. I deal with categories belonging to a state's nature never envisioned by theoretical treatments. . . . In short, I look at the state as our states really are."[61] The Aufklärers realized that the causal effect of time and tradition could be explicated only by examining the elements that, acting in conjunction, constitute the moral body. Increasingly, they directed their attention to problems of internal organization; their basic explanatory tools emphasized the *Primat der Innenpolitik.* Heeren summed up this newly won consciousness: "As long as this division [among monarchy, aristocracy, and democracy] is made the basis for the study of a state's constitution, then that study will remain extremely vague and ill defined because it describes only the various principles of government; totally omitted thereby are the *different relations between the government and the people* from which *alone* the different forms of state or types of constitution originate." As a final caution to those concerned with form alone, Heeren concluded: "The construction of a state form that contains within itself the guarantee for its permanence is a much greater absurdity than the desire to invent a perpetuum mobile that eternally propels itself."[62] The critical dissection of the relations between the government and the people became a primary goal.

4

One of the characteristic features in the development of Enlightenment thought is the decided shift of interest from politics and law to economics and sociology. This trend, already evident in France and England during the 1740s, reached Germany in the 1750s. It influenced the Aufklärers' standards of causal explanation and attested to a major change in social values. The trend is especially evident in the eighteenth-century development of the science of economics and the Aufklärers' realization of the important role economic development had played in the history of the state. The Aufklärers' awareness of the economic factor and their use of it in historical explanation are intriguing because they illustrate the manner in which the Enlightenment creatively restructured social thought and obtained thereby a new conception of history.

Though a study called economics had existed since antiquity, the science we call economics was first forged during the latter half of the eighteenth century. Scottish, English, and continental thinkers had taken the ancient concept of "oeconomics," shorn it of much of its original meaning and content, and redefined it so that it formed the kernel for two centuries of further development. This drastic revaluation occurred in part because of a change in social values; thinkers of the Enlightenment no longer accorded the way of life recently described by Otto Brunner as the "whole house [*ganze Haus*]" any self-evident validity.[63] The whole house had been the dominant pattern of Western social organization for more than two thousand years. It made little difference if the household was noble, peasant, or *bürger:* the same attitude and the same laws applied, ones that mirrored a lingering agrarian mentality. The unit was self-sufficient; its ideal was autarky; its rules of action and behavior were sanctioned by God's will, man's law, and natural right; its economy was modeled after the tradition of the community. Even the reach of the absolute state of the seventeenth century stopped at the door of the whole house. Absolutist laws dealt only with the relation of the whole house to the community at large. Only the *Hausherr* ("head of the household") had political rights; only he could enjoy the full benefits of the law. In more ways than one, a man's home was his castle, which he ruled as a sovereign lord. The tradition of the whole house embodied a complex of legal, religious, and social values and conventions which lay at the heart of ancient and medieval social structure and thought.

Until the eighteenth century, the study of economics meant the study of everything necessary to the functioning of the whole house: "Oeconomics ... included the totality of human relations and activities in the household — the relations between man and wife, parents and children, *Hausherrn* and apprentices, field hands, servants, or serfs [*Gesinde*], and the way in which the required duties in the house and fields were to be fulfilled."[64] From antiquity to the beginning of the eighteenth century, economic treatises presented an array of moralistic homilies, household suggestions, recipes ranging from the baking of bread to the brewing of beer, home cures, and descriptions of agricultural and manufacturing processes, all highly suggestive of the type of material still offered the American public by the *Old Farmer's Almanac.* The subjects we would expect to find in an economic study received slight treatment. When trade was discussed, it was done so from the assumption that a self-contained household was the desired ideal. Trade was tolerated if it served the goal of achieving autarky; it was roundly condemned if it became an end in itself, if it ever disintegrated into making money for profit's sake. The negative attitude toward trade was supported by the customs and religious traditions of the whole house and colored the historical evaluations of thinkers well into the eighteenth century. Its assumptions also applied to the state apparatus, which usually was treated as an enlarged household ruled over by the *Landesvater.* Trade, profit, and luxury were seen as forces leading to the moral and physical collapse of a nation. Pufendorf, for example, believed a concentration on commerce brought a nation to the brink of ruin by sapping its desire to fight and increasing its taste for depravity. He thought the English were becoming "effeminate and interested only in trade and profit."[65]

During the Enlightenment, the idea and conventions of the whole house were subjected to a thorough criticism, which led to the creation of the modern science of economics. As Otto Brunner has cautioned us, we cannot ascribe the destruction of the whole house to the Enlightenment alone; the process took a long time and had not been completed even by the end of the eighteenth century. Still, the movement toward modern economics first became a conscious ideal during the Enlightenment when the traditions of the whole house were questioned from all sides. The authority of the *Hausherr* was attacked in the same manner as that of the *Landesvater.* The religious justifications for the values of the whole house (drawn from numerous sources, including Mosaic law, the Roman idea of paterfamilias as formulated in the Vulgate and translated by Luther, and general Christian dogmatics and morality) fell in Protestant Germany before the historical onslaught of the Neologists. The familial relations of the whole house were undermined by ideas ranging from women's rights and childish innocence to human sensibility. This critique accompanied an important demographic change, as increasing numbers of small-city families left the shelter of the whole house and set up their own independent and limited households. The net result was redefinition of the household; the modern idea of the family (in Germany the word "family" did not acquire general recognition until the Aufklärung), with all its emotional overtones, replaced the legal and economic idea of the self-contained whole house. At the same time, the task of earning a living was located in a sphere outside of immediate family life and was subjected to critical analysis. The contradictions between the rational demands of earning a living and the moral and emotional demands of raising a family, which in the whole house had caused painful tension, were now resolved by separation. The late eighteenth-century image of the "warm, animated family nest" became the necessary counterpart to the rational science of economics.[66]

Economics, stripped of its moralistic and religious ties to the totality of family life, could not be studied without invoking the problems of the interrelations of Christian morality, household existence, and economic advantage. Enlightenment thinkers concentrated upon questions of trade, circulation of goods and money, the credit apparatus, and sources of wealth. In so doing they reversed the value judgments concerning the usefulness and function of trade. It became a truism that the wealth of a nation, when founded upon trade, manufactures, and agriculture, directly influenced the improvement of manners, morality, and science: "The more a nation has engaged in trade, the more its arts and sciences have flowered."[67] Healthy trade directed by enlightened self-interest laid the material foundations for the betterment of a nation. Trade, the "mother of the finest arts and sciences," was the golden chain that bound the world together; its history was "the history of man's ingenuity and powers of invention."[68] Trade was seen as a powerful force in the shaping of the nation's social life; it was, to use Johann Gottfried Eichhorn's phrase, "a powerful driving wheel of the . . . state machine."[69] Economic development was tied to fiscal organization, internal administration, technology, social structure, political power, and intellectual life and then applied to historical understanding. Throughout Europe, thinkers tackled these complex interrelations from various angles and employed whatever insights they believed they had culled from their studies to explain past and present.

Without going into the history of eighteenth-century economic thought, it can be said that two strategies of economic analysis, theoretical and historical, developed over the course of time. Theoretical analysis was best mirrored in the writings of François Quesnay and the Physiocrats, who strove to reduce the complexities of economic practice by deductively establishing a set of simple universal principles, such as the single tax on land. The historical school found its leading proponents among Scottish and English writers. They employed the empirical methods of Newton and Hume, beginning with observable relations and attempting to base a theory of economics on their observations. Many of its leaders, such as Hume, Ferguson, and Robertson, were historians in their own right, and its greatest thinker, Adam Smith, devoted the largest part of his epoch-making classic, *The Wealth of Nations,* to historical observation. Though differing in approach and method, the two models of analysis agreed upon certain principles; both opposed mercantilist restrictions, the concern with hard money, the idea that one nation's commercial gain necessarily implied another's loss, and the analogous application of household economics to national economics. Between the proponents of both schools there existed a host of eclectic thinkers who combined elements of both and grafted them onto earlier mercantilist propositions. Until the end of the century the majority of German thinkers could be called eclectic, but the historical element predominated. Almost all of them used a tactic of analysis postulated on historical observation and pragmatic application. And like the British, most attempted either to write economic history or to incorporate economic ideas into their own historical researches. With a few exceptions (Karl Friedrich von Baden and Isaak Iselin), the basics of the physiocratic method remained foreign to German thinkers.

Johann Jacob Schmauß was one of the many writers who called for the integration of economics and history. In his important study of modern European politics and diplomacy, *Einleitung zu der Staats-Wissenschaft,* Schmauß promised that the work would be capped by a volume devoted to the history of European commerce. The commercial structure of a state "is of such importance that the reputation and the power of European monarchs depends, to a great extent, upon it."[70] Although Schmauß never carried out his plan, others did seek to investigate commercial structure and administrative organization. Johann Heinrich Gottlob von Justi was a sensitive reflector of this trend. Justi, however, was not a typical Aufklärer. In many ways he resembled the hoard of adventurers who proliferated during the eighteenth century. What differentiated him from men such as Casanova, Cagliostro, Saint-Germain, and von Neurath, the ill-starred king of Corsica, was his devotion to serious scholarship. Born in Thuringia, probably an illegitimate child, Justi had an active and varied life which led him from the universities of Jena and Wittenberg to the battlefields of Bohemia and Moravia, to Weimar, Vienna, Göttingen, Denmark, and finally to Prussia; the subject matter of his numerous books and articles ranged from the theory of the monad to history, aesthetics, finance, and economics. Some scholars have even considered Justi "one of the fathers of German national economy,"[71] a judgment supported by the popularity of Justi's two major cameralistic works, *Staatswirthschaft* (2d ed., 1755) and *System des Finanzwesens* (1766), and by Joseph von Sonnenfels's praise and large-scale use of Justi's work.[72] But Justi's scholarly interests did not spare him the ignominious end of other eighteenth-century adventurers. He died in prison, blind, broken, and in disgrace.

In Justi's far-reaching and sometimes contradictory evaluations of economic, financial, and administrative structure, two elements typical of the Aufklärers' social thought emerge. The first is Justi's condemnation of speculation. As already noted, Justi was one of the most vocal opponents of Wolff. Like Schmauß, Schlözer, and Winckelmann, he leveled a scathing attack against the creations of ivory-towered academicians who were unwilling or unable to look at the world around them; among these creations Justi included the postulates of modern natural law, especially the idea of the social contract. In addition, his analytics emphasized the overriding concern with *Innenpolitik,* with the relation between the internal structure of society and the unique spirit of the nation. Hence Justi, like the rest of the Aufklärers, saw Montesquieu as one of the most important thinkers of his century. As Sonnenfels noted, Justi evaluated the whole complex of internal organization on the basis of its effect upon human *Glückseligkeit* – human happiness in its broadest context. The state's strength lay in the well-being of its citizens, not in the size of its armies or its dominions; its wealth lay in its citizens' activities, not in its hoard of silver and gold. Justi, like so many of his generation, thought it admirable to increase a state's population, providing the state had the necessary resources to feed more people. He estimated that Europe could safely increase its population sixfold before reaching its limit. Seeing the free play of human activity as the key to happiness, Justi contended that every manifestation of this activity – art, science, manufactures, trade, and agriculture – must be considered when evaluating a nation's past, present, and future. Each has an influence upon national wealth. If a state wishes to achieve the degree of power and stability of which it is capable, it must be administered according to an overall plan that includes all these elements, though "one would be mistaken if one believed that all people could be ruled according to a single plan and a single set of assumptions. The natural situation of the lands, the genius, and the disposition and customs of the people (which, following the example of the wise and noble author of the A-M [Frederick the Great's *Anti-Machiavel*], we may call the people's temperament) require a different plan for every nation."[73] Working from this assumption, Justi offered a number of suggestions aimed at eliminating contemporary commercial restrictions, aristocratic privilege, fiscal irresponsibility, and agricultural stagnation. He called for reform of taxation (reduced taxation equitably applied to all classes, abolition of tax-farming, maintenance of freedom and commerce); restructuring of peasant patterns of life (transformation of the peasant nucleated village to one based on the English model, abolition of serfdom, peasant ownership of land, abolition of strip farming, abrogation of village law requiring the planting of certain crops at certain times); and improvement of commerce and manufactures (breakdown of trade restrictions, abolition of price-fixing, guild reform, specialization of labor).

The extent to which Justi emphasized the importance of internal reform was evident when he attacked the ever popular eighteenth-century idea of the balance of power: "The power of a state does not depend upon the extent of its possessions, the size of its army, huge revenues, or the like. Rather, the degree of a state's power is determined solely by the perfection of its administration."[74] He showed how extensive lands more often than not were a drain on the mother country, how a large army would exhaust the resources of a poorly administered land, how a large population could be as much a burden to a shaky financial system as a benefit, and how large revenues were deleterious to a state unless they were properly reinvested. Each point was accompanied by numerous historical examples, the most prominent of which were drawn from the Spanish experience.

The Aufklärers were all fascinated by the dramatic decline of Spanish power since the time of Charles V. For Justi, the fatal flaw of the Spanish was their inability to forge a modern administrative state from the congeries of lands acquired by the Habsburgs. Blinded by the glory of their far-flung realm and the idea of resurrecting a universal Christian empire under the Habsburg aegis, the Most Catholic rulers stumbled from one misadventure into another. In the process they ruined their state, impoverished their subjects, and made Spain a veritable wasteland ruled by proud noblemen impervious to the people's needs. The loss of the Netherlands and Portugal did not cause the Spanish decline; rather, it attested to the weakness of the Spanish system itself. Even "the indescribable riches of the New World did nothing to secure the power of Spain after the days of Ferdinand the Catholic and Charles V. On the contrary, these riches further accentuated the pitiable weakness of the state. They made the Spanish proud, and pride engendered idleness, which allowed other nations to gain control of Spain's wealth. The rich West Indian mines were soon being worked by English, Dutch, Genoese, and French. Three-fifths of the Spanish silver fleets belonged directly to these nations and the other two-fifths came into their hands through commerce. In general, Spain, despite its American riches, did not become one farthing richer. Instead, its self-sufficiency was destroyed and Spain became the poorest land under the sun. In short, Spain was nothing but Europe's beast of burden; it carried the riches of the New World to the Old."[75]

Although the majority of the Aufklärers were reluctant to concentrate solely on *Innenpolitik* to the exclusion of foreign policy and intellectual and spiritual concerns, they agreed with the general thrust of Justi's causal reasoning. Gottfried Achenwall, Justi's contemporary, developed and popularized the study of "statistics," a historically oriented socio-politico-economic investigation of a state's constitution. According to Achenwall, statistics differed from political science in that the former described states as they actually were whereas the latter described them as they should be. The scope of statistics included both internal and external politics analyzed as to their effect upon the general good. Achenwall did not originate statistics in Germany (the seventeenth-century thinker Hermann Conring is usually accorded that distinction), but it was primarily through his efforts that the study "conquered the [German] world."[76] By the time of Achenwall's death (1772), statistics was taught at virtually every major German-speaking university, often with Achenwall's compendium *Staatsverfassung der heutigen vornehmsten europäischen Reiche und Völker in Grundriße* as the basic text; the text itself went through five editions during Achenwall's lifetime and achieved further longevity when Schlözer revised it (1781-1785).

Achenwall's inquiries were wide and sometimes discursive, owing in part to the wealth of material covered.[77] His organization in general followed the Aufklärers' hierarchy of causal connection; he began his study by describing the nation's climate and geography, proceeded to its constitutional form and foreign policy, and then described in detail the *Regierung des Reiches*. Under this general rubric he included everything from national character and religious belief and organization to legal structure and operation, manufactures, commerce, finance, agriculture, and military organization. Finally, in an attempt at summation, he portrayed the vital interests of each state. The topics he considered most important were agriculture, trade, and finance. "If," he said in his *Staatsklugheit*, "I have gone deeper in my observations of agricultural, commercial, and financial systems than in other subjects, . . . it is because these are the fundamental pillars of the well-being of the total populace [*der gesammten Bürger*] in addition, the present internal strength of a state depends, in part, on these categories."[78] In his investigation of these three systems, Achenwall combined elements drawn from all the economic theories of the time. He believed a well-organized agricultural structure "the most natural and lasting basis for the absorption and increase of trade and manufactures."[79] Nevertheless, a nation's wealth grows primarily through circulation of money, expansion of credit, and development of manufacturers — that is, through trade and industry. Financial administration either assured or negated the effects derived from benefits of trade, circulation of money, and expansion of credit. Consequently, he considered the financial operations of the state vital. Spain declined because of an inadequate financial policy. In a study of France's finances (published posthumously), Achenwall predicted dire consequences for the French unless their whole financial structure was reformed and simplified. In a rare touch of humor, he characterized French finances as being more confused than Wolffian philosophy.

The cross-sectional approach upon which statistics depended elevated the historical over the speculative; it assumed that a state's constitution could be apprehended only after extensive study of the temporal conjunction of economic, social, and political structures. It entailed the employment of what Pütter described as the *Einschaltungsmethode*, where history is "made to stand still in order that the whole can be surveyed."[80] Though Achenwall used statistics primarily to describe the states of modern Europe, other Aufklärers soon applied the statistical method to the remote past. Michaelis opened up a new field of inquiry when he employed it to study ancient Jewish history in an effort to explicate the Old Testament. In a similar manner, Pütter used statistics to interpret medieval German law, and

Christian Gottlob Heyne applied sociological and economic analysis to reinvigorate the study of the classics. Moreover, statistics was not limited to a study of individual states. Achenwall proposed to analyze the constitution of Europe, and Johann Christoph Gatterer even envisioned a study of universal statistics.[81]

5

The *Primat der Innenpolitik* was acclaimed even by experts in foreign policy. Schmauß, whose strength lay in diplomatic history, argued that all historical inquiries must start with an examination of a state's *innerliche Einrichtung,* its internal organization. Otherwise, any discussion of politics and diplomacy would be superficial and misleading.[82] Schmauß's explanation for the decline of Habsburg power paralleled that of the younger Justi. In *Einleitung zu der Staats-Wissenschaft,* Schmauß depicted the weaknesses of Charles V's realm and its two successor states. Despite their apparent strength, they consisted of scattered and dissimilar parcels, each with its own institutions, traditions, and interests. Their only bond was the feudal overlordship exercised by the Habsburg ruler, acting sometimes as emperor, sometimes as king, prince, or duke. Habsburg policy was basically a family policy, not a national one. In contrast, France had in the same period rationalized its strength; its constitution was well ordered, its population large, its commerce flourishing. Whenever threatened, it could act as a single body with concentrated force.[83] In this comparison, Schmauß demonstrated the quandary facing Germans who lived in small and middle-sized states. They were pro-Imperial, though not always pro-Austrian. They placed their hopes in the reformed *Ständestaat,* but they also realized the weakness of politics locked within the ambit of their medieval heritage. Schmauß, like others, felt the future belonged to the large, well-organized state supported by a viable economy.

Throughout the rest of the century, the importance of the economic motive continued to stimulate German thinkers, as evidenced by the number who turned to the history of trade, manufactures, or technology. Among those contributing essays on economic or colonial development were Schlözer, Sartorius, Semler, Sonnenfels, Eichhorn, Spittler, Hüllmann, and Heeren. Sometimes their investigations produced rather singular results, to say the least. A unique interpretation of the history of trade was offered by Friedrich Christoph Jonathan Fischer (1750-1797), professor of feudal law at Halle. In his four-volume *Geschichte des teutschen Handels* Fischer argued: "The Germans were the first modern Europeans to engage in trade on a large scale. It was from them that the southern peoples learned the principles of trade." In addition, the "Germans were the original creators of laws concerning exchange. . .: until the sixteenth century the rest of Europe, Italy included, drew their best artisans and artists from Germany; until then, our fatherland was the richest state in Europe."[84]

Far more worthy of note was the work of Johann George Büsch (1728-1780), founder of the Hamburger Handelsakademie and its director for almost thirty years. According to Roscher, Büsch was the leading representative of the liberal eclectics and a staunch defender of the northern German trading cities, particularly Hamburg. He was also one of the most important and prolific German economists of the last half of the century. His fame rests primarily upon his theoretical work (which deals with the circulation of money) and his history of Hamburg's trade.[85] Gottfried Achenwall had maintained that a major source of a nation's wealth lay in the circulation of money and an increase in consumption; Büsch expanded this idea and made the circulation of money pivotal. The more money in circulation, Büsch maintained, the larger the nation's wealth. Circulation itself was determined by two factors: size of the producing classes and total wages paid for all services. Because of the vital importance of monetary circulation, Büsch singled out trade as the prime producer of a nation's wealth. He drew attention to the importance of the middleman and clearly delineated the difference between passive and active trade. Unfortunately, he underestimated the importance of agriculture and manufacturing, a mistake probably traceable to his reliance upon the Hamburg experience. Whatever the merits and faults of Büsch's single-minded concentration on trade and money, one element in his thought characterizes the Enlightenment's developing standards of causal evaluation: the linkage of economic change to social development. Already in Justi's work we encounter the assumption that economic organization is closely related to social and intellectual patterns. The lack of money and the limited trade of the Middle Ages corresponded to a specific type of agrarian organization with its own code of law and way of life. A change in one of these elements would necessarily entail a change in the other; for Justi, it seemed easier to change the economic base than the ideological.

The assumption that quiet alterations in economic patterns deeply affect all aspects of life is evident in Schlözer's wide-ranging writings. It led him to pique some of his contemporaries by suggesting that the discovery of brandy and the introduction of the potato and of sugar, coffee, and tea had caused greater "revolutions" in Europe than the defeat of the Armada, the War of the Spanish Succession, and the Peace of Paris (1763).[86]

Schlözer's use of the word "revolution" seems, at first glance, highly unusual. Yet when we look at the assumptions supporting this view, the Aufklärers' idea of revolutionary change no longer appears so arbitrary. Working from the Leibnizian postulate of the universal interconnectedness of all life, which in effect denied accidental or catastrophic change,[87] the Aufklärers assumed that the often unnoticed changes affecting patterns of living revolutionized the given social conjunction and hence the course of history. Accordingly, the most important changes in history are social changes, which take place over an extended period of time. Schlözer expressed this belief when describing the early history of Leipzig: "During these princes' reigns other quiet and barely discernible revolutions occurred whose effects were more important than those already described. The hierarchy and the *poliarchie* [by which he meant a separation into distinct groups with certain privileges or rights] expanded. Before then there were, at most, three categories of people in the land: nobility, clergy, and slaves [serfs]. Now three new categories arose: monks, *Bürger,* and Jews. Real property passed into the hands of new holders."[88] Philosophes and Aufklärers alike argued that the "common" features of life were worthy of historical investigation,[89] a position Schlözer echoed in his famous statement that the real carriers of history were merchants, apostles, travelers, and inventors. This assumption, though sometimes ignored by later followers of Ranke (concerned with the *Primat der Außenpolitik* and the history of intellectual elites), remained a leitmotiv for a minority of German scholars, including Roscher, Riehl, Dilthey, and Hintze.[90] To my knowledge, one of the finest expressions of this type of historical mentality, first propagated by Enlightenment thinkers, was given by Thomas Carlyle who, despite his "romanticism," had much in common with the Enlightenment. It deserves repetition:

> Which was the greatest innovator, which was the more important personage in man's history, he who first led armies over the Alps, and gained the victories of Cannae and Trasymene; or the nameless boor who first hammered out for himself an iron spade? When the oak-tree is felled, the whole forest echoes with it; but a hundred acorns are planted silently by some unnoticed breeze. Battles and war-tumults, which for the time din every ear, and with joy or terror intoxicate every heart, pass away like tavern-brawls: and, except some few Marathons and Morgartens, are remembered by accident, not by desert. Laws themselves, political Constitutions, are not our Life, but only the house wherein our Life is led; nay, they are but the bare walls of the house: all whose essential furniture, the inventions and traditions, and daily habits that regulate and support our existence, are the work not of Dracos and Hampdens, but of Phoenician mariners, of Italian masons and Saxon metallurgists, of philosophers, alchymists, prophets, and all the long-forgotten train of artists and artisans.[91]

The Aufklärers saw a correlation between technological change and economic change. They went hand in hand, and both influenced social development. Throughout the Aufklärers' histories we encounter causal explanations founded on this belief. Nevertheless, some of the most prominent examples of technological change were not new and their direct tie to economic change was often tenuous. Gunpowder, one frequently cited example of technological change, basically altered methods of warfare and thereby helped undermine the feudal order. As Pütter wrote, "The use of guns and gunpowder effected a great change in warfare and even in the whole

German constitution."[92] According to Pütter's narrative such changes struck at the core of feudalism: through them the large standing professional army replaced the feudal fighting force, weakening the military function of the aristocracy and its claim to special privileges. They also led to the strengthening of the centralized state, to increases in taxation, to the creation of a bureaucracy to collect taxes, and to a change in the legal relations between the *Stände* and the monarch.[93] According to the Aufklärers, another technological change, the invention of printing, resulted in an expansion of learning; printing created a new and revolutionary means of mass communication, which in the long run made the dissemination of enlightenment possible and in the short run accelerated the spread of the Reformation. In the eyes of these good Protestants, the invention of printing had helped to shatter the Church's monopoly on learning.

Other technological innovations cited were more closely related to economic development because of their effect on transportation, especially shipping. Without such inventions as the astrolabe and the compass and the improvement of ships and sails, the great trade revolution of the fifteenth and sixteenth centuries would, they thought, have been impossible. That revolution altered for the first time since antiquity the patterns of East-West trade.[94] Not only were the traditional trading routes overshadowed, but the nature of trade also changed considerably: foodstuffs and other materials (e.g., rice, cotton, tobacco, sugar) transported in bulk replaced luxury articles; trade now affected a higher proportion of Europe's population than ever before. Improved transportation also made an efficient postal system possible. Besides offering the obvious advantage of speedy communication, an efficient postal system, the Aufklärers believed, was a necessary prerequisite to an effective credit system and consequently to expanded circulation of money. Countless other innovations, from the introduction of new foods and manufacturing processes to improvements in city management, captured their imagination and appeared in their historical writings as factors implementing changes in social patterns. Johann Beckman painstakingly described such innovations in his five-volume work, *Beyträge zur Geschichte der Erfindungen,* a work Roscher still found useful almost a century later.

In developing the theme of the relation between societal and economic change, the Aufklärers followed the model of French and British historians. They concentrated on the connection between trade and the formation of the middle class. Since trade was bascially an urban activity, the Aufklärers believed that the expansion of trade, the rise of the city, and the creation of the *Bürgerstand* were causally linked. Urban life differed qualitatively from life either on the land or in the village; *bürgerlich* obligations were fundamentally opposed to feudal ones: "Cities differed not only from *Dorfs* in their physical appearance – houses were built adjacent to one another, streets were laid, churches, hospitals, and cloisters were built, and the whole unit was protected by walls and gates – but also *morally*. The burgher enjoyed definite privileges, the foremost being his status as freeman. . . . He had the right to engage in trade, professions, and manufactures; *Bürgers* could brew their own beer, join guilds, and hold yearly fairs."[95] Since they were skeptical of, if not outwardly opposed to, aristocratic values, the Aufklärers equated the rise of *Bürgertum* with the destruction of the feudal system. Heeren succinctly summed up this attitude: "Basically, the *Bürgerstand* is an element completely alien to the feudal constitution."[96] Nevertheless, the origins of the *Bürgerstand* lay in the Middle Ages. Its development entailed a slow and tortuous process whereby cities grew with the increase in trade, won their rights after difficult conflicts with feudal lords, and finally "formed, for the first time, a nation in the political meaning of the word."[97] In effect, the study of the rise of the *Bürgerstand* was a chapter in medieval history; awareness of the history of the *Bürgerstand* and of the expansion of trade required the Aufklärers to revise many common Protestant assumptions concerning the Middle Ages. For example, Schlözer praised monasteries because of their economic activities; Wegelin credited the medieval papacy with establishing a certain degree of order, which had made increased trade possible; and Heeren, a devout Lutheran, examined the effects of the Crusades in a detached manner unthinkable a hundred years earlier.

For Heeren, the Crusades were the expression of a young and vibrant society naturally attracted to heroic undertakings: "They were the fruit of the awakened heroic spirit and religiosity of the Frankish-Germanic nation, the heroic period of Christianity. When the Crusades are looked at from this viewpoint, the viewpoint of that period, the reproaches usually leveled against them as senseless undertakings generated by superstition and bigotry disappear of themselves. The long-range results of the Crusades, however, prepared the ground for the destruction of the order that had begun them. During the era of the Crusades, trade with the East increased tremendously. If trade with the East can be called a moderately sized stream before the Crusades, after them it grew to a powerful river, which divided into many tributaries and expanded its distribution immensely."[98] The increase in trade led to the rise of cities, where the spirit of freedom awakened. In large commercial cities a new life began, free from the restrictions of the feudal order: personal freedom was ensured; men could dispose of their wealth; taxation was regulated; and communal law, which allowed the people to choose their own magistrates, was created.[99] In sum, "the rise of the communes may easily be seen as the most important and most effective result generated by the era of the Crusades."[100] Heeren summarized the effects of the Crusades by proclaiming, "*They did not create a better world immediately, but they prepared the way for one.* . . . It is always in the nature of great revolutions that their results are incalculable [*unabsehbar*]; but the vision of mortal men always remains limited. Still, a glimpse into the infinite distance has its attractions."[101]

Heeren's explanation reveals the basics of the Aufklärers' developing causal thinking: each age contains within itself the seeds of its own destruction; each event leads to results hardly envisioned by the participants and only darkly perceived by the inquiring historian. Certain large forces operate almost independently to establish the conditions for qualitative historical change, but they act in a manner beyond the total comprehension of limited human understanding. Trade was considered such a force and remained a favorite topic of investigation because the Aufklärers thought it a restless activity, almost a Promethean drive for expansion. As Wegelin maintained, trade cannot stand still, for its goal is the increase of wealth. With increased wealth, the Aufklärers believed, comes the improvement of society. Would the cultural achievements of the Renaissance have been possible without the riches of the Italian cities? Thinkers as different as Iselin, Schlözer, and Heeren thought not.

The Aufklärers' positive evaluation of wealth and trade led to a partial redefinition of social values in Germany. No longer was the *Bürger* the laughingstock of polite society, the bumbling, social-climbing boor so humorously portrayed by Molière. Instead, he became the archetype of the practical, free man whose fortune depended upon his own wits and talent, not on the accidents of birth; the aristocrat became the brunt of satirical attack. Writers as diverse as Lessing and Beaumarchais extolled the excellence of the bourgeois while casting scathing barbs at the run-of-the-mill aristocrat. During the Enlightenment, philosophes and Aufklärers alike proposed to reeducate the nobility in order to make its members useful to society; and the founding of such institutions as the Theresianum in Vienna, the *Ritterakademie* in Berlin, and the University of Göttingen offer ample evidence that such pleas did not fall on deaf ears. This attitude is mirrored in many of the Aufklärers' historical explanations. When Heeren tried to account for the unique development of the British Parliament, he looked to the relation of the British aristocracy to the bourgeoisie and singled out the fact that younger aristocratic sons as well as the majority of the gentry actively engaged in bourgeois pursuits. Accordingly, the lower house acquired a strength and a unity absent in the rest of Europe. [102] By the 1780s historians of the Aufklärung believed it vital to trace the rise of the middle class, as Spittler noted in the introduction to his popular compendium, *Entwurf der Geschichte der europäischen Staaten.* He proposed to answer the following questions: "When and how did the third estate arise? How have relations among the various *Stände* and between the *Stände* and the government been forged? How did the juridical system develop? And what happened to the states' financial and taxation systems?"[103]

The Aufklärers' first approach to causal explanation dealt with various external factors, each of which, when treated in isolation, evidenced a predictable effect of its own. In this sense they may be called the objective factors in the Aufklärers' structure of causal explanation; climate, topography, geography, constitutional form, technological innovation, and economic change each had a specific sphere of influence in the totality of social life. Nonetheless, though recognizing certain forces as predictably determinant, the Aufklärers refused either to single out one element as primary or to advance the proposition that all aspects of historical development could be subsumed under lawlike categories. At most, the Aufklärers used the objective categories in a negative way. Qualitative change could not occur unless certain objective preconditions existed; thus, the development of an independent *Bürgerstand* depended on the rise of the cities, which in turn depended on the expansion of trade. But neither of these objective preconditions sufficed to explain the specifics of Western urban development, which could be understood only by looking at another set of forces that were unique, unpredictable, and individual, the forces of internal, or spiritual, influence.[104]

VII
Categories of Causal
Explanation II: Spirit, Customs,
Values, and Ideas

1

The Aufklärers' explanation of external causation corresponded, by and large, to that of the western philosophes; in fact, virtually every causal explanation made by the Aufklärers could be traced to the writings of leading philosophes. Most Aufklärers willingly acknowledged this debt, though some groused about second-rate imitators of Hume, William Robertson, and Adam Ferguson, and all indulged in the almost mandatory attacks against Voltaire. It is only in the category of internal, or spiritual, causation and its relation to external causation that there was an independent, original development. Increasingly, the Aufklärers implemented a quasi-idealist explanation for historical change. To be sure, here too they learned from western thinkers, especially from Ralph Cudworth, Shaftesbury, Hume, and Rousseau. Yet the primary impetus for this development came from the inherent dynamics of German intellectual life. The Aufklärers struggled to forge a paradigm of historical understanding that would acknowledge the importance of material surroundings; at the same time, they sought to avoid the pitfalls of naturalism, materialism, and abstract speculation. The religious consciousness of the era, nourished by the postulates of eighteenth-century aesthetics and supported by universally held Leibnizian assumptions concerning the relation between the individual and the general, led the Aufklärers to proclaim the independent existence of nonmaterial factors, such as values, custom, and religious belief. They accorded individual spiritual acts, accomplished by "original geniuses," a major role in determining the form and direction of purposive change.

The Aufklärers confronted a problem that lay at the core of Rousseau's inquiries: the tension between change and communal being, between will and reason. Like Rousseau, Herder, and later de Tocqueville, the Aufklärers recognized that societies were regulated "by the feelings, the beliefs, the ideas, the habits of heart and mind of the men who compose them."[1] These shared communal feelings, embodied in custom, language, and law, formed the character, or spirit, of the times. They restricted change and served as the only true basis upon which effective change could be achieved. Consequently, the Aufklärers conceived of purposive change in terms of the conflict between the conservative forces of existing custom and the individual "revolutionary" activity of restructuring – but not abolishing – that custom when material conditions permitted. The true revolutionary (one who effects basic changes in society) was, in their eyes, the man or group of men who saved tradition from stagnation and breakdown by a creative reinterpretation of that tradition. In their evolving analysis, the Aufklärers differentiated among three types of spiritual influences: the vaguely defined *Geist der Zeit;* the more specific, though equally hazy, national character; and the active spirit, soul, or moral apprehension of the original genius, who acted within and against the other two. With these root concepts, the Aufklärers sought to describe the *Ideenwirkung* ("the rational and emotional effect of ideas") on history.

The major impulse to view historical change as the action of the spirit on a given social environment came from thinkers concerned with religious and ecclesiastical history. Here, more than anywhere else, a need for a creative reinterpretation of the past existed. The violent controversies of the first half of the eighteenth century that raged in Protestant Germany involving orthodox Christians, Pietists, and Wolffian rationalists, had left a deep impression on the Aufklärers. By the time the Aufklärers had reached manhood, most of them had gone through the crucible of religious assertion, followed by doubt, questioning, and rediscovery. For many the journey had been a difficult one, a psychological experience that had left deep and bitter scars. Some, such as Herman Samuel Reimarus, never recovered and led a Jekyll-and-Hyde life of inward disbelief masked by outward orthodoxy. Others emerged from the trials of youth as believing Christians but remained highly skeptical of dogmatic assertion or nonthinking piety. It was their goal to avoid the dangers of any one-sided evaluation of religion. They were, as Harnack said of Mosheim, "neither orthodox nor pietistic, nor rationalistic, but capable of appreciating all these tendecies."[2]

The Neologists (led by Mosheim, Semler, Johann August Ernesti, and Michaelis) tried to join the spiritual elements of Pietism to the recognition that all religions require rational exposition and formal ritual, though no one exposition or ritual could be valid for all times and all peoples. The first step, evident in Mosheim's work, entailed a redefinition of the church. Instead of seeing the church as the virgin bride of Christ, the Neologists considered it a human creation expressing a general religious impulse in forms determined by time and place: "The Church cannot be represented with more perspicuity and propriety than under the notion of a society, subjected to a lawful dominion, and governed by certain laws and institutions, mostly of a moral and spiritual tendency."[3] Like all societies, the church was a body in flux, changing, advancing, regressing, never the same at one time as it was at another. For Mosheim, heresies no longer were battles between the hosts of Christ and the Antichrist, but rather internal battles analogous to conflicts between estates in the realm: "As bodies politic are sometimes distracted

with wars and seditions, so has the Christian church, though designed to be
the mansion of charity and concord, been unhappily perplexed by intestine
divisions occasioned sometimes by points of doctrine, at others by a variety
of sentiments about certain rites and ceremonies."[4] That the organization,
ritual, and dogmatics of a church reflect the customs and *Denkungsart* of the
people who compose it was as true of the early church as it was in the
eighteenth century: "In those early times it was both wise and necessary to
show, in the establishment of outward forms of worship, some indulgence to
the ancient opinions, manners, and laws of the respective nations to whom
the gospel was preached . . . . In a word, the external forms of worship used
in the times of old, must necessarily have been regulated and modified
according to the character, genius, and manners of the different nations on
which the light of the gospel rose."[5] With a developed sense for the history of
ideas and action, Mosheim repeatedly described how changes in philosophy
and world view altered the interpretation of theology and the conception of
the church. In his *Historical Commentaries on the State of Christianity* and
his *Ecclesiastical History* he elaborated the idea suggested by Bayle that
Neoplatonic thought had recast Christianity in its own image. And in his
monographs on heresy (written as an answer to Arnold), Mosheim emphasized that religious beliefs were produced by man's desire to know and
explain systematically the causes of things; these beliefs were, in turn, shaped
by the spirit of the times.[6]

  The crucial element in Mosheim's redefinition of the church hinged on his
view of perception. Unlike western philosophes (e.g., Hume in his *Natural
History of Religion*), Mosheim refused to explain religious belief by reference
to sensation or experience alone.[7] He would have agreed with his slightly
younger contemporary Chladenius, who drew a distinction between sensation
(*Empfindung*) and experience (*Erfahrung*). According to Chladenius, experience was not direct perception but rather an interpretation of sensation,
achieved through the power of the *Einbildungskraft* acting on and from
sensation or formed by applying existing logic to make sensation comprehensible.[8] Consequently, experience was not primary but secondary, a
creation either of a deeper spiritual power or of accepted logical reasoning. In
an analogous fashion, Mosheim postulated a basic religious drive in human
nature, a universal spiritual category that preceded experience and directed it.
In effect, this spiritual drive was the unmoved mover, the inborn element that
continually impelled man to expand his religious consciousness. It was
definable not in positive answers embodied in church dogma but rather in a
cluster of basic questions, like those described in Mosheim's first essay on
heresy: "Who is the father and creator of Evil? Is Evil just as eternal as Good,
or was it created at a later time? . . . Through what strange occurrence is
Good so mixed with Evil that it is hard to decide which is which? . . . If the
forces of Evil have appropriated . . . areas from the forces of Good, where is
the Good's wisdom? Where is its power?"[9] The answers given to such

questions varied according to man's unique historical experience. In theory, though not always in practice, Mosheim proposed that all forms of worship are worthy of respect because they are concrete manifestations of man's eternal quest for religious understanding.[10] At the same time every temporal religious manifestation reflects man's basic weakness, his pettiness and his unfailing self-interest.

For Mosheim, the conflict between spiritual quest, institutionalized customs, and human weakness explained the continual process of struggle and renewal in ecclesiastical history, a dynamic clearly shown in his portrayal of the struggle between Calvin and Servetus.[11] Here Mosheim faced a topic that was eminently controversial and difficult enough to tax the powers of even a great historian. Contemporary judgments of Calvin and Servetus still mirrored the ideological and religious assumptions of the period. To the opponents of organized religion, Calvin was a cold-blooded killer and Servetus a guiltless martyr, one of the countless victims of religious intolerance. To the defenders of organized religion, Servetus was a *Schwärmer* ("religious fanatic") and a heretic who presented a real danger to religion. Mosheim refused to accept either view. He saw the struggle resulting from a unique conjunction of personal and suprapersonal forces; religious conviction, a universal feeling of uncertainty, personal character traits, and the particulars of Genevan politics all contributed to the tragic outcome. Mosheim approached his topic almost with the eyes of a Greek tragedian. No longer are there innocent martyrs and evil persecutors, no longer hypocritical men interested only in their self-interest; instead, idealistic belief, traditional reactions, and individual greatness and weakness all conjoin to push the conflict to its regrettable conclusion.

Mosheim employed every category of internal and external causation to set the scene for the conflict and define its parameters. With obvious sympathy he captured the mood of excitement, of indignation, of burning zeal that characterized the time and drove both Calvin and Servetus forward in their religious quest; he described the prevailing interest in witchcraft and astrology, which, acquired in childhood, affected even the greatest thinkers. Nor did he omit the political problems Calvin faced in his own city: "Calvin, despite the love and honor he had won in Geneva, did not have the whole city on his side. He saw himself surrounded by a strong group of enemies who would hardly let a chance slip by to pressure and provoke him. Some of them vehemently disagreed with his doctrine of predestination; others accused him of being despotic. Most of them were people who loved a free, uncontrolled, pleasant life and could not tolerate the strict regulations that Calvin in his zeal had introduced to battle disorder and depravity."[12]

But the battle between Calvin and Servetus could not be explained by general reasons alone; it was the individual characters of both participants which sealed the outcome. Mosheim recognized that both Calvin and Servetus were great men and great thinkers, impelled by a deep and valid religious concern. Yet their very greatness contained a demonic element that intrigued and frightened the Erasmian Mosheim, as is evident in the opening lines of his evaluation of Servetus's book on the Trinity. "What a furious passion! What a blind and shocking arrogance! But despite these faults, what impartial or fair reader could fail to see that the author of this book possessed an extraordinary mind. Who would not be amazed to learn that a young man of twenty or twenty-one had acquired so wide and deep a learning without the assistance of a teacher: so much had been read, digested, investigated, and reflected upon; so many things were sharply and correctly judged. Even more amazing, a total reformation of contemporary religion and philolophy is proposed with an extraordinary resoluteness."[13] Mosheim's evaluation of Calvin followed similar lines: Calvin too was brilliant and he too was driven by a passionate belief in the correctness of his views. In both these evaluations Mosheim reveals his attitude toward religious reformers, one that runs through all his writings on heresy. It was not their conception of religion alone which gave them power and made them effective, but also an unquenchable irrational drive that derived its power from an identification of God's will with their own individual self-interest. Herein lies the real tragedy of Calvin and Servetus: both equated their own feelings, emotions, and beliefs with the will of God.

Mosheim came to the conclusion that Calvin and Servetus were both *Schwärmer:* each transferred his hate of evil and sin to the other; each saw the other as an extraordinary heretic. In a sense, the two men were very similar; both loved honor more than anything else. "If even one of them had had the spirit of a Melanchthon or an Oecolampadius," the story would have been different.[14] But Mosheim sensed that such an "if" was impossible. A man of thought and action, such as Calvin, Servetus, or Luther, could not be a Melanchthon or an Erasmus. Visible in Mosheim's portrayal of the tragedy of Calvin and Servetus is the concept of the great historical figure; Mosheim disliked the characteristics of both leaders but he recognized their effect on history. At the end of his work he pleaded for forgiveness and understanding of these two major figures.[15]

2

The generation that followed Mosheim's extracted the emphasis upon spiritual causation from his writings, expanded it, and joined it to ideas derived from contemporary aesthetics, creating, in the process, a paradigm of historical explanation that could later be applied to secular history. One of the critical figures in this endeavor was Johann Salomo Semler, Halle theologian and New Testament scholar. Semler joined in his person the diverse religious strains of his time: he was the son of a Lutheran pastor with moderate leanings toward Pietism, a student of Sigmund Baumgarten, an admirer of Nicholas of Cusa, Calvin, and Richard Simon; he was drawn to spiritualist and mystical writers but repelled by unreflective Pietism. In his wide-ranging inquiries into New Testament exegesis, hermeneutics, and history, Semler breathed new life into the Halle theological faculty and hence into the university itself. He established a tradition of historical exegesis that broke both with the Pietism of August Hermann Francke and with the intellectualism of Wolff and his own mentor, Baumgarten. Along with Ernesti, Semler laid the foundations for historical hermeneutics and theology which led directly to Friedrich August Wolf, Schleiermacher, and Ferdinand Christian Baur.[16]

Four dominant themes establish the parameters of Semler's explanation of spiritual change: (1) his differentiation between "religion" and "theology" (e.g., between spirit and form), which assumed a reciprocal influence of one on the other; (2) his assumption that all products of human consciousness necessarily reflect the "local" conditions in which they are formed; (3) his idea that qualitative change entails a spiritual act against history and his belief that history can be overcome only through a knowledge of history; (4) his use of aesthetic concepts to explain Jesus' message. Semler announced and developed these themes in all his writings, sometimes emphasizing one, sometimes harmonizing all, but always with one major goal in mind: the idea that religion is a universal force in constant change. There is no such thing as a closed, immutable, perfect religion, just as there is no such thing as a perfect society. Religion, to be vital, must expand with man's consciousness, must answer the spiritual needs of each age in the language and thought of the age. If it does not, it remains an interesting, but lifeless, museum piece. Lurking beneath this belief was the assumption that religion, like every other product of man's consciousness, must be evaluated according to human standards. [17] The same hermeneutic principles and the same paradigm of explanation applied to both sacred and profane history. This assumption allowed German thinkers to apply ideas drawn from religious history to secular history. It also led to a later crisis in the Semler's theological thought; while he recognized the relativity of religious expression to historical situation, he still maintained that Christian revelation was divine and above rational explanation. His only recourse was an assertion of personal faith in Christ's resurrection and divinity.[18]

Semler's definition of religion established the context for his explanation of religious change. According to him, there are two sides to every religious manifestation, the external form embodied in dogma, organization, and ritual, and the internal, moral (or spiritual) apprehension of free individuals. Unlike Arnold, who saw a complete and irresolvable breach between the two, Semler felt that external forms were necessary and valid expressions of the universal moral drive; they were "absolutely indispensable,"[19] but they did not encompass the totality of man's moral experience: "The Christian religion includes the sum of the infinite levels of Christian conceptions and their application. . . . But each external religious community determines *one part* of these manifold conceptions, which it itself derived from the Bible, and expresses this part in a number of regulations determining the public and collective religious profession of its members. These doctrines are the immediate bands of such a community; the community, however, is and remains a single, special, immoral body, influenced by time and place and different from other communities."[20] Semler called these communities "immoral" in the sense that belonging to a certain confession does not ensure the moral excellence of the communicant. External form might help or hinder the attainment of an individual's moral awareness; it cannot assure it.[21] Each religious community (each objectified expression of a moral impulse) becomes a later hindrance to the further development of private moral expression. Man's concern with order, tranquillity, and uniformity makes specific historical forms oppressive to uninstitutionalized moral expressions. Consequently, tension between form and spirit eventually appears. Advocates of the inner religion develop their own vision and evolve their own language or dialect to express their convictions.[22] Religious change is effected through the conflict of the two parties, one representing accumulated historical tradition, the other, individual moral reinterpretation. This tension between community values and individual spirit, between form and freedom, provides the dynamic tension for historical change. It results in the creation of a new understanding of God's words which, when later institutionalized, serves as the historical tradition for further dynamic tension.

It might appear that Semler was here accepting Arnold's basic assumptions about the inevitable conflict between religion and theology, but actually he was contradicting them. Semler did not seek to portray the eternal battle between the forces of light and darkness; rather, he described the disagreements between people and groups with conflicting images of God's message. Though he opposed spirit to form, he recognized the existence of spirit in each form: "*Moral power, life, spirit, effect,* lie at the source of the Christian religion; history, memory, a dead stringing together of words and doctrines, cannot be held as the essence, as the finality and exercise, of the pure Christian teachings. Nevertheless, we must recognize that the *essentials* of the Christian religion — serious personal applications of Christian perception [*Erkenntnis*] — are and remain in all Christian parties, though in innumerable levels of *major* and *minor*."[23] The moral awareness, instead of existing in a hermetically sealed-off realm, is conditioned by and rooted in the historical tradition. It can be understood only within the context of that tradition, and because of its individual nature it cannot be adequately defined or described: "All historical or alien awareness handed down by tradition (historical belief) precedes the individual, living, moral, critical [*beurtheilende*] awareness (moral belief) .... The moral awareness, however, ... is never always the same, can never be the same, because of inevitable differences in individuals [*Individuorum*]."[24]

The nature of the conflict between spirit and historical form is further defined by Semler's second major assumption: every historical form mirrors the then existing conditions of life, and every theological formula applies traditionally accepted ideas to explain the mystery and majesty of God. [25] Since religion deals with man's relation to man, as well as with man's relation to God, extrareligious motives play a role in shaping every local religious form. The spirit of the times, climate, and social, political, and economic organization, the whole *Lebensart* ("life-style") of a people, leave their imprint on each objectified form of religion. At the same time, the forms of religious belief reciprocally influence and regulate social values. Society and religion cannot be separated: "All forms of public worship, the Jewish included, contain a single, accepted manner of worshiping God that reflects the unique experience of a nation from its origins on. Therefore, this religion belongs to the history of the nation or state and contains the invariable sum of its accumulated culture and the store of local interests that differentiate one people from another. Hence, public religion is unalterable, even for those who rule the people; for the rulers it was a means of maintaining a specified degree of external order within the state, insofar as possible." [26] Here Semler again transforms an idea propounded by Arnold: whereas Arnold denounced tying religion to society, Semler sees the coupling as an inevitable, though regrettable, fact of life.

Gottfried Achenwall and Johann David Michaelis also treated religion and society as interdependent phenomena. According to Achenwall, man can be investigated from three different angles: man as man (natural drives, passions, etc.), man as citizen, and man as an observer of religion. All three, however, are intertwined: "Here everything is in direct combination. The natural drives influence religion and the constitution, and these, in reverse, influence the natural drives. Each has an influence on the other." [27] Michaelis directed his investigations to showing how religious belief and organization are regulated by the local *sensus communis* and the *Lebensart* of the people, and how religious belief, in turn, limits social action. [28] In a like manner, Semler argued that even the greatest theologians, Luther and Calvin included, were constrained and influenced by the spirit of the times and the demands of civil polity and economic organization. [29]

Semler interpreted the history of religion in Leibnizian terms of process. The possible forms of religious comprehension consist of an infinite number of levels or steps; with the passage of time, there is a continual expansion of man's religious consciousness; the "continual change and succession in man's understanding" are part of God's plan. [30] "It is and remains God's wisest and most holy decree [*Ordnung*] that He rules and develops the human moral world as well as the physical world; hence, new conceptions, new combinations of reasons and proofs, must appear incessantly among Christians; it is, I repeat, God's order; it is the nature of a moral religion." [31] The human moral world, then is an analogue to the physical. It has its changes and revolutions just as does the physical world.[32] God's revelation is now seen as expansive, as a function of human development, embodied, in a sense, in history itself, and marked out by certain definite periods in which man's moral awareness broke the bounds of the temporal forms of historical religion. In effect, a change in religious consciousness entailed a wrenching denial of past history, a questioning of deeply ingrained values, attitudes, and traditions, which because of the interrelation between society and religion heralded a major social revolution.

All of the above assumptions meet in Semler's account of the birth and the early history of Christianity. Here Semler confronted the two crucial tasks facing Neologists: to incorporate historical relativism into a description of Christianity and to retain the divinity of Christ. As already mentioned, Semler was not totally successful. His solution to the second task resulted in a personal affirmation of his belief; to that he added an argument derived from his relativistic analysis of dogma: all proofs for or against Christ's divinity are ineffectual because all are founded on the presuppositions of the author and the intellectual assumptions of the time. Nevertheless, after making this point, Semler did offer a type of proof. If one wishes to advance some proof of Christ's divine mission, that proof lies in the moral (i.e., spiritual) nature of Christianity itself. Had not Christianity broken from the "national" awareness of the Jews to offer all mankind an expanded vision of God's plan, one capable of transcending its own historical limitations? In effect, Semler argued that the history of Christianity, its ability to offer continual material for an enhanced spiritual interpretation of its message, attested to its divine origins.[33] Even here we see how Neologists imparted a new meaning to Christian history. What once had to be explained away (the continual changes in Christian concepts, dogmatics, and ritual) now served as a sign of its perfection. Christianity was spiritual and hence divine because it could overcome each of its "historical, local, static forms [*stilstehenden Einkleidung*]."[34] Its perfection was a perfection-in-becoming, achieved through the action of the spirit on the given historical environment.

In his account of the rise of Christianity, Semler imaginatively used his newly won historical propositions to explain Christ's words and their effect. The New Testament, Semler contended, could be understood only when placed in its historical milieu. It was necessary to "portray the *actual ideas of the contemporaries* of Christ and the Apostles."[35] With an incomparable feeling for nuance, Semler did just that. He plunged into an investigation of the hopes, the fears, and the traditions of the Jewish sects that flourished immediately before Christ. He described the general atmosphere of crisis and the hopes for regeneration; he discussed the popularity of the messianic idea with all its variations, the increasing spiritualism of the Essenes, the general belief in magic and in raising the dead, the vague idea of a spiritual life after death contained in the concept of Elohim and the idea and use of baptism. According to Semler, two distinct groups of Jews existed prior to Christ's birth, the "Hebraic Jews, divided for a long time into many sects or parties, and the Hellenic, or foreign, Jews, who were also divided into many parties." [36] Despite intragroup differences, the two groups were distinguished from each other by the manner in which they interpreted the Bible. Hebraic Jews (e.g., Pharisees and Sadducees) used a literal interpretation, whereas Hellenic, or Alexandrian, Jews (e.g., Essenes) gave the Bible an allegorical meaning, applying its precepts "to all people." The contradiction between literal and allegorical interpretation (between history and spirit) set the stage for Christ's religious revolution, already presaged by John the Baptist.

Using an analytics derived from aesthetics, Semler boldly interpreted Jesus' words and the religious revolution Jesus wrought. Any effective revolution, Semler thought, must strike at a vital core of shared experience; it must use words, images, and ideas common to the people and reorder them so that a new awareness emerges. Moreover, it must affect not only the intellect but also the *Seelenkräfte*, the irrational, "voluntative" substance of life; its message must speak to all levels of feeling and experience. For this very reason, every effective revolution is also a limited one, constricted by the elements that led to its success. Hence, Semler maintained that Jesus began a new spiritual movement, which he did not, and could not, complete. [37] Christ's words were directed toward the Jews of his own time; they reflected the existing mentality of the period; they combined elements drawn from Hebraic and Greco-Jewish ideas and traditions. "The *Lehrart* and the manner of proof Jesus employed with the Jews obviously were particularly suited to them." [38] Jesus himself was both Jew and non-Jew; he was Jewish in the sense that his manner of speech, his clothing, and his character all accorded with the Jewish national character. [39] At the same time, he was a spiritual revolutionary who joined together a number of Jewish ideas to create an ideal different from any before. [40] Here Semler's reliance on aesthetics and Leibnizian philosophy is obvious. Jesus is evaluated in the same manner as the "original genius," the man who, according to Michaelis, is able to educate his people by combining knowledge with poetry, or who, in Iselin's words, is able to "influence the *Denkungsart* of a whole people and thereby effect a whole sequence of revolutions and events." [41] The new vision is determined not so much by the sum of its parts but by the total conjuction, by the *Zusammenhang*, of all its elements. To paraphrase Alexander Baumgarten, Jesus gave his generation a sensuous representation of a perfect spiritual religion. Because Jesus' teachings were phrased in the local conceptions of the time, it is necessary to separate the literal teachings from the spirit behind them; the divine kernel must be extracted from its dead historical shell.

What applied to Jesus applied even more to the apostles. They too were men of their times who propounded a new creed in language and images drawn from their own tradition or the tradition of their hearers. Each apostle conveyed Christ's message to diverse audiences from his own viewpoint. [42] The inevitable lack of agreement among the followers of Christ led Semler to advance an idea alien to earlier Lutheran writers; he expressly denied the idea of a pure and golden age of Christianity where every aspect of life operated according to the simple principles of primitive Christianity. There is nothing of the yearning for the past that was evident in Arnold and even, to a degree, in Mosheim. Luther's call to reestablish the Apostolic church in all its purity was a chimera; more than that, it was an impossibility. We may understand the past, but we cannot become first-century Christians again. And even if we could, we would not want to, for the spiritual understanding of Christ's message is deeper than it was in the early years of Christianity.

Unhampered by the need to describe a golden period of Christian purity, Semler showed that the same tensions existing in the pre-Christian era continued in the apostolic era. Just as there were two basic groups among the Jews, so were there two basic groups among the early Christians: the Hebraic, or Palestinian, Christians and the Hellenic, or Alexandrian, Christians. The Palestinian Christians, led by James, sought to preserve as much of the Jewish tradition as possible; the Alexandrian Christians, led by Paul, sought to join Christian concpets to the Greek ideas of *logos, monogenes,* and *prototokos* in order to make Christianity a universal spiritual religion. [43] Once again Semler returned to his apposition of individuality to community values, of freedom to form, and used the tension between them to explain Christian history. This theme is the constant in Semler's view of history. At all times there will be a majority who are satisfied with a "single external education," who prefer conformity to pluralism; there will also always appear a smaller group who recognize "the infinite inexhaustibility of God's power" in both the physical and the human moral world. [44] The latter, however, cannot exist without the former. It is only their reaction to the limitation of form which leads them to break with form. Thus one party defines the other; they stand in a symbiotic relation, and no matter how violently the break effected by the smaller group, enough of the old will remain for others to establish a new and repressive conformity. The revolutionaries of yesterday become the conservatives of tomorrow. Strangely enough, Semler himself suffered this fate. During the 1760s and 1770s, Semler, Michaelis, and Ernesti led the Neologist reformation of theology and hermeneutics. Semler's fame for free and independent thinking was so widespread that whenever scholars argued over which of the two most renowned eighteenth-century German universities, Halle or Göttingen, was freer, the defenders of Halle used Semler as their trump. By the late 1780s, however, Semler thought reform had gone too far, and he retreated. To almost everyone's amazement, he supported the repressive Wöllner Edict of 1788. He spent the rest of his life in relative obscurity, busying himself with an investigation of alchemy, distrusted by both his former conservative enemies and by his former liberal allies.

In Semler's work all the elements of spiritual causation employed by the Aufklärers in their historical explanations appear, sometimes explicitly, other times implicitly. In distinguishing between spirit and history, Semler rejected a realist (he called it a naturalist) explanation of historical change. The dynamics of change are explicable in terms of spirit acting on a given historical environment, even though environment limits and regulates the spirit. Semler did not treat spirit as a rational category; he never equated it with mind or with logic. Rationality was too limited; it constituted only a part of spirit, for it systematized the traditional knowledge of a given historical period. According to Semler, spirit is life, action, effect, *Gemüt*, terms he usually placed in apposition in order to create a general impression, not a rationally delineated definition. Spirit can probably best be described as an energy, a vital force encompassing the whole gamut of rational and irrational impulses. Here Semler stood on the same ground as Winckelmann, though his future-directed hermeneutics differed radically from Winckelmann's idealization of the past. Both men looked behind the creation (either a religious ideal or a work of art) in order to discern the energy that led to its creation.[45]

3

Semler's use of spirit as an active historical force attests to the strong irrational strain running through his work and that of his contemporaries. Spirit and its individual manifestations are inexplicable, indefinable, ineffable; they are there to be reexperienced, not rationally defined. It was this recognition of irrationality which led to the Aufklärers' use of spiritual causation, their conception of the *Ideenwirkung,* and their increasing fascination with the original genius. According to the Aufklärers' evolving pattern of historical explanation, qualitative historical change occurred through a combination of determinate and indeterminate forces. The determinate elements were those categories of external causation already discussed; the indeterminate were the spiritual elements. Material and external forces established the limits of possible change while spiritual elements gave it direction and impulse.

The Aufklärers believed effective change could occur only when material conditions allowed. To use their terminology, the times and the situation had to be right; basic contradictions between values and material life had to exist before qualitative change could take place. Thus, Gatterer could remark that had Muhammad appeared a hundred years earlier, he would not have been the founder of a major religion reaching from Lisbon to Samarkand. The Prophet's immense success stemmed from existing dissensions and divisions in religion and in the state.[46] Yet these contradictions alone did not determine the course of change; the spiritual act, serving as both catalyst and directing impulse, was "the spark that set everything afire."[47] In Heeren's words, every revolution (used in the broad sense) requires "a great moral impulse; it requires an idea that seems great and magnificent to the era, one that calls forth a united effort for its realization, in order to awaken the spirit and open up a new sphere for its activity."[48] The difference between this moral impulse and a logical conclusion lay in the freedom and irrationality of the moral impulse. It was free because it did not necessarily follow from the already given; in this sense, it was new. It was irrational because its effect was as visceral as it was intellectual, that is, it moved all the *Seelenkräfte*. It captured the imagination of high and low and gave people a path by which they could channel their hopes, their fears, and their frustrations. It allowed everyone to see in its fulfillment a realization of both self-interest and idealism. For this very reason, however, every great spiritual impulse leads to ends not originally proclaimed; the moral impulse provides the energy, the drive, for a goal never achieved.[49]

It was in this sense that Spittler explained the history of the medieval hierarchy and that Heeren, Spittler's student, described the effects of the Crusades.[50] Both men dealt with the same era (mid-eleventh to mid-sixteenth century), and while they investigated different, though related, subjects, their overall judgments were almost identical. Both saw the period immediately preceding the middle of the eleventh century as one of energy, unrest, and crisis. All the elements needed for revolution were present: increased trade was undermining agrarian patterns, traditional ties were being questioned, and new forms of education were emerging. The desire for reform was the ruling idea of the time. This desire was satisfied by Gregory VII, who through his actions and ideas gave Europe a new moral impulse. Gregory was "a genius, . . . a pope who finally had a plan, who acted from a grand design."[51] He "belonged to the small group of mortals. . ., who could understand their age in all its connections, who recognized all its strengths and weaknesses, and who built their bold plans upon this knowledge."[52] As with all moral revolutions, the effects of the one begun by Gregory were manifold and contradictory. They led to the Crusades, which Heeren, paraphrasing Gatterer, interpreted as a new *Völkerwanderung* ("migration of peoples").[53] The Crusades, in the long run, tied the three parts of the Mediterranean world together again; they expanded commerce and riches, led to the rise of the city, influenced the growth of the vernacular and the expansion of knowledge, and finally helped prepare the ground for the overthrow of the very system that had generated them. According to Spittler, Gregory's revolution also encouraged the growth of the universities, a development that had numerous effects: at first, the universities strengthened papal power; then (through the propagation of Roman law) they extended their support to the secular powers. The universities came to occupy a middle position between the contending powers; wooed by both, they were subject to neither, and hence they developed into the one institution from which an independent moral attack against the papacy could be launched.[54]

Nevertheless, the primary effect of Gregory's reforms was the strengthening and transformation of the papal hierarchy. Gregory gave the papacy a new mission, a great idea: "that the pope is the vicar of Christ, and as such is elevated above all secular powers."[55] Gregory's transformation of the papacy determined papal policies for hundreds of years despite variations of character and background in the popes that followed Gregory.[56] The papacy's new mission led, in turn, to the titanic battle between church and state, "a battle unique in history, because it was not so much a battle of arms as of talent."[57] Both Spittler and Heeren believed the contours of medieval history were established by the extension of papal power, with its far-reaching effects on belief, thought, action, and custom, and by the response of the medieval monarchies to this extension.

The history of Church and state became paradigmatic for the history of the Middle Ages. Both Spittler and Heeren traced the rise and decline of medieval papal power as beginning with Gregory, reaching its apogee under Innocent III, and declining during the Babylonian Captivity and the Great Schism; both men described the epic confrontations between Gregory and Henry IV, Innocent III and Frederick II, and Boniface VIII and Philip the Fair; and both portrayed the increasing feeling of despair, dissatisfaction, unrest, and energy at the end of the fifteenth century. The conditions for another revolution were present. Everywhere cries for reform were heard; there was an increase in mysticism, a series of attacks against the Church, unrest in the cities, and a recovery of learning. Spittler and Heeren agreed upon the one event that forced Europe into a new course: it was the Reformation as proclaimed by Luther. Like Gregory, Luther created a new moral impulse rooted in the experience of his whole society. Heeren and Spittler minimized the importance of the Renaissance in effecting this change and maintained that the new revolution was not inevitable. The reasoning behind these popular, though not universal, conclusions suggests how historians applied spiritual causal explanation (as used by Semler) to secular history.

Of all these assumptions, the one dealing with the Rennaissance is the most surprising. It has long been held that Enlightenment thinkers were fascinated by the Renaissance and saw themselves as its heirs and continuers. Evidence for this assumption can be found everywhere, especially in Voltaire's description of the Renaissance as one of the four golden ages of man. As Peter Gay has pointed out in his essay on the Enlightenment, there is little doubt that thinkers of the period admired the Renaissance. As to Germany, however, it is difficult to support two conplementary conclusions drawn by Gay: (1) that Enlightenment thinkers considered themselves heirs of the "pagan" Renaissance; (2) that Enlightenment historians credited the Renaissance with destroying the Middle Ages. The first proposition would have shocked the Aufklärers, most of whom spent considerable time combating anti-Christian assumptions. The second proposition could be maintained, but only through a shift in definition; instead of the Renaissance, "era of the Renaissance," or even better, "era when the recovery of learning occurred [*Wiederherstellung der Wissenschaften*]," should be used. The concept of the Renaissance we hold today was not the same as that contained in the weaker expression "recovery of learning." When the Aufklärers spoke of this recovery, they defined it as a quickening of interest in the classics. It was seen as one of the many factors working in conjunction to change the constitution of Europe. Schlözer described these factors in his usual pithy manner: "Then [in the fifteenth and sixteenth centuries] a host of new discoveries came together in our small part of the world, altered Europe's form [*Gestalt*], and through this transformation influenced the rest of the world. Paper, powder, and billbroking had already been developed, but only when joined to other discoveries and events did they lead to a revolution." Among these other developments Schlözer listed the following: "Gutenberg invented printing. The Osmanli Turks (already rulers of a majority of the lands wrested from Byzantium by the Arabs) finally conquered Constantinople itself. They created a power great enough to threaten Europe, and they chased Greek art and science to the West. . . . Diaz discovered the route to the East Indies around the Cape; Columbus discovered America; and the Reformation toppled the pope."[58]

Why were the discovery, editing, and circulation of a huge store of classical knowledge considered only a contributory factor in Europe's transformation? In Johann Christoph Gatterer's view, "These learned treasures came into circulation, but the capital was not noticeably increased; it remained mere *capital of the ancients*: one just divided it amongst each other. Soon there appeared all kinds of *monopolists* who dealt exclusively with ancient wisdom, sometimes naming themselves after Aristotle, Pythagoras, Plato, Cicero, or some other ancient author."[59] Spittler answered the question thus: "(1) Most of those who became enlightened by the classics became atheists, if not real heathens. . . . They considered contemporary religion as nothing but a tissue of errors and priestly deceit. One did not take the time to seek after nuggets of gold in such a terrible pile of rubbish. . . . (2) All those men enlightened by the classics chose the common theme of ridiculing the priests [*Pfaffen*] and the lazy-bellied monks. But if the clergy ever showed that they could have these *schönen Geister* burned, then the *schönen Geister* retreated. They were too *schön to allow themselves to be burned!* (3) Classical literature improves only forms of expression; moreover, it encourages one to think coextensively, allowing one to be at home in the classics and at the same time to be a totally unenlightened man. Classical literature is merely an inducement to further, true enlightenment; in itself it does not enlighten."[60]

Gatterer and Spittler, though differing in tone, make the same point. Classical knowledge, in itself, was ineffectual and, as propagated by Renaissance humanists, it was impotent, because it failed to generate the visceral reaction of great moral impulses. It remained merely a product of the intellect, leaving the emotions, the passions, and the dark feelings and intuitions untouched. It was a superrefined product of cold reason developed by a small and exclusive group, the beaux esprits, who, dependent upon their patrons and fearing the church, never really went to the root of the problems of their age. Instead of attacking the system they directed their critiques against externals, against abuses. The critiques themselves were made partly because it was the thing to do, partly from an intellectual commitment to truth, but never from the passionate conviction that would brave death. In the Aufklärers' eyes, classical humanists were guilty of the same faults as medieval Scholastics and the new scholastics of the seventeenth and early eighteenth centuries. They withdrew from life in its broader dimensions and thereby expended increasingly large amounts of energy investigating the miniscule and the unimportant. The humanists, the Aufklärers contended, failed to offer their generation pragmatic understanding, that is, direct experiential awareness, an *anschauende Erkenntnis*.

The negative description of the Renaissance served to highlight what the Aufklärers believed the Reformation had accomplished. The Reformation did proclaim a "great new interest." It made a new experiential framework possible because it provided a focal point for a cluster of feelings and frustrations generated over a long period of time and derived originally from a number of different sources. Thus its power sprang the bounds of the religious and the theological to touch and animate all aspects of life: "Religion replaced superficial personal interest as the driving force of politics; soon it was hard to find a political interest that was not at the same time more or less a religious interest, a political party that was not at the same time more or less a religious party, yes, even a war that was not at the same time more or less a religious war."[61] It did not matter, Heeren said, how correct his contemporaries found the teachings of the Reformation; his point was that people in that period saw religion as the vital core that informed all other endeavors. Hence the passion, the enthusiasm, the fanaticism engendered by the Reformation; hence its wide-ranging and indeterminate effects.

Heeren, Spittler, Gatterer, Wegelin, and Iselin, and all the other Aufklärers who saw the Reformation as critical approached the problem from the Protestant point of view. Despite the one-sidedness of their position, there is still something compelling about their vision. Though proclaiming the importance of ideas in history, they considered the *Ideenwirkung* as essentially irrational, as operating on the spirit, not on the mind alone. They rejected the catastrophe theory of causal explanation and maintained that qualitative historical change results from popular movements, which, though long in gestation, finally break with such force that nothing can contain or direct them. Such movements are like floods or earthquakes, whose extent defies immediate perception.[62] By tracing the power of popular movements to an overriding idea, these Aufklärers asserted that change was indeterminate, dependent upon the way the idea had been formulated and upon the character of those responsible for the formulation.

The Aufklärers also asserted the importance of the individual in history; it was the irreplaceable original genius, men such as Gregory VII and Luther, who, through words, actions, and character, forced their generations to look at the world with new eyes. The Aufklärers' conception of the original genius, derived directly from the religious and aesthetic assumptions of the time, lay at the core of their assertion of historical indeterminacy. Like Johann Gottfried Herder, who drew his ideas from the same source, the Aufklärers saw the original genius as "the creator of a people; he gives it a world to contemplate, he holds its soul in his hands." [63] While acknowledging the lawlike effect of certain causal factors and the importance of social environment, they could not accept the idea that Moses, Socrates, and Luther, let alone Jesus, were not unique, that their appearance could be explained merely as the concluding chapter to a predictable chain of events. Spittler made it a major theme of his *Geschichte der Hierarchie* to deny that Luther's reforms were "the final dosage of a cure" already begun by a number of fifteenth-century *testes veritatis* ("witnesses of truth") who had announced the same message. [64] Spittler confronted the difficult questions of defining what makes a "great historical figure" great and determining the degree to which a great or revolutionary figure is indebted to his predecessors and his time. He concentrated on the program and the character of three groups usually cited as Luther's predecessors — humanists, mystics, Hussites — and sought to demonstrate that while these groups prepared the ground for Luther, they lacked the necessary qualifications ever to have effected a positive revolution. Working from Spittler's answer, we can construct a picture of the characteristics he and his contemporaries ascribed to the revolutionary personality.

We have already seen why Spittler dismissed classical education as a possible starting point for effective change. In addition, Spittler believed that humanists lacked the necessary phsychological characteristics of the revolutionary personality. Claiming that most of them came to their critical stance only after a long and enervating grubbing through the classics, Spittler saw them as a group of aged men lacking the restless determination of youth. Because of age or temperament, humanists did not have "the fury [*das Stürmende*] and stubbornness to overcome all obstacles." They were too ready to "compromise for the sake of peace." [65] By emphasizing the inflexibility of great reformers, Spittler both confirmed Mosheim's evaluation of Calvin and Servetus and reversed Mosheim's value judgments. Whereas Mosheim looked to Erasmus and Melanchthon as true guides to religious improvement, Spittler dismissed them as ineffectual. They had lacked one of the necessary characteristics of the revolutionary personality, the quality of recklessness, of unflinching assuredness in the correctness of one's beliefs, of indifference to the consequences of one's acts. In Spittler's own words, the great reformer is by nature a *Stürmer*. [66] The difference between Mosheim's view and Spittler's shows how far the Aufklärung had gone in recognizing and accepting the inevitable irrational underpinning of action. By the 1780s German thinkers were agreeing that the actions of a true reformer must spring from the whole of his united powers, powers that defy logical explanation. And it must be remembered that Spittler cannot, by any stretch of the imagination, be placed in the camp of the *Stürmer und Dränger*. The real differences between the *Stürmer und Dränger* and the Aufklärers lay not in the opposition between reason and emotion, but rather in the degree of emphasis accorded each. As Hermann Hettner said long ago, the major theme in the literature and thought of the Aufklärung was the tension between head and heart.

Spittler's fascination with the unbridled energy and dogmatic determination of the man of action accounts in part for his criticism of mysticism. Mystics could never have energized a generation to rebel decisively against an existing structure because they renounced, or were indifferent to, participation in worldly affairs: "All *mystics,* especially the followers of great mystics, *are not active enough.* . . . He who has experienced the sweetness of remaining in the stillness of his speculations, of remaining in a sphere that is not in motion, in a sphere that does not turn, will never be great in the affairs of the world."[67] Spittler's second critique of mystics, founded on the Aufklärers' rejection of sensational theories of perception, emphasized apperception and intellectual construction. Not only were mystics inactive, but also their view of religion was too fleeting, too personal, too closely linked to their own sensations and experiences. Hence the mystical vision is locked within the ambit of indefinable sensate interpretation: "Mysticism is as temporally bound [*periodisches*] as the sentimental novel. Everything that is based on sensation alone is transitory; consequently, when it appears that a current of feeling is about to break forth, it soon loses its strength and subsides. The warmth of feeling is not of long duration."[68] Mysticism, claimed Spittler, lacked external intellectual form; it ignored dogma and theology and for that reason proved incapable of toppling existent structures. Spittler, like Semler, emphasized the necessity of combining form and freedom, of giving structure to one's sensations and feelings. The very word "reformation" attested to the necessity of creating an alternative form. As long as structure is not attacked at its roots, it has the power and the resiliency to survive. At best, mystics could have introduced a slightly better morality, which probably would have influenced the personal lives of the popes but would not have touched the hierarchical structure and the theology of the Church.[69]

True to the precepts of the Aufklärung, Spittler's image of the revolutionary envisioned a man combining the drive of the *Stürmer,* the spirit of the visionary, and the mind of the extraordinary intellectual. Mind, will, and spirit had to be equally strong and had to work in conjunction. This position explains Spittler's criticism of the Hussites. According to him, they failed to offer a viable alternative to Catholic theology and dogma. The cry for communion in both kinds did not have the universal power of attraction necessary to shake the foundations of papal power. The Hussites, Spittler claimed, were merely *Stürmer,* men who recognized the inequities of the time but who were unable to create a constructive and consistent structure to overcome these inequities. They were "negative thinkers" whose appeal was rooted in the local conditions of Bohemia.

By the end of the Aufklärung, German historians had evolved a typology of the great historical figure. It described both the figure's character and his sphere of action. According to the Aufklärers, great historical figures demonstrated certain recognizable characteristics, despite differences owing to time and place. Heeren gives an example in his comparison of Gregory VII and Luther: "Even if Luther toppled the structure Gregory had founded, were they not both reformers? Both had the same conviction, the same courage, the same crushing power [*zermalmenden Kraft*]. But the Italian joined to these a cunning and therefore a methodological bent [*Planmaßigkeit*] of which the ingenuous [*bieder*] German had no idea. Still, Luther's efforts achieved as much as those of Gregory. Is this not further proof that character is more dominant than cunning [*List*] in effecting great revolutions?"[70]

Character alone did not suffice to define the great historical figure. Equally important was the figure's sphere of action and effect. Like so many later thinkers who have confronted this problem, the Aufklärers could not, nor did they wish to, escape the moral dimensions of the question. No matter how *stürmisch,* brilliant, or original a historical personage, the Aufklärers refused to call him reformer, original genius, or great historical figure unless he had sought to resolve the basic spiritual, or moral, questions of the time. The Aufklärers were very careful to distinguish between famous conquerors, who acted merely from the dictates of pride, egotism, or self-interest, and spiritual leaders, who embodied in their persons the heart and soul of their times. Schlözer's disparaging remarks about the conqueror who marched to the beat of the drum and his praise of apostles, wise men, and inventors was one sentiment with which virtually all his contemporaries, including his archrival Herder, agreed.

Heeren incorporated Schlözer's distinction in his essay on the effects of the Reformation. He differentiated between revolutions instigated by conquerors, which he called purely martial [*rein-kriegerische*] revolutions, and revolutions whose causes lay in the moral nature of man, which he called moral-political revolutions. The causes and the nature of the former are simple to understand. They stem from the desires of individuals who, "slaves to their passions, appear as conquerors, subjugate states, and on the rubble erect a throne of greatness."[71] War initiates such revolutions and war remains their immediate effect; the first and last goal of martial revolutions is acquisition: "Events such as these can be interesting because of their effects; in their causes they are not, because they arise from a single, and at heart an impure, source, namely, the human lust for power."[72] Moral-political revolutions are "different because their source resides in the moral nature of man. Changes are effected through a slowly expanding *Volksidee* that becomes a ruling idea and stands in direct contrast to the existing order of things. As soon as the new reality is expressed and established, it causes enormous convulsions and great changes."[73] Unlike martial revolutions, moral-political revolutions are interesting not only for their effects but also for their causes: "In general, they are long in preparation, and this preparation goes unnoticed" until they break forth like a powerful torrent smashing all restraints.[74] It is the great historical figure who calls forth these revolutions by giving the general *Volksidee* form, content, and direction. He establishes parameters for a development that takes "centuries before all its effects are discernible to the eyes of the observer."[75]

As conceived by the Aufklärers, revolutionary, or qualitative, change occurred after a long period of gestation. Increasing contradictions between idea and reality, values and action, created an atmosphere of crisis that often led to a violent explosion and a reformation of existing structure. These changes were not normal, nor were they frequent. The Aufklärers' conception of revolutionary change faintly reminds one of Ortega y Gasset's explanation of critical change. And in the work of men such as Gatterer, Schlözer, Pütter, and Heeren, there is a hint that they envisioned the existence of long structural periods, beginning and ending with critical change, with each period having its own social, political, and intellectual configurations. I do not mean to imply that the Aufklärers were direct predecessors of later thinkers such as Fernand Braudel or Otto Brunner, but rather to suggest that the Aufklärers were beginning to grapple with problems common to modern historical thinking.

4

The model the Aufklärers evolved to deal with revolutionary change did not satisfy their need to explain normal historical change; one of their basic assumptions was that slow, imperceptible change can and must occur. When confronted with the task of describing change within a given structural framework, they placed less emphasis upon the work of specific individuals and more upon three differentiated, though interrelated, spiritual categories: the spirit of the times, national character, and the spirit of groups or corporations. All three categories were visible in the intellectual, psychological, and institutional developments of the age. Taken together, they constituted the historical tradition against which the group or the persons under study had to be measured. These categories, however, were not identical. Within any given historical tradition a number of contradictions existed among the spirit of the times, national character, and the spirit of corporations and groups. These contradictions created a continual dynamic tension which in its action and interaction helped to propel history forward. The interaction established what Gatterer called the spirit of events (*Geist der*

Begebenheiten), which the historian had to portray in an immediate manner (*anschauend darzustellen*).[76] As Spittler said, one should think himself into the times (*man denke sich in diese Zeiten hinein*) one was describing.[77] To think oneself into the past meant, above all, to grasp the general attitudes of the time, to understand the real psychological and spiritual determinants of the age. Only then can one appreciate the way in which ideas, values, and opinions are translated into action.

The attempts of the Göttingen jurist Johann Stephan Pütter to explicate German constitutional history offer a typical example of how the Aufklärers described the importance of values, ideas, and opinions in effecting normal historical change. In many ways, Pütter's effort to reform German legal studies forms an analogue to Semler's attempt to resolve the contradiction between dogmatic and Pietist theology. Like his contemporary (Semler and Pütter were both born in 1725), Pütter strove to avoid both a one-sided emphasis upon dogmatic theory and a present-minded concentration on practice. The first approach was advocated by the admirers of Pufendorf and especially by those trained by the Halle professor Ludewig, who consciously used speculative history to support the claims of the Prussian monarchy. The second approach found its most articulate spokesman in Johann Jakob Moser, whose legal academy at Hanau (founded in 1749) served as the focal point for those who denied the efficacy of theory and proclaimed the supremacy of practice.

Pütter chose a historical analysis of theory and practice as a means of resolving the contradiction between the two approaches. In his wide-ranging inquiries into German legal history, Pütter dealt extensively with the reception of Roman law in the Middle Ages and its enormous effect on the course of German historical development. The reception of Roman law appeared to him as central in understanding German constitutional history. Pütter employed all the Aufklärers' categories of spiritual causation to explain how and why Roman law became the general law of the land and what its acceptance meant for later constitutional development. According to Pütter, the necessary precondition for the reception of Roman law was made possible by the acceptance in the eleventh century of the translation theory: the kaiser was seen as the direct heir of the Roman emperors, the German Empire as the unbroken continuation of the Roman Empire. Only then could one accept Roman law as a local law instead of as a foreign importation.[78] Pütter, like Voltaire, Pufendorf, and Jean Bodin before him, denied the validity of the translation theory; to him it was a historical error propagated by an age with little sense for history.[79] Instead of a *translatio*, Pütter spoke of a *renevatio*, an *Erneuerung*, of the imperial idea.[80] That Pütter tied the introduction of Roman law to a *renevatio* of the imperial idea shows that, by the middle of the eighteenth century, the habit of assuming an unbroken continuity between the Holy Roman Empire and the Roman Empire had lost much of its force. Nevertheless, the fact that Pütter continually returned to the question in all his works, that he repeatedly asserted the fallacy of the translation theory, also shows that many Germans, even well-read ones, still tenaciously clung to the idea. The difference between Pütter's denial of the translation theory and Voltaire's is, however, that Pütter, while denying the juridical and political reality of the concept, recognized the psychological reality of the idea for medieval society. He saw it as his task to explain why the translation theory had achieved such widespread acceptance.

Pütter located the reason for the acceptance of the translation theory in the general religious and political ideas of the eleventh century, that is, in the spirit of those times. Although he traced the beginning of the concept to the coronation of Charlemagne in 800, Pütter argued that neither Charlemagne, the pope, nor the Roman populace considered the Frankish Empire the continuation of the Roman. On the contrary, Charlemagne and his contemporaries thought in terms of a renovation of the western Roman Empire. Charlemagne, Pütter contended, was always careful to distinguish among his titles of Roman Emperor, King of the Franks, and King of the Lombards. The empire ruled by Charlemagne was a German empire; the title Roman Emperor was something extra, a gift of the *populus Romanus,* who conferred upon him the title *advocati urbis et ecclesiae.* The tie between the Roman and German Empires was a personal, not a real, one.[81] As time went on, however, later Holy Roman emperors were not so careful to make these distinctions. Otto I, who renewed the German connections with Rome, let his other titles drop and called himself merely Roman Emperor.[82] By the late eleventh century, the equation of the German Empire with the Roman Empire had become complete. Nevertheless, Pütter ascribed the universal popularity of the imperial idea not to the actions of the kaisers but to the influence of two ruling opinions of the eleventh century: the idea of the four world monarchies as contained in the Book of Daniel and the theory of the two swords.

The idea of the four world monarchies, Pütter argued, had so strong an influence because it formed the core of the eleventh century's historical consciousness. It established the framework by which man ordered past, present, and future. Its strength derived from its religious underpinnings. In an age when religion infused all aspects of life, it was necessary to turn to an idea of history supported by biblical authority: "Once one begins fully to believe, as people at that time really did, that according to Daniel's prophecy Rome was the fourth monarchy, destined to exist until the end of the world," then it was inevitable that one would believe "that Augustus, Constantine, and Justinian were the predecessors of Charlemagne, Otto the Great, and all succeeding kaisers and that they all stood in the same relation to one another. To doubt the truth of this notion would have entailed the rejection of a universally accepted historical system [*Lehrgebäude der Geschichte*] which was inextricably intertwined with the structure of religious belief [*Lehrgebäude der Religion*]."[83] The theory of the two swords reinforced the tendency to equate the German and Roman Empire by singling out the kaiser as preeminent among rulers. It ascribed a dual responsibility for the affairs of the world: the pope was accountable for man's spiritual life, the kaiser for his earthly life. According to Pütter, the joining of these two religiously supported ideas invariably led to the acceptance of the translation theory and the image of the kaiser as ruler of the world. As Srbik has noted, Pütter was one of the first to probe the ideologic foundations of the medieval imperial idea and to show its basic religious kernel.[84]

Pütter saw the acceptance of the translation theory as the necessary condition for the reception of Roman law in Germany: "Justinian's code found entrance into Germany because people believed that Germany belonged to the Roman Empire and the kaiser was Justinian's successor. The kaiser was the ruler of the world and imperial law was the law of all Christendom."[85] Although the translation theory explained why the law was so readily acknowledged, it did not suffice to explain how Roman law was introduced into Germany; Pütter insisted that before the eleventh century Roman law was not indigenous to Germany, as it was to Italy. Consequently, he turned to a more specific explanation to account for its introduction. He singled out one group and one institution as critical for its propagation: the scholars and the newly founded Italian universities. Like Spittler after him, Pütter made the university one of the critically important institutions in the shaping of medieval life.[86]

Both Pütter and Spittler believed that the general corporate spirit of medieval universities emphasized rational models of thought. Each medieval university had its own specialities. The Germans who wished to study law streamed to the south, especially to Bologna. There the study of Roman law had been developed, partly because of a living tradition of that law, but also because Roman law offered a rationalistic alternative to the seeming chaos of customary law. In a sense, the wide popularity of Roman law corresponded to the medieval infatuation with scholastic philosophy; in both, speculation suppressed the study of history and custom. Needless to say, both Pütter and Spittler disapproved of this tendency, which lasted, Pütter said, well into the seventeenth century.[87]

According to Pütter, the young, eager, and generally city-bred medieval lawyers returned to Germany convinced of the excellence of Roman law and actively proclaimed its superiority over common usage. Soon Roman law was disseminated throughout Germany by those *Stände* whose *Denkungsart* was most amenable to the logical postulates of Roman law. The first to accept Roman law were scholars and clerics, men trained to think in logical and speculative categories. Roman law struck roots first in the cities, then on the land, earlier in the plains and lowlands than in the mountains. The *Stand* least receptive to Roman law proved to be the high aristocracy. The acceptance of Roman law was finally sealed by the establishment of the *Reichskammer-*

gericht as the general court of the Empire; in it Roman law ruled supreme. [88] Pütter explained the transmission of knowledge in terms suggestive of a sociology of knowledge.

In Pütter's description of the reception of Roman law, two elements basic to his conception of change are discernible. First, Pütter did not welcome the spread of Roman law. In his eyes indigenous German law, which drew its authority from custom and usage, served the needs of medieval Germany better than Roman law. German law reflected the German national character: "I think the true situation is that long before Roman law established itself, Germany had its own *Gewohnheitsrecht,* which sprang from the *Denkungsart* of the German peoples. The *Gewohnheitsrecht* was deeply rooted in Germany's whole constitution, partly in its climate, and in everything that was common to Germany's situation. Hence the Germans did not require written books of law." German law was natural, known to everyone through daily experience; Roman law, on the other hand, was strange and foreign to the common man. [89] Second, Pütter maintained that Roman law never totally supplanted indigenous German law. The reception of Roman law had created a dynamic conflict between custom and innovation: "It was unavoidable that these codes and their glosses, all of which stemmed from foreign soil, would immediately come into conflict with the totally different German customary law and soon even with the unique constitution of the German Empire." [90] According to Pütter, the conflict between foreign law and native law established the parameters of succeeding German legal development. In its intellectual implications it was a conflict between abstract reason and local experience, between oral tradition and written systematization, between general intellectual assumptions and *Lokalvernunft.* In human terms it entailed a conflict between the learned doctors of law and the historically minded "Teutsche Biedermänner." The former were dedicated to a rootless and sterile rationalism; the latter drew their wisdom from a tradition "passed on to them from a long line of forebears." That tradition was founded on "customs and usages that were, by nature, moderate." [91] In its most general terms, the conflict between Roman law and *Gewohnheitsrecht* was a conflict between totally different Weltanschauungen.

The results of the conflict were many. Pütter, like his colleague Michaelis, considered law, whether Roman law, German *Gewohnheitsrecht,* or the law of Moses, a reflection of a specific social order and national character. [92] With the increasing acceptance of Roman law, especially in the sphere of civil actions, Roman customs and habits of thought were grafted onto original German customs. [93] This process served to reinforce the tendency to accord Roman law preference over local law. Definite attempts were made by German "partiots" of the Middle Ages to preserve their original law through codification and glosses; nevertheless, the Roman example was so strong that the codifiers of the *Sachsenspiegel* and *Schwabenspiegel* unconsciously followed the Roman model. [94] In the long run, "the strange mixture of

Roman laws and German customs led to new and unusual offspring."[95] By the time of Maximilian I, German public and civil law consisted of an abstract, doctrinaire ordering of conjoined and disparate laws. It was a labyrinth from which rulers could pick and choose to suit their own needs. A crisis of understanding occurred, especially for the common man. Unaware of the intricacies of Roman law and no longer confident of *Gewohnheitsrecht,* the common man fell victim to the guild of lawyers, the *Pfaffen* of law.[96]

Moreover, the Roman legal model became so ubiquitous that it led to the recasting of systems of law which touched other spheres of life. The assertion of imperial supremacy latent in Roman law led to a reformation of Church law. In response to the challenge of Roman law, the Church adopted Gratian's commentaries on canon law. Gratian's commentaries were ordered and explicated in the same manner as Roman law and asserted the same type of universal pretensions. Encouraged by the legally trained popes of the thirteenth century, canon law conquered Germany and displaced the local collegiate custom of individual bishoprics. Hence, a second foreign law made its way into Germany and furthered the interminable conflict between custom and reason. Even feudal law, itself a product of the Middle Ages, did not escape the pervading influence of the methods of Roman law. According to Pütter, feudal law had had a general uniform structure which attested to its common origins. In its particular application, however, it varied according to the customs and the character of each European people. These variations irritated those who looked for a clear and universal set of laws to determine feudal relations. Hence, various scholars throughout Europe began to collect and systematize their local feudal law. In northern Italy, according to Pütter, this work was first undertaken during the reign of Frederick I by two Milanese mayors, Orbertus ab Orto and Gerhardus Niger. From their work, a third, unknown scholar produced a new compilation, the so-called *librum feudorum* (between the years 1158 and 1168). Although this new compilation was "in fact a private compilation composed only for Lombardy, it had the good fortune of being added as an appendix to the Justinian code at Italian universities. And that was enough to convince the Germans that it applied to the whole Roman Empire. It was blindly accepted whether or not it agreed with the German constitution."[97] Thus a third foreign law was introduced into Germany to confuse the development of the German constitution.

The interaction between foreign law and German *Gewohnheitsrecht* had precluded, Pütter asserted, continuous and purposive German constitutional development. Germany had remained in a constant state of confusion owing to the interminable conflicts among the various *Stände* and to internal contradictions in German manners and attitudes. Even more disastrous for Germany was the fact that imperial pretensions embroiled the kaisers in Italian politics. The destinies of Germany and Italy were so closely tied together that the natural development of both was impeded.[98] Germany became the battleground for the titanic struggle between the kaiser and the pope, which led, in turn, to the increase of *Faustrecht*. By the time of the Great Interregnum, *Faustrecht* had, Pütter claimed, sunk roots so deep that it became the source for late medieval and early modern German *Staatsrecht*.[99]

German *Gewohnheitsrecht* had been too weak to halt the spread of Roman, canon, and Lombardic fuedal law but too strong to give way totally to imported laws. Through time, a dualistic manner of thinking had become so well established in the German body politic that it resisted even the sharpest revolutionary changes. The effect of a previously accepted structure of thought far exceeded the life of the opinions and values that had led to its acceptance. Pütter voiced a belief analogous to that expressed by Marc Bloch a century and a half later: The past commands the present! "Conditions once formed, beliefs once held, remain realities even when the factors to which they owed their existence have disappeared. That a procedure has lost the rational function to which it owed its origins does not mean that the procedure no longer has a hold over the minds of men or that it is without influence or significance."[100] As Pütter observed, the Reformation denied the authority of the pope and hence the original cause for accepting canon law; still, German Protestants continued to accept canon law with the sole proviso that only those elements in direct contradiction with specific Lutheran doctrinal positions be dropped.[101] Pütter, aware of the irrational springs of action, continually argued that the unmasking of a false opinion did not eliminate the effects of that opinion.[102] It was this awareness that directed Pütter's plans for the reformation of German law and that made him, as Ernst Landsberg perceptively noted, one of the founders of the German historical school of law and one of the first to call for a reformation of the study of Roman law.[103]

Pütter's ties to the Germanic school are the most obvious. He continually argued that despite the penetration of foreign law into Germany, enough living remnants of customary law existed to allow a historically trained jurist to reconstruct its basic elements. The two richest fields for this reconstruction were German *Fürstenrecht* (laws regulating relations among princes and between princes and emperor) and local community law. *Fürstenrecht* proved valuable because the autonomous and almost sovereign position of the princes had allowed them to preserve a part of German private law; community law was important because Roman law had not totally filtered down to individual communities. If these sources were properly mined, Pütter believed it possible to reconstruct a set of legal principles founded on organic Germanic law which could again be applied to specific cases of German law. He summed up his ideas in the following outline:

I. The uncertainty of Germanic law was

    A. Not observable in earlier times before the acceptance of foreign law

    B. It first became uncertain for the following reasons:
       1. The courts were totally composed of jursits who had studied only
          Roman and canon law
       2. Hence the ignorance of Germanic law grew, especially in respect
          to the law of the high nobility, which still fully applied in
          Conring's time (mid-seventeenth century)
  II. No juridical grounds exist, however, to prefer foreign law to indigenous
     law because
     A. Germanic law is not, in itself, uncertain; the only difficulty arises
       from its mastery and its specific application
     B. This difficulty can be removed
       1. When the study of Germanic law is increasingly cultivated
          according to correct principles
       2. This has been done recently and if continued will permit
          increasing hope for the future.[104]

Given the benefit of hindsight, it is easy to see that Pütter's program was basically conservative, a fact supported by his monographs on differences among the German *Stände* (especially between the high and low nobility) and on misalliance [*Mißheiraten*]. [105] In the latter, Pütter offered the strictest interpretation possible for high noble misalliance, one that remained in effect for the whole of the nineteenth century. [106] But Pütter's conservatism was a radical conservatism that called for abandonment of existent legal methods. It was founded on an image of the future qualitatively different from the present. Like his contemporary and friend Justus Möser, a Göttingen-trained jurist and historian, Pütter asserted the superiority of local tradition and spirit over what he and his contemporaries would call a sterile rationalism. Germanic law was admirable because it alone embodied the spirit of the Germanic people. It alone corresponded to the Germanic *Volkscharacter*.

    Pütter's radical conservatism led him to champion the cause of reforming the study of Roman law. His program, founded on the assumption that law mirrored the unique historical experience of a single people and expressed their specific structure of thought and action, called for a gradual substitution of Germanic law for Roman law as contained in the Pandects. Hence the necessary complement to the Germanic program entailed a historical analysis of Roman law. To separate Germanic law from Roman law implied that the true sources of both must be uncovered. Roman law had to be explicated in terms of its own unique development, not, as was still common at many faculties of law, from the assumption that Roman law stood as a positive expression of an unchanging natural law. If it could be shown that Roman law had gone through its own organic development, that its dicta applied primarily to a different age and people, then a major support for its undifferentiated use in Germany would fall of itself. This hypothesis, in effect, parallels that of Pütter's colleague and contemporary Johann David

Michaelis, whose far-reaching investigations showed how Mosaic law applied to Moses' age and historical situation alone. The specific character of Mosaic law precluded, Michaelis argued, its universal application. Both Michaelis and Pütter attempted to distinguish between the universal process of creating law and the specific contents of positive law. Pütter argued that the scholar had to go beyond Justinian's code and look at older Roman law, to differentiate among the various periods of Roman legal development, and to develop a systematic description of that law in its relation to the Roman constitution and the Roman *Denkungsart*. Pütter himself did not complete this program. His student, colleague, and intimate friend Gustav Hugo did.

Gustav Hugo's pioneering efforts, as Ernst Landsberg has shown, established the direction of nineteenth-century German legal thought. [107] Hugo developed and perfected ideas latent in the Aufklärers' perception of the driving forces in the moral world. He continued the attack against abstraction and deduction; he refined their distinction between spiritual, or moral, understanding and mathematical reason; he came out squarely against natural law; and he emphasized the importance of irrational and "spiritual" causation in historical development. In this respect he clearly built upon the base established by the Aufklärers. Nevertheless, though Hugo shared the Aufklärers' temperament, he cannot be considered an Aufklärer in the same way that his colleague and coeval Arnold Heeren can; for, unlike Heeren, Hugo was one of the first historians to master and creatively employ the insights provided by Kantian philosophy. This distinction alone puts Hugo in a different world.

In Pütter, who definitely does belong to the Aufklärung, we encounter the same type of spiritual causation employed by Semler and propounded by Wegelin. Like them, Pütter attempted to mediate between a pure sociology of knowledge and an idealistic *Ideenlehre;* he recognized the creative action of ideas, values, and opinions without according them a fully metaphysical existence. He tried to show the interaction among various levels and kinds of ideas and he argued that the propagation of these ideas was carried on by specific *Ideenträger* (active social groups within society). He saw the conflict between ideas as containing both intellectual and sociological moments. The goal of Pütter's researches, the "Ideal," as Pütter, Schlözer, and later Hugo would express it, was to apprehend the totality of the phenomenon of German constitutional development by looking at it in terms of being and becoming. That Pütter never achieved this ideal cannot be denied. As later critics have consistently observed, Pütter's works lacked life; he did not have the ability to portray the past in immediate terms. But he did differentiate between the important and the unimportant, and he demonstrated a talent for creating a workable structure within which German constitutional history could be understood. [108]

Pütter's systematization was not an act of speculation; rather, it was founded on a mastery of the sources and an attempt to perceive the relation between disparate events. His system acknowledged the importance of the spiritual element in historical change and his whole approach denied the efficacy of the demonstrative method as applied to historical explanation. Pütter, like his contemporaries, defended the freedom of the spirit over the fatalism of rationalism. In so doing he propounded an idea that lay at the core of idealist historiography: freedom is a product of the spirit acting in and against history. Pütter's conception of this process was dim, much dimmer than that of Semler, who, in effect, stood on the brink of an idealist conception, for Semler believed that outworn institutions could be perfected only in and through history; Semler virtually gave history "a mission and a moral purpose." [109] Still, though Pütter was neither an original thinker nor a gifted philosopher, he was an artisan of history; one who helped to set a path for an altered understanding of the past.

VIII
Structure of Development and Appreciation of the Unique

1

The manner in which the Aufklärers employed the category of spiritual causation reveals the internal contradictions of their historical consciousness. On every level of explanation they were led to stress the conflict between form and freedom, between deterministic and nondeterministic historical creation. The Aufklärers never resolved this conflict adequately. At best, they pleaded for a harmonic joining of the elements of freedom and necessity. Their apprehension of the social world was, in effect, a dualistic one, the duality mirrored in their hermeneutic principles and strongly reminiscent of neo-Rankean historicism.[1] The Aufklärers were caught in the dilemma of denying the competency of deduction, though they still longed for an objective base from which they could evaluate historical change.

Because of their religious convictions, the Aufklärers refused to accept purely naturalistic, mechanistic, or sentimental explanations for historical change. Rather, they looked to spiritual, or moral, questions as normative for certain spheres of human activity. Values, ideas, opinions, and religious belief all had a real, though not an autonomous, existence. These products of the spirit could not be considered merely derivative reflections of material relations, yet it was equally obvious to the Aufklärers that the spiritual products themselves were not eternally immutable; all objectifications of religious life were temporally conditioned. Religion's "real reality" became the universal action of the spirit. This interpretation, which the Aufklärers extended to other spheres of human activity, led them ever closer to a relativistic appreciation of all human creation. They continually proclaimed that each epoch, each nation, and each set of values were unique in themselves. The Aufklärers emphasized the ridiculousness of present-directed value judgments, uninformed nationalism, and a one-sided eurocentricity, a position summed up by Justi:

> Although national pride is universally found in all peoples, we Europeans have surpassed all other nations in the world in developing this exaggerated conceit. Our superiority appears to us as self-evident. We boldly set ourselves above all other peoples in the rest of the world. Even when we accord others the honor of not being savages, they are, in our eyes, nothing more than incompetent, raw, and ignorant barbarians. All their customs, usages, and governments seem to us to be totally absurd, irrational, silly, and ridiculous. We believe our reason,

our understanding, our insights so superior that we look down on other peoples as we would upon pitiful little crawling worms. And, in fact, we behave toward them in this manner. We act as though we were the rulers of the whole world. We seize lands of people from the three remaining parts of the world without the least hesitation. We dictate laws and treat these people as though they were our slaves. If they show the least amount of resistance, we exterminate them. The strangest thing is that we do all this without anyone in Europe realizing that we are committing the most atrocious injustices [*himmelschreyenden Ungerechtigkeiten*].[2]

Everywhere the Aufklärers attacked the propensity to universalize the present; they called for a broader vision of the past and the present, a call that found its outlet in the restructuring of universal history, in the creation of the study of comparative religion, and in the Aufklärers' combination of cosmopolitanism and fascination with national uniqueness.

At the same time the Aufklärers readily indulged in making value judgments, some so patently narrow that it is difficult to see any tendency toward relativism at all. The examples of these judgments are so well known (they form the basis for the stereotypic portrayal of the Aufklärung) that a few should suffice. Virtually every thinker of the Aufklärung had nothing but disdain for the "learned doctors of Scholasticism." Scholasticism, or anything that in the Aufklärers' eyes resembled it, was dismissed as useless hairsplitting carried out by "spinners of philosophical webs," who had not the faintest acquaintance with life as it was lived. When the Aufklärers looked at the medieval Church, they seldom concealed their Protestant dislike for its pomp, ceremony, and organization, though they often praised the Church for its cultural contributions. Their evaluations of medieval politics were equally unsympathetic; almost all of them described it as a mass of confusion, violence, and error. In fact, they condemned all politics founded on conquest. Such diverse thinkers and personalities as Schlözer and Herder concurred in their evaluation of Alexander the Great as nothing but a destructive conqueror.

In the ongoing discussion concerning the degree to which the Enlightenment had a modern historical consciousness, a critical point of contention is the reason why these value judgments were made. Two fairly common answers may be proposed: (1) the judgments were the result of a necessary and unconscious subjectivism, a subjectivism inherent in the process of appreciating the past and consequently not in theoretical conflict with the relativist ideal; or (2) the judgments were made because the Aufklärers consciously believed that they alone possessed the objective key to true understanding and that they alone were enlightened by the rays of pure reason. Hence, they incorrectly applied abstract reason to concrete problems. The first answer exonerates the Aufklärers and the Enlightenment from the charge of being ahistorical. It focuses on the unique nature of historical understanding and argues that since history is value directed, if not value determined, it is impossible to expunge value judgment from historical analysis. The choice of subject matter, the delineation of problems and moods, the sympathy shown by one age for another, and even perhaps the historical evaluation itself are rooted in the existential needs of the interpreters. The second answer finds the Enlightenment guilty of the charge of being ahistorical; it concentrates on the obvious short circuits of historical reasoning present in the Aufklärers' historical work. It dismisses the pious claims of relativism and cosmopolitanism voiced throughout the period as inconsequential, if not dangerous, to the appreciation of historical uniqueness.

The fact that both contentions can be argued suggests a third conclusion, namely, that both are true. This possibility does not present a paradox; rather, it points to the existence of real contradictions in the Aufklärers' approach to the past which arose from their inability to propound a theory capable of mediating between normative and subjective understanding. The Aufklärers faced a quandary common to the modern historical consciousness. As I have attempted to show, the Aufklärers were well aware of the limited and subjective nature of historical understanding and of understanding itself. They certainly were not rationalists in the strict meaning of the word, for they heartily dismissed the idea that abstract reason alone was sufficient to comprehend the moral and social world of man. Their analytics was based on this assumption; however, they never went so far as to make relativism an absolute. In their eyes, truths and errors did exist. Granted, these were now considered far more difficult to perceive, but such perception was deemed possible, at least in ideal terms. Beneath the Aufklärers' recognition of relativism lay the assumption that an objective base existed that allowed one to uncover truth, even if it were only partial truth. They did not surrender the idea of a normative underpinning to historical judgment. They found themselves torn between the Scylla of normative thought and the Charybdis of relativism. In seeking a way out of their quandary, they introduced another normative element to mediate between relativism and ahistorical normative analysis. Faced with the duality of form and freedom, they historicized the problem of freedom by placing its achievement within time. Their solution accorded time its own distinct and normal structure of development built upon the popular metaphor of human growth and supported by Leibnizian metaphysics. This solution proved compelling because it allowed the researcher to recognize the validity of past historical action in and for itself without having to accord the specifics of that action contemporary moral approval or disapproval; one merely explained that this or that frame of reference or set of values was natural to men at a certain stage of their development. In effect, the Enlightenment's tendency to construct a philosophy of history arose from the hermeneutic problems inherent in Enlightenment thinking. And, despite the revulsion of later ages for such a strategy of analysis, it proved valuable to the Aufklärers. The conception of the autonomous development of all societies provided the historian with a new method of analysis, the comparative, and a new way of explanation, the analogical. Further, it paved the way for a wholesale revision of the history of ages, once maligned and neglected even by Enlightenment historians themselves.

As Frank Manuel has shown, the regnant desire to comprehend the meaning of ancient myth had an important impact upon the conception of societal development. It became clear that all societies undergo an analogous and autonomous growth pattern. Enlightenment thinkers, representing all stripes of religious belief and disbelief, saw myth as the primary source for uncovering the meaning of ancient religions. Myth was the key to understanding the nature of religion. Spurned by the elaborate and fanciful speculations of seventeenth-century allegorists and euphemerists and unwilling, or unable, to accept myth as literally true or patently false, Enlightenment thinkers throughout Europe struggled to apprehend the "reality" of myth and to reveal its human origins. The answers they proposed were varied, contradictory, and sometimes just as fanciful as those of the seventeenth-century authors against whom they rebelled. Among all the various eighteenth-century students of myth, the most original were those Professor Manuel called the "historico-psychological mythographers."[3] Their originality lay in the creative fusion of two dominant strains of eighteenth-century thought: the concern with man's irrationality and the historical recognition that a difference in time and social environment usually implies a qualitative difference in attitudes, values, and action. Working from these two propositions, the historico-psychological mythographers constructed a typology of the stages of human experience founded on the Augustinian metaphor of the ages of man. Society went through a growth pattern analogous to that of man's. Each stage in that pattern had its own mode of expression, its own psyche, which determined the way the age spoke, acted, thought, governed, and legislated. The period when myth was created could not be compared with the modern age; the mythic period's mentality was qualitatively different; it reflected the way men thought during the "childhood" of society. This assumption provided the theoretical base for the philosophes' discussion of the "primitive mind." As Professor Manuel rightly remarked, the Enlightenment's "psychologizing of religious experience in the historical context of the primitive world was one of the great intellectual revolutions of the age."[4]

The Aufklärers eagerly appropriated the ideas, images, and metaphors fashioned by the historico-psychological mythographers and applied them to their own historical explanations. The writings of Johann David Michaelis testifies to this tendency. The son of a prominent teacher of Near Eastern languages at Halle, Michaelis had undergone the same type of religious struggle as his slightly younger contemporary Semler. Because of the rationalist critique of revelation, Michaelis found it difficult to accept revelation as literally true. At the same time, his devotion to the general precepts of Christianity made it impossible for him to deny the truth of Judeo-Christian myth. Because Michaelis saw no way out of the quandary, his only solution was to change his career; he abandoned his plans to enter the ministry and chose to follow in his father's footsteps. In 1741 Michaelis vistied England and the stimulus offered by a different theological tradition led to a resolution of his problems. Influenced by the Oxford divines, especially by Lowth, whose lectures on *de poesi sacra Hebraoerum* made a lasting impression, Michaelis finally abandoned the idea that the whole corpus of Judeo-Christian myth was divinely inspired, that its total message was literally true and binding on all men. Armed with this insight, Michaelis proposed to use the tools of history and psychology to explicate the Old and New Testaments, to differentiate between the human and spiritual elements in both, and hence to create a new paradigm for the interpretation of the Bible. In 1745 he left Halle and accepted a position at Göttingen, where he came into close contact with Mosheim, Albrecht von Haller, and Johann Gesner. The four men met every week in Haller's home to discuss their work. Michaelis built up a strong base of knowledge concerning philology, the history of religion, and the natural sciences. By the 1750s he had mastered twelve languages, including Hebrew, Aramaic, Chaldean, Arabic, and Syrian; he had kept abreast of the latest discoveries in the natural sciences. As director of the *Göttingen-Gelehrten Anzeigen* (1753-1770), the Göttingen Gesellschaft, the library, and the philological seminar, he carried on extensive correspondence with the leading scholars of Europe. Everything that could be used to chart the unique conjunction of social, temporal, and physical factors influencing Old and New Testament times were incorporated into his explication of the Bible.

We have seen how Michaelis employed the categories of external causation to explain specific proscriptions of Mosaic law. However, Michaelis realized that environmental factors provided a limited explanatory tool. They were useful for specific explanation but failed to illuminate the critical eighteenth-century problem concerning the form, origin, and meaning of mythic expression. According to Michaelis, all mythic expression, including Judeo-Christian myth, revealed a general similarity that defied any explanation drawn from climate, geography, or unique historical experience. There was "an immediately recognizable similarity between the great Arab myths and those of Job, the songs of Moses and Deborah and the Psalms. Of course, the customs of the people and the nature of the land introduced differentia-tions. . . . Still, despite these differences, we can see a specific recognizable similarity between the best poems from the golden period of the Arabs and the Hebrew Old Testament."[5] Mythic expression differed qualitatively from rational understanding. It was poetry, usually produced during the nation's first golden age of poetic expression. It was rich in metaphors and images but poor in logical expression. Since Michaelis believed language the highest and most critical indication of a nation's *Denkungsart,* and since all early peoples seemed to have expressed their religion in poetic images, he propounded the view later summed up by his colleague Christian Gottlob Heyne: "Mythology is in itself the most ancient history and the most ancient philosophy. It is the conceptual world of the oldest legends of the *Volk* and the race expressed in rough speech. And in this respect it assumes a new significance as the residue of the most ancient way of imagining."[6]

Given Michaelis's assumption that mythic understanding differed in form and meaning from modern perception, it is not surprising that he leaped at the historico-psychological description of "primitive man." The metaphor of growth proved irresistible. "Peoples that are in their childhood appear identical, even if they inhabit different lands. Like children everywhere, they have certain customs and actions in common, ascribable to their age, which differ from those of adults and old people."[7] Like others of his era, Michaelis collected material about the practices and customs of primitive man. He searched through the endless stream of travel reports and learned dissertations on the peoples of newly discovered worlds; he bombarded his correspondents with questions about primitive societies and gloried, for example, when a friend conveyed to him Benjamin Franklin's knowledge of the American Indians for use in his "Jus Mosäicum."[8] He even persuaded the Danish minister Johann H. E. von Bernstorff to dispatch an expedition to explore and to collect material about the most inaccessible areas of the Near East (the ill-fated Carsten Niebuhr expedition). From all this material Michaelis constructed a rough typology of primitive society against which he measured the spirit of Mosaic law: "As long as one does not know this oldest law of the childhood of peoples, the genealogy of our own law remains incomplete."[9]

Michaelis conceived of primitive society as a collection of infinitesimally small states that "resembled families." These small states were ruled by elected judges famed for their honesty, men who exercised authority in the same manner as did parents. [10] Early societies demonstrated "more of a tendency toward despotism than larger and more mature ones."[11] This tendency was reinforced by an absence of class differentiation; since a hereditary nobility was alien to primitive society, no check on despotic power existed. But this defect was not overly important in early times. The limited size of the society and the simplicity of its organization allowed for less misuse of power than older, more complicated societies did. Justice was quick and honest because the customs, regulations, and actions of the community were known to all: "Herein lies the difference between the old and new worlds, between the ages of man. The Orient still has summary justice while Europe has a deliberate administration of justice. The ancient childhood of peoples favors more rapid administration of punishment; modern times, which are identical to the adult age of peoples, favor deliberate punishment. One can say that the more patriarchal a state, the more it resembles a large family, where one has an honest man, a father, to survey the whole; in that situation rapid punishment is desirable. The more a state grows to a size beyond the competence of one man to oversee it, the more dangerous is rapid punishment for the innocent." [12] The images of simplicity and honesty are central to Michaelis's description of the primitive state. Economic and social patterns reflected those of a simple pastoral or agrarian organization. Trade was minimal; contact between peoples, almost nonexistent. In primitive states a martial and patriotic spirit ruled (a theme borrowed from Montesquieu). Custom was the law of the land, recognized by everyone and passed from one generation to another by oral tradition. Mythic tradition, expressed in the form of divine poetry, bound the society together and gave voice to its religious consciousness.

This picture of primitive society was not in itself negative, not a bleak background designed to highlight the brilliance and achievements of the present as it so often seemed in Isaak Iselin's portrayal of primitive man. Michaelis did draw it, however, to illustrate the wide chasm separating early man from modern man. Everything that once had been appropriate for the normal operations of society — summary justice, patriarchal despotism, even the blood feud — would produce disastrous results in large and complex societies. What is common sense at one time is madness or error in another. [13] Michaelis did not condemn primitive societies; he praised the honesty, the nobility, and the "patriotism" of ancient men in a manner reminiscent of Pütter and Möser; but he also thought it impossible to recapture this "childlike simplicity." One cannot turn the clock back. The modern age was adult; it knew the benefits and disadvantages of complex patterns of life. It enjoyed the fruits of trade and suffered the bane of luxury, wantonness, and chicanery.[14] The primary message of his *Mosaisches Recht* is that the law of Moses was given by God and Moses for the people of Israel. It did not apply to the modern age. Michaelis still felt the burden of the past, the attempt to apply literally the legal and social sanctions of biblical times to the present. In eighteenth-century Germany many still called for the institution of Mosaic law to cleanse the body politic, and an even larger number felt that Mosaic law justified some of the gorier and more extreme forms of eighteenth-century punishments. Though Michaelis deemed the specifics of Mosaic law inapplicable to the eighteenth century, the spirit animating that law was, he argued, universal. Moses had drawn upon the accumulated customs and traditions of his people; he had taken cognizance of their temptations, their needs, and their desires and had framed the law inspired by God accordingly.

The metaphors of growth and childhood simplicity provided Michaelis with a general normative structure within which he could assess the unique experience of the Jews. Now he could compare their experience with that of other "primitive peoples" without being saddled with the perplexing problem of explaining how similar habits arose under dissimilar climatic and geographic conditions. In the process of according growth, or development, its own law, Michaelis and his contemporaries felt they could adequately resolve the dichotomy between freedom and determinism, between the unique and the general. The autonomous structure of societal growth established the general framework of historical possibility, calling forth in each stage of development a similar, though not identical, spiritual condition. The external categories of climate, geography, and political and economic organization channeled this mentality in a certain direction. Finally, the genius of the people, expressed in their national and sacred poetry, acted from and against these normative categories to determine the unique achievement of the Jews. For Michaelis, this explanation did not demean the Jews. On the contrary, by placing the ancient Jews in the stream of history, by showing how their solutions to a given set of problems were superior to those of other primitive peoples, Michaelis thought he had demonstrated their God-given message. The greatness of the Jews lay not in their exemption from normal historical development or in the specifics of their law, but rather in their creation of a religious vision and a process of lawmaking whose spirit could be reexperienced. In effect, Michaelis's conception of spiritual change is identical to Semler's.

Michaelis's application of contemporary tools of historical analysis to Old Testament exegesis effected a revolution in biblical exegesis in Germany. [15] To be sure, Michaelis was not the first to argue that the Old Testament should be analyzed as an ancient historical document of the Jewish people. That honor belongs to Spinoza. Nevertheless, the vary fact that Spinoza's name was associated with this approach tinged it with the air of heresy and atheism. For Germans such as Jacobi, who equated Spinoza's philosophy with fatalism, with a denial of free will, and hence with a denial of God, any analytics derived directly from Spinoza was suspect. [16] Michaelis, who was neither a Spinozian nor an atheist, gave the historical method respectability. Further, he pursued his studies with the painstaking research and sifting of evidence typical of the German academic. Even his sharpest critics, Hamann and Herder, did not deny the validity of Michaelis's approach. They rebelled against the specifics of his explication and the general tone of his work. They criticized Michaelis's lack of poetic feeling, his inability to really make himself one with the ancient Hebrew poets. Hamann, playing on Michaelis's name, disparagingly referred to him as the "archangel of Canaan's relics," [17] and Herder said that in *Mosaisches Recht:* "Nothing is explained in terms of the Oriental spirit of the times, the people, and the customs; rather, everything is a gloss of semi-Oriental and good European common sense." [18]

Despite real disagreements, both Michaelis and his German critics built their explanation of religion on a conception of psychology that differed from that of western thinkers. With the exception of Vico, whose influence on the Aufklärers was practically nonexistent, western mythographers of the historico-psychological school founded their analysis upon sensationalist psychology: "Religious sentiment was not inborn, but was acquired by men at a given moment in time – this is the basic postulate." [19] In western eyes, religion was a historical product created by man in response to certain sensations; it resulted from fear, or trauma, or psychic necessity, or from an incapacity to comprehend cause and effect adequately. According to the most radical western thinkers, especially Baron d'Holbach and his circle, religion was a *contagion sacrée* that deserved immediate abolition. Others, representing the typical posture of the Enlightenment, considered religion a necessary social prop, something to satisfy the ignorant masses, but certainly not applicable to the educated elite. Almost all the western historico-psychological mythographers viewed religion in negative terms, as an unfortunate product of history which could be overcome. The majority of the Aufklärers refused to accept this proposition. They opposed western sensationalist psychology with a psychology derived from Leibnizian metaphysics and contemporary aesthetics. Man's religious drive is inborn, a part of the spirit, which in its continual movement creates myriad forms of religious worship. Religion is primary, not secondary, for belief is natural to man. Disbelief is not an independent choice, but rather a state of disharmony, devoid of any norms, a state where man loses his spiritual contact with his fellowman. Thus, even when the Aufklärers explained history with the terms and the structure evolved by western historico-psychological mythographers, the basic assumptions underlying that explanation differed.

These contradictions notwithstanding, the Aufklärers still eagerly employed the metaphor of autonomous growth as a methodological and explanatory tool in the pursuit of historical understanding. They were particularly beguiled by the idea of comparative analysis, or interpretation from analogy, which the metaphor of autonomous growth suggested. Schlözer, Michaelis's student, considered the comparative approach an important means to untangle the knot of the past.[20] Throughout his works Schlözer sought to illuminate the condition of one society by reference to a better-known society at the same stage of development. Sometimes, as was his nature, Schlözer went a bit too far in piling comparison upon comparison until the value of the comparative method itself appeared questionable. For example, he suggested that ancient Germany "was a Canada before the rise of the Frankish Empire and that all the Germans who lived far away from the Roman boundaries were savages [*Wilde*]. Savages have no cities, no markets, no trade; they only barter. . . . The first inroads of trade made in Germany came from Roman merchants who sold the Germans Italian wine. In the same way, European brandy [*Branntwein*] acquainted the North American savages with trade, as tobacco did the Hottentots."[21] At other times Schlözer used the comparative approach to great effect in unraveling the complexities of ancient northern and Russian history.

Despite the pitfalls of the new method, it caught the imagination of countless historians, then and later. Gatterer used it to describe the tumultuous changes effected by the Crusades by drawing a parallel with the *Völkerwanderung*. Heeren purged the Crusades of the stigma attached to them by tracing their genesis to the mentality of a heroic age. Even as late as 1842, Wilhelm Roscher defended the use of such analogies in a letter to his mentor Ranke. After invoking Schlözer's example, the famous economic historian pleaded for a comparative study of political growth. Though he called analogy a "dangerous knife" when used by unskilled hands, he added: "But a knife that can not harm anyone is also useless to the surgeon. I believe everyone unconsciously uses analogies. I have developed two principles for the use of this tool. First, never consider it an end in itself, but rather a means to achieve a sharper, more lively [*lebendigen*] conception of the event under study. Second, compare only corresponding stages of a people's development, for example, the middle ages of the Greeks with the modern Middle Ages, the present condition in Turkey with the last period of the ancient Persian Empire."[22]

2

Writers who discuss the problem of historical explanation very often differentiate between history written to recreate the past for its own sake and history written to demonstrate how the past became the present. For the purpose of analysis this distinction is useful; yet, like other analytic constructs, it carries its own inherent dangers. Though it successfully warns us against the use of omnicompetent definitions of what real history is about, it also tends to exaggerate the incompatibility of both endeavors; this distinction sees developmental and static analysis as proceeding on two different planes with little or no interchange, especially if the developmental approach reveals too much concern for lawlike regularities governing human development. It is still modish to deny developmental approaches any efficaciousness in achieving an awareness of historical uniqueness and variety. But the stimulus provided by the idea of autonomous development, as adumbrated throughout the century by scores of diverse thinkers, led the Aufklärers to a deeper appreciation of national uniqueness. In the Aufklärung, diachronic and synchronic approaches, far from being mutually exclusive, dynamically reacted to affirm each other. Antiquarian delight with one's own unique past was expanded by reference to the autonomous development of other cultures (especially Greek culture). Speculative diachronic construction was continually grounded by reference to the manifold ways in which the form found expression in actual historical time. This interaction led thinkers of the Aufklärung to rediscover the grandeur of the Middle Ages.

The evolution of Johann Jacob Bodmer's thought illustrates the manner in which a concern for the Middle Ages was revived. Bodmer (1698-1783) may be classified as one of the founding fathers of the Aufklärung. His interests, attitudes, and responses clearly anticipated those of later thinkers and differed substantially from those prevailing during the first third of the eighteenth century. Bodmer's attack against Gottsched's aesthetics, his advocacy of the vital importance of metaphor and the "wonderful" in literature, his appeal to the sentiments, his almost pantheistic conception of nature, and his love for the simple joys of daily life became common themes sung by countless authors in the last half of the century. Bodmer was neither a great writer nor a great poet, but he was a gifted teacher, a guide who reveled in opening up new worlds to inquiring youth. Even when his writings became outmoded, his influence lived on through those who had received their first inspiration from him, men such as Friedrich Gottlieb Klopstock, Christoph Wieland, Salomon Gessner, Johann Sulzer, Wegelin, Johann Heinrich Pestalozzi, Johann Casper Lavater, Johannes von Müller, and Johann Heinrich Füssli. Bodmer's interests were healthily cosmopolitan; he corresponded with a host of foreign scholars throughout Europe, establishing close relations with the Haller circle in Bern, the Brockes circle in Hamburg, and with Rousseau and his admirers. Bodmer considered it his task to introduce the wonders of Milton, Dante, Spenser, and Shapespeare to the Swiss and German reading public.

Despite his wide contacts and his acknowledged learning, Bodmer remains one of the shadowy figures in most histories of eighteenth-century German thought. At best he is recognized for his role in the reformation of eighteenth-century aesthetics, but even in that capacity he is often viewed as an unsystematic precursor to Baumgarten, Lessing, Herder, and the Sturm und Drang. Except by a small number of writers, Bodmer's role in shaping a new German historical awareness has gone unmentioned.[23] Yet in interests and disposition Bodmer was, as the historian Fritz Ernst observed, "a born critical historian."[24] Beneath Bodmer's multitudinous efforts lay the historian's desire to recapture and reexperience past life, to which Bodmer joined the Aufklärers' goal of forging a new future anchored upon the sound tradition of the past.

Bodmer's original impetus to study the past derived from his Swiss background. He, like his contemporary Albrecht von Haller, was filled with deep veneration for his Swiss fatherland, its people, and its "romantic scenery."[25] Proud of Switzerland's role as mediator among French, German, and Italian cultures, Bodmer gloried in the mythic, linguistic, and historical traditions of Switzerland and neighboring Swabia. His love of Switzerland led him, almost unconsciously, to the conclusion that each people had its own unique genius and mode of expression. A literary discovery, made on a trip through France and northern Italy, reinforced this feeling. His parents had sent him on the trip in the hope that Bodmer would acquire enough knowledge about trade so that he could enter upon a mercantile career. In this respect the trip proved a total failure. Bodmer had not the slightest gift or inclination to become a merchant. Instead of "mercantile knowledge" Bodmer brought back a copy of Addison's *Spectator*.[26]

The *Spectator* offered Bodmer a conception of the nation corresponding to his own, as yet unexpressed, ideas. He was impressed by the variety of elegantly composed articles that dealt with all aspects of English life – dress, manners, eating habits, everything that made English or London society unique. He was beguiled by the journal's self-critical stance, by its tempering of a confident assertion of national excellence with a critique of national faults. Most of all, he sympathized with its *bürgerlich* ideal and moral purpose. The *Spectator* seemed the perfect vehicle for the creation of a national self-consciousness, and Bodmer lost no time in producing a Swiss equivalent. In 1721-22 he and his intimate friend Johann Jacob Breitinger proposed the publication of a "philosophic spectator of Switzerland."[27] Its scope would encompass the whole of Switzerland and its aim would be to "present specific information about the unknown customs and fashions of Swiss lands, whether they predominated in one city alone or throughout Switzerland." Articles would deal with "the different means of raising and educating children, habits of courtship, marriage ceremonies, means of maintaining a marriage, forms of conversation between men and women, the freedom of such conversations, the divertissements of men, women, and peasants, the ceremonies of politesse, forms of barbarism, the taste for eloquence, poetry, and scholarship, funeral and birthday customs, and dress and the like."[28] The moral purpose of the newly planned journal would be served by pointing out "local examples of steadfastness but also of faintheartedness in the face of misery, poverty, pain, death, and the loss of friends, children, mates, and amours"; it would also cite "examples of strong contempt or base admiration for wealth, passion, honor, and life." Bodmer concluded that the proposed journal "would make the uniqueness of the Swiss national character clear."[29]

The new journal, the second "moral" journal to appear in the German language, was entitled the *Discours der Maler.*[30] The title announced its function: Bodmer and Breitinger sought to reproduce faithfully the *Colorit* that animated Swiss society. And despite the lingering desire to improve Swiss morals via historical example, the general tone of the journal attests to Bodmer's immediate consciousness of participating in the life of a historical whole, "of belonging to a nation."[31] Therefore the tone of the *Discours der Maler* is slightly different from that of the *Spectator*. The cosmopolitan description of customs found in the *Spectator* is translated into an intensive description of local customs with an appeal to preserve and emulate them. Whereas the *Spectator* elevated individual good taste and judgment as primary, the *Discours der Maler* concentrated upon a morality founded upon historical and community values. For Bodmer, the rebirth of Switzerland, its moral and political betterment, could come only through an active confrontation with its living heritage. The path to the future was to be enlightened by the experience of the past.

The *Spectator* served as the first catalyst in forming Bodmer's historical consciousness. For the greater part of the twenties and thirties, this consciousness could be called "antiquarian," as defined by Nietzsche: "The history of his town becomes the history of himself; he looks on the walls, the turreted gate, the town council, the fair, as an illustrated diary of his youth, and sees himself in it all – his strength, industry, desire, reason, faults, and follies. 'Here one could live,' he says, 'as one can live here and now – and will go on living; for we are tough folk, and will not be uprooted in the night.' "[32] But the *Spectator* also opened a second door to Bodmer's appreciation of the past, for through it Bodmer discovered Milton. His confrontation with Milton's poetry had two effects: it forced him to define his aesthetic theories and it directed his attention to the intimate tie linking language, metaphor, and national character. As soon as Bodmer read Milton, he rushed out a translation of *Paradise Lost,* despite the almost universal German condemnation of Milton.[33] Gottsched greeted Bodmer's translation with a scathing attack on Milton, which in turn prompted Bodmer to defend Milton's merits. The exchange led Bodmer to break with Gottsched and settled the direction of his critical thought. Awed by Milton's poetical images and captivated by the richness and diversity of his language, Bodmer boldly asserted the primary role of metaphor in poetic understanding.

Unlike Gottsched, who relegated imagerial language to an ornamental role, Bodmer made it the essence of poetic composition. He asserted that metaphor alone proved capable of recapturing and recreating living images, for it alone spoke directly to the faculties of the soul. Poetry was a form of truth equal, if not superior, to philosophy and closely related in form and function to history.[34] Like history, poetry's truth was worldly, moral, and political.[35] And like history, poetry's truth could not be reduced to a set of logical and universal rules independent of time, place, and circumstance. The strength of poetry and history lay in their ability to recapture the individual in all its variety in an immediate, or evident, manner. Bodmer accomplished two things important for his mature conception of national uniqueness. First, by asserting a similarity between history and poetry, he suggested that the essence of a nation's traditions, its unique temporal character, can best be discovered in its poetic and mythic traditions, provided these traditions are experienced in their totality, with all the richness of language, belief, and custom left intact. Second, Bodmer concluded that poetry possesses great moral power; it operates directly upon the life of a nation.[36] It follows, therefore, that the great poet, especially the epic poet, occupies the position of creator and shaper of a nation's self-consciousness. It is the poet who creates the "truths" of a society and who, through his poetic fire, offers his people a new revelation. This is precisely what Milton accomplished. Milton's poem constitutes a new epic, a "Christian mythology," which expresses the truths of modern Christian society with a power and intensity equal to Homer's. Milton achieved this end by turning to the linguistic traditions of his people. His language is original in that it employs the new and the old, the obsolete and the ultramodern; it creates a broad fresco portraying the splendor of the Christian message. Milton's poem was successful because it creatively built upon the healthy tradition of the English nation.

While all these thoughts surged through Bodmer's mind, he still lacked a unifying or organizing idea that would allow him to merge his literary and antiquarian historical interests. During the late 1730s and early 1740s, Bodmer pursued both interests. He and Breitinger composed pamphlets, reviews, and disquisitions defending their aesthetic principles and laying siege to the "dark realm of the Teutobachs" — Gottsched and his followers.[37] The battle, a bitter conflict replete with personal invective and frustrating disappointment, raged through the German intellectual world. Bodmer and Breitinger also immersed themselves in probing the Swiss past. As early as 1727 they founded the *Helvetische Gesellschaft,* which was dedicated to collecting and publishing important material illuminating Swiss history. In 1735 they undertook the publication of the *Helvetische Bibliothek,* four volumes of which appeared between the years 1735 and 1741.[38] It consisted of excerpts from books dealing with Switzerland, original documents, and book reviews.

In 1743 Bodmer discovered a book that revolutionized his ideas: Thomas Blackwell's seminal work, *Enquiry into the Life and Writings of Homer* (1735). Blackwell offered a bold reinterpretation of Homer founded on a conception of autonomous historical development. He achieved what Bodmer was groping toward, a fusion of history with a theory of language, poetry, and hermeneutics which, at times, appears almost Vichian.[39] Blackwell provided Bodmer with a means of discovering a unity behind the diversity of his endeavors. Bodmer could now look at the medieval German past with new eyes.

In his study of Homer, Blackwell posed and sought to resolve a problem central to the thought of the Enlightenment: How and in what manner are individual works of genius influenced by circumstance, law, and Weltanschauung? Although Blackwell concentrated on the Homeric era, he implicitly proposed a universal scheme of historical interpretation applicable to eras and nations far removed from Greek antiquity. Blackwell was, in effect, searching for the generative principles underlying the infinite variety of observable historical phenomena. Like Vico and other theorists of autonomous historical development, he drew a direct relation between time-form and forms of consciousness and expression.[40] He focused on the problem of language development to illustrate this relation: "Whoever reflects upon the Rise and Fall of States, will find, that along with their Manners, their Language too accompanies them both in their Growth and Decay. Language is the Conveyance of our Thoughts; and as they are noble, free and undisturbed, our Discourse will keep pace with them both in Cast and Materials."[41]

The key to unlocking the meaning of language and thought lay in placing them in their corresponding stage of temporal development, called by Blackwell the "Progression of Manners": "There is, *My Lord,* a thing, which, tho' it has happened in all Ages and Nations, it is yet very hard to describe. Few People are capable of observing it, and therefore Terms have not been contrived to expresss a Perception that is taken from the widest View of Human Affairs. It may be called a *Progression of Manners;* and depends for the most part on our Fortunes: As they flourish or decline, so we live and are affected; and the greatest Revolutions in them produce the most conspicuous Alterations in the other: For the Manners of a People seldom stand still, but are either polishing or spoiling."[42] Later he concluded: "It is the *different Periods,* naturally succeeding in the *Progression of Manners,* that can only account for the Succession of Wit and Literature."[43] Blackwell regarded thought and language as intrinsically dependent upon the development of distinct mental, or psychological, states. These states followed one another in a natural, that is, a determined, order. Blackwell propounded a powerful analytics that asserted the conjunction and the reciprocity of thought, expression, and temporal condition. With this analytics one could intuit the general characteristics of a nation's language and form of consciousness from its temporal position or ascertain the time-form of a nation from its language and consciousness.

Blackwell employed a metaphor of growth that envisioned a conflict between spontaneity and reflection, between freedom and form; his ideal stressed the need to harmonize both. This metaphor determined Blackwell's appreciation of the steps in the progression of manners and, correspondingly, his view of language. Each step in the progression evidenced a different moment in the conflict between spontaneity and reflection, symbolized most immediately in language. Spontaneity dominated at the beginning of societal development; man looked at the world with childlike wonder. His language was "an *Alloy* of Simplicity and Wonder."[44] Naturally poetic in form, it was suffused with metaphor, "metaphor of the boldest, daring and most natural kind. For Words taken wholly from rough Nature, and invented under some Passion, as Terror, Rage, or Want . . . would be expressive of that Fanaticism and Dread, which is incident to creatures living wild and defenceless: we must imagine their Speech to be broken, unequal and boisterous."[45] Blackwell broke with traditional scholarship by proclaiming the primacy of poetry in the development of human expression, an idea advanced contemporaneously by Vico and Lowth and one that captured the imagination of later eighteenth-century writers. According to Blackwell, poetry and metaphor were natural to man, not products of long and "artificial" reflection.

If spontaneity dominated the first stage of the progression of manners, reflection ruled in the last. Polished language was the language of reflection. It was unfit for poetry. In everyday speech its hallmarks were "Prattle," "pretty Forms," and "Sheer Wit," all of which enervated a language. The process of "polishing a language" entailed a loss of its imagerial and metaphorical powers. When this process reached its conclusion – a conclusion corresponding to the complete ordering of a state – poetry became impossible. In describing the process, Blackwell wrote: "Your Lordship is so well acquainted with what passes for Politeness of Stile, that I need be at no pains to make out the Consequence. Let me only observe, that what we call *Polishing* diminishes a Language: it makes many Words obsolete; it coops a Man up in a Corner, allows him but one set of Phrases, and deprives him of many significant Terms, and strong and beautiful Expressions, which he must venture upon, like *Virgil,* at the hazard of appearing antiquated and homely."[46] Blackwell deemed both the first and the last stage in the progression of manners wanting: early society, though rich in natural feelings expressed in poetic metaphor, lacked the basic stability necessary to ensure a modicum of communal living; refined society, though ensuring order and stability, sacrificed the naturalness that man required for his spiritual well-being. In Blackwell's words, "We live within Doors, cover'd as it were, from Nature's Face; and passing our Days supinely ignorant of her Beauties, we are apt to think the Similies taken from her *low,* and the ancient Manners mean or absurd. But let us be ingenuous, *My Lord,* and confess, that while the Moderns admire nothing but Pomp, and can think nothing Great or Beautiful, but what is the Product of Wealth, they exclude themselves from the pleasantest and most natural Images that adorned the Old Poetry. *State* and *Form* disguise Man; and Wealth and Luxury disguise Nature. Their Effects in Writing are answerable."[47]

The age most congenial to the production of great heroic poetry stands between the two poles, at the juncture when reflection (and hence the ordering of the state) replaces spontaneity as the dominant mode. Homer was born in such a heroic age. Though experiencing the first fruits of an ordered society, Homer's age had not lost the naturalness of early society; everything was at the "proper pitch for Poetry."[48] Then man experienced the whole gamut of emotions; a poetic genius might "be a Spectator of all the various Situations of the human Race; might observe them in great Calamities, and in high Felicity."[49] Homer saw, as he wandered through the Greek countryside, "Towns taken and plundered, the Men put to the Sword, and Women made Slaves." He saw "Cities blessed with Peace, spirited by Liberty, flourishing in Trade, and increasing in Wealth. . . . Such Scenes afford extended Views, and natural ones too, as they are the immediate Effect of the great Parent of Invention, *Necessity,* in its young and untaught Essays."[50] The insecurity of these times created a feeling of liberty, of freedom, and of creation, unknown in its intensity to earlier and later periods.[51] During the heroic age the traditions of the past were still alive, the early religious beliefs still firmly and unquestioningly held: "*Philosophers* and speculative incredulous People had not sprung up and decryed Miracles and supernatural Stories."[52] Epic poetry, whose nerve was the "marvellous and the wonderful," necessarily rested upon a vibrant religious tradition, one fully developed, yet not overripe. Only at this time do references to religion have real meaning; only then do men naturally "introduce it into their *Business,* allude to it in their *Pleasures,* and abstain from it in no Part of Life; especially while the Doctrine flourishes and appears in Bloom."[53] The power of Homer's poetry derived from the fact that "he described from Realities." His recounting of Greece's mythic traditions was in no way contrived or artificial; rather, "such things" were "firmly believed, and generally received, for *Sacred Truths.*" And Homer "must have had a good Faith, or at least a *strong* Feeling of them himself, to be able to tell them with such Spirit and Complacency."[54]

Just as religion retained its original "novelty and youth" during the heroic age, so did language and manners. The heroic age was martial in spirit; arms were in repute and soldierly values dominant. "There was a Necessity for both. The *Man* who had bravely defended his City, enlarged its Dominion, or died in its Cause, was revered like a God: Love of Liberty, Contempt of Death, Honour, Probity and Temperance, were *Realities.*"[55] Homer was close enough in time to those about whom he sang to understand fully their motives, actions, and mentality. Along with the glories and the ethics of the warrior, the man in Homeric times "frankly owned the Pleasures of *Love* and *Wine;* he told how voraciously he *eat* [sic] and when he was hungry, and how horribly he was *frighted* when he saw an approaching Danger: He look'd upon no means as base to escape it; and was not at all ashamed to relate the *Trick* or *Fetch* that had brought him off."[56] The language of the Homeric era still contained the "boldest metaphors and glowing figures [that] cast a *Fire* and *Grace* into the Composition which no Criticism can ever supply."[57] Homer's language also had an advantage over the earlier Greek, for it reflected the improvements made in society before they led to a stultifying conformity.[58] During this period "the *Greek* language was brought to express all the best and bravest of human Feelings and retained a sufficient Quantity of its *Original, amazing, metaphorick* Tincture."[59]

Not only did the general characteristics of Homer's age prove conducive to the writing of great epic poetry, but so did Homer's own experiences. Blackwell drew a picture of Homer, the impoverished rhapsodist who wandered from court to court, entertaining a martial race of a wide and free country. Much of the fire, the heroism, and the drama of Homer's poetry stemmed, Blackwell argued, from the fact that it was sung to an assemblage of rapt listeners who treasured the accounts of their forebears' prowess and achievements.[60] Homer sang to men similar in character to the heroes he immortalized; the total involvement of his audience spurred him on to greater poetic achievement: "While he was impersonating a *Hero;* while his Fancy was warming, and his Words flowing; when he had fully entered into the *Measure,* was struck with the *Rythmus,* and seized with the Sound; like a Torrent, he would fill up the Hollows of the Work; the boldest Metaphors and glowing Figures wou'd come rushing upon him."[61]

Blackwell's exposition captivated Bodmer; on the simple level it provided him with ample historical and philosophical grist to enrich his attack against Gottsched's aesthetics. The *Enquiry* offered a historical paean to the excellence of the "original," the "primitive," and the "natural." It denied that epic poetry was preceded by an an act of reflection. Like Vico, Blackwell dismissed the whole corpus of traditional Homeric scholarship which "rested upon the idea that supreme poetry must express, or be a product of, the loftiest reflective consciousness; that poetry was an art based on reflection." [62] Blackwell appeared to Bodmer to be a fellow admirer of the rough, the simple, and the rustic, qualities Bodmer thought he had discovered in his fellow countrymen. Further, Blackwell's association of language, social order, and states of mind allowed Bodmer to place the question of aesthetic theory in a far wider context, that of the political; for now Bodmer equated the imposition of rules governing language with despotism and arbitrary rule. It could be accomplished only in an absolute state. The profusion of dialects and the unregulated development of language became, for Bodmer, a measure of a free state (which for him meant a *Ständestaat* with a republican constitution). Here the aesthetic ideals, moral stance, and political conviction of Bodmer and Blackwell met.

On a higher level, Blackwell's explication of the concept of autonomous historical development led Bodmer to the conclusion later drawn by English and Scottish admirers of Blackwell, namely, that each nation had its own Homeric, or heroic, age which produced great national poetry. [63] Blackwell's theory implied this conclusion, which he had explicitly suggested in numerous asides. Employing the idea that epic poetry is produced in a time of struggles, he observed:

It was when *Greece* was ill-settled, when Violence prevailed in many places, amidst the Confusion of wandering Tribes, that *Homer* produced his immortal Poem: And it was when *Italy* was torn in Pieces, when the little States were leagued against each other; in a word, in the Heat of the Struggle and Bloodshed of the *Guelfe* and *Ghibelline* Parties, that *Dante* withdrew from his Country and made the strongest Draught of Men and their Passions, that stands in the Records of modern Poetry. The Author of the *Eneid* lived in a Time of Disorder and publick Ruin: he saw the Mistress of the World become twice a Prey to lawless Power; her Constitution destroyed, and Prices set upon the Heads of her bravest Sons for opposing a Tyranny. And still, *My Lord*, it was when unhappy *Britain* was plunged in all the Calamities of *Civil Rage*, that our high-spirited Poem took its Birth. It is true, the *Plan of Paradise Lost*, has little to do with our present Manners; It treats of a sublimer Theme, and refuses the Measure of Human Actions: Yet it every where bears some Analogy to the Affairs of Mankind: and the Author (who had viewed the Progress of our Misery) has embellished it with all the proper Images his Travelling, Learning and Experience could afford him. [64]

Bodmer, struck by one of those lightning flashes of insight, applied this analogy to German history. In 1743 he announced the discovery of a heroic, or Homeric, period of German history and literature in an essay entitled: "Von den vortrefflichen Umständen für die Poesie unter den Kaisern aus dem schwäbischen Hause."[65] In this essay Bodmer lifted whole paragraphs from Blackwell and retained all his descriptive categories. Bodmer characterized the Hohenstaufen period as one of struggle between freedom and slavery, and he repeated Blackwell's injunction about the liberating effect such times had on the spirit.[66] Bodmer pictured the thirteenth-century Germans as no longer savage and devoid of all social institutions, but as not yet cramped by the restrictions of overdone propriety (*Zucht*), ceremony, and manners.[67] These Germans were warriors who retained much of their indefatigable spirit: "The bonds of religion and administration [*Policey*] had not dampened the natural and simple movement of the heart."[68] Like the wandering bards of the Homeric era, the medieval German benefited from far-flung travels to the Orient undertaken to free the Holy Land: "The Crusades gave him countless experiences. He could enrich his fantasy with a wonderful diversity of customs, manners, religions, and the like, which varied so widely from his own."[69] All these experiences found reflection in the German language, which was strong, natural, and metaphoric. The medieval Germans were free from the deleterious effects wrought by polish and refinement.[70]

There was one critical difference between Bodmer's and Blackwell's essays, a difference that demonstrates how the idea of autonomous historical development enriched the historical consciousness. Blackwell had proceeded from the given known (Homer's poetry) to the historically possible and then back to the known. In effect, he was a literary critic who sought a new set of principles by which he could measure and reinterpret the nature of Homer's greatness. He assessed the poet's stature by placing the poem within the context of when, where, and how it was written. Bodmer had no such given with which to work. Instead, he approached his problem by seizing upon the historical analogy Blackwell suggested; he hoped research would confirm his belief that medieval Germans had produced a poetry (and hence a society) comparable to the Homeric. It was a bold step, one that could easily be condemned as overly speculative; yet its results were immense both for the developing German awareness of national uniqueness and for the later shift in attitudes toward the Middle Ages. All Bodmer could do in 1743 was to suggest the possibility that such epic poetry could have been written in Germany during the Hohenstaufen period, that "Germany's condition in political, moral, and physical things was then at a correct and opportune temperature to produce great poets and that these poets were provided with adequate subject matter for their poetic works."[71] Bodmer had then known the names of a number of thirteenth-century poets, including Walther von der Vogelweide and Wolfram von Eschenbach, and he had read a few fragments of *Parzival* and *Gamuret;* but the vast bulk of Middle High German literature remained unknown to him. Everything was shrouded in the mist of an almost forgotten past. The most he could conclude was that, judging from the excellence of those few remnants, "much good had been lost."[72] Bodmer also knew of the existence of a parchment codex, number 7266, in the Royal Library in Paris, supposedly containing a large number of poems from the Hohenstaufen period.[73]

Once started on the track of unveiling the richness of a distant and neglected period, Bodmer spared no efforts in realizing his goal. He dispatched letters to his vast network of correspondents, asking them to help him obtain the Parisian codex, the famous Manesse manuscript. Finally, after a long and tortuous process, the French king agreed to let the codex be dispatched to Zurich. The long wait proved worthwhile. Bodmer, beguiled by the rich collection of minnesinger lyrical poetry, immediately brought out his *Proben der alten schwäbischen Poesie des dreyzehenten Jahrhunderts,* which contained excerpts from 82 of the 140 poets represented in the manuscript. The poems were accompanied by notes and a glossary, an integral part of all Bodmer's later publications. Bodmer's enthusiasm for the "noble simplicity" of the Middle High German writers infected his friends, and soon he had a number of like-minded men searching libraries and monasteries for further proofs of the excellencies of thirteenth-century poets. Within a short space of time Bodmer got to see the Florentine Tristan manuscript, the Jena codex of the minnesinger, and the Weingartner minnesinger manuscript. These led to the publication in 1757 of *Fabeln aus der Zeiten der Minnesinger* and in 1758 of the two-volume collection entitled *Sammlung von Minnesingern aus dem schwäbischen Zeitpuncte.* But Bodmer did not stop with the minnesinger; in 1753 he had published his own modernized version of *Parzival* done in hexameters,[74] and in 1757 he made literary history by publishing excerpts from the *Nibelungenlied* discovered by one of his correspondents in the Hohenem library.[75] Within the space of fourteen years Bodmer had changed a suggested possibility into a demonstrable actuality; he had rediscovered a new period of German historical greatness. It was, as Max Wehrli observed, "a recovery on the grand style which no longer had to do with mere scholarship, mere national or High German pride."[76] And in the process Bodmer gained a new and immediate feeling for the Hohenstaufen period, a feeling that transcended Blackwell's categories.

The more Bodmer immersed himself in Middle High German literature, the more his interests shifted from the typical to the unique, from the universal qualities found in all heroic periods to the individual character of the High Middle Ages in Germany. By slow degrees, a concern with the historically unique came to dominate his thoughts (though this tendency was reversed in his later life). Bodmer signalized his concern in a letter to Sulzer in 1747, where he commented on the usual run of German moral weeklies: "The majority of the German *Zuschauer* ["Spectators"] contain general, dry, verbose morals; the joyful ones, on the contrary, should be more historical;

they should transport the reader into the thousand circumstances of life." [77]
Everything Bodmer did conspired to this end. Even before he had read
Blackwell, Bodmer's antiquarian researches into Zurich's past had convinced
him that though the Middle Ages were barbarian with respect to religion and
learning, its political life was far from being barbaric. [78] Blackwell had taught
him to see that the feelings and expressions of that period – its *Geist* – were
also far from being barbaric; in fact, Bodmer now came to prefer the strong,
free, and metaphoric language of the time to that of an overrefined and
overstandardized German. The lyrical poems of the minnesinger, Wolfram von
Eschenbach's rendition of *Parzival,* and the drama of the *Nibelungenlied*
revealed a culture containing, Bodmer thought, the finest elements of the
German national character.

On one level the poems offered heady stuff to the social historian, for they
allowed him to uncover a wealth of information about the life-style of the
period. The minnesinger "provide one with the most complete information"
concerning the "disposition [*Gemütsart*], the way of thought [*Denkungsart*],
the customs, and the manners" of the nation. "We see in them the axioms
and rules pertaining to marriage, love, greatness, and valor which governed
one's daily life in dealings with one's liege lord, with strangers, with women,
with artists, and with friends and foes." And the moment such an insight is
achieved, the commonly held pejorative evaluations about the age will
disappear of themselves. [79] On this level of appreciation, Bodmer treated the
poems as valuable historical sources, capable of expanding knowledge about
the times in which they were composed and about the men who lived then. [80]

On a higher level of appreciation, the poems gave evidence to Bodmer of a
distinct state of mind, heroic in nature yet uniquely German in character, one
that still left marks on the German consciousness in Bodmer's own time.
Bodmer's self-appointed task was to resurrect this mentality by thoroughly
investigating the form, structure, and language of these newly recovered
works. He announced his goal in poetic form in his introduction to *Parcival:*

> Ob die worte von deiner sprach, ihr leben und adel,
> Unsern leuten gleich dunkel und alt und niederig scheinen,
> Seh ich die bilder darinn doch leben, und fyhl im gemythe
> Deinen ausdruk der angst und bewundre die neuen gedanken.
> Die will ich meinen zeiten entfalten und durch die entfaltung
> Wieder vor ihnen die freuden der alten Ahnen erneuern,
> Die sie von deinen gesaengen in ihrem herzen empfanden. [81]

Bodmer had initiated a revaluation in historical judgment which found its
final culmination in the triumph of historicism in Germany. He constructed a
new historical type, the medieval poet-knight, worthy to compete with the
existing images of the pagan philosopher and the Renaissance humanist so
fondly admired by men of the Enlightenment. As pictured by Bodmer, the
German medieval poet-knight was martial in spirit, genuinely and ingenuously
religious, honorable toward his fellowmen, and, above all, free. Natural, naive,

simple — these were the attributes Bodmer discussed and valued. They corresponded to his conception of the strengths residing in the Swiss character; by extension, they became the qualities that differentiated the German-speaking world from the overrefined, French-dominated world of eighteenth-century court life.

Not only did Bodmer praise his rediscovered poets, but he also called for a new interpretation of the High Middle Ages. He did not seek to expunge the medieval remains from German thought, culture, and even politics. Instead, he gloried in Germany's medieval past. He saw the medieval spirit as generative for all that remained sound in German thought and the structure of medieval politics as the foundation upon which the treasured German freedoms had been established. In Bodmer's view, the Hohenstaufen period was one of the great periods in European history. It was marked by vigorous energy and imaginative creation. Unlike the age in which Bodmer lived, it had not fallen prey to the passion for abstraction and standardization. The minnesinger Wolfram von Eschenbach and the unknown composer of the *Nibelungenlied* had grasped the manifold variety of life and had portrayed that variety in a strong, vibrant, and immediate language. Both the form and the structure of their language testified, Bodmer contended, to a society equally strong and vibrant; Bodmer had learned Blackwell's lessons well. He accepted without reservation the proposition that great poetry springs from the character of a people and of an age. The individual poet does not invent the images and pictures he uses; rather, he takes them from the natural speech of his nation and his times. [82] The great poet becomes the spokesman for his times, and through his works one can grasp the spirit of a people separated from us by "many days distance." [83]

Armed with this insight, Bodmer, the cosmopolitan defender of patriotic values, directed his glance beyond the Alps and rediscovered the greatness of Dante, a poet generally demeaned in Germany and even in France. The argument and analogies Bodmer used in his evaluation of Dante were the same he employed in praising medieval Germans. Dante had lived in a heroic age; he had captured the true color of his times and had created a poetic work that shaped the future of the Italian national consciousness. In the second of Bodmer's two essays on Dante, he demonstrates how far his historical consciousness had developed since his initial confrontation with Blackwell. The major thrust of Bodmer's argument centered on the idea of historical relativism. He mocked those "critics of our polite [*artigen*] world" who "assume their times superior in enlightenment and thoroughness to all others." They fall into the trap of "employing contemporary standards as universal norms to judge the character and forms of thought of all people in all times." [84] At best, these critics recognized a few passages of fire and brilliance embedded in what they considered the morass of Gothic barbarisms. "They complain about the poem's disorder and confusion because either they are unable to perceive its art and understand the effort and thus fail to follow the plan [*Grundrisse*] in every detail, or they find the proportions too intricate and too base for their limited comprehension." [85] The fault did not lie in the poem: it arose from the narrow-mindedness of the critics. They had failed to understand that a great poetic creation partook of the spirit of the times. The language of the poem, filled with passion, symbols, images, and conviction, was immediately vital. Otherwise, the poem would have remained a lifeless, mechanical exercise in stringing together rhymes and rhythms, doomed by its very nature to early oblivion. To understand a great poetic creation one must perceive the milieu in which it was written; only then can the originality and the beauty of such a work become evident. Instead of regretting Dante's so-called Gothicisms, Bodmer savors them: "That which one names obscure, Gothic, contradictory, and affected in its plan and execution could, with a little bit of justice, be called new, unusual, and original." [86] As a final warning to those overly impressed by their own era, Bodmer took the idea of historical relativism formulated in the Enlightenment and turned it back on its creators: "Dante was justified in imparting the tincture of the sciences, customs, and tastes of his contemporaries to his work, just as poets living today make it a duty to compose according to the character of our time. If Dante's poem has become too learned, too obscure, too tiresome, for the contemporary reader, so the leading poets of today may appear to a later age of the human race as too artificial, too superficial, too empty." [87]

Conclusion

Traditional interpretations have found the Enlightenment guilty of wholesale antipathy to the Middle Ages. The indictment has often been levied that such an antipathy demonstrates the poverty of the Enlightenment's historical consciousness. In simple terms, it has been claimed that the Enlightenment was not interested in the past as such. Bodmer's fascination with the Middle Ages directly contradicts this assumption, and modern research has shown that Bodmer's concerns were not unique. Although many Enlightenment thinkers did look back at the medieval past and saw nothing but deceit, error, and barbarism, there were those who did not share these negative feelings. As Lionel Gossman has recently demonstrated, medievalism played an integral role in Enlightenment thought: "Medievalism was part of a wider movement of curiosity about and sympathy for earlier and more 'primitive' cultures."[1] In this sense, medievalism was as natural to Enlightenment thought as the widespread infatuation with the ancient cultures of Greece, Israel, Rome, and China, or with the culture of newly appreciated lands such as Russia. If one of the hallmarks of modern historical thought is a deep-seated interest in and sympathy for the past, then the Enlightenment shared this feeling. Bodmer's medievalism, Winckelmann's worship of the Greeks, Michaelis's lifetime concern with the ancient Hebrews, and Schlözer's fascination with the Phoenicians, the Siebenbürgern Germans, and Russia all testify to the Aufklärung's concern for the past. A vibrant historical imagination was a central element of the Aufklärung's world view.

The recognition of the Aufklärung's basic concern with the past does not alone prove that its historical thought coincided with the form of historical thinking encompassed by the word "historicism." At best it allows us to discount the traditional evaluation that Enlightenment thought was antihistorical or ahistorical. If we are to ascertain the relation between Enlightenment historical thought and the rise of historicism, the function of historical understanding is of critical importance. If, for a moment, we forget the many specific definitions, historicism may be defined as a way to look at the world "whereby the truth, meaning or value of anything is to be found in history."[2] In this definition two central concerns can be detected: (1) history is the means by which one acquires an understanding of the human condition; (2) historical understanding serves as a challenge to confront and to transvalue the burden of the past. Historicism operates on a dualistic principle in that it attempts to mediate between conflicting ideas such as change and continuity, individuality and communal being, freedom and necessity, and value and causality. In eighteenth-century Germany, these dichotomies

[213]

assumed especial importance because of the unresolved tensions in German life. More than France and Great Britain, Germany was a battleground where contending intellectual and political traditions struggled for supremacy. Throughout the last half of the century, German thinkers were compelled to steer a path between a religion of the heart and a rational religion, between the claims of the absolute and the feudal state, between cosmopolitan universalism and provincial localism, and between a literature modeled after French classical forms and one mirroring sentimental expressionism. Increasingly, German thinkers and writers sought to resolve these mutually exclusive positions through the application of historical analysis.

Despite the real difference in attitudes between the thinkers and the historians I have discussed, all viewed history as the key to unlock the meaning of life. History dissolved the absolute claims of conflicting solutions; further, it functioned as a moral critique of the narrowness and pettiness of contemporary existence. Past experience, present realities, and future possibilities were seen as intimately related. Historical understanding served as the necessary prologue to meaningful reform. To overcome the present one had to understand how the present had been shaped by the past; only then could an image of the future founded upon concrete reality be constructed. Historical understanding provided a critique that denied the efficacy of abstract reason and arbitrary standardization; it condemned the superficial customs and conventions associated with polite society of the time by recognizing the primacy of what Bodmer, Semler, Möser, Pütter, Gatterer, and even Schlözer called *Lokalvernunft,* a concrete, historically conditioned, understanding of a particular situation. None of these writers urged the Germans to imitate the past blindly; rather, they called for a renewal of the spirit. They justified the possibilities of such a renewal by arguing that historical understanding enabled people to reexperience emphatically the heroic spirit of past ages. In this sense, historical understanding entailed an intuitive grasp of the unique moment. This intuitive understanding, which approximated that experienced by the poet or the artist, enabled people to understand their own humanity by apprehending the humanity of others. For the Aufklärers, history became the guide in their search for an understanding of things human.

This function of historical understanding reveals two categories central to the historicist mentality: the concept of development and the idea of individuality. Each, when taken to its logical conclusion, excludes the other. If this occurs, history is seen either as an unending developmental chain where every moment is determined by what preceded it or as an aggregate of unique individual moments with little or no causal connection. The Aufklärers were able to avoid both extremes and still assert the reality of both categories. They constructed their idea of history upon two assumptions derived from Leibnizian philosophy: the idea of perfectibility and the theory of the monad. Both had played central roles in Leibniz's attempt to formulate a philosophical system that would avoid the pitfalls of mechanistic explanation. Unlike many western thinkers who defined perfection in normative, positive terms, German thinkers viewed perfection as a potentiality toward which a body could strive. History was the story of a genetic process wherein each stage was viewed as unique, informed by its own spirit, yet symbiotically related to its past and its future. Those stages were often seen as analogous to the monad. The monad theory was Leibniz's answer to the atomic theory. The monad, as differentiated from the atom, is a basic entity that is organically individual, self-containing, and self-sufficient. Each monad is the expression of unity in diversity and each monad is a "point of view," an aspect of the totality of the world: "Each one of these is not only a fragment of the universe, it is the universe seen from a particular viewpoint."[3] Thus the Aufklärers came to recognize periods and cultures as points of view, as discrete perspectives of history, which can be apprehended only by seeing them as necessary and constitutive parts of the whole.

These formulations were not accepted merely because they were Leibnizian, for Leibniz was an extremely controversial figure during most of the eighteenth century; nor were they the result of an inherent tendency of German intellectual history, attended by its own independent and autonomous development. Rather, the Aufklärers appropriated these Leibnizian metaphors because they seemed to resolve problems central to the Enlightenment as a whole and to the Aufklärung in particular. The Aufklärers' idea of history sprang from an interaction between intellectual tradition and existential condition. The overriding existential problems confronting eighteenth-century thinkers were religious and political. In the religious realm, the Aufklärers participated in the Enlightenment's analysis of the phenomenon of religion.[4] Yet, unlike many leading western philosophes, they sought to "save" revealed religion. In so doing they attempted to reconcile the dialectic between Pietism and rationalism. In the political sphere, the Aufklärers struggled to resolve the basic political question of the Enlightenment within the context of the German experience: How can one construct a polity that is both free and efficient? The strategies the Aufklärers employed to resolve these religious and political problems helped shape the specific outline of their idea of history.

A ubiquitous religious impulse impelled the Aufklärers to question the absolute dictates of autonomous reason. First implicitly and then with quickening awareness, the Aufklärers drew a distinction between nature and grace and between their correlates, reason and spirit. As noted above, they did so in response to the contending claims of Pietism and rationalism.[5] The former emphasized an irrational and highly personal religion of the heart; the latter sought simple universal truths. In Pietism, grace or spirit dissolved reason; rationalism made grace, or spirit, reasonable. Neither the Pietist nor the rationalist answer satisfied the Aufklärers, since either claim assumed a primacy of one over the other. Instead, the Aufklärers attempted to evolve a mode of appreciation that incorporated elements of both Pietism and rationalism. According to the Aufklärers, reason and spirit were distinct yet joined. They were not identical, at least not in a simple manner. The Aufklärers directed their attention to probing the manner in which reason and spirit were related. In this endeavor they historicized the concept of reason. Reason became the concrete manifestation of an age's appreciation of truth. Beneath this manifestation the Aufklärers discerned the action of an inborn energy − spirit − which, they contended, defines man's freedom. Thus every product of reason contains a spiritual element. Reason, in its broader context, is that which binds a community together. Combined with necessary forms of ritual, it defines a religious body. But since spirit strives for its own self-fulfillment, spirit continually acts in and against reason. The moment reason acquires a repressive or tutelary quality − as it must at each stage of its development − spirit conspires to break reason's hold. For the history of religion, this meant that each religious phenomenon was both unique and universal, unique in its concrete historicity, universal in that it reflected the operation of spirit or grace. It further implied that no final religious answer is possible, for spirit or grace is active, not static; it is universal and individual at the same time.

Politically, the Aufklärers faced a situation analogous to the religious one. They confronted a set of conflicting positions that either sacrificed individuality to abstract formulations or abandoned the application of reason in favor of irrational individualism. In simple terms these choices were to restructure the body politic along the lines established in France and supported by modern theories of natural law, or to accept the bewildering status quo. They balked at the first choice, fearing a destruction of the vaunted German liberties and the abrogation of the religious guarantees established by the Peace of Westphalia. They rejected the second because they realized the inability of the existing political units to deal effectively with the immensely difficult political and economic problems of the time. In the Aufklärers' opinion, the absolute state denied freedom by its very nature; the traditional feudal state had allowed the suppression of freedom because of its weakness and inefficiency. They opted for a solution designed to realize the possibilities of freedom inherent in the *Ständestaat* through a program of concrete reform, that is, through the application of *Lokalvernunft*. In other words, they hoped for a harmonic resolution of change and continuity. Practical reforms directed to the abolition of the abuses of serfdom, to the reorganization of the agrarian system, to the alleviation of poverty, to the partial introduction of free trade, and to the reorganization of the legal system were to be joined to a revived *Ständestaat* constitution in which the "constituted bodies" were to play an active role in the formulation of internal policy. In this way the Aufklärers hoped to effect a revolution without destroying the uniqueness of the German national character.

The Aufklärers' religious and political views both saw change in terms of the tension between tradition and innovation, which Wegelin designated as "the dead and the living forces of society." In this change tradition is transformed but not destroyed. Each new historical creation contains a strong admixture of whatever preceded it. The Aufklärers employed the image of education to describe this process. The education of humanity was seen as analogous to the education of the individual. Both were to be directed by the light of historical understanding. In the Aufklärers' view, education was not a passive process, conditioned solely by reflection on past and present. Rather, historical understanding had to be nourished by action, by continual application of historical reason to concrete situations. This attitude is both optimistic and progressive, but it does not reflect the naive optimism often ascribed to Enlightenment thinkers or the concept of automatic progression propounded by a minority of French philosophes. The Aufklärers advanced a view of history that envisioned the possibility of progress, provided man directs his energies to achieving such progress. Their vision of progress was reformist, where their sense of future time was regulated by their feeling for past time and was modified by the recognition that every nation, every historical epoch, had its own worth, its own unique spirit. Their image of the future was the creation of a *Bildungstaat* – a state animated by an ethical or spiritual ideal by which the inner life of man was enriched.

2

Until now I have dealt with historicism as a general Weltanschauung and as an approach to history that accepts the reality and the mutual interdependence of the ideas of development and individuality. This concept by itself does not encompass the complexity of the historicist mentality. Equally important is a theory of understanding that justifies historicism as both viable and objective. Georg Iggers, a leading interpreter of historicism, clarifies the point: "The core of the historicist outlook lies in the assumption that there is a fundamental difference between the phenomena of nature and those of history, which requires an approach in the social and cultural sciences different than those of the natural sciences."[6] Though the terms Professor Iggers employs are recent (derived from Dilthey), the impulse he describes is clearly evident in the epistemological inquiries of the Aufklärers. A central problem in the Aufklärers' historical thinking was to establish an independent hermeneutic region for the study of man in society.

Impelled by their religious convictions, the Aufklärers evolved a paradigm of historical explanation characterized by two basic propositions: (1) man and the social world that man constructs are composed of material and spiritual natures; (2) the spiritual nature that fashions man's experience in the world cannot be totally explained by the material world in which man subsists. From Chladenius to Heeren, eighteenth-century German thinkers clarified and elaborated these propositions; they received instruction along the way from parallel developments in aesthetics and psychology.

The close conjunction between the Aufklärers' developing conception of history and their researches into aesthetics, psychology, and religion stemmed from the basic impulse animating these endeavors: the desire to mediate between normative and subjective modes of understanding. In both aesthetics and psychology a concerted effort was made to apprehend forms of perception that eluded a rationlist or sensationalist formulation. In psychology, the problem was to distinguish reason, will, and sensation; in aesthetics, between form, imagination, and effect. In both, the middle element of the triad was seen as dominant. Will directed reason, while imagination created form. Slowly these two dominant terms, will and imagination, were joined and expanded to define the element of human nature that distinguished man from other species. Generally, this element was called spirit, which in its action attested to man's freedom.

The conclusion that spirit was original and free (not totally explicable by normative means) led the Aufklärers to draw a distinction between rational or abstract understanding and moral or immediate understanding. The former was best suited to investigate a world external to man; the latter allowed one to understand the human world. Abstract understanding isolates elements and divides them into their constitutive parts; it eliminates everything that cannot be expressed in quantitative terms and then reconstructs the world through the use of deductive reasoning. Its goal is to establish a chain of causal relations. Moral understanding, seeking to comprehend the world in its interrelations, tries to "see everything in everything."[7] It proceeds by an intuitive grasp [*anschauende Erkenntnis*] of the individual in the totality, a grasp that is impelled by the action of the spirit. Mathematics is the ideal notational system for abstract understanding; poetry, the ideal form for intuitive understanding. History, which stands poised between both forms because of its dual concern with the external world and the spiritual world, has to draw from both. In its analysis of the natural world it should be guided by the causal principle; yet, since its object of investigation is man in the world, its highest goal is to present an intuitive understanding of the past. In other words, the historian has to employ both the truths of science and the truths of poetry in order to formulate an independent logic of historical explanation. According to the Aufklärers, every historical phenomenon contains an infinite conjunction of complex and individual elements. It is beyond the competence of any one person or age to comprehend fully the totality of a past age. Hence, every historical generalization entails an intuitive understanding of this totality made from a specific perspective or point of view. Total historical understanding is an impossible ideal; at most the historian can integrate former perspectives into his own consciousness through an act of intuitive understanding and attain, thereby, an expanded awareness of the past and the present.

The Aufklärers evolved an idea of history that envisioned historical change as the result of a continual interaction between transmitted social values and intellectual forces and a spiritual drive that sought to transform them. In so doing, the Aufklärers borrowed the idea of original genius from contemporary aesthetics to account for the specific manner in which qualitative change occurs. The original genius becomes the central agent in effecting spiritual revolutions. The genius, as conceived by the Aufklärers, is not the great speculative thinker; rather, the genius is the great poet. Working from the idea expressed by such thinkers as Blackwell, Bodmer, Lowth, and Michaelis, that poetry both preceded and was superior to reflection, the Aufklärers characterized genius as supra- or irrational. The great poet provides his people with an intuitive representation of the truths of their times at a level approaching divine understanding.[8] The genius forms a people by shaping its national character through his intuitive understanding. Hence, a historian has to uncover a people's national character by investigating its sacred and creative writings. Only when this character is reexperienced can a historian adequately understand the context in which events took place.

Taken together, these positions contain elements central to historicism. In the broadest sense, the world was conceived in historical terms and historical analysis became the means to unlock the secrets of man's existence. In more specific terms, the Aufklärers attempted to maintain the dual ideas of genetic development and individuality without subsuming one in the other. The idea of individuality is used on the simplest level to describe the original genius; his specific formulations mirror his own unique character which cannot be explained by purely normative means. But the idea of individuality is also expanded to encompass larger units such as groups, nations, peoples, civilizations, and epochs. In their writings the Aufklärers affirmed the irrational substratum of life. And, finally, they formulated a theory of historical understanding that established a duality between nature and spirit and recognized that all historical understanding is relative to the milieu in which it is generated.[9] Granted, these positions were not always explicated in a coherent system, certainly not by any one individual. In certain respects, ideas implicit in their formulations were not taken to their logical conclusions. Thus, for example, we do not encounter the concentration upon the state as an ethical entity which was to be so prevalent in full-blown historicism. The nationalistic impulses of their historical thinking were always modified by the Aufklärers' cosmopolitan outlook, by their belief that the general category of humanity transcends national affiliation. Yet, like Herder, they did believe that humanity can be realized only within the traditions in which one is nourished.

Many real contradictions can be found in the Aufklärers' writings, contradictions resulting from their attempts to mediate between the normative postulates of scientific thought and the subjective implications of their own discoveries. Still, it is my contention that the joint efforts of these scholars, publicists, and clergymen, each cultivating his own limited sphere of interest, produced the general presuppositions from which the most famous figures of later eighteenth-century German history operated. If, as Friedrich Meinecke asserts, the rise of historicism is one of the great intellectual revolutions of the modern age, then the larger part of this revolutionary activity was carried out in the Enlightenment by Enlightenment thinkers. To paraphrase Georg Lukács, the great achievements in late eighteenth- and early nineteenth-century German thought were not achieved in opposition to the Enlightenment but flowed directly from it.

Notes

Introduction

1. Max Wundt, *Die deutsche Schulphilosophie im Zeitalter der Aufklärung*, Heidelberger Abhandlungen zur Philosophie und ihrer Geschichte, vol. 32 (Tübingen: J. C. B. Mohr, 1945), p. 1.

2. *Goethe and His Age*, trans. Robert Anchor (London: Merlin Press, 1968). Besides pointing out the continuity between the German Enlightenment and German idealism, Lukács also argues (p. 15) that Goethe, at least the young Goethe, "was a participant in the general evolutionary process of the Enlightenment and in the German Enlightenment within it."

3. See Janine Buenzod, "De l'Aufklärung au Sturm und Drang: continuité au rupture?" in *Studies on Voltaire and the Eighteenth Century*, ed. Theodore Besterman, XXIV (Geneva: Institut et Musée Voltaire les Delices, 1963), 289-314, who convincingly argues that the Sturm und Drang did not signal a break with the Aufklärung.

4. An example of the parameters of this debate may be seen in three recent works. Lionel Gossman emphasizes the difference between the French Enlightenment's historical consciousness and the type of consciousness associated with the word "historicism" in his excellent study, *Medievalism and the Ideologies of the Enlightenment: The World and Work of La Curne de Sainte-Palaye* (Baltimore: Johns Hopkins Press, 1968). In a different vein, Louis Althusser shows the modern aspects of Montesquieu's historical consciousness in *Politics and History: Montesquieu, Rousseau, Hegel and Marx*, trans. Ben Brewster (London: New Left Books, 1972). Martin Göhring also draws a connection between Montesquieu and the modern historical consciousness in *Montesquieu: Historismus und moderner Verfassungsstaat* (Wiesbaden: Max Steiner, 1956).

5. Gossman, *Medievalism*, p. viii.

6. Throughout the text I retain the German word *Stand*, pl. *Stände*, and its various compounds. *Stände*, roughly translated, refers to the orders, corporations, and estates derived from medieval and early modern European social and political practice. It carries with it the connotation of a specific social and legal mentality associated with one order [*Stand*] or with the complex of all. A *Ständestaat* is a state where corporate orders, constituted bodies, and a juridical system postulated upon the *Stände* predominate.

7. Helen P. Liebel, *Enlightened Bureaucracy versus Enlightened Despotism in Baden, 1750-1792*, Transactions of the American Philosophical Society, n.s., vol. 55, pt. 5 (Philadelphia, 1965), pp. 6-8.

8. Although no study of eighteenth-century European universities exists, it is generally accepted that most western universities were in a state of

decline. In Catholic countries, the universities carried on the same curriculum that had been forged to further the Counter-Reformation. The English universities were also in a rather sad state, at least if one accepts Gibbon's harsh characterization of Oxford as containing a kernel of truth. The only place in western Europe where a vibrant intellectual life existed in the universities was Scotland.

9. Thomasius's attitude clearly approximated that of the Aufklärung. Since Thomasius preceded Wolff, there is a difficulty in periodization. Unlike Wolff, however, Thomasius never dominated the thought of his generation. In fact, his philosophy of life did not even conquer the University of Halle, where he taught. Although Thomasius had a number of outstanding students, especially in the faculty of law, the Halle of his time was dominated more by the Pietism of Francke. When Wolff arrived at Halle he displaced Thomasius. From then on, Halle housed the two opposing strains of extreme rationalism and self-conscious Pietism. These were the very strains the Aufklärers sought to reconcile.

I. The Crisis of Historical Consciousness
at the Dawn of the Aufklärung

1. 3 vols. (Paris, 1935); *The European Mind, 1680-1715*, trans. J. Lewis May (London: Hollis and Carter, 1952).

2. This idea persisted because it provided one of the major supports for the translation theory, which saw the Holy Roman Empire as the direct successor to Rome, despite Jean Bodin's devastating attack on both. The first major theorist in Germany to deny the translation theory was the brilliant seventeenth-century Helmstedt professor Hermann Conring.

3. Erich Seeberg, *Gottfried Arnold: Die Wissenschaft und die Mystik seiner Zeit* (1923), reprint ed. (Darmstadt: Wissenschaftliche Buchgesell-schaft, 1964), p. 459.

4. This view of history prevailed at the Protestant universities of Germany which had incorporated Melanchthon's reforms. For Melanchthon, the major task of history was to inculcate correct religious belief and to teach correct principles of composition. See Josef Engel, "Die deutschen Universitäten und die Geschichtswissenschaften," *Historische Zeitschrift*, 189 (1959):239, 245-246, 249, 255-256; Heinrich Ritter von Srbik, *Geist und Geschichte: Vom deutschen Humanismus bis zur Gegenwart*, 2 vols. (Salzburg: Müller, 1950), 1:63-70; Friedrich Paulsen, *Geschichte des gelehrten Unterrichts, auf den deutschen Schulen und Universitäten vom Ausgang des Mittelalters bis zur Gegenwart*, 3d ed., 2 vols. (Berlin: Walter de Gruyter, 1919-1921), 1:234, 254.

5. Adalbert Klempt, *Die Säkularisierung der universalhistorischen Auffassung* (Göttingen: Musterschmidt, 1960), pp. 127-128.

6. René Descartes, *Discourse on Method and Other Writings*, trans. Arthur Wollaston (London: Penguin Books, 1960), pt. 1, p. 40.

7. In general, *érudits* were concerned with literary evidence and antiquarians with nonliterary evidence. For an excellent discussion of their goals and their differences see Arnaldo D. Momigliano, "Ancient History and

the Antiquarian," in *Studies in Historiography* (London: Weidenfeld and Nicolson, 1966), pp. 1-39. See also David Knowles, *Great Historical Enterprises* (London: Nelson, 1963).

8. Momigliano, "Ancient History and the Antiquarian," p. 16.

9. Quoted by Ernst Cassirer, *The Philosophy of the Enlightenment,* trans. Fritz C. A. Koelln and James P. Pettegrove (Princeton: Princeton University Press, 1951), p. 209.

10. Christian Wolff, *Preliminary Discourse on Philosophy in General* (1728), trans. Richard J. Blackwell (Indianapolis: Bobbs-Merrill, 1963), p. 7.

11. Wolfgang Philipp, *Das Werden der Aufklärung in theologie-geschichtlicher Sicht,* Forschungen zur systematischen Theologie und Religionsphilosophie, vol. 3 (Göttingen: Vandenhoeck and Ruprecht, 1957), pp. 87-97. I use the term "new philosophers" to designate those who denied traditional scholastic thinking. It applies also to those who believed the natural and social worlds could be studied mathematically.

12. Leo Strauss, *Natural Right and History* (Chicago: University of Chicago Press, 1953), p. 178.

13. Pierre Bayle, "Pyrrho," in *Historical and Critical Dictionary Selections,* trans. Richard H. Popkin (Indianapolis: Bobbs-Merrill, 1965), pp. 205-206 n. C.

14. See the discussion of two abbés in ibid., pp. 196-204 n. B.

15. Bayle, "Third Clarification," in *Dictionary,* p. 435.

16. Ibid., p. 429.

17. Bayle offers a duality that is virtually absolute, so absolute that many later commentators could not believe that Bayle expected anyone to opt for "incomprehensibility." To them Bayle's proposition was nothing more than a hidden attack on Christianity. It could be argued that Bayle in this instance was playing the "judicious historian [who] imitates the grape-gatherers and gardeners. Before speaking of certain facts he waits for time to ripen them. . . . temporal death is the almost inevitable consequence of obedience to the lawgiver of historians" ("Bonfadus," in *Dictionary,* p. 31 n. D). Modern scholarship has questioned this interpretation. K. C. Sandberg has shown that Bayle was not endangered by the dire consequences often visited on a writer who was too honest ("Pierre Bayle's Sincerity in His View on Faith and Reason," *Studies in Philology,* 61 [1964]:74-84). The question concerning the nature of Bayle's faith is still open, but I believe that Bayle accepted the choice of "incomprehensibility" to be both correct and, given the direction of his critique, more intellectually honest.

18. Johann Huizinga suggests the same: "Der historische Skeptizismus, der nicht mit dem philosophischen Skeptizismus gleichgesetzt werden darf, ist schon eine alte Krankheit. . . . Er taucht anscheinend immer wieder auf, wenn eine neue kräftige Strömung des Geistes eine Zeit zwingt, ihren Standpunkt gegenüber der Geschichte aufs neue zu bestimmen. . . . Im 17. Jahrhundert erscheint der Skeptizismus von neuem: Pierre Bayle und Fontenelle legen dafür Zeugnis ab. Der Skeptizismus trat damals in einer feineren und einer Gröberen Form auf. In der letzteren leugnet er überhaupt die Echtheit der Quellen. . . . Die feinere Form des Skeptizismus dagegen leugnet nicht a priori die Echtheit der Quellen, aber sie bestreitet die Möglichkeit, daß die

Wiedergabe der Tatsachen, sogar wenn sie durch Zeitgenossen oder Augenzeugen erfolgt, richtig sein könne" (*Im Bann der Geschichte: Betrachtungen und Gestaltungen* [Basel: Pantheon, 1943], pp. 68-69).

19. The best works on Pufendorf are Hans Welzel, *Die Naturrechtslehre Samuel Pufendorfs* (Berlin: Walter de Gruyter, 1958); Leonard Krieger, *The Politics of Discretion: Pufendorf and the Acceptance of Natural Law* (Chicago: University of Chicago Press, 1965); Eric Wolf, *Grotius, Pufendorf, Thomasius: Drei Kapitel zur Gestaltgeschichte der Rechtswissenschaft,* Heidelberger Abhandlungen zur Philosophie und ihrer Geschichte, vol. 11 (Tübingen: J. C. B. Mohr, 1927); Friedrich Meinecke, *Die Idee der Staatsräson in der neueren Geschichte* (1924), vol. 1 of *Werke,* 3d ed., ed. Walter Hofer (Munich: Oldenbourg, 1963).

20. Welzel, *Naturrechtslehre,* p. 14; Krieger, *Politics of Discretion,* p. 51; Seeberg, *Gottfried Arnold,* p. 325.

21. Strauss, *Natural Right and History,* p. 171.

22. Ibid., p. 183.

23. Wolf, *Grotius, Pufendorf, Thomasius,* pp. 85-96; Seeberg, *Gottfried Arnold,* p. 325.

24. Samuel von Pufendorf [Severinus von Monzambano], *Ueber die Verfassung des deutschen Reichs,* trans. Harry Bresslau (Berlin, 1870), sec. 6, par. 9, pp. 106-107 (hereafter cited as Monzambano).

25. Welzel, *Naturrechtslehre,* p. 79.

26. Samuel von Pufendorf, *Einleitung zu der Historie der vornehmsten Reiche und Staaten,* 4 vols. (Frankfurt, 1718), vol. 1, "Vorrede."

27. Krieger, *Politics of Discretion,* pp. 131-132.

28. Monzambano, sec. 6, par. 1, p. 98.

29. Ibid., sec. 6, par. 3, p. 99; Pufendorf, *Historie der vornehmsten Reiche,* "Vorrede."

30. *The Spectrum of Social Time,* trans. Myrtle Korenbaum (Dordrecht: Reidel, 1964), pp. 31-32. Gurvitch referred to this sense of time as predominant in times of uncertainty: "It is the time of *social roles* and of *collective attitudes,* where regulated social roles collide with repressed, aspired, fluctuating and unexpected social roles. . . . This is the time of global societies in transition, as our society of today so often is" (p. 32). The same idea has been brilliantly employed by George Armstrong Kelly in his analysis of Rousseau (*Idealism, Politics and History: Sources of Hegelian Thought* [Cambridge: Cambridge University Press, 1969]). Rousseau himself was deeply influenced by Pufendorf (see Robert Derathé, *Jean-Jacques Rousseau et la science politique de son temps* (Paris: Presses Universitaires de France, 1950).

31. *Discourse on Method,* pt. 1, p. 40.

32. *Standesperson,* as used here, refers to a member of a legally recognized estate of the realm.

33. Kelly, *Idealism, Politics and History,* pp. 71-72.

34. For an extensive discussion of the historical role of the image of the future see Fred L. Polak, *The Image of the Future: Enlightening the Past, Orientating the Present, Forecasting the Future,* trans. Elise Boulding, 2 vols.

(Leyden: Sythoff, 1961), vol. 1, *The Promised Land: Source of Living Culture.*

35. Pufendorf, *Historie der vornehmsten Reiche,* 1:917-918.

36. Ibid., p. 1019.

37. Ibid., pp. 986-987.

38. See Meinecke, *Staatsräson,* p. 295; Hans Rödding, *Pufendorf als Historiker und Politiker in den "Commentarii de Rebus Gestis Friderici Tertii"* (Halle, 1912), pp. 45-60, 82; Johann Gustav Droysen, "Zur Kritik Pufendorfs," in *Abhandlungen zur neueren Geschichte* (Leipzig, 1876), pp. 307-386.

39. "Diese Methode des Systematisierens, die eine gedachte Geschichte mit Hilfe der Logik ordnet und konstruiert, dürfte die Überwindung der annalistischen Geschichtschreibung befördert haben. . . . Alles drängt über das bloße Nacherzählung hinaus auf Stoffbeherrschung und Stoffgestaltung, d.h. auf wirkliche Geschichte hin" (Seeberg, *Gottfried Arnold,* p. 325).

40. Lewis White Beck, *Early German Philosophy: Kant and His Predecessors* (Cambridge, Mass.: Belknap Press, 1969), pp. 148-149.

41. The phrase, used by the Catholic theologian Karl Adam, is quoted by William Nicholls, *Systematic and Philosophical Theology* (London: Penguin Books, 1969), p. 75.

42. Karl Barth, *Die protestantische Theologie im neunzehnten Jahrhundert: Ihre Vorgeschichte und ihre Geschichte* (Zurich, 1947).

43. Gottfried Arnold, *Unparteyische Kirchen- und Ketzer-Historie, von Anfang des Neuen Testaments biß auf das Jahr Christi 1688,* 2 vols. in 1 with consecutive pagination (Frankfurt, 1700), p. 475 (hereinafter cited as *K. u. K.*).

44. Albrecht Ritschl, *Geschichte des Pietismus in der Lutherische Kirche des siebzehnten und achtzehnten Jahrhunderts,* 4 vols. (Bonn, 1884), vol. 2, bk. 1, p. 302.

45. *K. u. K.,* "Vorrede," par. 25.

46. *K. u. K.,* p. 99.

47. *K. u. K.,* p. 31.

48. *K. u. K.,* p. 236.

49. *K. u. K.,* "Vorrede," par. 15.

50. *K. u. K.,* pp. 258-260.

51. *K. u. K.,* pp. 30-39, 160.

52. *K. u. K.,* "Vorrede," par. 31, and p. 223.

53. *K. u. K.,* p. 237.

54. "Die Sophia ist 'die offenbahrende, verklärende, ankündigende Kraft der gantzen hochheiligen Dreyeinigkeit'" (quoted by Seeberg, *Gottfried Arnold,* p. 26).

55. This basic assumption of Pietist hermeneutics later formed the basis of the theory of emphatic understanding (Joachim Wach, *Das Verstehen: Grundzüge einer Geschichte der hermeneutischen Theorie im neunzehnten Jahrhundert,* 3 vols. [1926-1933]; reprint ed., 3 vols. in 1, [Hildesheim: Georg Olms, 1966], 1:15-16 n. 2). One must remember, however, that Arnold's formulation is far more radical than traditional Pietist hermeneutics, which sought to combine rational and emphatic standards.

56. Quoted by Beck, *Early German Philosophy*, p. 151.
57. *K. u. K.*, p. 153.
58. Wolff, *Preliminary Discourse*, p. 3.
59. Bayle, "Arriage," in *Dictionary*, p. 27 n. C.

II. Form and Goal of the Aufklärung's Idea of History

1. Benedetto Croce, *History: Its Theory and Practice*, trans. Douglas Ainslie (New York: Russell and Russell, 1960), p. 26.
2. Cassirer, *Freiheit und Form: Studien zur deutschen Geistesgeschichte*, 3d ed. (Berlin: Bruno Cassirer, 1916), p. 101.
3. The connection between the Aufklärung and Thomasius is emphasized by Wundt, *Die deutsche Schulphilosophie*, pp. 264-351. What I call the Aufklärung, Wundt labels the third generation of the Aufklärung.
4. The difficulty of uncovering all of Leibniz's ideas may be illustrated by the controversy between Maupertuis and König. König had criticized Maupertuis's *principe de la moindre action* and remarked that whatever was valid in it had already been proposed by Leibniz in a letter to Jacob Hermann in 1707. This critique, with its hint, though not charge, of plagiarism, enraged the overly sensitive Maupertuis and led to a violent clash in which Maupertuis forced the Berlin Academy to take his side and condemn König as a liar because König could not produce the original letter. The controversy assumed European importance when Voltaire defended König and virtually ruined Maupertuis by making him the laughingstock of Europe. For details of the controversy see Adolf von Harnack, *Geschichte der Königliche Preussischen Akademie der Wissenschaften zu Berlin*, 4 vols. (Berlin: Reichsdruckerei, 1900), 1:331-345.
5. The degree to which Wolff considered himself a Leibnizian is open to question. He repeatedly said that he owed more to Aristotle and the Spanish scholastics than to Leibniz. Leibniz disassociated himself from Wolff's philosophy. See Walther Arnsperger, *Christian Wolffs Verhältnis zu Leibniz* (Weimar, 1887). Be that as it may, Wolff's contemporaries thought of him as a Leibnizian and referred to his philosophy as the Leibniz-Wolffian philosophy.
6. Eric A. Blackall, *The Emergence of German as a Literary Language, 1700-1775* (Cambridge: Cambridge University Press, 1959), pp. 2-11. Blackall gives an excellent appraisal of Wolff's achievement in forging a German philosophic vocabulary (pp. 27-48).
7. Johann Georg Sulzer, *Lebensbeschreibung von ihm selbst aufgesetzt*, ed. Johann B. Merian and Friedrich Nicolai (Berlin, 1809), pp. 11-15. Sulzer (1720-1779) was born and trained in Switzerland; he later moved to Berlin where he did most of his work. Originally a professor of mathematics, he was most famous for his writings on aesthetics and psychology. He was closely allied to the Bodmer-Breitinger-Haller circle in Switzerland and on close terms with Nicolai and Mendelssohn.
8. The tendency to equate mathematical knowledge with the unreal, the imaginative, was forcefully argued by one of the first major anti-Wolffians, Christian A. Crusius, in *Entwurf der nothwendigen Vernunft-Wahrheiten*

(Leipzig, 1745), and *Weg zur Gewissheit und Zuverlässigkeit der menschlichen Erkenntniss* (Leipzig, 1747).

9. Sulzer, *Lebensbeschreibung*, p. 21.

10. Sulzer's regard for nature is analogous to what Wolfgang Philipp has called "physicotheology" (*Das Werden der Aufklärung in theologiegeschichtlicher Sicht*, Forschungen zur systematischen Theologie und Religionsphilosophie, vol. 3 [Göttingen: Vandenhoeck and Ruprecht, 1957]). Hegel took cognizance of this approach, which he characterized in the following manner: "Es war eine zeitlang Mode, Gottes Weisheit in Tieren, Pflanzen, einzelnen Schicksalen zu bewundern." The physicotheologians themselves, however, were addicted to the polyhistorical assumptions of exemplar history. The Aufklärers combined the basic religious outlook of the physicotheologians with the Leibnizian idea of harmonic conjunction. In a sense, Hegel did the same. After his comment on physicotheology, he asked: "Wenn zugegeben wird, daß die Vorsehung sich in solchen Gegenständen und Stoffen offenbare, warum nicht aber in der Weltgeschichte?" Later he added: "Unsere Betrachtung ist insofern eine Theodizee, eine Rechtfertigung Gottes, welche Leibniz metaphysisch auf seine Weise in noch unbestimmten, abstrakten Kategorien versucht hat . . ." (Georg Wilhelm Friedrich Hegel, *Vorlesungen über die Philosophie der Geschichte*, vol. 12 of *Werke* [Frankfurt: Suhrkamp, 1970], p. 28).

11. Johann David Köhler, *Erneuerter Entwurf eines Collegii über den gegenwärtigen Zustand von Europa und die jetzigen Welt-Händel* (Göttingen, 1736), pp. 2-3. Köhler (1684-1750) was one of the most respected historians of the first half of the eighteenth century. Educated at Wittenberg, he taught at Altdorf and Göttingen. His major concerns were German history, European history, and especially the ancillary sciences.

12. Fontenelle quoted by Carl L. Becker, *The Heavenly City of the Eighteenth-Century Philosophers* (New Haven: Yale University Press, 1932), p. 91; Montesquieu, *The Persian Letters*, trans. George R. Healy (Indianapolis: Bobbs-Merrill, 1964), Letter LXVI, pp. 110-111.

13. Henry St. John Bolingbroke, *Letters on the Study and Use of History*, vols. 3 and 4 of *Collected Works* (London, 1809), Letter 4, 3:403-405.

14. Gibbon on Voltaire, quoted by Arnaldo D. Momigliano, "Gibbon's Contribution to Historical Method," in *Studies in Historiography*, p. 45.

15. August Ludwig von Schlözer, *Stats-Gelartheit: Zweiter Theil: Theorie der Statistik nebst Ideen über das Studium der Politik überhaupt* (Göttingen, 1804), p. 92. Schlözer (1735-1809), famous as a historian and as a publicist, was one of the most prominent Aufklärers. He was educated at Wittenberg and Göttingen. After a stay in Russia, he returned to Göttingen, where he was a professor for the rest of his life.

16. Johann Salomo Semler, *Johann Semlers Lebensbeschreibung von ihm selbst abgefaßt*, 2 vols. (Halle, 1781, 1782), 1:15. Semler (1725-1791), educated at Halle, taught at Altdorf and Halle. He was one of the most famous theologians of his generation and a leader of the group commonly called the Neologists. His major concerns were New Testament history and hermeneutics, though he also wrote on such subjects as medieval German

history and the history of crafts. He helped his mentor, Sigmund Jacob Baumgarten, translate and edit the *English World History.*

17. Johann Jacob Schmauß, *Kurze Erleuterung und Vertheydigung seines Systematis Juris Naturae* (Göttingen, 1755), p. 11. Schmauß (1690-1757) was a highly gifted teacher and an original, though controversial, thinker. He was educated at Halle, where he studied with Thomasius and Gundling; he served for awhile in the court of Baden-Durlach before he accepted a professorship at Göttingen. He also taught at Halle. His major concerns were European political history, German history, and natural law.

18. *Kurze Erleuterung,* p. 12.

19. Carl Justi, *Winckelmann und seine Zeitgenossen* (1866), 5th ed., reprint ed., 3 vols. (Cologne: Phaidon, 1956), 1:88.

20. Johann Stephan Pütter, *Litteratur des teutschen Staatsrechts,* 4 vols. (Göttingen, 1776-1791), 1:443-445. Pütter (1725-1809), educated at Halle, Jena, and Marburg, taught at Marburg and Göttingen. During his long stay at Göttingen he was one of its most famous teachers and jurists. His courses in German constitutional history were known throughout Germany and his textbooks on that subject were widely used in Protestant and Catholic universities alike. Among his students were the founders of the "historical school of law," Savigny, Hugo, and Eichhorn.

21. Isaak Iselin, *Über die Geschichte der Menschheit,* 4th ed., 2 vols. (Basel, 1779), 2:406-408. Often these thinkers were among the later followers of Wolff. Iselin listed Mendelssohn, Lambert, Reimarus, Sulzer, and Baumgarten.

22. Quoted by Momigliano, "Gibbon's Contribution," p. 43.

23. Johann Christoph Gatterer, ed., *Historisches Journal, von Mitgliedern des Königlichen Historischen Instituts zu Göttingen,* 2 (1773), 120. Gatterer (1727-1791) was educated at Altdorf and taught at Göttingen. He and Schlözer were the most famous historians at Göttingen during the 1760s and 1770s. He is most renowned for his work in universal history and the ancillary sciences. Similar attacks on the reliability of French scholarship were voiced by the famous church historian Johann Lorenz von Mosheim and the orientalist Johann David Michaelis. Mosheim, in his important study of Servetus, remarked: "Allein was achten die ordentlichen und meisten französischen Geschichtsschreiber dergleichen Kleinigkeiten, die wir übrigen so genau beobachten, damit die Wahrheit der Geschichte nicht verfälschet werde? Diese Herren dichten, wenn sie die leeren Plätze in der Geschichte aus Büchern und guten Nachrichten nicht füllen können. . . . Und was ihre hitzige Einbildung sich als wahrscheinlich vorstellet, das wird ohne Bedenken als eine zuverläßige Wahrheit in diejenigen Bücher hineingerücket, die sie unter dem Namen einer Historie in die Welt schicken" (Johann Lorenz von Mosheim, *Neue Nachrichten von dem berühmten spanischen Artzte Michael Servets der zu Geneve ist verbrannt worden* [Helmstedt, 1750], p. 22). And in reply to Jacobi's suggestion that a society for the critical study of the Bible be founded, Michaelis wrote: "Ich sollte suchen, grosse Gelehrte in Frankreich und Italien zu ermuntern: Das ist nicht möglich. Denn in diesen Ländern sind keine grosse Gelehrte" (Johann David Michaelis, *Literarischer Briefwechsel*

von Johann David Michaelis, ed. Johann Gottlieb Buhle, 3 vols. [Leipzig, 1794-1796], 1:118).

24. "Die Katastrophentheorie ist gleichsam das normale Seitenstück zu dem geschichtsphilosophischen Systeme, das Religionen und Staatsverfassungen durch einen einmaligen Willensakt aus dem Nichts entstehen ließ" (Eduard Fueter, *Geschichte der neueren Historiographie,* 3d ed., vol. 3, sec. 1 of Handbuch der mittelälterlichen und neueren Geschichte, ed. Georg von Below, Friedrich Meinecke, and Albert Brackmann [Berlin: Oldenbourg, 1936], p. 345).

25. Quoted by Cassirer, *Philosophy of the Enlightenment,* p. 217.

26. Montesquieu, *Considerations on the Causes of the Greatness of the Romans and Their Decline,* trans. David Lowenthal (Ithaca: Cornell University Press, Cornell Paperbacks, 1968), chap. XVIII, p. 169.

27. Schlözer, "Ideal," in *Vorstellung seiner Universal-Historie,* 2 vols. (Göttingen, 1772-1773), 1:45. (This edition, the first of two, is hereafter cited as *Universal-Historie I.*)

28. *Der gegenwärtige Zustand der Göttingischen Universität in zweenen Briefen an einem vornehmen Herrn im Reiche* (Göttingen, 1748), p. 77.

29. Cassirer, *Freiheit und Form,* p. 62.

30. Even those who claimed to be anti-Leibnizian, largely because they were opposed to Wolff, expressed this idea. Nicholas Gundling, Thomasius's most able student, employed a similar argument: "When a German grapevine is planted in Spanish soil, some of the old color always remains; the fruit will always retain some of its tartness even though it takes on something of the Spanish sweetness. When I, therefore, see what Tacitus wrote of the ancient Germans and compare it with the Germany of today, I must admit that there is still something remaining of the old. And even when more generations pass there will always be a great deal, or at least something, of the past left" (Nicholas H. Gundling, *Ausführlicher Discours über den ietzigen Zustand der europäischen Staaten,* 2 vols. [Frankfurt, 1733-1734], 1:6).

31. Claude Lévi-Strauss, *La pensée sauvage* (Paris, 1962), pp. 89-99, 306-323. Schlözer expressed the ideal in the following manner: "Der Zusammenhang der Begebenheiten ist zweyerlei, entweder ein *Realzusammenhang,* oder ein blosser *Zeitzusammenhang.* Man verstatte mir diese Namen, oder weise mir schicklichere an. Mit andern Worten, jede Reihe von Begebenheiten muß auf eine gedoppelte Art gelesen werden: einmal in die *Länge,* vor-und rückwärts; und dann in die *Breite,* seitwärts oder synchronistisch" (*Universal-Historie I,* 1:46).

32. Quoted by Meinecke, "Deutung eines Rankewortes," in *Zur Theorie und Philosophie der Geschichte,* vol. 4 of *Werke,* ed. Eberhard Kessel (Stuttgart: Koehler, 1965), pp. 119-120. Meinecke referred to this double interest as "horizontal" and "vertical" history, a distinction confusing to the American reader. By "horizontal" he meant "die Kausalverkettung der einzelnen Gebilde." Vertical history was defined as "aufwärts zu Gott und wieder abwärts auf das historische Gebilde." Although Meinecke recognized both tasks, his specific interests were with vertical history. His method of taking a "Gratwanderung durch das Gebirge" made any causal analysis extremely difficult. Only at the end of his life, after the disaster of World

War II, did Meinecke attempt to revise his attitude toward horizontal history, as shown by his *Deutsche Katastrophe* and his increasing preference for Burckhardt — the Burckhardt of the *Weltgeschichtliche Betrachtungen* — over Ranke.

33. Pütter, *Grundriß der Staatsveränderungen des teutschen Reichs, nebst einer Vorbereitung worinn zugleich ein Entwurf einer Bibliotheck und gelehrten Geschichte der teutschen Historie enthalten*, 2d ed. (Göttingen, 1755), "Vorrede." Pütter used the word *constitution* in its broadest meaning, as the complex set of institutions, laws, habits, traditions, and opinions which formed the state's character at any given time.

34. Johann Martin Chladenius, *Allgemeine Geschichtswissenschaft, worinnen der Grund zu einer neuen Einsicht in allen Arten der Gelahrheit gelegt wird* (Leipzig, 1752), pp. 218-240. Chladenius (1710-1759), was trained at Wittenberg, taught there and at Erlangen. Although a theologian, he is considered one of the most important eighteenth-century theorists of history.

35. *Handbuch der Universalhistorie nach ihrem gesamten Umfange von Erschaffung der Welt bis zum Ursprunge der meisten heutigen Reiche und Staaten* (Göttingen, 1761), p. 61.

36. *Entwurf der allgemeineren europäischen Staatshändel des siebzehnten und achtzehnten Jahrhunderts als der europäischen Geschichte zweyter Theil* (Göttingen, 1756), "Vorrede."

37. *Ancient Greek Historians* (1908), reprint ed. (New York: Dover, 1958), p. 45.

38. Sigmund Jacob Baumgarten, *Uebersetzung der allgemeinen Welthistorie die in Engeland durch eine Geselschaft von Gelehrten ausgefertiget worden, nebst den Anmerkungen der holländischen Uebersetzung*, 30 vols. (Halle, 1744-1767), vol. 1, "Vorrede."

39. Gatterer's entire statement, to which I will refer again, deserves quoting because it clearly indicates the degree to which Leibnizian conceptions were accepted in the last half of the eighteenth century: "Der *höchste Grad des Pragmatischen* in der Geschichte wäre die Vorstellung des allgemeinen Zusammenhangs der Dinge in der Welt (*Nexus rerum universalis*). Denn keine Begebenheit in der Welt ist, so zu sagen, *insularisch*. Alles hängt an einander, veranlaßt einander, zeugt einander, wird veranlaßt, wird gezeugt, und veranlaßt und zeugt wieder. Die Begebenheiten der Vornehmen und der Geringen, der einzelnen Menschen und aller zusammen, des Privatlebens und der grossen Welt, ja selbst der unvernünftigen und leblosen Geschöpfe und der Menschen, alle sind in einander verschlungen und verbunden. Daß ein Mensch diesen höchsten Grad des Pragmatischen in der Historie erreichen könne, wird kein Vernünftiger erwarten . . ." (Gatterer, ed., *Allgemeine Historische Bibliothek von Mitgliedern des Königlichen Instituts der Historischen Wissenschaften zu Göttingen*, 16 vols. [Halle, 1767-1771], 1:85-86 [hereafter cited as *AHB*]). Gatterer's ideal was also expressed by Heeren: "Die Weltgeschichte in ihrem ganzen Umfange, was ist sie anders als ein fortlaufendes Gewebe von Ursachen und Wirkungen, wo die Wirkungen wieder die Ursachen neuer Wirkungen werden? Die Entwicklung dieses unermeßlichen Gewebes, sey es im Ganzen, sey es in einzelnen Theilen, ist die Aufgabe für den Geschichtschreiber. . . . Er wird es sich selber gestehen, daß

das vollständige Erforschen der Begebenheiten in ihrem Zusammenhange weit über seine Kräfte, ja weit über die Kräfte jedes menschlichen Wesens gehe; er wird also das ihm vorgesteckte Ziel als ihm unerreichbar erkennen; aber er wird es sich doch auch gestehen dürfen, daß er ihm sich nähern mehr oder weniger sich nähern kann; *und daß eben dieses Annähern Geschichte schreiben heißt*" (Arnold Hermann Ludwig Heeren, "Andenken an deutsche Historiker aus den letzten fünfzig Jahren," in vol. 6, *Historische Werke* [Göttingen, 1823], pp. 434-436.

40. Johann Heinrich Gottlob von Justi, *Untersuchung der Lehre von den Monaden und einfachen Dinge worinnin der Ungrund derselben gezeigt wird* (Berlin, 1748), p. xiv.

41. For an excellent study of the contours of the problem of the application of the mathematical model to other sciences see Giorgio Tonelli, "Der Streit über die mathematische Methode in der ersten Hälfte des achtzehnten Jahrhunderts und die Entstehung von Kants Schrift über die 'Deutlichkeit,'" *Archiv für Philosophie* 9/1-2 (1959):37-66. The eighteenth-century desire to differentiate between mathematical knowledge and real knowledge was evident in the writings of both Vico and Buffon. For Vico's evaluation of mathematics see Antonio Corsano, "Vico and Mathematics," in *Giambattista Vico: An International Symposium,* ed. Giorgio Tagliacozzo and Hayden V. White (Baltimore: Johns Hopkins Press, 1969), pp. 425-438: Yvon Belaval, "Vico and Anti-Cartesianism," in *Giambattista Vico,* ed. Tagliacozzo and White, pp. 77-92. For Buffon's distinction between physical and mathematical truths see Peter Gay, *The Enlightenment: An Introduction,* 2 vols. (New York: Knopf, 1967, 1969), vol. 2, *The Science of Freedom,* p. 154.

42. Carl Becker put forth this interpretation in his controversial little essay, *The Heavenly City,* pp. 71-118. It is hard to resist the temptation to stereotype the Enlightenment's idea of history as philosophy teaching by example, especially since Bolingbroke specifically used the Plutarchian term to describe history. Even those favorable to the Aufklärung regret the use of the term and consider it antihistorical. Fueter offered a contradictory set of defenses of the Enlightenment's fascination with pragmatic history. His first defense was that the Enlightenment did not invent the concept but used it in a more honest and open manner. His second defense argued that only the minor figures of the Enlightenment practiced a one-sided pragmaticism. The leaders of thought had already overcome it (Fueter, *Neueren Historiographie,* pp. 342-343). By far, those most critical of the Aufklärung's use of the word have been the German commentators.

43. *Johann von Müller der Historiker* (Leipzig, 1809), p. 68.

44. *Historisches Journal,* 6 (1776), 165-166. The different set of definitions the author in question proposed were the following: (1) a history whose narrative allows us to deduce truths about mankind; (2) a history that unearths the causes and effects of important events; (3) a history in which the writer successfully achieves what he has set out to do.

45. *AHB* 1:80-81.

46. "Zerstreute Anmerkungen über das Gedächtniß," in *Vermischte Schriften,* 2 vols. (Frankfurt, 1766, 1769), 1:48.

47. Ulrich Im Hof, *Isaak Iselin: Sein Leben und die Entwicklung seines Denkens bis zur Abfassung der "Geschichte der Menschheit" von 1764,* 2 vols. (Basel, 1947), 1:424. Schmauß described earlier history thus: "Die Historie ist ehemals fast durchgehends nur als eine solche Wissenschaft angesehen worden, die dienlich seye, Gottes unergründliche Gerichte in den vielfältigen und wunderbaren Zufällen, so sich an Frommen und Gottlosen von Anbeginn der Welt bis zu unserer Zeit ereignet, zu erkennen; oder auch sonst nur einige *Moralien* aus denen Geschichten zu ziehen, und die Tugend daraus zu lernen; so daß der Nutzen derselben fast allein in Schul-Reden und Predigten erkannt worden" (Schmauß, *Kurzer Begriff der Reichs Historie in einer accuraten chronologischen Ordnung, von den ältesten Zeiten, bis auf die gegenwärtigen,* 2d ed. [Leipzig, 1729], "Vorrede," p. 9).

48. (Leipzig, 1766), First Collection, 2:247.

49. Pütter, *Grundriß der Staatsveränderungen des teutschen Reichs,* 3d ed. rev. (Göttingen, 1764), "Vorrede."

50. Wundt, *Die deutsche Schulphilosophie,* p. 285.

51. *Uebersetzung der Welthistorie,* vol. 1, "Vorrede." In addition, Baumgarten presented a grab bag of reasons to justify the study of history. The idea of useful examples was included among those reasons. Baumgarten's most devoted and brilliant student, Johann Salomo Semler, himself testified to Baumgarten's transitional position (*Semlers Lebensbeschreibung,* 1:210).

52. Chladenius, *Das Blendwerk der natürlichen Religion,* trans. Urban Gottlob Thorschmid (Leipzig, 1751).

53. *Allgemeine Geschichtswissenschaft,* "Vorrede."

54. Semler, *Zur Revision der kirchlichen Hermeneutik und Dogmatik* (Halle, 1788), pp. 86-87.

55. It does not follow that the Neologists' assumptions were universally accepted. Reimarus still used history to discredit the Bible. Following the example of Spinoza, Reimarus tried to show that the doctrinal interpretations of Christianity could not be sustained by historical analysis. He dismissed the Neologists' attempts with the simple argument that it seems impossible to believe that God intended a sincere Christian to be first a good philologist (Henry E. Allison, *Lessing and the Enlightenment: His Philosophy of Religion and Its Relation to Eighteenth-Century Thought* [Ann Arbor: University of Michigan Press, 1966], p. 47).

56. *Universal-Historie I,* 1:33-34.

57. "Every nation, . . . whether Greek or barbarian, has had the same conceit that it before all other nations invented the comforts of human life and that its remembered history goes back to the very beginning of the world" (Giambattista Vico, *The New Science,* trans. Max Harold Fisch and Thomas Goddard Bergin [Garden City: Anchor-Doubleday, 1961], p. 19).

58. *Letters,* Letter 2, 3:332-333.

59. "Hr. Herder hat völlig recht, daß sich etwas *leichter sagen als thun* lasse. Aber hier, wo von Weltgeschichte die Rede ist, meine ich, muß es auch *gesagt* werden, ehe es *gethan* wird. . . . aber um den Streitenden auseinander zu bringen, müssen diese Grundsätze *entwickelt,* muß ein *Plan,* eine *Theorie,* ein *Ideal* dieser Wissenschaft, verfasset werden" (*Universal-Historie I,* vol. 2, "Vorbericht"). Later in the same work Schlözer remarked: "Es wäre

nunmehro Zeit, einen Blick auf das Ganze zu werfen, um wenigstens zu übersehen, ob und wo irgend noch ein Stück Feld unbebaut seyn möchte, und um allmälig den Weg dazu zu bahnen, daß einmal ein vollständiges Lehrgebäude der Revolutionen des Erdbodens und Menschengeschlechts darauf gebauet werden konnte" (ibid., 2:265-266). Gatterer expressed the same concern for the future of historiography and the same belief that his efforts would help overcome the inadequacies in German historical writing. He looked forward to the day when the Germans would no longer "be the laughingstock of Europe because of their pedantry, their love of minutiae, their exaggerated use of footnotes, and their desire to demonstrate learning when it was least needed" (*AHB* 1:36).

III. The Aufklärung's Image of the Future and Its Concept of Historical Development

1. Becker, *Heavenly City*, p. 97. This derivative assumption animates Becker's critique of the Enlightenment's historical consciousness. Typical of Becker's approach is the following statement: "Do not, therefore, ask the Philosophers that question so dear to the nineteenth century: 'How did society come to be what it is?' Almost without exception they will reply with Rousseau: 'We do not know.' And at once we feel that they have it on the tip of their tongues to dismiss us with an impatient 'and we do not care'" (p. 98).

2. Polak, *Image of the Future,* 1:47.

3. Gay, *Enlightenment,* 2:6.

4. Ibid., p. 3.

5. Ibid., p. 8.

6. Gay's concentration upon the centrality of the anti-Christian element of the Enlightenment is obvious even from his definition of the recovery of nerve. He defines it as a rejection of the negative attitude produced by Christianity which ruled until the end of the seventeenth century (ibid., pp. 5-6).

7. Ibid., p. 5.

8. Georges Gurvitch, *The Spectrum of Social Time,* trans. Myrtle Korenbaum (Dordrecht: Reidel, 1965), p. 50. Gurvitch differentiates seven realms of social life, which he calls ecological surface, organization, conventions, social roles, collective attitudes, symbols-ideas-values, and collective mentality.

9. In fact, if one looks closely at Professor Gay's explanation for the recovery of nerve, the real cause turns out to be a nonmaterial and highly controversial improvement in the quality of life. In the last analysis, Professor Gay really ascribes the recovery of nerve to the supposed eighteenth-century decline of Christianity: that is, to what he sees as a process of secularization finally effected by the "little family of the philosophies." He does so through a simple device. By blaming Christianity for a "failure of nerve" that suffused the whole Christian period from the end of antiquity to the seventeenth century, he hints that only a "modern paganism" can produce the opposite effect. Whatever the merits of Professor Gay's interpretation, it does not

show that the Enlightenment's image of the future was a companion of realism.

10. Gay, *Enlightenment*, 2:12.

11. Ibid., p. 7.

12. Fred Polak defines the utopian mentality along similar lines (see *Image of the Future*, p. 19). The term *Noch-Nicht-Sein* was coined by Ernst Bloch to describe utopian thinking. For a short, but comprehensive, introduction to the interpretations of utopian thought see the introduction to *Utopias and Utopian Thought,* ed. Frank E. Manuel (Boston: Houghton Mifflin, 1966). Since I was unable to obtain the original edition while working in Vienna I have used the German translation, *Wunschtraum und Experiment: Vom Nutzen und Nachteil utopischen Denkens,* trans. Otto Kimminich (Freiburg: Rombach, 1970), pp. 7-23. My definition of the utopian image of the future resembles what Kelly called a chimera when he discussed the visions of Rousseau, Kant, Fichte, and Hegel in *Idealism, Politics and History:* "A 'chimera' is not identical with the ideal state . . . but . . . it signifies any conceivable situation where man can feel intact, harmonious, a valid part of the world" (p. 15).

13. Semler, *Neuer Versuch die gemeinnützige Auslegung und Anwendung des Neuen Testaments zu befördern* (Halle, 1786), p. 14.

14. Ibid., p. 118.

15. Achenwall, *Die Staatsklugheit nach ihren ersten Grundsätzen* (Göttingen, 1761), "Vorrede," par. 10.

16. Iselin, *Geschichte der Menschheit,* 1:xxiii.

17. Schlözer, *Stats-Gelartheit nach ihren Haupt Theilen. Erster Theil: Allgemeines Stats Recht und Stats Verfassung* (Göttingen, 1793), p. 11.

18. Judith Shklar, "Die politische Theorie der Utopie," in *Wunschtraum,* ed. Manuel, p. 145.

19. Kelly, *Idealism, Politics and History,* p. 1.

20. Shklar, "Theorie der Utopie," p. 147.

21. Schlözer, *Universal-Historie I,* 2:273.

22. "Die *Einbildung* ist noch in unsern *Monarchien* und in unsern *Freystaaten,* wie bey den *Griechen* und bey den *Römern,* das grosse Gesetz, das die meisten Seelen beherrschet. Obgleich sie durch eine erleuchtetere und ausgebreitetere *Vernunft* mehr gemässiget wird, so ist ihre Uebermacht doch noch unendlich groß: so sind wir doch wahrscheinlicher Weise, wie es die *Griechen* und die *Römer* auch waren, der *Barbarey noch näher als der wahren Menschlichkeit*" (Iselin, *Geschichte der Menschheit,* 2:463).

23. "Abhandlung vom Standort und Gesichtspunct des Geschichtschreibers oder der teutsche Livius," *AHB* 5 (1768):18-19.

24. Semler, who was fascinated by these people, punctuated his *Lebensbeschreibung* with valuable portrayals of the beliefs of the Harz Mountain miners.

25. For example, Christian Gottlob Heyne was frightened merely by hearing about ghosts.

26. Montesquieu, *The Spirit of the Laws,* trans. Thomas Nugent (New York: Hafner, 1949), Bk. XIX, chap. 4, p. 293.

27. It is true that Montesquieu offered fragmentary suggestions about the influence of time on society, but they were undeveloped and often inadequate. Especially difficult were his regulative, or energizing, principles for each type of government and the manner in which they decayed. Germany as a political unit just could not be explained by any of them. In fact, as Franz Neumann points out, they even contradicted Montesquieu's idea of a mixed government (*Spirit of the Laws*, p. xlii).

28. The harmonic metaphor is present in Montesquieu's writings: "What is called union in a body politic is a very equivocal thing. The true kind is a union of harmony, whereby all the parts, however opposed they may appear, cooperate for the general good of society — as dissonances in music cooperate in producing overall concord" (*Considerations*, chap. ix, pp. 93-94). One could also find Montesquieu opting for an explanation of change based on human drives. He argues (in ibid., chap. xi) that political structures are upset because of man's incessant drive to acquire power. Thus many Aufklärers could accept both Montesquieu and Hume.

29. For the controversy over the applicability of the mathematical method to other fields of inquiry, see Tonelli, "Der Streit über die mathematische Methode," pp. 37-66.

30. Schmauß, *Vorstellung des wahren Begriffs von einem Recht der Natur* (Göttingen, 1748), pp. 7-8.

31. Schmauß, *Kurze Erleuterung*, p. 15. In the same work Schmauß ridicules Wolff for having "proven" that "when one wishes to eat, natural law decrees that the mouth should not be open too wide or too little" (p. 12). Wolff's fixation on demonstration invites ridicule. One of the most hilarious examples was his proof that German coffeehouses should be made like English ones so that they would be comfortable for scholars (cited by Beck, *Early German Philosophy*, p. 262).

32. Schmauß, *Vorstellung Recht der Natur*, pp. 12-13.

33. Ibid., p. 15.

34. Quoted by Cassirer, *Philosophy of the Enlightenment*, p. 332.

35. Quoted by Basil Willey, *The Eighteenth Century Background: Studies on the Idea of Nature in the Thought of the Period* (Boston: Beacon, 1961), p. 58.

36. Michaelis, *Mosaisches Recht*, 1st ed., 6 vols. (Frankfurt, 1770-1775), 2:223-225. Diderot also denied the validity of the natural aversion in his *Supplément au voyage de Bougainville*.

37. *Neues Systema des Rechts der Natur* (Göttingen, 1754), p. 465.

38. Because of the close tie between aesthetic and historical concerns, Alfred Baeumler went so far as to call aesthetics the *Vorläufer der Historiographie*, but I believe he goes too far in seeing a causal relation between history and aesthetics. The fascinating thing about the Aufklärung is that it expands both fields and that both sets of inquiry have a reciprocal effect upon each other. See Alfred Baeumler, *Kants Kritik der Urteilskraft: Das Irrationalitaetsproblem in der Aesthetik und Logik des achtzehnten Jahrhunderts bis zur Kritik der Urteilskraft* (Halle: Max Niemeyer, 1923).

39. Gillo Dorfles, "Myth and Metaphor in Vico and in Contemporary Aesthetics," in *Giambattista Vico*, Tagliacozzo and White, p. 577.

40. The creative role of philosophical analysis, which envisioned an *Überwindung* of irrationality through a consciousness of irrationality, has led Alfred Baeumler to call the eighteenth century the classic age of irrationalism: "Insofern ist das 18. Jahrhundert die klassische Zeit des Irrationalismus: es hat nicht nur das Erlebnis des Individuellen, sondern auch noch den Mut, es auf die ratio zu beziehen. Die ganze philosophische Fruchtbarkeit des 18. Jahrhunderts beruht darauf, daß in ihm die entgegengesetzten Prinzipien zugleich sich entfalten; der Rationalismus erhielt sich in ungebrochener Kraft, während der Irrationalismus sich erhob: aus dem Widerstreit und der Versöhnung dieser Prinzipien ist die deutsche klassische Philosophie hervorgegangen" (Baeumler, *Irrationalitaetsproblem*, p. 5).

41. Perhaps it is even an exaggeration to call late eighteenth-century aesthetics Wolffian. As Baeumler acknowledged (ibid., pp. 211, 217), it was more Leibnizian than Wolffian in content, and its basic concern with the *menschlichen* accorded more to the concerns of Wolff's great rival, Thomasius.

42. Alexander Baumgarten (1714-1762) was the younger brother of Sigmund Jacob Baumgarten (1706-1757), the famous Halle theologian and church historian and the teacher of Semler. Alexander Baumgarten was educated at Halle, where he accepted Wolff's philosophy. From 1738 until 1740 he was a professor at Halle, and from 1740 until his death a professor at Frankfurt on the Oder. Besides his aesthetic works, he was most known for his *Metaphysica*.

43. Baeumler, *Irrationalitaetsproblem*, pp. 6-8.

44. Cassirer, *Philosophy of the Enlightenment*, p. 341.

45. Ibid., p. 348.

46. Alexander Baumgarten first promulgated some of his views in his *Meditationes philosophicae de nonnullis ad poema pertinentibus* (Halle, 1735), translated as *Reflections on Poetry* by Karl Aschenbrenner and W. B. Holther (Berkeley and Los Angeles: University of California Press, 1954). The ideas contained therein were then popularized by Georg Friedrich Meier, *Anfangsgründe aller schönen Wissenschaften* (Halle, 1748). The two volumes of Baumgarten's *Aesthetica* appeared later (1750 and 1758), but they were never so widely read as Meier's popularization. Baumgarten's retention of the Wolffian term "confused ideas" to explain the aesthetic experience angered the Swiss Wolffian, Johann Jacob Bodmer. In reviewing Baumgarten's *Aesthetica* he said: "It seems that the opinion is getting out of hand that taste is a lower form of judgment whereby we can have only confused and dark knowledge. In this sense it will be no great praise to have a taste which is so uncertain, and it is scarcely worth striving for" (quoted by Cassirer, *Philosophy of the Enlightenment*, p. 340).

47. Baeumler, *Irrationalitaetsproblem*, pp. 80-82. In this definition Bodmer was guided by Leibniz's idea of harmonic conjunction; he went so far as to claim that "Leibniz's system of pre-established harmony . . . struck a mortal blow at sensation. . . . he deposed it from the judgeship which it had usurped for so long and made it simply a ministering and occasional cause of a judgment of the soul" (quoted by Cassirer, *Philosophy of the Enlightenment*, p. 333; and by Baeumler, *Irrationalitaetsproblem*, p. 81).

48. Carlo Antoni, *Der Kampf wider die Vernunft: Zur Entstehungsgeschichte des deutschen Freiheitsgedankens,* trans. Walter Goetz (Stuttgart: Koehler, 1951), pp. 37-54. Antoni makes Bodmer a central figure in the process of overthrowing abstract rationalism (which he incorrectly labels the Aufklärung). Like Croce, Antoni had a very low opinion of Baumgarten's aesthetics and therefore slighted Baumgarten's importance. Baeumler and Cassirer, seeing a close tie between Baumgarten and Kant, make Baumgarten the central figure in eighteenth-century aesthetics, but I believe they slight the importance of those who were also engaged in hammering out a new approach to aesthetics, often without knowledge of Baumgarten's work.

49. Antoni, *Kampf wider die Vernunft,* p. 51.

50. Moses Mendelssohn, *Über die Empfindungen* (Berlin, 1755), pp. 192-193n.

51. Ibid., p. 52.

52. Baeumler, *Irrationalitaetsproblem,* p. 186.

53. Johann Georg Sulzer, "Observations sur les divers états où l'ame se trouve en exerçant ses facultés primitives, celle d'apercevoir et celle de sentir," in *Histoire de l'Académie Royale des Sciences et Belles-Lettres de Berlin* (Berlin, 1763), pp. 407-420.

54. Ibid., p. 409.

55. Chladenius also used the visual analogy in his discussion of historical understanding (see his *Allgemeine Geschichtswissenschaft,* esp. the chapter, "Von Zuschauer und Sehepunkte," pp. 91-115).

56. Here Sulzer consciously denies the Leibniz-Wolffian one-faculty theory and seemingly returns to the classical idea of two faculties.

57. Sulzer, "Observations," p. 409.

58. Ibid., p. 410.

59. Ibid.

60. Ibid., p. 417.

61. Ibid.

62. To illustrate the tentative nature of these categories, the fuzziness of the term *Einbildungskraft* should suffice. For some thinkers, *Einbildungskraft* was actually the term used to describe experience; it was a composite of the conscious and unconscious memory which correctly reflected the experienced object. Others used it to describe the creative power of the soul which is capable of rearranging individual experience and to create a differentiated image of the past and the future. Further difficulty in understanding the Aufklärers came from their use of terms from four different languages — sometimes not equivalent — to describe one thing. For example, not only did the Germans employ the words *Vernunft* and *Verstand* for "reason"; they were also prone to use *raison,* "understanding," *ingenium, iudicium, ratiocinatio, intelligentia, génie, sagacité, esprit fort,* and "common sense." All these were used alongside the German technical and common terms such as *Witz, Scharfsinn,* and *Urteilskraft.* It was not until Kant that a real distinction was made between *Vernunft* and *Verstand.* The same confusion applies to the three-faculty theory. Although the distinction between these two terms is implicit in the writings of many thinkers of the Aufklärung, Kant was the first to establish it clearly.

63. Wilhelm Körte, ed., *Briefe der Schweitzer Bodmer, Sulzer, Geβner aus Gleims litterarischen Nachlasse* (Zurich, 1804), p. 254.

64. Baeumler, *Irrationalitaetsproblem,* pp. 235-237.

65. Perhaps in no other century have Swiss thinkers played so important a role in European thought. Everywhere one went in Europe, one encountered Swiss intellectuals, professors, and teachers. For decades the Swiss members (Beguelin, Bernoulli, de Catt, Euler, Lambert, Merian, Passavant, Sulzer, and Wegelin) dominated the Berlin Academy (Harnack, *Geschichte der Akademie,* 1:327). To realize their importance for the Aufklärung, one has only to mention the following names: von Haller, Bodmer, Breitinger, Sulzer, Geβner, Wegelin, Zimmermann, von Müller, and Iselin.

66. Iselin, *Geschichte der Menschheit,* 1:xiv.

67. Ibid., p. 4.

68. Ibid., p. 167.

69. Ibid., p. 168. Montesquieu gives a similar definition in *Spirit of the Laws,* Bk. I, chap. 1, p. 3.

70. Iselin, *Geschichte der Menschheit,* 1:7-8.

71. Iselin's image of woman as the educator of humanity was based on an idealization of his own experience. He had a sensitive and well-read mother who educated him as a youth and continually spurred him on to continue his studies. Iselin believed that his age was on the right track because the feminine drives were becoming more predominant: "Seit dem Anfange unsers Jahrhunderts hat auch in diesem Stücke der Zustand von Europa sich fast durchgehends verändert. Die weibischen Triebe und Neigungen erhalten täglich eine merklichere Uebermacht" (*Geschichte der Menschheit,* 2:431). Iselin's skeptical attitude toward Swiss politics and his championship of the cause of women's rights probably received reinforcement from the younger Schlözer, with whom Iselin came into contact at Göttingen. Schlözer's critique of the Swiss oligarchs and his successful efforts to provide his daughter with a first-class education have already been mentioned.

72. *Geschichte der Menschheit,* 2:250-251.

73. For an excellent development of this theme see Kelly, *Idealism, Politics and History.*

74. Ibid., p. 55.

75. Schlözer, *Universal-Historie I,* 1:10-13.

76. Ibid., p. 6.

77. Gatterer, *Ideal einer allgemeinen Weltstatistik* (Göttingen, 1773), pp. 26-27.

78. Gatterer, *Abriβ der Universalhistorie in ihrem ganzen Umfange,* 2d ed. rev. (Göttingen, 1773), pp. 393-404.

79. Iselin called education the greatest of man's endeavors: "Die Erziehung ist die grösste Wohlthat, welche der Mensch dem Menschen gewährten kann. Ihr erster, ihr grosse Endzweck ist, die verschiedenen Triebräder der menschlichen Seele in die vollkommenste Harmonie zu bringen, und ihrem unersättlichen Bestreben nach Thätigkeit diejenige Richtung zu geben, durch welche ihre wohlthätigen Neigungen unaufhörlich erleichtert, erweitert, erhöhet werden, durch welche sie immer fähiger wird,

die Glückseligkeit, und die Vollkommenheit andrer zu befördern"
(*Geschichte der Menschheit*, 1:88).

80. "Gelehrte von Profession . . . sind, wie die Geschichte lehrt, eben so
wie Geistliche, natürliche Freunde der Despotie: aber wol zu verstehen, wenn
sie *mit am Ruder sitzen.* Denn eben weil sie sich ihrer Einsichten bewußt sind,
so wünschen sie *menschenfreundlich,* daß zum Glücke des Stats alles, mit dem
geringsten Widerstande und Widerspruche, nach ihrem Kopfe gehe; dieser
geringste Widerstand aber ist bekanntlich in der Despotie – Vergl. mit der
Geschichte des jetzigen Premier-Ministers (vormals Professors), Hrn Marquis
Tanucci in Neapel, und des Hrn Turgot in Versailles" (Schlözer, *Briefwechsel,*
16 vols. [Göttingen, 1774-1782], vol. 1: *Meist statistischen Inhalts*
[1774-1775], pp. 147-148n).

81. Achenwall, *Staatsklugheit,* "Vorrede," par. 26.

82. Michaelis, *Mosaisches Recht,* 2:14: "Darf ich hierbey die Anmerkung
machen, daß die Gesetzgebende Klugheit sich auch mit der Zeit ändert, oder
eigentlicher zu reden, für jedes Zeitalter der Völker ihre besondern
Vorschriften eben so gut, als für die verschiedenen Himmelsstriche hat?"

83. Montesquieu, *Considerations,* chap. XVII, p. 160.

84. *Spirit of the Laws,* Bk. XIX, sec. 14, pp. 298-299.

85. Pütter, *Beyträge zum teutschen Staats- und Fürsten-Rechte,* 2 vols.
(Göttingen, 1777), 2:57-58. For Pütter's discussion of the incorporation of
the three "foreign laws" see ibid., 2:34-58, and his *Litteratur des teutschen
Staatsrechts,* 1:34-43.

86. *Patriotische Abbildung des heutigen Zustandes bey der höchsten
Reichsgerichte worin der Verfall des Reichs-Justitzwesens samt dem daraus
bevorstehenden Unheile des ganzen Reichs und die Mittel wie demselben
noch vorzubeugen der Wahrheit gemäß und aus Liebe zum Vaterland*
(Göttingen, 1749), p. 35. The disease in question here was the deplorable
state of the Empire's two courts, the Reichskammergericht and the
Reichshofrat.

87. "Ueberhaupt muß das Genie der Bürger dem Zweck des Staats gemäß
gebildet werden. Dieses wird hauptsächlich durch Unterricht, Exempel und
Direction bewürket. Mittelst dieser dreyen Dinge kann der Character einer
Nation gar sehr verbessert, wenn gleich nicht völlig verändert werden, indem
sich die Natur nicht ausrötten läßt" (Achenwall, *Staatsklugheit,* pp. 156-157).

88. The German word *Bildung* connotes more than its English equiva-
lents, "education" and "formation." It refers not only to the process of
education but also to the goal of education, of cultivating the qualities and
faculties that characterize humanity. Ideally, it connotes both mastery of
knowledge and development of the self.

89. Pütter expressed this sympathy in his autobiography by relating a
discussion he had had with a Frenchman who had difficulty grasping the
freedom in the German Freedoms: "Er sehe doch, sagte er, daß er sich von
der Teutschen Freyheit, die ihm oft sehr geruhmt worden wäre, nicht richtige
Begriffe gemacht habe. Er finde jetzt gegen seine Erwartung, daß er mehr
Freyheit der Teutschen Fürsten und Reichsstände als der Unterthanen sey.
Ganz konnte ich ihm diesen Scrupel nicht benehmen. Doch begriff er, daß in
der Hülfe, die des Adels Hintersassen bey den Landesherren, und landesherr-

liche Unterthanen theils bey den Landständen, theils bey den Reichsgerichten finden könnten, zwischen der Teutschen und Französischen Verfassung noch immer ein großer Unterschied sey" (*Selbstbiographie zur dankbaren Jubelfeier seiner fünfzigjährigen Professorsstelle zu Göttingen*, 2 vols. [Göttingen, 1798], 2:667). And Schlözer declared: "Politische Kenntnisse haben angefangen, die alte WeltGeschichte, vorzüglich in den Begriffen von den Griechen, zu reformieren. . . . Politische Kenntnisse sind das erprobteste Präservatif gegen Projectur-und Revolutions Sucht: sie schaffen Malcontenten zu ruhigen, willigen und dankbaren Bürgern um" (*Stats-Gelartheit: Erster Theil*, p. 28).

IV. Human Origins and Historical Development

1. Hübner's book was first published in 1714 and went through numerous German editions. It was also translated into French, Italian, Hungarian, Swedish, and Polish.

2. In his autobiography Semler gives a powerful description of the effects extreme Pietism sometimes had on youth. He relates how his older brother spent many a sleepless night imploring the Almighty to save his soul and how he grew more despondent every day because he could not proclaim that he was among the reborn. Johann David Michaelis also tells how he became despondent because he could not accept everything in the symbolic books. It was only after a trip to England that he resolved his problems. Of course, there always were those who never recovered their belief, especially if they were born before 1715. One was Hermann Samuel Reimarus (1694-1768), who early in his life was so disturbed by the Pietist criticism of Wolff and by Wolff's own doctrines that he resigned his position in Wittenberg and returned to his native city of Hamburg. Reimarus accepted a position as professor of Hebrew in the gymnasium there which, oddly enough, was run by Hübner. Reimarus was the author of the "Wolffenbüttel Fragments" (published as *Fragmente eines Ungenannten* [1774-1778] by Gotthold Ephraim Lessing), one of the most thorough German attacks on Christianity. Reimarus was one of the few to carry physicotheology to its logical conclusion, a conclusion that could easily dispense with Christian revelation.

3. Charlotte von Einem, *Aus dem Nachlaß Charlottens von Einem: Ungedruckte Briefe von Hölty, Noss, Boie, Overbeck u. a., Jugenderinnerungen*, ed. Julius Steinberger (Leipzig: Vereinigung Göttingen Bücherfreunde, 1923), p. 142.

4. Harnack, *Geschichte der Akademie*, 1:6.

5. It was equally difficult for the western Enlightenment to shake off Christian chronology. Antoine Augustin Calmet's *Histoire universelle sacrée et prophane* (1754), the *English Universal History from the Earliest Account of Time to the Present* (1737), Hardion's *Histoire universelle sacrée et prophane* (1754), Vernet's *Abrégé d'histoire universelle* (1753), and Turgot all retained the traditional biblical chronology and history (J. H. Brumfitt, *Voltaire, Historian* [London: Oxford University Press, 1958], pp. 85-86).

6. *Sculptura Historiarum et Temporum Memoratrix: Das ist, Gedächtnüß-Hülfliche Bilder-Lust der Merkwürdigsten Welt-Geschichten aller Zeiten von Erschaffung der Welt biß auf gegenwärtige* (Nuremberg, 1726), p. 2.

7. *Abriß der Universalhistorie,* p. 586.

8. *Abriß der Chronologie* (Göttingen, 1777), p. 88.

9. Bolingbroke, *Letters,* Letter 3, 3:375; Letter 1, 3:319.

10. Ibid., Letter 3, p. 382.

11. Chladenius, *Blendwerk,* p. 31.

12. Semler, *Revision der Hermeneutik,* p. 78.

13. Philipp, *Werden der Aufklärung,* p. 84.

14. The comparison was made in Semler's *Beantwortung der Fragment eines Ungenanten insbesondere vom Zweck Jesu und seine Jünger,* 2d ed. (Halle, 1780), p. 290. The correspondence between the fields of aesthetics and hermeneutics was strengthened by the Neologists' belief that Holy Scripture was "sacred poetry" and therefore should be studied as a work of art. The term "sacred poetry" was taken from Robert Lowth but was really developed by Michaelis.

15. Michaelis, "Schreiben an Herrn Professor Schlötzer die Zeitrechnung von der Sündflut bis auf Salomo betreffend," in *Zerstreute kleine Schriften,* 2 vols. (Jena, 1794), 1:262-263.

16. Michaelis, *Introduction to the New Testament,* trans. from the 4th ed. (1788) by Herbert Marsh, 4 vols. in 6 (Cambridge, 1793-1802), vol. 3, pt. 1, p. 100.

17. "Schreiben an Schlötzer," 1:267-268.

18. Ibid., pp. 220-221.

19. *Beurtheilung der Mittel, welche man anwendet, die ausgestorbene hebraische Sprache zu verstehen* (Göttingen, 1757), pp. 97-101.

20. Schlözer, *Probe russischer Annalen* (Bremen, 1768), p. 51.

21. *Universal-Historie I,* 2:349-350. Schlözer here agrees with Voltaire that we could have no knowledge about the process of creation and disagrees with him by accepting Buffon's explanation for the seashells: "Voltaire refuses to believe that the sea could ever have covered the Alps or the Pyrenees, asserting that such an idea is contrary to all the laws of gravity and hydrostatics" (Brumfitt, *Voltaire,* p. 87).

22. Schlözer, *Universal-Historie I,* 1:62-63.

23. Schlözer, *Allgemeine nordische Geschichte: Fortsetzungen der allgemeinen Welt-Historie durch eine Gesellschaft von Gelehrten in Teutschland und Engeland ausgefertiget,* pt. 31 (Halle, 1771), p. 263.

24. Ibid., p. 256.

25. "The Concept of History: Ancient and Modern," in *Between Past and Present: Six Exercises in Political Thought* (New York: Viking Press, 1968), p. 68.

26. *Nordische Geschichte,* p. 263.

27. *Tableau de l'histoire de Russie* (Gotha, 1769), pp. 13-15.

28. The literature on secularization is vast and eminently contradictory. For a recent and concise summary of the various uses of the word see Harmann Lübbe, *Säkularisierung: Geschichte eines ideenpolitischen Begriffs* (Freiburg: Karl Alber, 1965). I have learned a great deal from my colleague

Kees Bolle, who has written an excellent article on the nature of secularization, "Secularization as a Problem for the History of Religions," *Comparative Studies in Society and History*, 12 (July, 1970):242-259.

29. See Mircea Eliade, *The Sacred and the Profane*, trans. Willard R. Trask (New York: Harper and Row, 1961), and *The Quest: History and Meaning in Religion* (Chicago: Chicago University Press, 1969). Also see Kees Bolle, *The Freedom of Man in Myth* (Nashville: Vanderbilt University Press, 1968).

30. This point is clearly made by Leo Strauss in his important work, *Natural Right and History*. Historians are too often prone to see the theories of Hobbes and Locke as natural continuations of the classical and scholastic past. If they do, then the confrontation the Aufklärung had with modern natural law cannot be seriously perceived. For example, Meinecke writes: "Ja diese Aufklärung kann sogar als die höchste Steigerung des alten, aus der Antike stammenden Naturrechts gelten. Denn der Glaube an die zeitlose menschliche Vernunft gewann jetzt eine Kraft und Sicherheit wie nie zuvor, weil er bestätigt zu werden schien durch die großen naturwissenschaftlichen Entdeckungen des späten 17. und 18. Jahrhunderts und weil die christlich-religiösen Einschränkungen, mit denen er bisher behaftet gewesen war, in Mißkredit kamen durch das Ende der Religionskriege, durch das Erlöschen der religiösen Fanatismen" ("Klassizismus, Romantizismus und historisches Denken im achtzehnten Jahrhundert," in *Zur Theorie und Philosophie der Geschichte*, pp. 266-67).

31. Cassirer, *Philosophy of the Enlightenment*, p. 242.

32. Ibid., p. 240.

33. Wilhelm Dilthey, *Weltanschauung und Analyse des Menschen seit Renaissance und Reformation* (1913), 9th ed. (Göttingen: Vandenhoeck and Ruprecht, 1970), pp. 378-382.

34. Franz Neumann, "Types of Natural Law," in *The Democratic and the Authoritarian State: Essays in Political and Legal Theory* (Glencoe: Free Press, 1957).

35. *Enlightenment*, 2:455-461.

36. Achenwall, *Staatsklugheit*, pp. 26-27.

37. Ibid.

38. Johann Stephan Pütter, *Anleitung zum teutschen Staatsrecht*, trans. Carl Anton Friedrich Graf von Hohenthal, 2 vols. (Bayreuth, 1791), 1:1.

39. Schlözer, *Stats-Gelartheit: Erster Theil: Allgemeines Stats Recht und Stats Verfassung* (Göttingen, 1793), pp. 13-14.

40. Pütter, *Anleitung zum teutschen Staatsrecht*, p. 1.

41. "Um in dieser Wissenschaft auf den Grund zu kommen, muß man bis auf solche Vorstellungen zurückgehen, da weder Staaten, noch andere Gesellschaften, oder willkürlich eingegangene Verbindungen, den Zustand des Menschen bestimmen; Man muß sich erst zwey oder mehrere Menschen *ohne alle Verbindung* vorstellen, und alsdann erörtern, was einer gegen den andern für Rechte und Verbindlichkeiten habe, ohne noch eine verbindliche Handlung (*factum obligatorum*) vorgenommen zu haben, um sodann bestimmen zu können, was solche Handlungen für neue Gerechtsamen und Obliegenheiten hervorbringen, und was in diesem ursprünglich natürlichen

Zustande der Mensch für Rechte und Mittel habe, zu Erhaltung seines Rechts zu gelangen, und gegen Beleidigungen sich sicher zu stellen" (Pütter, *Neuer Versuch einer juristischen Encyclopädie und Methodologie* [Göttingen, 1767], pp. 8-9.
   42. Pütter, *Anleitung zum teutschen Staatsrecht*, pp. 65-66.
   43. Pütter, *Beyträge Fürsten-Rechte*, 2:20.
   44. See Pütter, *Der einzige Weg zur wahren Glückseeligkeit deren jeder Mensch fähig ist* (Göttingen, 1772).
   45. Pütter, *Neuer Versuch einer Encyclopädie*, pp. 63-64.
   46. Quoted by Beck, *Early German Philosophy*, p. 274.
   47. Johann Heinrich Gottlob von Justi, *Die Chimäre des Gleichgewichts von Europa: Eine Abhandlung worinnen die Richtigkeit und Ungerechtigkeit dieses zeitherigen Lehrgebäudes der Staatskunst deutlich vor Augen gelegt* (Altona, 1758), p. 1.
   48. Ibid., pp. 5-6.
   49. Schmauß had more than the usual experience with the nonacademic world. Before accepting a professorship he had served as *Hofrat* and later as *Geheimer Cammerrat* at the court of Baden-Durlach. He had established many contacts with prominent diplomats and was very well regarded by the Habsburgs. His major historical work, *Einleitung zu der Staats-Wissenschaft*, was originally designed as a guide for the Habsburg ambassador at the court of England, Count Phillip Joseph v. Kinsky.
   50. "Es ist aber dabey den Anfängern sehr nöthig, zu mercken, was Thomasius vielfältig erinnert, daß in der menschlichen Natur Verstand und Wille, als die zwey vornehmste Kräften der Seele, nicht als völlig von einander *separirte Theile* müssen angesehen werden; sondern sie stehen in einer genauen Verknüpfung miteinander, dergestalt, daß zwar, was die menschliche würckliche *Actiones* betrifft, der Wille eigentlich der Meister bleibt und der Verstand sich demselben mehrentheils, gleichwie ein Knecht seinem Herrn, nur *accommodiret*, oder doch auch in den Willen oft grossen Einfluß hat" (Schmauß *Vorstellung Recht der Natur*, pp. 17-18).
   51. Ibid., pp. 29-30.
   52. Ibid., p. 25.
   53. Charles Coulston Gillispie, *The Edge of Objectivity: An Essay in the History of Scientific Ideas* (Princeton: Princeton University Press, 1960), pp. 184-186. Gillispie offers a brilliant portrayal of the rise of an anti-Newtonian view of nature during the eighteenth century.
   54. For a good capsule summary of this controversy see Beck, *Early German Philosophy*, pp. 352-360.
   55. Michaelis, *Mosaisches Recht*, 6:219.
   56. Gillispie, *Edge of Objectivity*, p. 170.
   57. Semler, *Revision der Hermeneutik*, pp. 84-87.
   58. Schlözer, *Stats-Gelartheit: Zweiter Theil*, p. 27.

V. Historical Causation

   1. One merely has to look at the dispute between neopositivists and neo-idealists concerning the use of general laws in history.

2. I use this term for want of a better one. By it, I mean those historians who have derived their hermeneutic principles from Ranke's own statements and from an analysis of his writings. This group may also be called historical idealists or historicists, but both terms include a wider variety of thinkers than the term "neo-Rankean" would imply. Modern thinkers such as Dilthey, Cassirer, Baeumler, and Antoni who have drawn their inspiration from Kant or Hegel have contributed valuable reappraisals of the Aufklärung's historical consciousness. The neo-Rankeans, on the other hand, still judge the Aufklärung as the age of positivism and natural law par excellence. They view the great revolution in historical thinking as an act against the Enlightenment effected by the German romantics and the *Klassiker,* where the so-called preromantics served as midwives. In other words, the neo-Rankeans see a radical conflict between *Aufklärung* and Romanticism which they sometimes stereotype as the difference between Goethe and Kant. Probably the greatest neo-Rankean of the twentieth century was Friedrich Meinecke, who despite his ties to Dilthey offered the most famous and influential neo-Rankean portrayal of the rise of modern historical thinking on his *Die Entstehung des Historismus,* vol. 3 of *Werke,* ed. Carl Hinrichs (Munich: Oldenbourg, 1953).

3. "Vorrede," in *Kurzer Begriff der Reichs Historie.*

4. Mosheim, *An Ecclesiastical History Ancient and Modern: From the Birth of Christ to the Beginning of the Eighteenth Century in which the Rise, Progress and Variations of Church Power are Considered in Their Connection with the State of Learning and Philosophy and the Political History of Europe during that Period,* trans. Archibald MacLaine, 2d ed., 6 vols. (London, 1819), 1:7-8. The *Ecclesiastical History,* originally written in Latin, was finished just before Mosheim's death. Three editions of the Latin edition appeared (1755, 1783, 1801). There were also three editions of the German translation (1769, 1773, 1770-1796). A French translation was published in 1776. The work enjoyed its greatest success, however, in the English-speaking world. The first English translation by MacLaine went through seven editions between 1765 and 1825 in England. Two American editions were published before 1800. James Murdock, an American clergyman, retranslated the work in 1832; this translation saw at least seven English and American editions, the last in 1892. The last three of these were edited by Bishop Stubbs, who generally praised Mosheim, but who also expressed his dissatisfaction with Mosheim for his impartiality. The good bishop did not think Mosheim avid enough in his defense of the Protestant religion.

5. Gatterer, "Vom historischen Plan und der darauf sich gründenden Zusammenfügung der Erzählungen," *AHB* 1:80-81.

6. Schlözer, *Neuverändertes Rußland oder Leben Catharinä der zweiten Kayserinn von Rußland, aus authentischen Nachrichten beschrieben* (Riga, 1767), pp. 3-7, and *Stats-Gelartheit: Erster Theil,* pp. 3-5.

7. Arnaldo D. Momigliano, "Time in Ancient Historiography," in *History and the Concept of Time: History and Theory,* Beiheft 6 (Middletown, Conn.: Wesleyan University Press, 1966), p. 14.

8. Schlözer made this clear in *Stats-Gelartheit: Erster Theil* when he used the machine metaphor to discredit the position taken by Karl Friedrich von Moser that the *Obrigkeit ist von Gott* ("Anhang," p. 181).

9. "Vorrede," in *Neuverändertes Rußland.*
10. Pütter, *Beyträge Fürsten-Rechte,* 1:20.
11. *Universal-Historie I,* 2:358. Schlözer also discussed the best way to study the history of Icelandic literature: "Doch die *Entstehungsart* der Gelehrsamkeit auf Island, ihr *Verfall,* ihre *Paligenesie,* und die *Gegenstände,* auf deren Bearbeitung die Neigung dieser Isländer vorzüglich fiel, verdienen eine nähere Anzeige" (*Isländische Litteratur und Geschichte* [Göttingen, 1773], p. 5).
12. Quoted by Charles Coulston Gillispie, *Edge of Objectivity,* p. 225.
13. "Jeder Satz ist entweder ein historischer oder ein dogmatischer satz. . . . Nun wird eine andere Erkänntniß bey einer dogmatischen Stelle, eine andere Erkänntniß bey einer historischen Stelle, eine andere bey einer trockenen dogmatischen oder historischen Stelle, eine andere bey einem Gesetze, eine andere bey einem Wunsche oder Versprechen vorausgesetzt, folglich hat auch ein Ausleger bey jeder Art von Stellen, nach der Beschaffenheit ihres Inhalts etwas anders zu thun" (*Einleitung zur richtigen Auslegung vernünfftiger Reden und Schriften* [Leipzig, 1742], "Vorrede"). Here, in outline, Chladenius defines the task of hermeneutics.
14. Wach, *Das Verstehen,* 3:22-23. As far as I know there is not a single work in English that deals with Chladenius, which is a pity, for not only is his work bold and original, but it also testifies to the close tie between the thinking of the Aufklärung and the strong religious sensibilities of the time. For a while Chladenius was also ignored by German historians. Strangely, he is not even treated in the *ADB.* It was not until the end of the nineteenth century that Chladenius was rediscovered. Bernheim, for example, characterized him as "der erste, der das Verhältnis der historischen Methode zur allg. Erkenntnistheorie und zur Logik eingehender zu bestimmen versucht hat" (quoted by Wach, *Das Verstehen,* 3:21, n. 2). Rudolf Unger dealt perceptively with Chladenius in his important article, "Zur Entwicklung des Problems der historischen Objectivität bis Hegel," *Deutsche Vierteljahrsschrift für Literaturwissenschaft und Geistesgeschichte,* 1 (1923):104-138. And the new *ADB* has corrected the failure of the first by dealing with Chladenius in detail. It also gives a good bibliography.
15. Wach maintains that Chladenius's equation of the state with a moral body is suggestive of Hegel and Droysen (*Das Verstehen,* 3:27 n. 5). It must be remembered, however, that Wolff also defined the state as a moral body. The definition was a commonplace one for most of the Aufklärung. Chladenius also used Wolff's definition of history as knowledge of things that are or occur; he did not, however, accept the consequences Wolff drew from this definition, namely, that historical knowledge consists of "the bare knowledge of fact."
16. "Es kommt bey den Geschäften der Menschen hauptsächlich auf ihren Willen und Freyheit an" (Chladenius, *Allgemeine Geschichtswissenschaft, worinnen der Grund zu einer neuen Einsicht in allen Arten der Gelahrtheit gelegt wird* [Leipzig, 1752], p. 270).
17. Ibid., p. 215.
18. Ibid., p. 206.
19. Ibid., pp. 222-223.

20. Chladenius reveals the influence of Wolff in his use of the word "confused." Like Baumgarten, Chladenius also meant "fused" events, ones that form an integrated whole.

21. *Allgemeine Geschichtswissenschaft*, pp. 218-219.

22. Thomas Reid, as quoted by Hans-Georg Gadamer, *Wahrheit und Methode: Grundzüge einer philosophischen Hermeneutik*, 2d ed. (Tübingen: J. C. B. Mohr [Paul Siebeck], 1965), p. 22.

23. F. M. Barnard, "The 'Practical Philosophy' of Christian Thomasius," *Journal of the History of Ideas*, 32 (1971):226.

24. See n. 16, above.

25. Barnard, "Practical Philosophy," p. 225.

26. The most evident example was the founding of the University of Göttingen; Gerlach Adolf von Münchhausen, the guiding spirit of the new university from 1735 until 1771, was a student of Thomasius's and envisioned the university as a *Pflanz-Garten* for future men of the world. The same attitude was reflected in the new statutes of the universities of Helmstedt, Erlangen, Vienna, Kiel, Strasbourg, and Königsberg.

27. *Allgemeine Geschichtswissenschaft*, p. 129.

28. "Denn die Geschichte an und vor sich hat kein Ende: sie ziehet allemahl Folgen nach sich . . ." (ibid., p. 147).

29. "Von Zuschauer und Sehepunkte," in ibid., pp. 91-115.

30. *Allgemeine Geschichtswissenschaft*, p. 225.

31. Ibid., pp. 275-276.

32. Ibid., p. 262.

33. Dilthey, "Die Entstehung der Hermeneutik," in *Gesammelte Schriften*, 12 vols. (Stuttgart: B. G. Teubner, 1962), 5:334-335.

34. *Allgemeine Geschichtswissenschaft*, pp. 275-276.

35. Gatterer, "Vom historischen Plan," p. 81.

36. "Abhandlung vom Standort und Gesichtspunct des Geschichtschreibers oder der teutsche Livius," *AHB* 5:6.

37. Gatterer, "Von der Evidenz in der Geschichtkunde," in *Die allgemeine Welthistorie die in England durch eine Gesellschaft von Gelehrten ausgefertiget worden*, ed. D. F. E. Boysen (Halle, 1767), 1:6-7.

38. Ibid., p. 6.

39. Ibid., pp. 5-6.

40. Ibid., p. 5.

41. Ibid., pp. 20-21.

42. The Halle historian Johann Peter Miller, teacher and friend of the famous Neologist Thomas Abbt, expressed a similar view in the same year. In his "Vorrede" to the second edition of Abbt's *Fragment der ältesten Begebenheit des menschlichen Geschlechts* (Halle, 1767), Miller stated: "*Man kan durch die Geschichte am leichtesten jene Kentnisse erlangen, welche jedem Menschen wichtig seyn müssen, oder es wenigstens bey einem weisen Gebrauche werden können.* Wenige Seelen haben die Stärke, oder die Gedult, daß sie allgemeine Wahrheiten in dem genauen Zusammenhange mit dem ganzen Umfange der Wahrheiten mit einer philosophischen oder gar mathematischen Schärfe einsehen oder überdenken konten, und die, welche die Alten, unsere witzigen Nachbarn und unsere neuesten Schriftsteller gelesen

haben, können unmöglich ihren Geschmack so sehr entwöhnen, daß sie so viele Regeln und Anmerkungen, welche noch dazu unsere Philosophen so roh und ungebildet, als sie selbst dieselben nur immer für sich denken mögen, der Welt sagen, mit einiger Begierde lesen oder behalten sollten. Aber die Geschichte beschäftiget nicht blos unsern Verstand. Wir können, indem wir denken sollen, zugleich sehen und empfinden. Die Bilder drücken sich von selbst in die Seele, besonders wo die Begebenheit selber eine unserer Leidenschaften intereßiret, ein. . . . Bey diesem Anblick kommen die Sinnen, die Fantasie und das Herz selbst dem Verstande zu Hülfe. Wir erlangen eine anschauende Erkentnis und eine solche Bekantschaft mit den entferntesten Orten, Zeiten und Personen, daß wir an Kentnissen und Erfahrung Nestors werden; gleich als wir etliche hundert Jahre die Welt durchreiset wären" (quoted by Gatterer, *AHB* 1:237-238).

43. Johann Heinrich Gottlob von Justi, *Untersuchung der Lehre von den Monaden,* p. xiv.

44. Gatterer, *Abriß der Universalhistorie,* p. 4.

45. With the exception of histories written by critics of Christianity, nothing incurred Gatterer's wrath more than those that dealt with history mechanically. He mocked the writers of such histories: "With chronological tables in hand, they proceed from one year to the next, observing in each year the very same ordering of material. For example, they first tell us what happened in the cabinets, then they take us to the battlefield, then they describe commerce and wars, first of Europe, then of Asia, Africa, and America — one after the other" ("Vom historischen Plan," pp. 77-78).

46. Johann Joaquim Winckelmann's works on the art of the Greeks had already appeared when Gatterer stated his position on classical historians, and Johann Matthias Gesner and Christian Gottlob Heyne had given new life to the study of the classics. Gatterer and Heyne were colleagues and friends.

47. Gatterer, "Vom historischen Plan," pp. 77-78.

48. "Es war endlich Zeit, daß nach fast 300 Jahren jemand sich daran machte, ein System der antiken Kunst aufzustellen, nicht um die unsere zu verbessern, sondern um zu zeigen, wie man jene zu betrachten und zu bewundern habe" (quoted by Antoni, *Kampf wider die Vernunft,* p. 67, n. 2).

49. Gatterer, *Historisches Journal,* 1 (1772):58.

50. Gatterer, "Standort und Gesichtspunct," p. 17.

51. Gatterer, "Vom historischen Plan," p. 20.

52. Gatterer, "Evidenz," pp. 8-9.

53. Ibid., pp. 20-21.

54. Gatterer, *AHB* 2 (1767):32.

55. Gatterer, "Vom historischen Plan," p. 86.

56. Gatterer, "Evidenz," p. 23.

57. Ibid., pp. 10-11.

58. In this section I have drawn upon two good monographs on Wegelin's idea of history: Hermann Bock, *Jakob Wegelin als Geschichtstheoretiker,* Leipziger Studien aus dem Gebiet der Geschichte, vol. 9, pt. 4 (Leipzig: B. G. Teubner, 1902); Lutz Geldsetzer, *Die Ideenlehre Jakob Wegelins: Ein Beitrag zum philosophisch-politischen Denken der deutschen Aufklärung,*

Monographen zur philosophischen Forschung, vol. 33 (Meisenheim am Glan: Anton Hain, 1963). Wach gives an excellent summary of Wegelin's hermeneutic principles in *Das Verstehen*, 3:42-52.

59. As noted earlier, Swiss scholars played a prominent role in German intellectual life. Of those here mentioned, von Haller had an important position in Göttingen, Sulzer was one of the important members of the Berlin Academy, Iselin received the major impetus for his historical studies while in Göttingen, and von Müller was intimately involved in German political and intellectual life during the revolutionary period.

60. Wegelin had made many enemies in Switzerland through two of his early publications. His *Religiöse Gespräche der Toten* (1763) was a strong plea for Erasmian toleration and religious improvement, and his *Dialogues par un ministre suisse* (1763) was one of the few Swiss defenses of Rousseau. In it he called for a religion of morality and brotherly love, not one based on sterile dogmatism.

61. Wegelin's major works are *Sur la philosophie de l'histoire* in the *Mémoires* of the Berlin Academy (1770-1776) and especially his *Briefe Über den Werth der Geschichte* (Berlin, 1783).

62. Despite a similarity in approach, it is difficult to establish any direct influence upon Wegelin by Gatterer or Chladenius. I think it can be shown that the ideas propagated by Wegelin were already common to eighteenth-century thought. Probably the most important influences on Wegelin were Bodmer, Sulzer, and perhaps Mendelssohn, sources likely used by Gatterer. The idea of a differentiation between forms of scientific inquiry was brought out in Kant's and Mendelssohn's answers to the famous Berlin Prize Question of 1763: "On demande, si les vérités métaphysiques en général et en particulier les premiers principes de la Theologie naturelle et de la Morale sont susceptibles de la même évidence que les vérités mathématiques, et en cas qu'elles n'en soient pas susceptibles, quelle est la nature de leur certitude, à quel degré elle peut parvenir, et si ce degré suffit pour la conviction?" The question itself was suggested to the Berlin Academy by Sulzer, who was then president of the Class for Speculative Philosophy. It was this same question that impelled Gatterer to write his essay, "Von der Evidenz in der Geschichtkunde." Of course, it is entirely possible that Wegelin read Gatterer's article, which appeared as an introduction to an important edition of the *English World History* published in Halle.

63. Bock, *Jakob Wegelin*, pp. 49-52.

64. Wegelin, *Briefe*, p. 128.

65. "Wollte man eine solche historische Ausführung bis auf die kleinsten veranlassenden Ursachen zurückführen, so würde man eine unmögliche Sache unternehmen, und Gefahr laufen, daß man gewissen besondern Umständen mehr zuschriebe, als man ihnen zuschreiben sollte, so daß daraus eine historische Hypothese entstünde" (ibid., p. 132).

66. The reference to Wegelin as the Prussian Montesquieu is taken from Wach, *Das Verstehen*, 3:46. According to Wach, Wegelin was also dubbed the Descartes of history. Although the latter description might vaguely apply, the former is a bit misleading. If anything, Wegelin, influenced by both Sulzer and Bodmer, was more favorable to Hume than to Montesquieu, though he

revered both. Sulzer was Hume's German translator and Bodmer took Hume's side in his essay, *Beobachtung den National-Charakter,* against Montesquieu and Jean Dubos. See Antoni, *Kampf wider die Vernunft,* p. 62. The same preference for Hume in the question of causation was evident in Iselin's *Geschichte der Menschheit.*

67. "Weil der Mensch ein thätiges Wesen ist, und den Werth seines Bestehens in die Wirksamkeit des Geistes und Willens setzt, so hört er niemals auf thätig zu seyn . . ." (Wegelin, *Briefe,* p. 31).

68. Ibid., p. 12.

69. "Das Eigene, und, so zu sagen, Eigenthümliche einer Nation besteht in einer Art zu handeln, deren Erscheinungen ihr allein zugeschrieben werden können, und bey ihr nur deswegen sichtbarer als bey einer jeden andern sind, weil die Entstehungsart eines solchen Volks, seine Maximen, Einrichtungen, Gebräuche und Angelegenheiten, keine andern Handlungsarten hervorbringen konnte. Alles Willkürliche wird also dadurch ausgeschlossen, indem der wahre Charakter eines Volks nichts als die stuffenweise geschehene Ausbildung und Entwickelung seiner ursprünglichen Anlagen, und die Summe derselben enthält" (ibid., p. 13).

70. Ibid., p. 12.

71. Ibid., p. 13. Wegelin's use of the terms "character" and *Colorit* points to the influence of Bodmer, who frequently used the same terms. For example, in an article printed in 1763 on Dante, Bodmer made the following observation: "Dante hatte ebensosehr das Recht, seinem Werke das Kolorit der Wissenschaften, der Sitten und des Geschmackes seiner Zeitgenossen zu geben, wie die Dichter von heute es sich zur Pflicht machen, im Charackter ihrer Zeit zu dichten" (quoted by Antoni, *Kampf wider die Vernunft,* pp. 53-54). The use of these metaphors drawn from the visual arts corresponds to the general tendency of eighteenth-century hermeneutics to employ the metaphor of seeing instead of cognition.

72. Again, it must be emphasized that the Aufklärers did not say they were living in an enlightened age, but rather that the dawn of enlightenment was visible; hence their frequent use of the metaphors *Morgenröte* or *Morgenstunden.*

73. "Durch die Policey . . . verstehe ich alles dasjenige was, ausser den ersten Bedürfnissen der Natur, für eine jede Nation erforderlich ist, welche ihren gesellschaftlichen Zustand sicher, dauerhaft, angenehm, und beglückt zu machen gedenkt" (Wegelin, *Briefe,* p. 240).

74. "Ein jeder Stand, eine jede Classe, ja ein jeder Charakter, hat seine eigene Vernunftlehre, Moral und Politik, an deren Regeln er selten zweifelt, und sich nur in den seltensten Fällen die Mühe giebt, etwas weiter nachzudenken, und einige allgemeine Vorstellungen zu Hülfe zu Rufen" (ibid., p. 257).

75. "Der gesellschaftliche Mensch . . . bringt in seine öffentlichen Verbindungen alle Verhältnisse und daraus entspringenden pflichtmäsigen Begriffe seines innern und äussern Zustandes. Als Mensch, oder als ein der Ueberlegung fähiges Wesen, hat er Vorstellungen von Recht und Unrecht, Wohlwollen, Zuneigung, Haß, Abneigung und Widersetzlichkeit gegen alles, was ihm Nutzen, oder Schaden, Vortheil oder Nachtheil bringen kann. Dieser

Vorstellungen macht er aber niemals überhaupt, und allgemeiner Weise wirksam und thätig, sondern ihre Richtung wird nach den gesellschaftlichen Verhältnissen bestimmt, in welche er zu Beförderung seiner Glückseligkeit zu treten genöthigt ist" (ibid., p. 292).

76. "Denn nichts gleicht der Empfindlichkeit eine eingeschränkten Geistes, weil er immer fürchtet, daß man ihm zu nahe trete; weswegen auch seine Geschäftigkeit unendlich gros ist" (ibid., p. 107). Or the following: "Hat nun ein solcher den wahren Geist seines Amts und Standes, oder ist seine Vernunft mit dem gleichförmig, was seine Pflichten von ihm erfordern, so ist sein öffentlicher Charakter der wahre Ausdruck seiner innern Gemüthsbeschaffenheit. Wenn auch Unvollkommenheiten und Fehler dieser seiner öffentlichen Beziehung anklebten, so wird dennoch ein mit seinem Schicksale zufriedener Mensch dieser fehlerhafte Seite seiner Amtsobliegenheiten eher zu vermindern als zu erweitern suchen" (ibid., p. 85).

77. "Da die Kaufmannschaft niemals auf gleichem Punkte bleibt, sondern durch den Zusammenfluß der Kräfte und Nationalbetriebsamkeit immer mehr erweitert wird: so fällt das eine Volk mit dem andern oft in Streitigkeiten und Widersprüche, welche man nicht blos durch Strafgesetze endigen kann, sondern die in öffentliche Kriege ausschlagen, zu deren Führung eine Seemacht mit allen Künsten und Wissenschaften des Seewesens erforderlich ist. Die kaufmännische Eifersucht ist oft allein hinlänglich, eine Nation mit der andern in Streit zu verwickeln; und weil es in allen diesen Streitigkeiten darauf ankommt, welches Volk die meiste Emsigkeit und Geschichtlichkeit miteinander verbindet: so werden alle Nationalkräfte zu deren Erlangung angewendet; dadurch wird alsdann der Nationalgeist verfeinert, verstärkt und erweitert, weil die Regierung ihre wichtigste Angelegenheit darin setzt, durch die beßten Verordnungen alle Hindernisse dieser Nationalbetriebsamkeit aus dem Wege zu räumen, Fleis und Arbeitsamkeit zu ermuntern, Unredlichkeit, Betrug, und alle Arten der Vernachtheilungen empfindlich zu bestrafen; welches in die allgemeine Policey der Nation den wichtigsten Einfluß hat" (ibid., pp. 255-256).

78. Ibid., p. 249. Wegelin's positive evaluation of Roman law ran counter to a growing trend among eighteenth-century German jurists to locate the true source of freedom and justice in ancient Germanic law. Here Wegelin probably reflects the general Prussian attitude toward imperial institutions and traditions and the French orientation of the Berlin Academy. The opposing position was usually advanced by those desirous of retaining and reforming the imperial structure, men who represented the middle and smaller units of the empire such as Möser and the Göttingen jurist, Johann Stephan Pütter.

79. "Durch das Originelle, . . . verstehe ich eine jede Unternehmung, deren innere Schwierigkeiten jeden andern hätten abschrecken können, den Begriff ihrer Möglichkeit abzufassen, und sich zu derselben zu entschliessen" (ibid., p. 195).

80. Bock, *Jakob Wegelin,* p. 100.

81. "Dis ist auch der wahre Begriff, welchen wir uns von solchen Männern machen müssen, die unter dem Namen der Grosen bekannt sind. Sie hatten alle nicht nur eine grose Erfindsamkeit, sondern auch eine solche Stärke in

ihrer Handlungsweise, die von einer Menge wohl verbundener Vorstellungen herrührte" (Wegelin, *Briefe*, p. 99).

82. "Da nun kein Publikum vorhanden war, welches die öffentlichen Lehren nach der Vorschrift der gesunden Vernunft beurtheilen konnte, so muß man die Schullehrer als gänzlich abgesondert von der Gesellschaft, und ihre gelehrten Arbeiten auf eben die Art ansehen, nach welcher und die Nachforschungen der Mystagogen aller Nationen bekannt sind, welche ganz im Dunkeln arbeiteten, und sich nur in dem eingeschränkten Kreise ihrer eigenen und besondern Begriffe bewegten. Je weniger wirkliche Wahrheit in einem Vortrage ist, desto feinere und verschiedenere Bedeutungen giebt man den Worten; und da die Auslegungen derselben überhaupt willkürlich sind, so entsteht aus der Verschiedenheit dieser Auslegungen ein unaufhörliches Gezänke" (ibid., p. 130).

83. "Denn die Wirksamkeit der Begriffe hängt von ihrer Anschaulichkeit ab, und es streitet mit der Natur aller Vorstellungen des reinen Verstandes, daß sie bildlich, und dadurch recht einleuchtend gemacht werden. . . . So war dennoch der Begriff beschaffen, welchen Moses zum Grunde seiner Gesetzgebung legte, und da er zu den Aeltesten in Israel kam, sagte er ihnen: Jehova, das selbstständige Wesen, das Wesen alle Wesen, derjenige, der beständig seyn wird, was er gewesen ist, hat mich zu euch gesandt. Auf diesem Begriffe beruhete die Lehre der Unsichtbarkeit, der Einheit, und Unveränderlichkeit dieses Wesens, oder war darin begriffen" (ibid., p. 197).

84. Ibid., p. 131.

85. Ibid., p. 85.

86. As an example, Wegelin listed the development of the church hierarchy. At the time it was, he argued, a good solution to the problems facing religion and society. If we now see something wrong with it, it is only because we have been formed in a different atmosphere.

87. "Am schlimmsten kommt man zurechte, wenn man nach gewissen Voraussetzungen eine herrschende Meinung verdammt, ehe man alle Ursachen ihrer Einführung genau erwogen hat. Immer sollte dieser Grundsatz für unfehlbar angesehen werden, daß nichts in der Welt eingeführt worden, ohne daß seine Veranlassung mit einem gegenwärtigen Nutzen begleitet gewesen, und daß die Dauer einer Einrichtung, die auf blosen Meinungen beruhet, von ihrer Uebereinstimmung mit den Lokalangelegenheiten der Gesellschaft abhängt" (Wegelin, *Briefe*, p. 132).

88. Bock, *Jakob Wegelin*, pp. 100-101.

VI. Categories of Causal Explanation I: Climate, Geography, and Political, Social, and Economic Structure

1. In addition to *Zweymahl zwey und fünffzig auserlesene biblische Historien aus dem Alten und Neuen Testamente, der Jugend zum Besten abgefasset* (Leipzig, 1714), mentioned in chapter IV, Hübner wrote a work on geography, *Kurtze Fragen aus der alten und neuen Geographie* (numerous editions, including translations into French, Dutch, Italian, Swedish, and Russian); a ten-volume universal history, *Kurtze Fragen aus der politischen Historie* (numerous editions); a review of historical literature, *Hamburgische*

Bibliotheca Historica, 11 vols. in 6 (Leipzig, 1715-1729); and two immensely popular lexicons, *Reales Staats-Zeitungs und Conversations Lexicon* (numerous editions) and *Curieuses Natur-Kunst-Gewerck und Handels Lexicon* (numerous editions). Hübner was probably the most popular historical writer of the first third of the eighteenth century despite, or perhaps because of, his obvious shallowness and mediocrity. The only later comment favorable to Hübner which I have seen is one made by Heeren: "Seine *biblische Geschichten,* seine *kurze Fragen aus der politischen Historie* bis zum Ausgang des siebzehnten Jahrhunderts, in zehn Theilen ... sind von ihm und seinen Sohn in so vielen Auflagen erschienen, daß sie zu den am meisten verbreiteten Schriften gehören. Ist gleich die Wissenschaft durch sie nicht erweitert worden; so haben sie doch außerordentlich gewirkt. Durch sie ward die Geschichte in den allgemeinen Jugendunterricht gezogen; eine große Masse historischer Kenntnisse ward in dem großen Publikum in Umlauf gesetzt; und man gewöhnte sich an den deutschen Vortrag in Unterrichte. Unbestritten bleibt daher Hübner das Verdienst, seinen Nachfolgern dadurch den Weg gebahnt zu haben, daß er das Deutsche Publikum empfänglich für die Geschichte und ihre Hülfswissenschaften ... machte. Wenn wir noch jetzt mit Wahrheit sagen können, daß es kein anderes Publikum in Europa giebt, unter dem eine solche Masse von Kenntnissen der allgemeinen Geschichte verbreitet ist, als das Deutsche, so verdanken wir dieß keinem jener frühern Schriftsteller mehr als ihm" (*Historische Werke,* 6:443-444).

2. *Kurtze Fragen aus der politischen Historie biß auf gegenwärtige Zeit continuiret,* 10 vols. (Leipzig, 1715), 7:37-39.

3. Schlözer, *Universal-Historie I,* 2:265.

4. *Introduction to the New Testament,* 3:108-109.

5. Mosheim, *Ecclesiastical History,* 2:446-447. Spittler advanced the same argument: "Dem Papste, unter welchem Kreuzzüge zuerst aufkamen, konnte man keinen Plan zutrauen, und, wie konnte man möglicher Weise voraussehen, was sich hernach ereignete, daß der von ihm veranlaßte Kreuzzug 200 Jahre lang Folgen von ähnlicher Art haben würde?" (Ludwig Timothy Spittler, *Geschichte der Kreuzzüge: Zweiter Anhang zur Geschichte des Papstthums aus dem literarischen Nachlasse des D. Gurlitt,* ed. Cornelius Müller [Hamburg, 1827], p. 1).

6. *Ecclesiastical History,* 2:447.

7. Moses Mendelssohn, *Über die Empfindungen,* p. 127.

8. *Kurtze Fragen aus der politischen Historie,* 1:11.

9. Ibid., 1:16-19.

10. "Denn was bleibt wol noch dem Verfasser einer Staatsgeschichte übrig, wenn er nichts von Religionssachen, nichts von der Lage, der natürlichen Beschaffenheit und den Producten der Länder, und der daraus zu beurtheilenden Emsigkeit, Handlung und Macht der Nationen, nichts endlich von den Künsten und Wissenschaften derselben sagen darf? Soll es etwa ein chronologisches Verzeichnis der Regenten seyn, das allenfalls noch mit einigen, entweder unerheblichen, oder in eine Biographie gehörigen Lebensumständen durchwebt, oder mit Erzählungen von Einzügen, Geburts—Krönungs-Vermählungs-Begräbnis-Feyerlichkeiten, oder wie die artigen Staatsceremonien alle heissen, aufgeputzt, oder mit gewöhnlichen Hof- und

Liebesränken erbaulich unterbrochen, oder durch Beschreibungen von Kriegen und Schlachten schröcklich gemacht, oder mit andern Nachrichten angefüllet ist, die entweder ohne die losgerissenen Stücke nicht verstanden und beurtheilet werden können, oder den grösten Theile nach gar nicht in die grosse Historie gehören, sondern in derselben mehr berüht, als beschrieben werden sollen?" (Gatterer, "Vom historischen Plan," pp. 24-25).

11. "Der Mensch bestehet aus Leib und Seele, die aufs genaueste mit einander verbunden sind, so daß die Begebenheiten dieser wesentlichen Theile, als Begebenheiten einer einigen Sachen angesehen werden: wie sie denn auch so genau an einander hangen, daß es nicht möglich ist, nur eine Begebenheit des Leibes anzugeben, daran die Seele nicht Antheil nähme; und so auch mit den Veränderungen der Seele. Doch *äussern* sich diese Begebenheiten bald hauptsächlich in der *Seele*, bald hauptsächlich im *Leibe*. Denn so kommen in Ansehung der *Verstandes*, Erkenntniß und Unwissenheit, Irrthum und Wahrheit; in Ansehung des *Willens*, Tugend und Laster, Affecten und Entschlüssungen vor; in Ansehung des *Leibes* aber Kranckheit und Gesundheit" (Chladenius, *Allgemeine Geschichtswissenschaft*, pp. 76-77).

12. "Die Begebenheiten der moralischen Wesen sind mithin von den Begebenheiten eintzelner Menschen ganz unterschieden; ob wohl die Geschichte *eintzelner* Menschen in jene den grösten Einfluß haben. Eine *Handlung* bestehet zwar noch immer, wenn sie gleich ihren treuen und klugen Directeur verlohren hat, aber sie *leidet* doch dadurch. Hingegen sind die Geschichte derjenigen Menschen, welche mit einem moralischen Wesen zu thun haben, grossen theils auch nicht zu den Geschichten der moralischen Wesen selbst zu rechnen: als ob der Directeur eine Frau gehabt, wie vieler Kinder gehabt usw." (ibid., p. 64).

13. Achenwall, for example, used the same definition of the state as a moral person: "Der Staat ist ein moralischer Körper, weil in dem Staat vereinigte Kräfte von einem Willen zu einerley Zweck geleitet werden" (*Staatsklugheit*, p. 25). Also see Pütter, *Neuer Versuch einer Encyclopädie*, pp. 10-11.

14. "Die Begebenheiten der moralischen Wesen gründen sich zwar auf den vereinigten Willen der Menschen; da sie aber äusserliche Dinge zu ihren Vorwurf haben: so entstehen ihre Veränderungen und Begebenheiten auf zweyerley Art: *einmahl in* und *an* den Willen der Menschen, der veränderlich ist; und so wohl eyfriger, als nachläßiger, besser und schlimmer werden kan; ingleichen daß mehrere Menschen ihren Willen mit der Zeit vereinigen, oder *im* Gegentheil von ihrem vorigen Willen *abgehen;* wie bey allen Dingen geschiehet, bey welchen es auf den Beyfall der Leute ankommt. *So dann* werden auch die moralischen Wesen verändert, durch die Begebenheiten der *Cörper*, welche mit den moralischen Dingen verbunden sind; als welche den menschlichen Willen und dessen Ausführung fördern, hindern, ändern und gar aufheben können" (Chladenius, *Allgemeine Geschichtswissenschaft*, p. 63).

15. See, for example, Henri Barckhausen, *Montesquieu: Ses idées et ses oeuvres d'après les papiers de la Brède* (Paris: Hachette, 1907); Gustav Lanson, *Montesquieu* (Paris: F. Alcan, 1932); Lawrence Meyer Levin, *The Political Doctrine of Montesquieu's "Esprit des Lois"* (New York: Columbia University Press, 1932). Brumfitt gives a good summary of Voltaire's reaction

to *The Spirit of the Laws,* showing how Voltaire was both influenced by some of Montesquieu's ideas and repelled by his lack of systematic presentation and uncritical use of source material (*Voltaire,* pp. 117-121).

16. *Spirit of the Laws,* Bk. IX, chap. 4, p. 293.
17. Chladenius, *Allgemeine Geschichtswissenschaft,* p. 72.
18. For Voltaire's reaction see Brumfitt, *Voltaire,* pp. 118-120.
19. *Spirit of the Laws,* Bk. XIV, chap. 10, p. 228.
20. Ibid., chap. 12, p. 231.
21. Ibid., Bk. XVI, chap. 2, p. 251.
22. Ibid., Bk. XVII, chap. 2, p. 264.
23. As an example of the use of climatic causal explanation in early eighteenth-century Germany, the following statements by Nicholas H. Gundling and Jacob August Franckenstein, respectively, should suffice: "Denn gleichwie kein eintziger Mensch dem andern gleich ist ratione voltus noch auch ratione Morum & Inclinationum; also sind auch gantze Republiquen unterschieden, ratione Intentionum, finium & propensionum Moralium, wozu das unterschiedliche Clima vieles thut; daher müssen sich auch auf unterschiedene Art gouverniret werden. Manche Nationes sind sehr servilisch, und müssen servilisch beherrschet werden, als die Türcken und Indianer, und fast alle Morgenländer überhaupt; Andere aber, sonderlich die Septrionales, lassen sich nicht so tractiren.... Dass Lufft und Clima vieles zum Unterschied der Nation thue, können wir daraus abnehmen: Wenn schön Wetter ist, so sind wir munter, und haben Courage, aber wenn es trübe und kalt ist, so sind wir auch nicht aufgeräumet, und unsere Affecten exeriren sich gantz anders" (*Ausführliche Discours,* 1:7-8). The two-volume work was the posthumous collection of Gundling's lectures. Franckenstein, who edited the first volume, expanded on Gundling's observations in his introduction: "Die Nordlichen Völcker sind lebhafft, und starck vom Leibe, Gebeinen und Kräfften, wobey die kalte Lufft ein grosses würcket; die Südlichen aber haben ein weit grösseres Nachsinnen und Beurtheilungs-Kraft, wozu die hitzige Witterung nicht wenig beyträgt" (ibid., p. 24).
24. Michaelis, *Mosaisches Recht,* 1:2.
25. Michaelis's student and admirer, Johann Gottfried Eichhorn, called *Mosaisches Recht* an "original work; hardly anything of comparable quality existing today deals with the constitution of either an ancient or a modern state" (*Johann David Michaelis: Einige Bemerkungen über seinen litterarischen Character* [Leipzig, 1791], p. 20).
26. Mosheim, *Ecclesiastical History,* 1:22.
27. Iselin, *Geschichte der Menschheit,* 1:55-56.
28. *Spirit of the Laws,* Bk. XVIII, chaps. 2-4, pp. 272-273.
29. "Das geographische Datum, dass England eine Insel ist, wird erst dadurch statistisch; wenn es als ein HauptGrund der Allmacht der Briten dargestellt wird: Unterschied zwischen reiner trockner Geographie, und— wenn man den Namen dulten will— politischer Geographie" (Schlözer, *Stats-Gelartheit: Zweiter Theil,* p. 38).
30. Achenwall, *Staatsverfassung der heutigen vornehmsten europäischen Reiche und Völker im Grundriße,* 5th ed. (Göttingen, 1768), p. 567.

31. "Ueber die Entstehung, die Ausbildung und den praktischen Einfluß der politischen Theorien in dem neueren Europa," in *Kleine historische Schriften*, 3 vols. (Göttingen, 1803-1808), 2:249-250.

32. Franco Venturi, *Utopia and Reform in the Enlightenment* (Cambridge: Cambridge University Press, 1971).

33. Ibid., p. 70.

34. Ibid., p. 62.

35. Johann Heinrich Gottlob von Justi, *Vergleichungen der europäischen mit den asiastischen und andern vermeintlich barbarischen Regierung* (Berlin, 1762), p. 6.

36. The *Staatsanzeigen* had, at its peak, a subscription list of more than 4,400, a very large figure for the time. For a quick comparison, Christoph Martin Wieland's influential *Der Teutsche Merkur* never sold more than 2,500 copies and usually had difficulties maintaining a rate of 2,000. The degree of Schlözer's influence may be quickly summed up by relating two anecdotes frequently used by his commentators. In the first, the Austrian minister and professor Joseph Freiherr von Sonnenfels told his students that the only place one could hear a free discussion of politics was in Schlözer's Göttingen. In the second anecdote, the Empress Maria Theresa criticized one of her ministers and then asked him: "Was würde Schlözer dazu sagen?" The impression the *Staatsanzeigen* made on Schlözer's German contemporaries may also be illustrated by the title of an anonymous pamphlet written against Schlözer during the height of the German reaction to the French Revolution: *Sanscüllottismus des Herrn Hofraths und Professors Ludwig August* [sic] *Schlözer zu Göttingen* (1794); already in 1793 a frightened Hannoverian government forced Schlözer to stop printing the *Staatsanzeigen*.

37. Schlözer, *Neuverändertes Rußland*, "Vorrede."

38. "Die ganze Menschheit verunedelt sich oft bei dieser Reg. Form: alles kriecht, bekömmt TitelSucht, lernt HundesDemut, wird LöwenLecker. Und sässe auch eine Grazie auf einem solchen Thron? – Da unten am Thron, von ihr ungesehen, schleicht ein OtternGezücht herum, das in dieser unnatürlichen RegierungsForm so natürlich, wie Gewürm in dem sonst woltätigen Schlamm des Rils, nistet" (Schlözer, *Stats-Gelartheit: Erster Theil*, pp. 143-144).

39. Schlözer, *Staatsanzeigen* (Göttingen), vol. 3, pt. 11, p. 258.

40. Schlözer, *Stats-Gelartheit: Erster Theil*, pp. 140-141.

41. Ibid.

42. *Staatsanzeigen*, vol. 3, pt. 12, p. 410.

43. Ibid., vol. 16, pt. 62, p. 233.

44. Heeren, "Entstehung der politischen Theorien," p. 178.

45. Schlözer, *Briefwechsel*, vols. 2-16: *Meist politischen und historischen Inhalts* (1776-1782), 2:147-148.

46. Even the location of the German universities strengthened the feeling of academic independence. With the exception of Vienna, none of the major universities were in capital cities under the direct watch of the court.

47. Mosheim, *Ecclesiastical History*, 1:256.

48. Schlözer, *Stats-Gelartheit: Erster Theil*, p. 128.

49. "Entstehung der politischen Theorien," p. 247.

50. Gatterer, *Abriß der Universalhistorie,* pp. 208-209.

51. "Die meisten griechischen Staten waren, Macedonien und Syrakus abgerechnet, klein und ohnmächtig, und hatten eine unglückliche demokratische Regierungsform: beides setzte sich ausser Stand, einen langen Zeitraum hindurch die Werke großer Staten zu thun. Nächstdem dachten sie von je her zu sinnlich: ihr Geist heftete sich zu sehr an geringfügige Gegenstände, und ihre Feinheit ward darüber Frivolität. Ihre Achtung gegen körperliche Vorzüge und Künste war übertrieben: sie zeichneten die schönsten Leute in ihren Annalen auf, ordneten Wettspiele der Schönheit an, setzten Preise auf den gelehrtesten Kuß, und errichteten Ehrensäulen den besten Ringern; selbst Pythagoras, Plato, und Ckrysipp, mußten vorher in die Wette ringen, ehe ihre Landsleute auf ihre Weisheit aufmerksam wurden. Ihre Religion war albern, und ohne Wirkung auf das Herz. Ihr Naturrecht war zum Theil grausam und unmenschlich. Ihre Sitten begünstigten den Flor der Kunst, das Gefühl der Schönheit, und die unnatürliche Wollust, gleich stark. Die Spectakel-Wuth war in Athen aufs höchste gestiegen: drei Tragödien des Sophokles aufführen zu lassen, kostete hier mer, wie jemand erzält, als der ganze peloponnesische Krieg. Und diese Unsterblichsten aller Griechen, die Athener, welch ein verächtlicher Pöbel waren sie schon zu Demosthenis Zeiten! wie eifersüchtig und verräterisch unter sich, ohne aller Gefühl von Patriotism, blos für Eigennutz und Faction wirksam, und immer bereit, Vaterland und alles jedem Mächtigeren, und wenn es auch der persische Erbfeind war, aufzuopfern" (Schlözer, *Vorstellung der Universal-Historie,* 2d ed. rev. [Göttingen, 1775], pp. 63-65).

52. Venturi, *Utopia and Reform,* p. 65.

53. Schlözer, *Staatsanzeigen,* vol. 5, pt. 13, p. 143; vol. 7, pt. 25, p. 52.

54. Venturi, *Utopia and Reform,* p. 88.

55. "Der Geist der Freiheit, den man damals in Rom, wie heut zu Tag in Genua und Paris, *Rebellion* nannte, zeigte sich bei ihnen immer aufs neue wieder" (Schlözer, *Geschichte von Corsica* [Göttingen, 1769], p. 12).

56. The similarity of the Aufklärers' views to those of Madison is seen in an excerpt from *The Federalist Papers:* "From this view of the subject it may be concluded that a pure democracy, by which I mean a society consisting of a small number of citizens, who assemble and administer the government in person, can admit of no cure for the mischiefs of faction. A common passion or interest will, in almost every case, be felt by a majority of the whole; a communication and concert results from the form of government itself; and there is nothing to check the inducements to sacrifice the weaker party or an obnoxious individual. Hence, it is that such democracies have ever been spectacles of turbulence and contention; have ever been found incompatible with personal security or the rights of property; and have in general been as short in their lives as they have been violent in their deaths." Or the following: "Among the numerous advantages promised by a well-constructed Union, none deserves to be more accurately developed than its tendency to break and control the violence of faction. The friend of popular governments never finds himself so much alarmed for their character and fate as when he contemplates their propensity to this dangerous vice. He will not fail, therefore, to set a due value on any plan which, without violating the

principles to which he is attached, provides a cure for it. The instability, injustice, and confusion introduced into the public councils have, in truth, been the mortal diseases under which popular governments have everywhere perished" (Alexander Hamilton, James Madison, and John Jay, *The Federalist Papers*, New American Library [New York: Mentor, 1961], pp. 81, 77).

57. Achenwall, *Staatsklugheit*, p. 48.

58. Their attitude toward the weaknesses of the monarchical and democratic forms further attests to their dislike of aristocracy as a form of rule; one of the weaknesses ascribed to both forms was the tendency to "disintegrate" into an aristocracy.

59. Achenwall, *Staatsklugheit*, pp. 35-36.

60. Venturi, *Utopia and Reform*, p. 112.

61. Achenwall, *Staatsklugheit*, "Vorrede," par. 4.

62. Heeren, "Entstehung der politischen Theorien," pp. 207-208, 250.

63. The term *ganzes Haus* was originally made popular by W. H. Riehl in the nineteenth century. Otto Brunner used it in his important article, "Das 'ganze Haus' und die alteuropäische 'Ökonomik,'" in *Neue Wege der Sozialgeschichte: Vorträge und Aufsätze* (Göttingen: Vandenhoeck and Ruprecht, 1956), pp. 33-61, upon which the following paragraphs are based.

64. Brunner, "Das 'ganze Haus,'" p. 35.

65. Pufendorf, *Historie der vornehmsten Reiche*, 1:302.

66. "Erst im 18. Jahrhundert dringt das Wort Familie in die deutsche Umgangsprache ein und gewinnt jene eigentümliche Gefühlsbetontheit, die wir mit ihr verbinden. Voraussetzung ist offenbar die Herauslösung der engeren ständischen Kleinfamilie aus der Gesamtheit des Hauses. Im 'ganzen Hause' wurden Ratio und Gefühl in immer wiederkehrenden, sicherlich oft schmerzlichen Spannungen gegeneinander ausgeglichen. Mit seiner Aufspaltung in Betrieb und Haushalt tritt der 'Rationalität' des Betriebs die 'Sentimentalität' der Familie gegenüber. . . . 'Rationale' und 'irrationale' Strömungen stehen in einer bisher unbekannten Weise gegeneinander" (Brunner, "Das 'ganze Haus,'" p. 42).

67. Johann David Köhler, *Historische Münzbelustigung: Darinnen allerhand merkwürdige und rare Thaler, Ducaten, Schaustücke, und andere sonderbarer Gold und Silbermünzen von mancherley Art, accurat in Kupfer gestochen, beschreiben, und aus der Historie umständlich erklaret werden*, 22 vols. (Nuremberg, 1729-1750), 17:282.

68. Schlözer, *Versuch einer allgemeinen Geschichte der Handlung und Seefahrt in den ältesten Zeiten* (Rostock, 1761), "Vorrede," pp. 6-7.

69. Eichhorn, *Geschichte des ostindischen Handels vor Mohämmed* (Gotha, 1775), p. viii.

70. Schmauß, *Einleitung zu der Staats-Wissenschaft*, 2 vols. (Leipzig, 1741-1747), vol. 1, *Die Historie der Balance von Europa* (1741), "Vorrede."

71. F. Frensdorf, "Die Vertretung der ökonomischen Wissenschaften in Göttingen vornehmlich im achtzehnten Jahrhundert," in *Festschrift zur Feier des hundertfünfzigjährigen Bestehens der Königlichen Gesellschaft der Wissenschaft zu Göttingen* (Berlin, 1901), p. 528.

72. According to Roscher, Sonnenfels considered Justi "Als den Ersten, welcher alle Staatswissenschaften auf Ein oberstes Princip, Beförderung der

allgemeinen Glückseligkeit, zurückgeführt habe" (Wilhelm Roscher, *Geschichte der National-Oekonomik in Deutschland* [Munich, 1874], p. 444).

73. Johann von Justi, *Chimäre des Gleichgewichts,* pp. 39-40.

74. Ibid., p. 27.

75. Ibid., p. 33.

76. Vincenz John, *Geschichte der Statistik: Ein quellenmässiges Handbuch für den akademischen Gebrauch wie für den Selbstunterricht* (Stuttgart, 1884), pp. 85-86.

77. Nothing escaped Achenwall's notice; his *Nachlasse* have long notes on such subjects as the relation between national character and diet, clothing, work habits, marriage and courting customs, and educational policy.

78. Achenwall, *Staatsklugheit,* "Vorrede," par. 11.

79. Ibid., p. 96.

80. Pütter, *Historisch-politisches Handbuch von den besonderen teutschen Staaten,* pt. 1 (Göttingen, 1758), pp. xvii-xviii.

81. Gatterer, *Ideal einer allgemeinen Weltstatistik.*

82. Schmauß, *Einleitung zu der Staats-Wissenschaft,* vol. 1, "Vorrede."

83. "Die Haupt-Ursach ist der eigenen Stärcke des Königreichs Franckreich zuzuschreiben, welches einem ramassirten Cörper gleichet, der seine gantze Kräften allezeit gleichsam beysammen hat; welche Kräften von seiner eigenen Situation und innerlichen Verfassung herkommen, und nicht auf zufälliger oder erborgter Hülffe bestehen, mithin beständig dauerhafft sind. Da hingegen die gantze Macht Caroli V, so fürchterlich sie auch äusserlich schiene, aus allerley zerstreuten Stücken bestund, deren eines von dem andern seiner Einrichtung und Interessen nach, so wohl als nach der Situation, allzuweit entfernet und dem Feind zu Diversionen allzusehr bequem war, daß Carolus V sich einer rechten Zusammensetzung aller Kräfte seiner vielen Länder auf einmahl hätte bedienen können; wie dann auch Franckreich durch die Diversion des Teutschen Religions-Kriegs die Projecten der Oesterreichischen Universal-Monarchie 2 mahl gäntzlich zernichtet hat. Dieser grosse Unterschied der Oesterreichischen und Frantzösischen Stärcke ist meines Bedünckens niemahl tief genug eingesehen oder erwogen worden" (Schmauß, *Einleitung zu der Staats-Wissenschaft,* 1:626).

84. Friedrich Christoph Jonathan Fischer, *Geschichte des teutschen Handels,* 4 vols. (Hanover, 1785-1792), 1:v, vii.

85. Johann Georg Büsch, *Abhandlung von dem Geldumlauf in anhaltender Rücksicht auf die Staatswirtschaft und Handlung,* 3 vols. (Hamburg, 1780-1784), and *Versuch einer Geschichte der hamburgischen Handlung nebst zwey kleineren Schriften eines verwandten Inhalts* (Hamburg, 1797).

86. Schlözer, *Briefwechsel,* 8:93-94.

87. "Mit der allgemeinen Verknüpfung der Dinge hebt man zugleich die Kräfte aller Wesen, hebt man die Wesen selbst auf. Eine zufällige Kraft, deren Einschränkung nicht bestimmt sind, kann nichts *wircken.* Wodurch aber sind die Kräfte in der Welt bestimmt, als durch den Zusammenhang der Dinge?" (Mendelssohn, *Über die Empfindungen,* p. 72).

88. Schlözer, *Kleine Chronik von Leipzig: Erster Theil, biß zum Jahre 1466* (Leipzig, 1776), pp. 58-59.

89. Dilthey, "Das achtzehntenjahrhundert und die geschichtliche Welt" (1901), in *Gesammelte Schriften*, 3:264.

90. Many scholars interested in social history recognized their debt to the Aufklärung. For example, Wilhelm Roscher, though a student of Ranke's, openly expressed his admiration for Schlözer, crediting him with joining history to *Staatswissenschaft* (*Geschichte der National-Oekonomik*, p. 582). Writing to Ranke in 1842, Roscher stated: "Since Schlözer's time it has become a custom at Göttingen to combine history and political science, which, to me, seems the only possible way to cultivate the study of *Staatswissenschaft* correctly" (reprinted in *Preussischer Jahrbücher*, 133 [1908]:385-386). It was a fine compliment from one who has been credited with directing the attention of his age to social and economic history (George Peabody Gooch, *History and Historians in the Nineteenth Century* [Boston: Beacon Press, 1959], p. 534). Dilthey's efforts to reinterpret the eighteenth century are well known; his emotional and intellectual ties to the Aufklärung have been finely and sensitively portrayed by Carlo Antoni, *From History to Sociology: The Transition in German Historical Thinking*, trans. Hayden V. White (Detroit: Wayne State University Press, 1959), pp. 1-38.

91. Quoted by Fritz Stern, ed., *The Varieties of History: From Voltaire to the Present* (Cleveland: World Publishing Co., 1956), pp. 93-94.

92. Pütter, *Vollständigeres Handbuch der teutschen Reichs-Historie*, 2d ed., 2 vols. (Göttingen, 1772), 1:362, and *Grundriß der Staatsveränderungen des teutschen Reichs*, p. 272.

93. Pütter built his argument upon an assumption long accepted as self-evident by European scholars. There is, however, a difference between the Aufklärers' evaluation of the importance of gunpowder and that made by earlier thinkers. As Roy S. Wolper has shown ("The Rhetoric of Gunpowder and the Idea of Progress," *JHI*, 30 [1970]:589-598), earlier thinkers had attempted to interpret the invention of gunpowder as proof of modern progress. By the mid-eighteenth century the "Quarrel of the Ancients and Moderns" had been exhausted and the Aufklärers no longer felt compelled to view the new methods of warfare as a positive contribution to society. They were content to show that it had important societal effects.

94. "Es giebt in der Geschichte des Welthandels im Großen nur einen einzigen allgemein Epoche machenden Zeitpunct, den der Entdeckung von Amerika, und der fast gleichzeitigen Auffindung des Seewegs nach Ostindien, am Ende des funfzehenten Jahrhunderts. Er ist dieß allein, weil er nicht blos eine Veränderung in dem Gange des Handels von einem Volke oder Lande zum andern, sondern in seiner ganzen Natur bewirkte, *indem er ihn vom Landhandel zum Seehandel umformte*. . . . So lange diese Ordnung der Dinge dauerte, ergiebt sich auch von selbst, was sowohl in dem ganzen alterthum, als in dem ganzen Mittelalter Veränderungen des Welthandels seyn konnten; Veränderungen seiner Straßen und seiner Stapelplätze, nicht aber seiner Natur und seines Wesens. Die Caravenenstraßen in Asien konnten sich ändern (wiewohl sie, gewissermaßen von der Natur selber vorgezeichnet, sich wenig änderten); ihre ziele blieben immer die Ufer des Mittlemeers, oder des schwarzen Meers. Hier waren bald die Phönicischen, bald die Griechischen Städte Vorderasiens, bald Alexandrien die Stapelplätze; so wie wiederum an

der Europäischen Küste Corinth, Constantinople, oder die Italiänischen Häfen in dem Empfange der Waaren entweder wechselten, oder auch sich theilten; — es war doch immer ein und derselbe Handel, dessen Straßen sich nur änderten" (Heeren, *Versuch einer Entwickelung der Folgen der Kreuzzüge*, vol. 3 of *Kleine historische Schriften*, pp. 303-306.

95. Pütter, *Anleitung zum teutschen Staatsrecht*, 1:240.

96. Heeren, *Folgen der Kreuzzüge*, p. 134.

97. Ibid., p. 264.

98. Ibid., p. 339.

99. "Aber freylich waren es noch weit mehr die *mittelbaren* Folgen der Kreuzzüge, welche das Aufkommen der Communen und des Bürgerstandes begünstigen. Sie hatten den Schutz der Personen und des Eigenthums zum Ziel; und je mehr dieses sich vergrößerte, je reicher die Städte wurden, um desto wichtiger wurden ihnen nicht nur ihre erhaltenen Privilegien, sondern um desto mehr fühlten sie sich auch im Stande, sich neue zu verschaffen. Dieser steigende Reichthum war aber eine Frucht des Handels; und dieser steigende Handel wiederum eine Frucht der Kreuzzüge" (ibid., p. 267).

100. Ibid., p. 249.

101. Ibid., pp. 438-439.

102. "Auch war es weder die Entstehung eines Bürgerstandes, noch die bloße Zulassung seiner Deputirten zu dem Parlement, oder ständischen Versammlung, welche der Brittischen Verfassung ihre Eigenthümlichkeiten gab; denn alle jene Erscheinungen zeigen sich ja auch in Frankreich sowohl als den Spanischen Reichen. Die Ursachen lagen vielmehr in der *verschiedenen Form die der Adel hier erhielt,* in den verschiedenen Verhältnissen desselben gegen den Bürgerstand, und die dadurch möglich gewordene *Bildung des Unterhauses* in seiner spätern Gestalt. . . . Die Absonderung des höhern Adels, (der Peers), von dem niedern, geschah auch in andern Ländern Europas; aber in keinen andern Ländern dieses Welttheils verschmolz sich so der niedere Adel mit dem Bürgerstande, daß er in der Versammlung der Stände des Reichs von jenem sich abgesondert und mit diesem sich zu Einem Hause verbunden hätte" (Heeren, "Entstehung der politischen Theorien," pp. 167-168).

103. Ludwig Timothy Spittler, *Entwurf der Geschichte der europäischen Staaten*, 3d ed., ed. Georg Sartorius (Berlin, 1823).

104. Schlözer summed up the Aufklärers' multicausal method in his first work, devoted to the history of Phoenician trade: "Indem wir aber die Ursachen von dessen Anwachse erzählen, so handeln wir zugleich (1) von der Lage des Landes; (2) von den Manufacturen der Phönicier, dem Glase und Purpur; (3) von ihren Erfindungen zur Erleichterung der Handlung und Seefahrt, da sie zuerst die eigentlich sogenannte Münze erfunden, und zuerst ihre Seefahrten nach dem Laufe der Sterne eingerichtet haben; (4) von ihrer Seemacht; (5) von ihrer Staatsverfassung; (6) von ihrem Character und Gemüthsart. Alle diese Stücke verdienen, für sich selbst untersuchet zu werden sie müssen aber um so vielmehr unsere Aufmerksamkeit reizen, weil sie die Ursache sind, die durch eine glückliche Verbindung etwas in seiner Art recht Großes hervorgebracht haben" (*Geschichte der Handlung*, pp. 138-139).

VII: Categories of Causal Explanation II: Spirit,
Customs, Values, and Ideas

1. De Tocqueville as quoted by Kelly, *Idealism, Politics and History*, p. 61.

2. Adolf von Harnack, *History of Dogma*, trans. Neil Buchanan, 7 vols. in 4 (New York: Dover Press, 1961), 1:27.

3. Mosheim, *Ecclesiastical History*, 1:1.

4. Ibid., 1:6.

5. Ibid., 1:124-125.

6. Mosheim, *Anderweitiger Versuch einer vollständigen und unpartheyischen Ketzergeschichte* (Helmstedt, 1748), pp. 50-51.

7. In this position Mosheim was following Ralph Cudworth, whose work he translated. Hume's explanation of the rise of religion is best summed up in the following: "The primary religion of mankind arises chiefly from an axious fear of future events. . . . Every image of vengeance, severity, cruelty, and malice must occur and must augment the ghastliness and horror which oppresses the amazed religionist. A panic having once seized the mind, the active fancy still further multiplies the objects of terror; while that profound darkness, or what is worse, that glimmering light with which we are envisioned, represents the spectres of divinity under the most dreadful appearances imaginable (David Hume, *The Philosophical Works of David Hume*, vol. 4, *The Natural History of Religion* [Boston, 1854], p. 478).

8. "Eine *Erfahrung ist,* wenn man aus Empfindungen einen allgemeinen Satz macht: es mag derselbe nun entweder allgemein seyn, oder nur von einem Hauffen gelten. Die Erfahrung ist daher von der Empfindung unterschieden, und entstehet aus derselben, entweder durch die Einbildungskraft, oder durch Schlüsse. Die Empfindungen haben in Ansehung der *Wahrheit* gar keine Schwierigkeit, wenn nur die Empfindung selbst vorhanden ist: Die *Erfahrung* aber kan dennoch falsch seyn, wenn gleich die Empfindungen richtig sind, worauf sich dieselbe gründet; weil noch gar nicht ausgemacht ist, wie man auf eine Art, die Bestand hat, aus eintzeln Fällen eine *allgemeine* Anmerkung, oder einen allgemeinen Satz zu machen befugt seyn. Am wenigsten aber thut es gut, daß man *Empfindungen* und *Erfahrungen* mit einander vermenget, welches bisher beständig geschehen" (Chladenius, *Allgemeine Geschichtswissenschaft*, pp. 55-56).

9. Mosheim, *Ketzergeschichte*, p. 9.

10. Although Mosheim was latitudinarian in his beliefs, he could not refrain at times from taking potshots at the papacy. For example, he implied that Pope Gregory VII and Matilda of Tuscany had been on very intimate terms, and he even repeated the early Protestant claim that there had been a Pope Joanna. Still, Mosheim was successful enough in sympathetically portraying various religious beliefs to induce Harnack, looking back into the eighteenth century, to see in him a kindred spirit and to characterize him as "the Erasmus of the eighteenth century" (Harnack, *History of Dogma*, 1:26).

11. See Mosheim, *Ketzergeschichte*, and *Neue Nachrichten von Michael Servets*.

12. Mosheim, *Ketzergeschichte*, pp. 191-192.

13. Ibid., p. 29.

14. Ibid., p. 239.

15. "Servet schiene dem Kalvin ein ausserordentlicher Ketzer, und nicht nur ein Ketzer, sondern gar ein muhtwilliger Gotteslästerer zu seyn, ein Mann, der die Gründe des Glaubens und die Ehre Gottes freventlich antastete. Und der Spanier war so blind und unsinnig, daß er ihn in dieser Meinung von sich durch seinen Stolz, durch seinen Eigensinn, durch seine Unbescheidenheit und Heftigkeit befestigte. Ist es zu verwunden, wenn man sich dieses alles vorstellet, daß Kalvin sich eingebildet hat, er würde nicht nur ohne Schuld bleiben, sondern Gott und seiner Gemeinde ein Theil seiner Pflicht abtragen, wenn er den Tod eines solchen Bösewichtes beförderte? Die göttliche Gerechtlichkeit hat ihn sonder Zweifel nach seinem Herzen und Absichten, und nicht nach seinem Werken gerichtet: diese sind sträflich; jene sind rühmlich. Laßt uns eben so urtheilen und ihm eine Sünde vergeben, die er nicht würde begangen haben, wenn entweder sein Eifer um Gott und seine Ehre kleiner, oder sein Erkenntniß grösser gewesen wäre" (Mosheim, *Neue Nachrichten von Michael Servets*, p. 239).

16. Wach, *Das Verstehen*, 1:18, n., 2:98.

17. Johann Gottfried Herder summarized this point of view: "Menschlich muß man die Bibel lesen, denn sie ist ein Buch von Menschen für Menschen geschrieben" (quoted by Wach, *Das Verstehen*, 2:54).

18. "Ich wil die Hauptsache viel deutlicher und kürzer sagen: die Aufgabe, ob Jesus auferstanden ist, oder nicht, theilet die Menschen in Christen und Deisten. Jene sagen, die Auferstehung Jesus ist kein Object gewöhnlicher sinlichen Empfindungen gewesen, wie Wolken, Berge, Bäumen; Jesus lies sich nur von einigen sehen, wie er selbst wolte; er veränderte dadurch ihre vorige Denkungsart; er entdeckte ihnen eine Reihe geistlicher Begriffe, die alle vorige Dunkelheit vertreiben und den Zusammenhang mit seinen Lehren auf einmal aufklären sollen. Die Deisten aber setzen ganz andre Prämissen von Jesu voraus, womit eine solche übernatürliche Begebenheit keinesweges zusammen hängen kan; darum leugnen und bestreiten sie diese Begebenheit. Das mögen sie thun; so bleiben wir stets geschieden. Sie müssen aber nicht sich rümen, sie hätten das Christenthum völlig widerlegt und uns alle unsre Ueberzeugung genommen; die Auferstehung Jesu hängt mit dem Leben und Endzweck Jesu zusammen; wer seine Lehren erfaren hat, der wird auch glauben, daß ihn Gott von den Todten erweckt hät" (Semler, *Beantwortung der Fragment*, pp. 265-266).

19. Semler, *Lebensbeschreibung*, 2:42.

20. Semler, *Revision der Hermeneutik*, pp. 46-47.

21. "Aber alle andern Christen, welche selbst mehr *moralische* Einsicht haben und unterhalten, wissen es, und gestehen es zur Ehre Gottes, daß es neben der kirchlichen Religionsordnung, worin alle, auch Buben und Bösewichte einstimmen können, noch eine moralische fortgehende innere Religion gebe, die nicht an *Festtage* oder an die Clerisey, an Cärimonien, an Redensarten gebunden ist, wozu alle diejenigen Christen nun noch *verbunden* sein, welches *dieses wissen und einsehen*" (Semler, *Revision der Hermeneutik*, p. 73).

22. "Sie machen eine besondre Classe aus, welche in der moralischen Welt durchaus nicht ganz fehlen kan. Ihre vornehmsten Gegenstände nemen sie aus der körperlichen Welt; ihre Grundsäze darüber sind gleichsam ihr Heiligtum und feierliches Geheimnis. . . . Ihre *mystische* Sprache hat gleichsam verschiedene *Dialekte*. . . . Alle diese Personen rechnen darin auf ihres Gleichen, daß die *äusserlichen* Uebungen der Religion und die Mittel dazu, nur einen sehr geringen Anfang zum *moralischen* guten Stande ausmache; der freilich für sehr viele auch hinlänglich und genug seie" (Semler, *Lebensbeschreibung*, 1:267-268).

23. Semler, *Revision der Hermeneutik*, p. 88.

24. Semler, *Auslegung des Neuen Testaments*, pp. 275-276.

25. "Weil ihre geselschaftliche Religionssprache, Kirchensprache eben so verschieden ist, als sie selbst durch *physischen* und bürgerlichen Unterschied, ohne irgend einen Nachtheil ihres Menschenlebens, noch jetzt eben so getheilt sind, und bleiben, wie Gott selbst es ordnet, wie lang und breit die Menschen und unter was für häuslicher Ordnung in welchen Clima sie wonen sollen!" (Semler, *Revision der Hermeneutik*, p. 45).

26. Semler, *Auslegung des Neuen Testaments*, pp. 1-2.

27. Achenwall, *Vorbereitung zur Staatswissenschaft der heutigen fürnehmsten europäischen Reiche und Staaten worinnen derselben eigentlichen Begriff und Umfang in einer bequemen Ordnung entwirft* (Göttingen, 1748), p. 17.

28. Michaelis, *Mosaisches Recht*, 1:170-171. The following quotation indicates the importance Michaelis attached to the influence of the *Lebensart:* "Es ist nöthig, daß wir hier die Lebensart erwähnen, auf die Moses seinen ganzen Staat gründete, und zugleich anzeigen, wie sich seine Gesetze gegen die übrigen Lebensarten verhielten. Weder der Regierungsform, noch auch das, was ich bisher von einigen Grundmaximen des Staats gesagt habe, werden wir hinlänglich verstehen, ohne den Israelitischen Bürger, ohne das Volk zu kennen, welches den Stoff des Staates ausmachte" (ibid., 1:198-199).

29. "Eben diese unvermeidliche Einschränkung füret die Zeit ferner mit sich, hinter *Luthern* und hinter allen *theologischen Verfassern*, noch viel mehr, als es in allen *bürgerlichen, öconomischen* — Geschäften sichtbar ist; worin doch die Zeit unvermeidlich immer andere Vortheile und Entschliessungen für aufmerksame Zeitgenossen mit sich bringt" (Semler, *Lebensbeschreibung*, 2:258).

30. Ibid., 2:156.

31. Semler, *Auslegung des Neuen Testaments*, p. 93.

32. "Ich zweifle gar nicht an einer solchen Offenbarung und Belehrung Gottes, wodurch die moralische Welt ähnliche Perioden hat, als in der physischen große Revolutionen nicht fehlen können" (ibid., p. 18).

33. Semler, *Beantwortung der Fragment*, pp. 248-251.

34. Semler, *Auslegung des Neuen Testaments*, pp. 64-65.

35. Ibid., p. 242.

36. Semler, *Revision der Hermeneutik*, pp. 3-4.

37. "Aller Unterricht, auch der christlich göttliche, oder aus Gottes Anstalt und Offenbarung durch Christum, ist doch stets *Anfang;* war nie, und

konte nie seyn, das schon volkommenste unveränderliche Maas der folgenden Erkenntnisse für alle künftige Menschen, die Christen werden solten" (Semler, *Auslegung des Neuen Testaments*, p. 51).

38. Ibid., p. 7.

39. Semler, *Beantwortung der Fragment,* p. 118.

40. Ibid., p. 11.

41. Michaelis, *Beantwortung der Frage von dem Einfluß der Meinungen in die Sprache und der Sprache in die Meinungen* (Berlin, 1760), pp. 81-82; Iselin, *Geschichte der Menschheit,* 1:77.

42. Michaelis went even further, claiming that if the Evangelists agreed in every point the authenticity of their accounts would be in doubt, for each man sees and hears what he is ready to see and each interprets from his own personal experience.

43. "Da finden wir Anfange der neuen Religion an eine doppelte *Auslegung;* gewesene Juden, zumal die in Palästina noch woneten, auch in *Rom* und *Klein Asien,* behalten freilich noch ihre ganze jüdische Ordnung, *Sabbate,* Reinigungen, Unterschied der Speisen u. weil sie als Nation fortdauerten, und *eine geringere Erkentnis* von der geistlichen volkommeneren Religion haben. Die Lehrer geben auch hierin eine Zeitlang nach, um sie nicht zu sehr anzustossen. Dagegen *alexandrinische* Juden, (die schon, wie *Philo* klagte, besser dachten) und nicht mehr zur Nation gehören wolten, und alle aus den Heiden, welche Schüler *Pauli* heissen, die gänzlich Unnützlichkeit *jüdischer* Gebräucher einsahen, da sie, diese Christen selbst, gar nicht zum *jüdischen* Staat als Mitglieder und Bürger gehörten" (Semler, *Beantwortung der Fragment,* p 117). Or again, "*Die Hauptsache* ist also: gleich von Anfang der christlichen Religion an haben die Christen sich in zwey Parteyan getheilet; eine hat Jesum als sehr vorzüglichen volkommenen Menschen zum Meßias angenommen; die andere setzt schon lange vor diesem Menschen Jesus, den Sohn Gottes, voraus, der nun eben mit diesem Menschen Jesus unsichtbarer Weise, auf Menschen durch Lehren, und auf Geister, durch Macht Gottes gewirket, und die nachtheilige Gewalt der Geister über die Menschen aufgehoben habe" (ibid., p. 64).

44. Semler, *Lebensbeschreibung,* 2:161-163.

45. "Wenn eine der tiefsten und fruchtbarsten ästhetischen Einsichten, die das Zeitalter gewonnen hatte, darin bestand, daß die Gesetzlichkeit des Schönen, nicht aus den fertigen Werken, sondern aus der 'Energie' des künsterlischen Schaffens abzuleiten und zu erklären sei.... Wenn in der psychologischen Kunstlehre der Engländer, bei Klopstock und den Schweizern, bei Lessing und Herder die Darstellung und Erregung der Leidenschaft als das letzte Ziel aller Kunst gefaßt wurde – so spricht sich das Ideal Winckelmanns in der Forderung der 'Einfalt und Stille' aus" (Cassirer, *Freiheit und Form,* pp. 204-205).

46. Gatterer, *Abriß der Universalhistorie,* p. 622.

47. Iselin, *Geschichte der Menschheit,* 2:356-357.

48. Heeren, *Folgen der Kreuzzüge,* pp. 206-207.

49. Heeren characterized these moral impulses in the following manner: "Ideen, die allgemein verbreitet und allgemein wirksam werden sollen, müssen von der Art seyn, daß Jedermann, daß auch die große Masse des Volks für sie

empfänglich ist, und durch sie zum Handeln gebracht werden kann. Es giebt nur *zwey* Arten solcher Ideen, die religiösen und die politischen. Die gelehrten Kenntnisse können nur der Antheil einer beschränkten Anzahl von Menschen seyn; die Systeme der Philosophen haben noch keine Kriege zwischen Nationen erregt, wenn gleich ihrer Meynungen, zu Volksbegriffen ausgeprägt, darauf Einfluß haben konnten. Die Ideen dagegen von Religion und Vaterland sind zu tief in unsere moralische Natur verflochten, als daß sie blos Gegenstand der Vernunft bleiben, und nicht auch Gegenstand des Gefühls werden sollten. Je dunkler sie blieben, um desto stärker schient eben ihre Kraft zu seyn; und so sind sie es, die auch den ungebildeten Haufen zu elektrisiren vermögen, und ihm eine Wirksamkeit geben, die leicht den Charakter des Enthusiasmus, ja selbst des Fanatismus, annimmt. . . .

"Wie furchtbar aber auch diese Erschütterungen sind, so schient doch durch sie vorzüglich das Schicksal der Menschheit bestimmt zu werden. Die moralische Welt bedarf zu ihrer Reinigung and Erhaltung der Stürme nicht weniger als die physische. Allein es gehören Generationen, es gehören Jahrunderte dazu, ehe sich ihre Wirkungen so weit entwickeln, daß das blöde Auge des Sterblichen sie einigermaaßen umfassen kann . . . (*Folgen der Kreuzzüge,* pp. 8-9).

50. Spittler, *Geschichte der Hierarchie von Gregor VII bis auf die Zeiten der Reformation aus dem literarischen Nachlasse D. Gurlitt,* ed. Cornelius Müller (Hamburg, 1828). These were lecture notes taken by Gurlitt in Spittler's courses at Göttingen in the early 1780s.

51. Ibid., p. 1.

52. Heeren, *Folgen der Kreuzzüge,* p. 80.

53. Gatterer made the comparison in *Abriß der Universalhistorie,* pp. 530-531.

54. Spittler, *Geschichte der Hierarchie,* pp. 7-23.

55. Heeren, *Folgen der Kreuzzüge,* p. 82.

56. "Gregor bildete sich eine Schule, die nicht ausstarb; und wenn auch ein Schwächerer zuweilen die Tiara erhielt, so lebte der Geist doch fort, der in einem Corps, wie das der Römischen Curie – so wie einst des Römischen Senats – sich erzeugen mußte" (ibid., pp. 95-96).

57. Ibid., p. 96.

58. Schlözer, *Universal-Historie I,* pp. 73-75.

59. Gatterer, *Historisches Journal,* 1:268.

60. Spittler, *Geschichte der Hierarchie,* pp. 113-114.

61. Heeren, "Entwickelung der politischen Folgen der Reformation für Europa," in *Kleine historische Schriften,* 3 vols. (Göttingen, 1803-1808), 1:20-21. Heeren, who was at his prime when the French Revolution broke out, considered it another major change, this time, however, with politics at its core. Thus, the above point could be reversed: in 1800, there was scarcely a religious party that was not more or less political.

62. "Wer vermag dem durchgebrochenen Strom seine Bahn, wer dem Erdbeben seine Gränzen zu bezeichnen?" ("Entwickelung der Reformation," p. 9).

63. Herder as quoted by Isaiah Berlin, "Herder and the Enlightenment," in *Aspects of the Eighteenth Century,* ed. Earl R. Wasserman (Baltimore: Johns Hopkins Press, 1965), p. 93.

64. Spittler, *Geschichte der Hierarchie*, p. 119.
65. Ibid., p. 116.
66. Ibid., p. 110.
67. Ibid.
68. Ibid., p. 111.
69. Ibid., pp. 86, 110-111.
70. Heeren, *Folgen der Kreuzzüge*, p. 84, n.
71. Heeren, "Entwickelung der Reformation," p. 5.
72. Ibid., p. 6.
73. Ibid.
74. Ibid., p. 7.
75. Ibid., p. 9.
76. Gatterer, *Historisches Journal*, 9 (1769):119.
77. Spittler, *Geschichte der Hierarchie*, p. 10.
78. Pütter, *Litteratur des teutschen Staatsrechts*, 1:36-37.
79. "Aus Mangel historischer und philosophischer Kentniβ konnte man leicht auf die Gedanken kommen, das Reich, das den Römischen Kaiser zum Oberhaupt habe, sey das Römische Reich" (Pütter, *Beyträge Fürsten-Rechte*, 2:33).
80. "So war nur eine Erneuerung der westlichen Kaiserwürde, so wie sie ehemals schon in Osten und Westen abgetheilt gewesen war. So hieβ es auch auf dem damaligen Münzen ganz richtig: *Renevatio imperii*, nicht *translatio*" (Pütter, *Historische Entwickelung der heutigen Staatsverfassung des teutschen Reichs*, 3 vols. [Göttingen, 1786-1787], 1:65).
81. Pütter, *Entwickelung des teutschen Reichs*, 1:61-65.
82. Ibid., 1:116.
83. Pütter, *Beyträge Fürsten-Rechte*, 2:34-35.
84. Srbik, *Geist und Geschichte*, 1:128. "Er begriff den religiösen Kern der Kaiser- und Reichidee, der ihm nicht wie Voltaire eine bloße Verbrämung von Macht und Interessensstreben war" (ibid.).
85. Pütter, *Beyträge Fürsten-Rechte*, 2:53.
86. This opinion came naturally to both Pütter and Spittler. As eighteenth-century university professors and advocates of the *Ständestaat*, they believed the university alone capable of shaping a nation's intellectual life: it was a constituted body drawing vast numbers of students to its lecture halls. Pütter, as the first historian of the University of Göttingen, was especially aware that a certain esprit de corps animated the whole body of scholars and students, and he assumed the same to have been true at the birth of the universities.
87. Pütter, *Beyträge Fürsten-Rechte*, 2:136, and *Entwickelung des teutschen Reichs*, 1:180-183.
88. Pütter, *Grundriβ der Staatsveränderungen des teutschen Reichs*, p. 330. "Zuverlässig ist es in Städten eher als auf dem Lande geschehen, und von Gelehrten und Geistlichen mehr als von Laien unterstützt, unter dem Adel aber weniger als in anderen Ständen, befolget worden" (Pütter, *Beyträge Fürsten-Rechte*, 2:45).
89. Pütter, *Beyträge Fürsten-Rechte*, 2:85.
90. Pütter, *Litteratur des teutschen Staatsrechts*, 1:56.

91. Ibid., 1:57. Pütter's use of the word *bieder* is typical for the eighteenth century. Lessing had made the word popular and it achieved almost immediate acceptance because it best expressed a growing feeling of German self-identification; it offered a contrast between the good, ingenious German and the sly, subtle, and superficial Frenchman or Italian.

92. "Eben so ist klar am Tage, daß unzehlige Dinge im Römischen Rechte vorkommen, die entweder auf die ganz eigne Römischen Staatsverfassung, oder auf den besonderen Nationalcharacter der Römer eine besondere Beziehung haben" (Pütter, *Beyträge Fürsten-Rechte*, 2:99-100).

93. Ibid., 2:63; Johann Stephan Pütter, *Neuer Versuch einer juristischen Encyclopädie und Methodologie* (Göttingen, 1767), p. 32.

94. Pütter, *Litteratur des teutschen Staatsrechts*, 1:57.

95. Pütter, *Neuer Versuch einer Encyclopädie*, p. 33.

96. Pütter, *Litteratur des teutschen Staatrechts*, 1:57.

97. Ibid., 1:51-52.

98. "Endlich mußte schon Otton über diese neue Verbindung mehr als einmal nach Italien ziehen, und mehrere Jahre dort verweilen, wie seitdem auch fast alle seine Nachfolger thun mußten. Darüber konnte unser gutes Teutschland in solcher Entfernung und anhaltenden Abwesenheit seines Oberhauptes nicht anders als in Verwirrung gerathen, und in Anstalten, die zur Aufklärung und Aufnahme der Nation erforderlich gewesen waren, ganz vernachläßigt zurückkommen; ohne zu gedenken, wie viel Teutsches Blut seitdem in Italien aufgeopfert werden müßen, und was vollends für neuer Stoff zu Mißhelligkeiten zwischen Staat und Kirche daraus erwachsen, der zuletzt in die unglücklichsten Folgen für Teutschland und für alle weltliche Mächte ausgebrochen ist" (Pütter, *Entwickelung des teutschen Reichs*, 1:119).

99. "In diesen unruhigen Zeiten, da fast beständig *zwistige Kayserwahlen* des Reich trenneten, auch bey den oftmahligen *Entfernungen der Kayser* Teutschland seines Oberhaupts so gut wie beraubet war, und da ohnehin die Faction der *Welfen und Gibellinen* immer weiter um sich griff, faßte das *Faustrecht* so tiefe Wurzeln, daß es als eine Haupt-Quelle des Staatsrechts mittlere Zeiten anzusehen" (Pütter, *Grundriß der Staatsveränderungen des teutschen Reichs*, p. 201).

100. Felix Gilbert, "Three Twentieth Century Historians: Meinecke, Bloch, Chabod," in John Higham, Leonard Krieger, and Felix Gilbert, *History* (Englewood Cliffs, N.J.: Prentice-Hall, 1965), p. 368.

101. Pütter, *Beyträge Fürsten-Rechte*, 2:58-59.

102. "So können oft die größten Irrthümer in gewissen Folgen, die einmal daraus erwachsen sind, so tiefe Wurzeln fassen, daß man, wenn auch der Irrthum nachher an Tag kömmt, nicht mehr im Stande ist, diese einmal eingewurzelten Folgen zu heben. Das ist insonderheit der Fall, wenn sowohl die gesetzgebende Gewalt als das Ansehen der Gerichtsstühle und Rechtsgelehrten Irrthümer unterstützt, und wenn unvermerkt eine ganze Nation oder doch ein grosser Theil derselben selbst ihre Sitten und Geschäffte nach solchen Grundsätzen einzurichten gewöhnt wird" (ibid., 2:59).

103. Ernst Landsberg, *Geschichte der deutschen Rechtswissenschaft* (Munich, 1898), pt. 3, 1:349.

104. Pütter, *Beyträge Fürsten-Rechte*, 2:136.

105. Pütter, *Ueber den Unterschied der Stände: Besonders des hohen und niedern Adels in Teutschland zur Grundlage einer Abhandlung von Mißheirathen teutscher Fürsten und Grafen* (Göttingen, 1795), and *Ueber Mißheirathen teutscher Fürsten und Grafen* (Göttingen, 1796).

106. Landsberg, *Geschichte der Rechtswissenschaft*, 1:343.

107. "Hugo erschient damit als der Begründer der neueren Rechtswissenschaft überhaupt, soweit dieser historische, d. h. empirische Auffassung und Behandlung durchgehends eigenthümliche ist. Es darf dagegen, falls man genau reden will, nicht bezeichnet werden als der Begründer der "historische Schule" im engeren Sinne, derjenigen Schule, für die dieser Name durch Übung feststeht. Von Hugo datiert die neue deutsche historische Rechtswissenschaft überhaupt; er hat für sie positiv diejenige Methode und diejenige Richtung festgestellt, die seither im wesentlichen innegehalten worden sind: er ist der erste Autor in der Kette der literärgeschichte, bei dem wir Heutigen vollständig das Gefühl haben, ohne weiteres zu Hause zu sein. . . . er ist Fleisch von unserem Blute" (ibid., 2:40).

108. Despite Pütter's pioneering work, he has received scant attention from modern scholars. The reasons for this neglect are many. Some German scholars, evaluating Pütter by later standards, dismissed him as a superficial thinker, a merely formal talent (the judgment in general of Johann C. Bluntschli, *Geschichte des allgemeinen Staatsrechts und der Politik seit dem sechzehnten Jahrhundert bis zur Gegenwart* [Munich, 1864]. Pütter's attachment to the German Empire and his hopes for a reformed *Ständestaat* did not endear him to those who saw the *deutsche Erhebung* as the signal for the revitalization of German life. Finally, Pütter's own autobiography has hurt his reputation; of all his works, it is the worst. In it he spent an inordinate amount of time describing his meetings with his social superiors and listing aristocrats who had attended his lectures. If one only had a passing acquaintance with Pütter's work and had turned to his autobiography for help, it would be difficult not to reach the conclusion that Pütter was a guileless sycophant. Despite these criticisms, Pütter is recognized by some as the author of the first German *Verfassungsgeschichte* (Fritz Hartung, *Zur Entwicklung des Verfassungsgeschichtschreibung in Deutschland* [Berlin: Akademie Verlag, 1956], p. 3). He was also the most famous teacher of law in his time. During his long period of activity at Göttingen, Pütter trained two generations of students, many of whom became the leading figures in law and politics at the end of the eighteenth and in the first part of the nineteenth century; they included Gustav Hugo, Karl Friedrich Eichhorn, Ernst Brandes, August Wilhelm Rehberg, the Baron vom Stein, and Karl August von Hardenberg.

109. Kelly makes moral purpose one of the central points in the German idealist conception of history (*Idealism, Politics and History*, p. 294).

VIII. Structure of Development and
Appreciation of the Unique

1. For an excellent analysis of neo-Rankean dualism see Walter Hofer, *Geschichtschreibung und Weltanschauung: Betrachtungen zum Werk Friedrich Meineckes* (Munich: Oldenbourg, 1950).

2. Johann von Justi, *Vergleichungen der europäischen mit den asiastischen und andern vermeintlich barbarischen Regierungen* (Berlin, 1762), "Vorrede."

3. Frank E. Manuel, *The Eighteenth Century Confronts the Gods* (Cambridge, Mass.: Harvard University Press, 1959), p. 132.

4. Ibid.

5. Michaelis, "Vom Arabischen Geschmak: Sonderlich in der poetischen und historischen Schreibart," in *Erpenii Arabische Grammatik* (Göttingen, 1771), p. xxxv.

6. Quoted by Manuel, *Eighteenth Century Confronts the Gods*, p. 302. Professor Manuel maintains that Heyne's conception of myth was drawn from Herder. It is true that Herder and Heyne were friends. It is also true that during the 1770s Heyne and Michaelis were not on very good terms, partly because of Michaelis's opposition to offering Herder a professorship at Göttingen, partly because of differences about the running of the library and the *Göttingen Gelehrte Anzeige*. Still, the fact of the Herder-Heyne friendship alone does not suffice to explain Heyne's conception of myth. In fact, his basic views had already been established before that friendship was sealed. According to Heyne's son-in-law, Arnold Heeren, the most important influence on forming Heyne's appreciation of myth came from Robert Wood's *Essay on the Original Genius of Homer* (London, 1775). Wood had six copies of the work printed privately in 1769 for a select group. One of these was sent to Michaelis, who immediately recognized its importance and showed it to Heyne, who then summarized it in the *Göttingen Gelehrte Anzeige* in 1770. Michaelis and his son translated the book into German and it appeared in Germany before it appeared publicly in England (Heeren, "Christian Gottlob Heyne," *Werke*, 6:181-82; Michaelis, *Literarischer Briefwechsel*, 2:238; Michaelis, *Mosaisches Recht*, 2:184).

7. Michaelis, *Mosaisches Recht*, 2:388.

8. Sir John Pringle to Michaelis, May 2, 1774, in *Literarischer Briefwechsel*, 2:381-386.

9. Michaelis, *Mosaisches Recht*, 1:3.

10. Ibid., 6:88-89.

11. Ibid., 1:290.

12. Ibid., 6:164.

13. Ibid., 1:170-171.

14. Ibid., 1:3.

15. Eichhorn summarized Michaelis's achievement: "Man hatte vor ihm schon bemerkt, daß Sitten, wie das A. T. sie schildert, oben von der Zeit der Patriarchen an, und so der Reihe nach herab auch in den folgenden Jahrhunderten aus Sitten anderer, von Geschlecht und Sprache ganz verschiedenen Völker, die unter ganz verschiedenen Klimaten wohnten, aus

Berichten von Amerika, von Indien und Grönland u.s.w. Erläuterungen, mehr
und minder nehmen könnten. . . . Nur durch diese so genau gezogene Gränze
entgieng doch seinem sonst so philosophischen Blick ein wichtiger Punkt —
die wahre Quelle der bemerkten Aehnlichkeiten. Er sah sie wohl für bloßen
Zufall an; und doch ein Zufall, so weit fortgehend und so ausgebreitet, bleibt
wohl kein Zufall mehr. So dringt sich die Bemerkung auf, daß gleiche Lage
der Cultur und gleicher Geistes-Zustand zu gleicher Denk- und Sinnes Art, zu
gleichen Sitten und Gebräuchen führe; und daß, sich überlassen und in ihrem
Stufen-Gang der Bildung durch fremden Einfluß nicht gestöhrt, die Menschheit überall nach einerley Gesetzten sich erhebe, und nach allgemeinen fest
bestimmten Schritten vorwärts schreite. Diese durch den Gang der menschlichen Cultur durch alle Zeiten der Geschichte bestätigte Bemerkung scheint
für das hohe Alterthum ganz neue Bahnen zu eröffnen und zu Resultaten
hinzuführen, durch die sich, wie es scheint, viel tiefer als bisher in den Geist
der Schriften der Hebräer dringen laßt" (*Michaelis*, pp. 32-34).

16. Otto Friedrich Bollnow, *Die Lebensphilosophie F. H. Jacobis* (1933),
2d ed. (Stuttgart: W. Kohlhammer, 1966), pp. 150-158.

17. Rudolf Unger, *Hamann und die Aufklärung: Studien zur Vorgeschichte des romantischen Geistes im achtzehnten Jahrhundert,* 2d ed., 2 vols.
(Halle: H. Niemeyer, 1925), 1:242.

18. "Denn nichts ist eigentlich aus dem orientalischen Geist der Zeit, des
Volks, der Sitte erklärt, sondern nur überall Blumen eines halb Oriental-
ischen, gut Europäischen *common sense* herüber gestreut" (Johann Gottfried
Herder, "Michaelis Mosaisches Recht," in *Frankfurter gelehrte Anzeigen,* 34
[April, 1772], 267).

19. Manuel, *Eighteenth Century Confronts the Gods,* p. 134.

20. "So war es natürlich, eine kurze Geschichte derselben einzuschalten,
sie zu erklären, die Interpretation zu beweisen, die weisen Ursachen der
erteilten Rechte, zur Ehre des Erteilers, aufzusuchen, und den Einwendungen
der Gegner, durch Schlüsse zu begegnen, die 1. aus dem Menschen Verstande,
2. aus dem Sprach Gebrauch alter Zeiten, und 3. aus der Analogie, dem
Parallelism, oder der Vergleichung . . . geschöpft werden konnten und
mußten" (Schlözer, *Kritische Sammlungen zur Geschichte der Deutschen in
Siebenbürgen,* 3 vols. in 1 [Göttingen, 1795-1797], 3:3).

21. Schlözer, *Chronik von Leipzig,* pp. 13-14,

22. Roscher to Ranke, 1842, printed in *Preussische Jahrbücher,* 133
(Feb. 1908):384.

23. The best works dealing with Bodmer's importance for history are
Antoni, *Kampf wider die Vernunft,* pp. 38-64, and Max Wehrli, *Johann Jakob
Bodmer und die Geschichte der Literatur* (Frauenfeld: Huber, 1936). Also
important is Fritz Ernst's introduction to his edition of Bodmer's *Schriften:
Ausgewählt* (Frauenfeld: Huber, 1938).

24. *Schriften,* ed. Ernst, p. 11.

25. "Persönliche Anekdoten," in ibid., p. 21.

26. Ibid., p. 23.

27. Johann Jacob Bodmer and Johann Jacob Breitinger, "Ein Plan
eidgenössischer Sittenbeschreibung," in Max Wehrli, ed., *Das geistige Zürich*

im achtzehnten Jahrhundert: Texte und Dokumente von Gotthard Heidigger bis Heinrich Pestalozzi (Zurich: Atlantis, 1943), p. 59.

28. Ibid.

29. Ibid., pp. 59-60.

30. The first moral journal patterned after the *Spectator* and the *Tatler* to appear in Germany was the *Patriot*, published in Hamburg by the Brockes circle.

31. Wehrli, *Bodmer und die Geschichte der Literatur*, p. 16.

32. *The Use and Abuse of History*, trans. Adrian Collins (Indianapolis: Bobbs-Merrill, 1949), p. 18.

33. Johann Jacob Bodmer, *Johann Miltons Verlust des Paradieses: Ein Heldengedicht in ungebundene Rede übersetzt* (Zurich, 1732).

34. Bodmer, "Probe Uebersetzung Milton," in *Sammlung critischer, poetischer, und andrer geistvollen Schriften, zur Verbesserung des Urtheils und des Wizes in den Wercken der Wolredenheit und der Poesie*, 5 pts. in 2 vols. (Zurich, 1741-1742), vol. 1, pt. 1, p. 14.

35. Antoni, *Kampf wider die Vernunft*, p. 38.

36. Ibid., p. 50.

37. Bodmer to Herzel, in *Briefe der Schweizer*, ed. Körte, p. 45.

38. Bodmer and Johann Jacob Breitinger, eds., *Helvetische Bibliothek: Bestehend in historischen, politischen, und critischen Beyträgen zu den Geschichten des Schweitzerlandes*, 6 vols. in 2 (Zurich, 1735-1741).

39. It has been suggested that Blackwell, among others, was influenced by Vico because of the many similarities between their ideas of poetry, metaphor, the primitive, and historical development. Typical is the statement made by Max H. Fisch in the introduction to his and Thomas A. Bergin's translation of *The Autobiography of Giambattista Vico* (Ithaca: Cornell University Press, 1944 [I have used the paperback edition, which has the same pagination]), p. 82: "It is scarcely creditable that the Vichian ideas scattered through the writings of Blackwell, Ferguson, Hume, Wollaston, Warburton, Hurd, Monboddo, Wood, Blair, Duff, Mason, Brown, Lowth, Warton and Burke, are due solely to their having been in this or that respect *animae naturaliter Vicianae*, or to a gradual unfolding of Shaftesbury's seminal thoughts, or even to an indirect and diluted Vichian influence through Italian and French authors mentioned in previous sections." Professor Fisch's conclusion has been disputed by René Wellek, who argues that more than enough modern and classical precedents were available to Scottish and English thinkers to allow them to arrive at the Vichian ideas these men espoused. Wellek concludes: "Very similar ideas, we have to admit, can be arrived at independently, and, as a case in point, 'Vichian' ideas were developed from their pre-Vichian forms in directions that often came close to the actual statements of Vico. But no one in the eighteenth century, least of all in Great Britain, absorbed or even discussed the totality of Vico's stupendous scheme of history" (René Wellek, "The Supposed Influence of Vico on England and Scotland in the Eighteenth Century," in *Giambattista Vico*, ed. Tagliacozzo and White, p. 223). I am inclined to agree with Professor Wellek, especially in the case of Blackwell. Although there are similarities between Blackwell's and Vico's thought, the dissimilarities are

even more striking. Not only did Blackwell's theory of aesthetics differ radically from Vico's so too did his view of Homer. Blackwell showed no awareness whatsoever concerning Vico's contention that the *Iliad* and the *Odyssey* were composed at different periods, or that Homer as a man or even as two different men did not exist. It is my belief that Blackwell's view, as well as that of Robert Wood, can easily be explained by reference to the dyanmics of Enlightenment thought without reference to the deus ex machina of an omnipresent, though universally unacknowledged, Vichian influence.

40. Thomas Blackwell, *An Enquiry into the Life and Writings of Homer* (London, 1735), p. 73.

41. Ibid., p. 36.

42. Ibid., pp. 13-14.

43. Ibid., p. 76.

44. Ibid., p. 44.

45. Ibid., p. 42.

46. Ibid., pp. 58-59.

47. Ibid., p. 25.

48. Ibid., p. 72.

49. Ibid., p. 22.

50. Ibid., pp. 23-24.

51. Blackwell described the spirit of freedom: "Besides, the Times of such Struggles have a kind of *Liberty* peculiar to themselves: They raise a free and active Spirit, which overspreads the Country: Every Man finds himself on such Occasions his own Master, and that he *may be* whatever he can *make* himself: He knows not how high he may rise, and is unawed by Laws, which are then of no Force. He finds his own Weight, tries his own Strength, and if there is any hidden Worth, or curbed Mettle in him, certainly shews and gives it vent. Accordingly we see, that the Genius's produced at these Times, give great Proofs of *Reach* and *Capacity,* especially in politick Managements and civil Affairs, in the largest Sense. The abstract *Sciences* are generally the Product of *Leisure* and *Quiet;* but these that have respect to *Man,* and take their Aim from the human Heart, are best learned in Employment and Agitation" (ibid., pp. 64-65).

52. Ibid.

53. Ibid., p. 52.

54. Ibid., pp. 143-144.

55. Ibid., p. 53.

56. Ibid., p. 329.

57. Ibid., p. 117.

58. According to Blackwell, "The Necessity of Labour and Contrivance; a growing Commerce, and more than any thing besides, the Number of free Cities and independent Governments, soon raised a nobler Language than either of the Originals. It was at first *simple, unconfined* and *free,* as was their own Life" (ibid., pp. 45-46).

59. Ibid., p. 46.

60. Ibid., p. 119.

61. Ibid., p. 117.

62. A. Robert Caponigri, *Time and Idea: The Theory of History in Giambattista Vico* (1938) (Notre Dame: University of Notre Dame Press, 1968), p. 160. Blackwell made the point clear when he stated that by reflection Homer "had converted the Principles of all the Sciences, natural and moral, into *human* or *divine* Persons, and then wrought them into the underparts of his Poem. This is beginning at the wrong end; and however proper the Method may be, or rather necessary in *Philosophy,* it wou'd spoil all in the hands of the Muses" (*Enquiry into the Life of Homer,* p. 314).

63. Donald M. Foerster surveys the development of English and Scottish Homeric criticism in *Homer in English Criticism: The Historical Approach in the Eighteenth Century,* Yale Studies in English, vol. 105 (New Haven: Yale University Press, 1947). From the 1750s on Scottish writers argued that "Ossian was the Scottish Homer," that "the two poets, besides living in the same stage in the progress of society, derived their ideas of the epic from the same source" (ibid., p. 55). And Englishmen used Blackwell's analysis to extol the merits of Spenser and Shakespeare. The weakest part of Foerster's book is the section on Germany. Foerster believes that Herder "was the first to call attention to Blackwell's *Enquiry* and the first to espouse Blackwell's arguments. Bodmer clearly has that honor, preceding Herder and most English commentators by two decades. The book was well known in Germany during the fifties; for example, Winckelmann had referred to it as one of the best books ever written (Meinecke, *Die Entstehung des Historismus,* p. 248, n. 2).

64. Blackwell, *Enquiry into the Life of Homer,* pp. 65-66.

65. In *Sammlung critischer Schriften,* pt. 7, pp. 25-53; reprinted in Wehrli, ed., *Das geistige Zürich,* pp. 67-76.

66. Wehrli, ed., *Das geistige Zürich,* pp. 67-68.

67. Ibid., p. 68.

68. Ibid., p. 69.

69. Ibid., p. 71.

70. Ibid., p. 70.

71. Ibid., p. 73.

72. Ibid., p. 75.

73. Ibid.

74. Bodmer, *Der Parcival, ein Gedicht in Wolframs von Eschilbach Denckart: Eines Poeten aus den Zeiten Kaiser Heinrich des VI* (Zurich, 1753).

75. *Chriemhilden Rache und die Klage: Zwey Heldengedichte aus dem schwaebischen Zeitpuncte samt Fragmenten aus dem Gedichte von den Nibelungen und aus dem Josaphat* (Zurich, 1757).

76. Wehrli, *Bodmer und die Geschichte der Literatur,* p. 26.

77. Körte, ed., *Briefe der Schweizer,* p. 67.

78. Bodmer, *Helvetische Bibliothek,* vol. 1, pt. 2, pp. 5-6.

79. Bodmer, *Sammlung von Minnesingern aus dem schwaebischen Zeitpuncte,* "Vorrede," in *Sammlung critischer Schriften,* p. 41.

80. *Proben der alten schwäbischen Poesie des dreyzehnten Jahrhunderts aus der Maneßischen Sammlung* (Zurich, 1748), p. vi.

81. Bodmer, *Parcival,* pp. 6-7. Translated, the lines read:

Though the words of your language, their life and nobility,
Appear to our people both vulgar and obscure,
I see their images still living; I experience in my spirit
Your expression of anguish and I wonder at your new ideas.
These to my time do I desire to unfold, and through this unfolding
Again renew the delight in our ancient ancestors
That we perceive in our hearts through your sons.

82. "Das Nibelungenlied," in *Das geistige Zürich,* ed. Wehrli, p. 97.

83. Bodmer, "Von dem Werte des dantischen dreifachen Gedichtes," in *Sammlung critischer Schriften,* p. 39.

84. Bodmer, "Über das dreyfache Gedicht des Dante," in *Das geistige Zürich,* ed. Wehrli, p. 97.

85. Ibid., p. 98.

86. Ibid., p. 100.

87. Ibid.

Conclusion

1. *Medievalism and the Ideologies of the Enlightenment: The World and Work of La Curne de Sainte-Palaye* (Baltimore: Johns Hopkins Press, 1968), p. 334. Franco Venturi has also shown how medievalism was a natural stance for a number of eighteenth-century Italian historians and publicists ("History and Reform in the Middle of the Eighteenth Century," in *The Diversity of History: Essays in Honour of Sir Herbert Butterfield,* ed. John Huxtable Elliott and Helmut George Koenigsberger [London: Routledge and Kegan Paul, 1970], pp. 223-244).

2. Dwight E. Lee and Robert N. Beck, "The Meaning of Historicism," *American Historical Review* (April, 1954), p. 577. Other commentators have given similar definitions. For example, Hayden V. White defines historicism as *"the tendency to interpret the whole of reality, including what up to the romantic period had been conceived as absolute and unchanging human values, in historical, that is to say relative, terms."* (introduction to Carlo Antoni, *From History to Sociology: The Transition in German Historical Thinking,* trans. Hayden V. White [Detroit: Wayne State University Press, 1959], p. xvii). The German scholar, Reinhard Wittram, defines historicism as "alle Erscheinungen des menschlichen Lebens wesentlich als Geschichte und damit als zeitbedingt und veränderlich darstellen" (*Das Interesse an der Geschichte* [Göttingen: Vandenhoeck and Ruprecht, 1958], p. 58).

3. Ernst Cassirer, *The Philosophy of the Enlightenment,* p. 32.

4. Karl Barth and Frank Manuel document this movement in their respective works: *Protestant Thought: From Rousseau to Ritschl,* trans. H. H. Hartwell (New York: Harper and Row, 1959), and *The Eighteenth Century Confronts the Gods.*

5. Carlo Antoni sees the conflict between reason and spirit as one of the basic themes in the development of eighteenth-century German historical thought (*Der Kampf wider die Vernunft*).

6. Georg C. Iggers, *The German Conception of History: The National Tradition of Historical Thought from Herder to the Present* (Middletown, Conn.: Wesleyan University Press, 1968), pp. 4-5.

7. Georg Christoph Lichtenberg, *Lichtenberg: Aphorisms and Letters,* trans. Franz Mautner and Henry Hatfield (London: Jonathan Cape, 1969), p. 40.

8. In late eighteenth-century German aesthetics, God's knowledge is usually described as an *anschauende Erkenntnis* of all things. At the same time the understanding of a genius is also described as an *anschauende Erkenntnis.* The difference was one of degree, not nature.

9. These general categories are proposed by Walter Hofer in his seminal study of Friedrich Meinecke, *Geschichtschreibung und Weltanschauung: Betrachtungen zum Werk Friedrich Meineckes* (Munich: Oldenbourg, 1950), p. 370.

Bibliography

PRIMARY SOURCES

Abbt, Thomas. *Fragment der ältesten Begebenheit des menschlichen Geschlechts.* Intro. Peter Miller. Halle, 1767.

Achenwall, Gottfried. *Abriß der neuesten Staatswissenschaft der vornehmsten europäischen Reiche und Republiken zum Gebrauch in seinen academischen Vorlesungen.* Göttingen, 1749.

————. *Anzeige seiner neuen Vorlesungen über die grössere europaische Staatshändel des siebzehnten und achtzehnten Jahrhunderts, das ist über die Geschichte des europäischen Staats-Systems seit 1600 als den zweyten Theil der europäischen Geschichte.* Göttingen, 1755.

————. *Entwurf der allgemeineren europäischen Staatshändel des siebzehnten und achtzehnten Jahrhunderts als der europäischen Geschichte zweyter Theil.* Göttingen, 1756.

————. *Französischer Finanz-Staat, aus dem königlichen Steuer-Edict vom November 1771.* Ed. J. C. Spamer. Göttingen, 1774.

————. *Geschichte der allgemeineren europäischen Staatshändel des vorigen und jetzigen Jahrhunderts im Grundriße.* 2d ed. Göttingen, 1761. 3d ed. Göttingen, 1767.

————. *Geschichte der heutigen vornehmsten europäischen Staaten im Grundriße.* 2d ed. Göttingen, 1759. 3d ed. rev. Göttingen, 1764.

————. *Geschichte der heutigen vornehmsten europäischen Staaten im Grundriße.* Ed. Johann Philipp Murray. 4th ed. rev. Göttingen, 1773.

————. "Observations on North America." Trans. J. G. Rosengarten. *Pennsylvania Magazine of History and Biography* (Jan., 1903).

————. *Die Staatsklugheit nach ihren ersten Grundsätzen.* Göttingen, 1761.

————. *Staatsverfassung der europäischen Reiche im Grundriße.* 3d ed. Göttingen, 1756.

————. *Staatsverfassung der heutigen vornehmsten europäischen Reiche im Grundriße.* 4th ed. Göttingen, 1762.

————. *Staatsverfassung der heutigen vornehmsten europäischen Reiche und Völker im Grundriße.* 5th ed. Göttingen, 1768. 6th ed. Ed. August Ludwig Schlözer. 2 vols. Göttingen, 1781-1785.

————. *Vorbereitung zur Staatswissenschaft der heutigen fürnehmsten europäischen Reiche und Staaten worinnen derselben eigentlichen Begriff und Umfang in einer bequemen Ordnung entwirft.* Göttingen, 1748.

Arnold, Gottfried. *Unparteyische Kirchen- und Ketzer-Historie, von Anfang des Neuen Testaments biß auf das Jahr Christi 1688.* 2 vols. in 1. Frankfurt, 1700.

Baumgarten, Sigmund Jacob. *Uebersetzung der allgemeinen Welthistorie die in Engeland durch eine Geselschaft von Gelehrten ausgefertiget worden, nebst den Anmerkungen den holländischen Uebersetzung.* 30 vols. Halle, 1744-1767.

Bayle, Pierre. *Historical and Critical Dictionary Selections.* Trans. Richard H. Popkin. Library of Liberal Arts. Indianapolis: Bobbs-Merrill, 1965.

Beckman, Johann. *Beyträge zur Geschichte der Erfindungen.* 2d ed. 5 vols. Leipzig, 1786-1805.

Blackwell, Thomas. *An Enquiry into the Life and Writings of Homer.* London, 1735.

Bodmer, Johann Jacob. *Bodmer's Tagebuch (1752-1782).* Offprint from *Jubiläumsschrift der Allgemeinen Geschichtsforschenden Gesellschaft der Schweiz* (1891), pp. 191-216.

—————. *Chriemhilden Rache und die Klage: Zwey Heldengedichte aus dem schwaebischen Zeitpuncte samt Fragmenten aus dem Gedichte von den Nibelungen und aus dem Josaphat.* Zurich, 1757.

—————. *Conradin von Schwaben: Ein Gedicht mit einem historischen Vorberichte.* Karlsruhe, 1771.

—————. *Fabeln aus der Zeiten der Minnesinger.* Zurich, 1757.

—————. *Litterarische Pamphlete aus der Schweiz, nebst Briefen an Bodmern.* Zurich, 1781.

—————. *Der Parcival, ein Gedicht in Wolframs von Eschilbach Denckart: Eines Poeten aus den Zeiten Kaiser Heinrich des VI.* Zurich, 1753.

—————. *Proben der alten schwäbischen Poesie des dreyzehnten Jahrhunderts aus der Maneßischen Sammlung.* Zurich, 1748.

—————. *Sammlung critischer, poetischer, und andrer geistvollen Schriften, zur Verbesserung des Urtheils und des Wizes in den Wercken der Wolredenheit und der Poesie.* 5 pts. in 2 vols. Zurich, 1741, 1742.

—————. *Schriften: Ausgewählt.* Schriften der Corona XXI. Ed. Fritz Ernst. Frauenfeld: Huber, 1938.

Bodmer, Johann Jacob, and Breitinger, Johann Jacob, eds. *Helvetische Bibliothek: Bestehend in historischen, politischen, und critischen Beyträgen zu den Geschichten des Schweitzerlandes.* 6 vols. in 2. Zurich, 1735-1741.

Bolingbroke, Henry St. John. *Letters on the Study and Use of History.* Vols. 3 and 4 of *Collected Works.* London, 1809.

Boysen, D. F. E., ed. *Die Allgemeine Welthistorie die in England durch eine Gesellschaft von Gelehrten ausgefertiget worden.* Preface by Johann Christoph Gatterer. 10 vols. Halle, 1767-1772.

Büsch, Johann Georg. *Abhandlung von dem Geldumlauf in anhaltender Rücksicht auf die Staatswirtschaft und Handlung.* 3 vols. Hamburg, 1780-1784.

—————. *Versuch einer Geschichte der hamburgischen Handlung nebst zwey kleineren Schriften eines verwandten Inhalts.* Hamburg, 1797.

Chladenius, Johann Martin. *Allgemeine Geschichtswissenschaft, worinnen der Grund zu einer neuen Einsicht in allen Arten der Gelahrtheit gelegt wird.* Leipzig, 1752.

—————. *Das Blendwerk der natürlichen Religion.* Trans. Urban Gottlob Thorschmid. Leipzig, 1751.

—————. *Einleitung zur richtigen Auslegung vernünfftiger Reden und Schriften.* Leipzig, 1742.

Claproth, Johann E. *Der gegenwärtige Zustand der Göttingischen Universität in zweenen Briefen an einem vornehmen Herrn im Reiche.* Göttingen, 1748.

—————. *Schreiben von dem gegenwärtigen Zustand der Göttingischen Universität an einen vornehmen Herrn im Reiche.* 1746.

Crusius, Christian A. *Entwurf der nothwendigen Vernunft-Wahrheiten.* Leipzig, 1745.

—————. *Weg zur Gewissheit und Zuverlässigkeit der menschlichen Erkenntniss.* Leipzig, 1747.

D'Alembert, Jean le Rond. *Preliminary Discourse to the Encyclopaedia of Diderot.* Trans. Richard N. Schwab. Library of Liberal Arts. Indianapolis: Bobbs-Merrill, 1963.

Descartes, René. *Discourse on Method and Other Writings.* Trans. Arthur Wollaston. London: Penguin Books, 1960.

Dobrovský, Josef, and Anton, Karl Gottlob von. *Der Briefwechsel zwischen Josef Dobrovský und Karl Gottlob von Anton.* Ed. Miloslav Krbec and Vêra Michálová. Berlin: Universitäts Verlag, 1959.

Eichhorn, Johann Gottfried. *Geschichte des ostindischen Handels vor Mohämmed.* Gotha, 1775.

—————. *Johann David Michaelis: Einige Bemerkungen über seinen litterarischen Character, besonders, eigentlich nur für Freunde abgedruckt.* Leipzig, 1791.

—————. *Weltgeschichte.* 2 vols. 2d ed. rev. Göttingen, 1804.

Einem, Charlotte von. *Aus dem Nachlaß Charlottens von Einem: Ungedruckte Briefe von Hölty, Noss, Boie, Overbeck u. a., Jugenderinnerungen.* Ed. Julius Steinberger. Leipzig: Vereinigung Göttingen Bücherfreunde, 1923.

Eines Anonymi eilfertige doch unpartheyische Gedancken über das in Hrn. D. Chladenius wöchentlichen biblischen Untersuchungen gefällte scharfe Urtheil von des Hrn. Hoffrath Schmauß neuen Systemate des Rechts der Natur. Göttingen, 1754.

Fischer, Friedrich Christoph Jonathan. *Geschichte des teutschen Handels.* 4 vols. Hanover, 1785-1792.

Fleischhauer, Johann Jacob. *Zufällige Gedenken von dem Alter, Wachsthum und Nutzen der Oeconomic.* Academica Gottingensia, pt. 2. Göttingen, 1750.

Freyherr von Moser und Schlözer über die oberste Gewalt im Staat mit Anmerkungen eines Unpartheyischen und ein Versuch über Staats-Verbindung. Meissen, 1794.

Gatterer, Johann Christoph. "Abhandlung vom Standort und Gesichtspunct des Geschichtschreibers oder der teutsche Livius." In *Allgemeine Historische Bibliothek von Mitgliedern des Königlichen Instituts der Historischen Wissenschaften zu Göttingen.* Vol. 5, pp. 3-29. Halle, 1768.

—————. *Abhandlung von Thracien nach Herodot und Thucydides aus dem Lateinischen übersetzt und mit einer Uebersicht und dem nöthigen Register.* Intro. Hermann Schlichthorst. Göttingen, 1800.

—————. *Abriß der Chronologie.* Göttingen, 1777.

—————. *Abriß der Diplomatik.* Göttingen, 1778.

—————. *Abriß der Geographie.* Göttingen, 1775.

————. *Abriß der Heraldik.* Göttingen, 1773.

————. *Abriß der Universalhistorie in ihrem ganzen Umfange.* 2d ed. rev. Göttingen, 1773.

————. *Abriß der Universalhistorie nach ihrem gesamten Umfange von Erschaffung der Welt bis auf unsere Zeiten.* Göttingen, 1765.

————. *Antwort auf die Schlözersche Species Facti.* Göttingen, 1773.

————. *Einleitung in die synchronistische Universalhistorie zur Erläuterung seiner synchronistischen Tabellen.* Göttingen, 1771.

————. *Handbuch der neuesten Genealogie und Heraldik worinnen aller jezigen europäischen Potentaten Stammtafeln und Wappen.* Nuremberg, 1763, 1764.

————. *Handbuch der Universalhistorie nach ihrem gesamten Umfange von Erschaffung der Welt bis zum Ursprunge der meisten heutigen Reiche und Staaten.* Göttingen, 1761.

————. *Ideal einer allgemeinen Weltstatistik.* Göttingen, 1773.

————. *Synopsis Historiae Universalis, Sex Tabulis.* Göttingen, 1769.

————. "Vom historischen Plan und der darauf sich gründenden Zusammenfügung der Erzählungen." In *Allgemeine Historische Bibliothek von Mitgliedern des Königlichen Instituts der Historischen Wissenschaften zu Göttingen.* Vol. 1, pp. 15-89. Halle, 1767.

————. "Von der Evidenz in der Geschichtkunde." In *Die Allgemeine Welthistorie die in England durch eine Gesellschaft von Gelehrten ausgefertiget worden.* Ed. D. F. E. Boysen. Vol. 1, pp. 3-38. Halle, 1767.

Gatterer, Johann Christoph, ed. *Allgemeine Historische Bibliothek von Mitgliedern des Königlichen Institus der Historischen Wissenschaften zu Göttingen.* 16 vols. Halle, 1767-1771.

————. *Historisches Journal, von Mitgliedern des Königlichen Historischen Instituts zu Göttingen.* 16 vols. Göttingen, 1772-1781.

Gebauer, George Christian. *Anzeige zu der vor kurzem entstandenen Frage: Was vor einem Herzog Heinrich zu Lüneburg, das in die Capelle A. L. Fr. zu Alt-Oetting in Bayern verlobte silberne Schiff zuzueignen sey?* Frankfurt, 1751.

————. *Grund-Riß zu einer umständlichen Historie der vornehmsten europäischen Reiche und Staaten mit einer Vorrede von dem mannigfaltigen Nutzen der historischen Wissenschaft und nöthigen Registern versehen.* 2d ed. rev. Leipzig, 1738. 3d ed. Leipzig, 1749.

————. *Portugisische Geschichte, von den ältesten Zeiten dieses Volks bis auf itzige Zeiten; mit genealogischen Tabellen und vielen Anmerkungen versehen, in denen die Belege und allerhand Untersuchungen der historischen Wahrheiten anzutreffen sind.* 2 pts. Leipzig, 1759.

Gebauer, George Christian, ed. *Corpus Juris Civilis.* Spangenberg ed. Göttingen, 1776, 1796.

Gesner, Johann M. *Biographia Academica Gottingensis.* Ed. J. N. Eyring. Vols. 1, 2. Halle, 1768. Vol. 3. Göttingen, 1769.

Goethe, Wolfgang. *Dichtung und Wahrheit.* In *Goethes Werke: Hamburger Ausgabe.* Vol. 9. Hamburg: Christian Wegner, 1955.

Gottsched, Johann Christoph. *Gottsched und seine Zeit: Auszüge aus seinem Briefwechsel.* Ed. Thomas W. Danzel. Leipzig, 1848.

Grotius, Hugo. *Florumsparsio ad jus judinianeum.* Ed. with preface by George Christian Gebauer. Halle, 1729.

Gundling, Nicholas H. *Ausführliche Discours über den ietzigen Zustand der europäischen Staaten.* 2 vols. Frankfurt, 1733-1734.

Haller, Albrecht von. *Tagebuch seiner Beobachtungen über Schriftsteller und über sich selbst.* 2 vols. Bern, 1787.

Haller, Gottlob Emanuel von. *Erster Versuch einer critißchen Verzeichniß aller Schriften welche die Schweiz ansehen.* 3 vols. Bern, 1759-1762.

—————. *Schweizerisches Münz- und Medaillenkabinet.* 2 vols. Bern, 1780-1781.

—————. *Vertheidigung des Wilhelm Tell.* Fluelen, 1824. Originally published in 1772.

Heeren, Arnold Hermann Ludwig. "Entwickelung der politischen Folgen der Reformation für Europa." In *Kleine historische Schriften.* Vol. 1. 3 vols. Göttingen, 1803-1808.

—————. *Historische Werke.* Vol. 6. Göttingen, 1823.

—————. *Ideen über die Politik, den Verkehr und den Handel der vornehmsten Völker der alten Welt.* 2 vols. 4th ed. Göttingen, 1824.

—————. *Johann von Müller der Historiker.* Leipzig, 1809.

—————. "Ueber die Entstehung, die Ausbildung und den praktischen Einfluß der politischen Theorien in dem neueren Europa." In *Kleine historische Schriften.* Vol. 2, pp. 145-250. 3 vols. Göttingen, 1803-1808.

—————. *Versuch einer Entwickelung der Folgen der Kreuzzüge.* Vol. 3 of *Kleine historische Schriften.* Göttingen, 1808.

Heeren, Arnold Hermann Ludwig, and Hugo, Gustav. *Spittler.* Berlin, 1812.

Hegel, Georg Wilhelm Friedrich. *Vorlesungen über die Philosophie der Geschichte.* Vol. 12 of *Werke.* Frankfurt: Suhrkamp, 1970.

Herder, Johann Gottfried. "Michaelis Mosaisches Recht." *Frankfurter Gelehrte Anzeigen.* No. 34, pt. 1 (April 28, 1772).

—————. "Schlözer's Nordische Geschichte." *Frankfurter Gelehrte Anzeigen.* Nos. 16, 17, pp. 121-136.

—————. "Schlözer's Vorstellung seiner Universalhistorie." *Frankfurter Gelehrte Anzeigen.* No. 60 (July 28, 1772), pp. 473-478.

Heyne, Christian Gottlob. *Akademische Vorlesungen über die Archäologie der Kunst des Altertums insbesondere der Griechen und Römer.* Brunswick, 1822.

Hübner, Johann. *Curieuses Natur-Kunst-Gewerck und Handels Lexicon.* Leipzig, 1712.

—————. *Hamburgische Bibliotheca Historica der Studierenden Jugend zum Besten zusammen getragen.* 11 vols. in 6. Leipzig, 1715-1729.

—————. *Kurtze Fragen aus der Genealogie nebst denen dazu gehörigen Tabellen zur Erläuterung der politischen Historie zusammen getragen.* 5th ed. 4 vols. Leipzig, 1737-1744.

—————. *Kurtze Fragen aus der neuen und alten Geographie biß auf gegenwärtige Zeit continuiret und mit einer nützlichen Einleitung vor die Anfänger auch mit einer ausführlichen Vorrede von den besten Land Charten.* Leipzig, 1719.

—————. *Kurtze Fragen aus der politischen Historie biß auf gegenwärtige Zeit continuiret.* 10 vols. Leipzig, 1715.

—————. *Reales Staats-Zeitungs und Conversations Lexicon, darinnen so wohl die Religionen und geistlichen Orden, die Reiche u. Staaten, Meere, Seen, Flüsse, Städte, Festungen, Schlösser, Häfen, Berge, Vorgebürge, Pässe, und Wälder, die Linien Deutscher hoher Häuser, die in verschiedenen Ländern übliche so geistliche als weltliche Ritter-Ordern, Wapen, Reichstäge, gelehrte Societaten.* Leipzig, 1711.

—————. *Zweymahl zwey und fünffzig auserlesene biblische Historien aus dem Alten und Neuen Testamente, der Jugend zum Besten abgefasset.* Leipzig, 1714.

Humboldt, Wilhelm von. *Wilhelm von Humboldt.* Ed. Heinrich Weinstock. Frankfurt: Fischer Bücherei, 1957.

Hume, David. *Natural History of Religion.* Vol. 4 of *The Philosophical Works of David Hume.* Boston, 1854.

Iselin, Isaak. *Über die Geschichte der Menschheit.* 4th ed. 2 vols. Basel, 1779.

Justi, Johann Heinrich Gottlob von. *Abhandlung von dem Zusammenhang der Vollkommenheit der Sprachen mit dem blühenden Zustand der Wissenschaften: Wobey zugleich zu Anhörung einer Rede von dem unzertrennlichen Zusammenhang eines blühenden Zustands der Wissenschaften mit denjenigen Mitteln, welche einen Staat mächtig und glücklich machen.* Vienna, 1750.

—————. *Die Chimäre des Gleichgewichts von Europa: Eine Abhandlung worinnen die Richtigkeit und Ungerechtigkeit dieses zeitherigen Lehrgebäudes der Staatskunst deutlich vor Augen gelegt.* Altona, 1758.

—————. *Historische und juristische Schriften.* 2 vols. Frankfurt, 1760.

—————. *Untersuchung der Lehre von den Monaden und einfachen Dingen worinnen der Ungrund derselben gezeigt wird. Abhandlungen welche den von der Königlichen Preußischen Akademie der Wissenschaft auf das Lehr-Gebäude von dem Monaden gesetzten Preis erhalten hat.* Berlin, 1748.

—————. *Vergleichungen der europäischen mit den asiastischen und andern vermeintlich barbarischen Regierungen.* Berlin, 1762.

Köhler, Johann David. *Anweisung für reisende Gelehrte: Bibliothecken, Münz-Cabinette, Antiquitäten-Zimmer, Bilder-Sale, Naturalien- und Kunst Kammern u. d. m. mit Nutzen zu besehen.* Frankfurt, 1762.

—————. *Ehren-Rettung Johann Guttenbergs: Eingebohrnen Bürgers im Mayntz aus dem alten rheinländischen adelichen Geschichte derer von Horgenloch, genannt Gänsefleisch wegen der ersten Erfindung der nie genug gepriesenen Buch-drucken-Kunst in der Stadt Mayntz, mit gäntzlichen und unwiedersprechlicher Entscheidung des darüber entstandenen dreyjahrhundertjährigen Streits, getrenlich und mit allem Fleiß ausgefertiget.* Leipzig, 1741.

—————. *Erneuerter Entwurf eines Collegii über den gegenwärtigen Zustand von Europa und die jetzigen Welt-Händel.* Göttingen, 1736.

—————. *Gezeigter und bestärckter Nutz der Wappenkenntnüß zur Entdeckung einer historischen Wahrheit in der Untersuchung der zur Erläuterung der Braunschweig-Lüneburgischen Historie dienlichen Frage:*

Was für einen Herzog Heinrich zu Lüneburg das A 1518 in die Capelle U. L. Fr. zu Alt-Oetting in Bayern verlobte silberne Schiff zuzueignen sey? Göttingen, 1749.

—————. *Historische Münzbelustigung: Darinnen allerhand merkwürdige und rare Thaler, Ducaten, Schaustücke, und andere sonderbarer Gold und Silbermünzen von mancherley Art, accurate in Kupfer gestochen, beschreiben, und aus der Historie umständlich erkläret werden.* 22 vols. Nuremberg, 1729-1750.

—————. *Historische Nachricht von den Erb-Land-Hof Aemtern des Herzogthums Braunschweig und Lüneburg, und dazu gehöriger Lande, sowohl insgesamt als besonders, größten Theils aus archivischen Urkunden.* Göttingen, 1746.

—————. *Kurze Geschichte von alten geschnittenen Steinen.* Nuremberg, 1760.

—————. *Kurze und gründliche Anleitung zu der alten und mittlern Geographie, nebst dreizehn Land-Kärtgen.* Nuremberg, 1745.

—————. *Sculptura Historiarum et Temporum Memoratrix: Das ist, Gedächtnüß-Hülfliche Bilder-Lust der merkwürdigsten Welt-Geschichten aller Zeiten von Erschaffung der Welt biß auf Gegenwärtige.* Nuremberg, 1726.

Körte, Wilhelm, ed. *Briefe der schweitzer Bodmer, Sulzer, Geßner aus Gleims litterarischen Nachlasse.* Zurich, 1804.

Lowth, Robert. *Lectures on the Sacred Poetry of the Hebrews, to which are added the Principle Notes of Professor Michaelis and Notes by the Translator and Others.* Trans. G. Gregory. London, 1847.

Malby, Abbe. *Von der Art die Geschichte zu schreiben oder über die historische Kunst.* Ed. A. L. Schlözer with notes by F. R. Salzmann. Strasbourg, 1784.

Mendelssohn, Moses. *Über die Empfindungen.* Berlin, 1755.

Michaelis, Johann David. *Abhandlung von den Ehegesetzen Mosis welche die Heyrathen in die nahe Freundschaft untersagen.* 2d ed. Frankfurt, 1786.

—————. *Abhandlung von der syrischen Sprache, und ihrem Gebrauch: Nebst dem ersten Theil einer syrischen Chrestomathie.* 2 vols. Göttinger, 1786.

—————. *Agamemnon: Ein Trauer-Spiel aus dem Englischen übersetzt.* Göttingen, 1750.

—————. *Beantwortung der Frage von dem Einfluß der Meinungen in die Sprache und der Sprache in die Meinungen, welche den, von der Königlichen Academie der Wissenschaften für das Jahr 1759, gesetzten Preis erhalten hat.* Berlin, 1760.

—————. *Beurtheilung der Mittel, welche man anwendet, die ausgestorbene hebraische Sprache zu verstehen.* Göttingen, 1757.

—————. "Briefe von der Schwierigkeit der Religions-Vereinigung." In *Syntagma Commentationum,* pp. 121-170. Göttingen, 1759.

—————. *Einleitung in die göttlichen Schriften des Neuen Bundes.* 1st ed. Göttingen, 1750. 2d ed. 2 vols. Göttingen, 1765. 3d ed. Göttingen, 1777.

—————. *Erklärung des Briefes an die Hebräer.* 2 pts. Frankfurt, 1762, 1764.

————. "Erläuterung der Alterthumer des unter den morgenländischen Völckern bey Machung eines Bundes ehemals gebräuchlichen Opfers, Blutes und Weins." *Wöchentliche Hallische Anzeigen.* No. 23 (Aug. 9, 1745), pp. 530-538; no. 24 (Aug. 16, 1745), pp. 544-555. In Code MS Michaelis 340, with author's comments in Göttingen Library.

————. *Erpenii arabische Grammatik, abgekürtzt vollständiger und leichter gemacht nebst den Anfang einer arabischen Chrestomathie aus Schultens Anhang zur Erpenischen Grammatik.* Göttingen, 1771.

————. *Etwas von der ältesten Geschichte der Pferde und Pferdezucht in Palästina und benachbarten Ländern sonderlich Aegypten und Arabien.* Frankfurt, 1776.

————. *Fragen an eine Gesellschaft gelehrter Männer die auf Befehl Ihro Majestät des Königs von Dännemark nach Arabien reisen.* Frankfurt, 1762.

————. *Introduction to the New Testament.* Trans. from 4th German Ed. (1788) by Herbert Marsh. 4 vols. in 6. Cambridge, 1793-1802.

————. *Lebensbeschreibung von ihm selbst abgefaßt.* With commentary by Hassencamp. Rinteln, 1793.

————. *Literarischer Briefwechsel von Johann David Michaelis.* Ed. Johann Gottlieb Buhle. 3 vols. Leipzig, 1794-1796.

————. *Moral: Herausgegeben und mit der Geschichte der christlichen Sittenlehre.* Ed. Carl Friedrich Stäudlin. 2 vols. Göttingen, 1792.

————. *Mosaisches Recht.* 1st ed. 6 vols. Frankfurt, 1770-1775. 2d ed. Reutlingen, 1785.

————. *Raisonnement über die protestantischen Universitäten in Deutschland.* 4 vols. Frankfurt, 1768-1776.

————. "Schreiben an Herrn Professor Schlötzer die Zeitrechnung von der Sündflut bis auf Salomo betreffend." In *Zerstreute kleine Schriften.* Vol. 1, pp. 219-282. 2 vols. Jena, 1794.

————. "Selbstbiographie," *Allgemeiner Magazin für Prediger.* Vol. 6, pp. 93-122. Leipzig, 1790.

————. *Vermischte Schriften.* 2 vols. Frankfurt, 1766, 1769.

————. "Von der Verpflichtung der Menschen die Wahrheit zu Reden: Und zeigt zugleich an, wie er künftig seine Arbeit auf der Georg-Augustus-Universität einzurichten gedenke." In *Academica Gottingensia.* 1750. Pt. 2.

————. *Vorrede zur arabischen Grammatik und Chrestomathie: Vom arabischen Geschmak sonderlich in der poetischen und historischen Schreibart.* Göttingen, 1771.

Montesquieu, Charles Louis de Secondat. *Considerations on the Causes of the Greatness of the Romans and Their Decline.* Trans. David Lowenthal. Ithaca: Cornell University Press, 1968.

————. *The Persian Letters.* Trans. George R. Healy. Library of Liberal Arts. Indianapolis: Bobbs-Merrill, 1964.

————. *The Spirit of the Laws.* Trans. Thomas Nugent. Intro. Franz Neumann. New York: Hafner, 1949.

Mosheim, Johann Lorenz von. *Anderweitiger Versuch einer vollständigen und unpartheyischen Ketzergeschichte.* Helmstedt, 1748.

──────. *Beschreibung der grossen und denckwürdigen Feyer die bey der allerhöchsten Anwesenheit des Allerdurchlauchtigsten, Größmächtigsten Fürsten und Herren, George des Andern, etc. auf Deroselben Georg Augustus hohen Schule in der Stadt Göttingen im Jahr 1748 am ersten Tage des Augustmonates begangen ward.* Göttingen, 1749.

──────. *An Ecclesiastical History Ancient and Modern: From the Birth of Christ to the Beginning of the Eighteenth Century in which the Rise, Progress and Variations of Church Power Are Considered in Their Connection with the State of Learning and Philosophy and the Political History of Europe during that Period.* Trans. Archibald MacLaine. 2d ed. 6 vols. London, 1819.

──────. *Erzählung der neuesten chinesischen Kirchengeschichte.* Rostock, 1748.

──────. *Gutachten über den theologischen Doktorat 9 August 1749.* Ed. Paul Tschackert. Leipzig, 1905.

──────. *Historical Commentaries on the State of Christianity during the First Three Hundred and Twenty Five Years.* Trans. R. S. Vidal and James Murdoch. 2 vols. New York, 1852.

──────. *Institutes of Ecclesiastical History, Ancient and Modern: A Literal Translation from the Original Latin with Copious Additional Notes.* Trans. James Murdock and Henry Soames. Ed. William Stubbs. 3 vols. London, 1863.

──────. *Neue Nachrichten von dem berühmten spanischen Artzte Michael Servets der zu Geneve ist verbrannt worden.* Helmstedt, 1750.

──────. *Streittheologie der Christen: Nach den Grundsätzen des seeligen Heern Kanzlers ausgeführet.* Ed. Christian Ernst von Windheim. Erlangen, 1763.

──────. *Versuch einer unpartheiischen und gründlichen Ketzergeschichte.* Helmstedt, 1746.

Müller, Johannes von. *Vier und zwanzig Bücher allegemeiner Geschichten besonders der europäischen Menschheit.* Stuttgart, 1810.

Niebuhr, Barthold G. *The Life of Carsten Niebuhr, the Oriental Traveller, with an Appendix by J. D. Michaelis.* Trans. Robinson. Edinburgh, 1836.

Pufendorf, Samuel von. *Briefe Samuel von Pufendorfs an Christian Thomasius, 1687-1693.* Ed. Emil Gigas. Munich, 1897.

──────. *Einleitung zu der Historie der vornehmsten Reiche und Staaten.* 4 vols. Frankfurt, 1718.

──────. [Severinus von Monzambano.] *Ueber die Verfassung des deutschen Reichs.* Trans. Harry Breßlau. Berlin, 1870.

──────. *Von Natur und Eigenschafft der christlichen Religion und Kirche in Ansehung des bürgerlichen Lebens und Staats.* Trans. Immanuel Webern. Leipzig, 1692.

Pütter, Johann Stephan. *Anleitung zum teutschen Staatsrecht (1770).* Trans. from Latin by Carl Anton Friedrich Graf von Hohenthal. Preface by Friedrich Wernhard Grimm. 2 vols. Bayreuth, 1791.

──────. *Beyträge zum teutschen Staats- und Fürsten-Rechte.* 2 vols. Göttingen, 1777.

————. *Der einzige Weg zur wahren Glückseeligkeit deren jeder Mensch fähig ist.* Göttingen, 1772.

————. *Entwurf einer juristischen Encyclopädie nebst etlichen Zugaben.* Göttingen, 1757.

————. *Geist des Westphälischen Friedens nach dem innern Gehalte und wahren Zusammenhange der darin verhandelten Gegenstände historisch und systematisch dargestellt.* Göttingen, 1795.

————. *Grundriß der Staatsveränderungen des teutschen Reichs, nebst einer Vorbereitung worinn zugleich ein Entwurf einer Bibliotheck und gelehrten Geschichte der teutschen Historie enthalten.* 2d ed. Göttingen, 1755.

————. *Grundriß der Staatsveränderungen des teutschen Reichs.* 3d ed. rev. Göttingen, 1764. 4th ed. Göttingen, 1769.

————. *An Historical Development of the Present Political Consitution of the Germanic Empire.* Trans. Josiah Dornford. 3 vols. London, 1790.

————. *Historische Entwickelung der heutigen Staatsverfassung des teutschen Reichs.* 3 vols. Göttingen, 1786-1787.

————. *Historisch-politisches Handbuch von den besonderen teutschen Staaten.* Pt. 1. Göttingen, 1758.

————. *Kurzer Begriff des teutschen Staatsrechts.* Göttingen, 1764.

————. *Litteratur des teutschen Staatsrechts.* 4 vols. Göttingen, 1776-1791.

————. *Neuer Versuch einer juristischen Encyclopädie und Methodologie.* Göttingen, 1767.

————. *Patriotische Abbildung des heutigen Zustandes beyder höchsten Reichsgerichte worin der Verfall des Reichs-Justitzwesens samt dem daraus bevorstehenden Unheile des ganzen Reichs und die Mittel wie demselben noch vorzubeugen der Wahrheit gemäß und aus Liebe zum Vaterland.* Göttingen, 1749.

————. *Selbstbiographie zur dankbaren Jubelfeier seiner fünfzigjährigen Professorsstelle zu Göttingen.* 2 vols. Göttingen, 1798.

————. *Tabulae Genealogicae ad Illustrandam Historiam Imperii Germaniamque Principem.* Göttingen, 1768.

————. *Ueber den Unterschied der Stände: Besonders des hohen und niedern Adels in Teutschland zur Grundlage einer Abhandlung von Mißheirathen teutscher Fürsten und Grafen.* Göttingen, 1795.

————. *Ueber Mißhierathen teutscher Fürsten und Grafen.* Göttingen, 1796.

————. *Unpartheyische Gedanken über die in dem Cammergerichts-Visitations-Berichte.* Göttingen, 1769.

————. *Versuch einer academischen Gelehrten-Geschichte von der Georg-Augustus-Universität zu Göttingen.* 2 vols. Göttingen, 1765, 1788.

————. *Versuch einer richtigen Bestimmung des kayserlichen Ratifications-Rechts bey Schlüssen reichsständischer Versammlungen insonderheit der Visitation des Cammergerichts.* Göttingen, 1769.

————. *Vollständige Anleitung zur Geschichte des teutschen Reichs* (1760). In Code MS Achenwall 89, no. 257 in Göttingen Library.

————. *Vollständigeres Handbuch der teutschen Reichs-Historie.* 2d ed. 2 vols. Göttingen, 1772.

————. *Vorbereitung zur Kenntniß der vornehmsten teutschen Staaten.* Göttingen, 1750.

————. *Zu einer öffentlichen Rede welche bey der Feyer des allgemeinen Friedens.* Göttingen, 1763.

Ranke, Leopold von. *Geschichte der romanischen und germanischen Völker.* Leipzig, 1824.

Roscher, Wilhelm. "Wilhelm Roscher an Leopold von Ranke (1842)." In *Preussische Jahrbücher,* no. 133:3 (Sept. 2, 1908), pp. 383-386.

Rössler, Emil, ed. *Die Gründung der Universität Göttingen: Entwürfe, Berichte und Briefe der Zeitgenossen.* Göttingen, 1855.

Sanscüllottismus der Herrn Hofraths und Professors Ludwig August [sic] *Schlözer zu Göttingen.* 1794.

Schlözer, August Ludwig von. *Allgemeine nordische Geschichte: Fortsetzungen der Algemeinen Welt-Historie durch eine Geselschaft von Gelehrten in Teutschland und Engeland ausgefertiget.* Pt. 31. Halle, 1771.

————. *August Ludwig von Schlözer und Russland.* Ed. L. Richter and L. Zeil. Berlin: Akademie-Verlag, 1961.

————. *Geschichte von Corsica.* Göttingen, 1769.

————. *Isländische Litteratur und Geschichte.* Göttingen, 1773.

————. *Kleine Chronik von Leipzig: Erster Theil, bis zum Jahre 1466.* Leipzig, 1776.

————. *Kleine Geschichte von Russland: Bis auf die Erbauung von Moskau im Jahre 1147.* Göttingen, 1769.

————. *Kritische Sammlungen zur Geschichte der Deutschen in Siebenbürgen.* 3 vols in 1. Göttingen, 1795-1797.

————. *Neuverändertes Rußland, oder Leben Catharinä der zweiten Kayserinn von Rußland aus authentischen Nachrichten beschrieben.* Riga, 1767.

————. *Oskold und Dir: Eine russische Geschichte.* Göttingen, 1773.

————. *Probe russischer Annalen.* Bremen, 1768.

————. *Species Facti.* Göttingen, 1773.

————. *Stats-Gelartheit nach ihren haupt Theilen. Erster Theil: Allgemeines Stats Recht und Stats Verfassung.* Göttingen, 1793.

————. *Stats-Gelartheit. Zweiter Theil: Theorie der Statistik nebst Ideen über das Studium der Politik überhaupt.* Göttingen, 1804.

————. *Systema Politices.* Göttingen, 1771.

————. *Tableau de l'historie de Russie.* Gotha, 1769.

————. *Versuch einer allgemeinen Geschichte der Handlung und Seefahrt in den ältesten Zeiten.* Rostock, 1761.

————. *Vorstellung seiner Universal-Historie.* 2 vols. Göttingen, 1772, 1773.

————. *Vorstellung der Universal-Historie.* 2d ed. rev. Göttingen, 1775.

Schlözer, August Ludwig von, ed. *Briefwechsel: Meist statistischen Inhalts, 1774-1775; Meist historischen und politischen Inhalts, 1776-1782.* 16 vols. Göttingen, 1774-1782.

—————. *Schwedische Biographie, enthaltend eine Sammlung von Lebensbeschreibungen berühmter Schwedischer Kriegs- und Staatsmänner.* Altona, 1760.

—————. *Staatsanzeigen* (Journal). 16 vols. Göttingen, 1782-1793.

Schlözer, Karl von. *Zur Ehrenrettung Schlözers, des Historikers und Publicisten.* Lübeck, 1846.

Schlözer, Leopold von. *Dorothea von Schlözer: Ein deutsches Frauen-Leben um die Jahrhundertwende 1770-1825.* Göttingen: Vandenhoeck and Ruprecht, 1937.

Schmauß, Johann Jacob. *Corpus Juris Publici S. R. Imperii Academicum: Enthaltend des Heiligen Römischen Reichs teutsche Nation Grund-Gesetze.* 5th ed. Leipzig, 1759.

—————. *Einleitung zu der Staats-Wissenschaft, und Erleuterung des von ihm herausgegebenen Corporis Juris Gentium Academici.* Vol. 1. *Die Historie der Balance von Europa: Der Barriere der Niederlande, die Oesterreichischen Sanctionis pragmaticae, und anderer dahin gehörigen Sachen und Tractaten in sich haltend.* Leipzig, 1741. Vol. 2. *Die Historie aller zwischen den nordischen Potentzen: Dänemarck, Schweden, Rußland, Polen und Preussen geschlossenen Tractaten in sich haltend.* Leipzig, 1747.

—————. *Einleitung zur allerneuesten Staats-Wissenschaft, zum Unterricht der academischen Jugend.* Leipzig, 1745.

—————. *Kurze Erleuterung und Vertheydigung seines Systematis Juris Naturae.* Göttingen, 1755.

—————. *Kurzer Begriff der Historie der vornehmsten europäischen Reiche und Staaten zum Gebrauch der academischen Lectionen.* Göttingen, 1755.

—————. *Kurzer Begriff der Reichs Historie in einer accuraten chronologischen Ordnung, von den ältesten Zeiten, bis auf die Gegenwärtigen.* 2d ed. Leipzig, 1729.

—————. *Neues Systema des Rechts der Natur.* Göttingen, 1754.

—————. *Patriotischer Vorschlag zu einem Frieden zwischen Bayern und Oesterreich: Wodurch nicht allein beyde Partheyen ihren besondern Vortheil erreichen sondern auch die Balance von Europa und die Sicherheit und Ruhe des teutschen Reichs befestiget wird.* Göttingen, 1743.

—————. *Vorstellung des wahren Begriffs von einem Recht der Natur.* Göttingen, 1748.

Schmauß, Johann Jacob, ed. *Corpus Juris Gentium Academicum enthaltend die vornehmsten Grund-Gesetze, Friedens- und Commercien-Tractate, Bündnüsse und andere Pacta der Königreiche, Republiquen und Staaten von Europa.* 2 vols. Leipzig, 1730.

Schröck, Johann Matthias. *Abbildungen und Lebensbeschreibungen berühmter Gelehrten.* First collection. Vol. 2. Leipzig, 1766.

Semler, Johann Salomo. *Beantwortung der Fragment eines Ungenanten insbesondere vom Zweck Jesu und seine Jünger.* 2d ed. Halle, 1780.

—————. *Historische Abhandlungen über einige Gegenstände der mittlern Zeit bey Gelegenheit eines Aufsatzes der in München das Accessit erhalten.* Dessau, 1782.

————. *Johann Semlers Lebensbeschreibung von ihm selbst abgefaßt.* 2 vols. Halle, 1781, 1782.

————. *Neuer Versuch die gemeinnüzige Auslegung und Anwendung des Neuen Testaments zu befördern.* Halle, 1786.

————. *Zur Revision der kirchlichen Hermeneutik und Dogmatik.* Halle, 1788.

A Short Account of his Majesty's Late Journey to Goettingen and of the State of the New University There in a Letter to my Lord. 1748.

Spittler, Ludwig Timothy. *Geschichte der Hierarchie von Gregor VII bis auf die Zeiten der Reformation aus dem literarischen Nachlasse D. Gurlitt.* Ed. Cornelius Müller. Hamburg, 1828.

————. *Geschichte der Kreuzzüge: Zweiter Anhang zur Geschichte des Papstthums aus dem literarischen Nachlasse des D. Gurlitt.* Ed. Cornelius Müller. Hamburg, 1827.

————. *Vermischte Schriften über deutsche Geschichte, Statistik und öffentliches Recht.* Vol. 11 of *Sämmtliche Werke.* Ed. Karl Wächter, 15 vols. Stuttgart, 1827-1837.

Sulzer, Johann Georg. *Lebensbeschreibung von ihm selbst aufgesetzt.* Ed. Johann B. Merian and Friedrich Nicolai. Berlin, 1809.

————. "Observations sur les divers états où l'ame se trouve en exerçant ses facultés primitives, celle d'apercevoir et celle de sentir." In *Histoire de l'Académie Royale des Sciences et Belles-Lettres de Berlin.* Mémoires de l'Académie de Berlin. Berlin, 1763.

Vico, Giambattista. *The New Science.* Trans. Max Harold Fisch and Thomas Goddard Bergin. Garden City: Anchor-Doubleday, 1961.

————. *On the Study Methods of Our Time.* Trans. Elio Gianturco. Library of Liberal Arts. Indianapolis: Bobbs-Merrill, 1965.

Wegelin, Jakob. *Briefe über den Werth der Geschichte.* Berlin, 1783.

Wehrli, Max, ed. *Das geistige Zürich im achtzehnten Jahrhundert: Texte und Dokumente von Gotthard Heidigger bis Heinrich Pestalozzi.* Zurich: Atlantis, 1943.

Wolff, Christian. *Preliminary Discourse on Philosophy in General.* Trans. Richard J. Blackwell. Library of Liberal Arts. Indianapolis: Bobbs-Merrill, 1963.

————. *Vernünftige Gedanken von den Kräften des menschlichen Verstandes und ihrem richtigen Gebrauche in Erkenntnis der Wahrheit [Deutsche Logik].* Vol. 1 of *Gesammelte Werke.* Ed. Hans Werner Arndt. Hildesheim: Georg Olms, 1965.

Wood, Robert. *An Essay on the Original Genius and Writings of Homer, with a Comparative View of the Ancient and Present State of Trade.* London, 1775.

————. *Versuch über das Originalgenie des Homers aus dem Englischen.* Trans. Johann David [?] Michaelis. Frankfurt, 1773.

SELECTED SECONDARY SOURCES

Books

Allison, Henry E. *Lessing and the Enlightenment: His Philosophy of Religion and Its Relation to Eighteenth-Century Thought.* Ann Arbor: University of Michigan Press, 1966.

Aner, Karl. *Die Theologie der Lessingzeit.* Halle: Max Niemeyer, 1929.

Antoni, Carlo. *From History to Sociology: The Transition in German Historical Thinking.* Trans. Hayden V. White. Detroit: Wayne State University Press, 1959.

————. *Der Kampf wider die Vernunft: Zur Entstehungsgeschichte des deutschen Freiheitsgedankens.* Trans. Walter Goetz. Stuttgart: Koehler, 1951.

Auerbach, Erich. *Mimesis: The Representation of Reality in Western Literature.* Trans. Willard Trask. Garden City: Anchor Books, 1957.

Baeumler, Alfred. *Kants Kritik der Urteilskraft: Das Irrationalitaetsproblem in der Aesthetik und Logik des achtzehnten Jahrhunderts bis zur Kritik der Urteilskraft.* Halle: Max Niemeyer, 1923.

Baur, Ferdinand Christian. *Die Epochen der kirchlichen Geschichtschreibung.* Vol. 2 of *Ausgewählte Werke in Einzelausgaben.* Ed. Klaus Scholder. Stuttgart: Frommann, 1963.

Beck, Lewis White. *Early German Philosophy: Kant and His Predecessors.* Cambridge, Mass.: Belknap Press, 1969.

Becker, Carl L. *The Heavenly City of the Eighteenth-Century Philosophers.* New Haven: Yale University Press, 1932.

Benz, Trude. *Die Anthropologie in der Geschichtschreibung des achtzehnten Jahrhunderts.* Bonn: Wuppertal-Elberfeld, 1932.

Blackall, Eric A. *The Emergence of German as a Literary Language, 1700-1775.* Cambridge: Cambridge University Press, 1959.

Bluntschli, Johann C. *Geschichte des allgemeinen Staatsrechts und der Politik seit dem sechzehnten Jahrhundert bis zur Gegenwart.* Munich, 1864.

Bock, Hermann. *Jakob Wegelin als Geschichtstheoretiker.* Leipziger Studien aus dem Gebiet der Geschichte. Vol. 9, pt. 4. Ed. Gustav Buchholz, Karl Lamprecht, and Gerhard Seeliger. Leipzig: B. G. Teubner, 1902.

Bruford, Walter H. *Germany in the Eighteenth Century: The Social Background of the Literary Revival.* Cambridge: Cambridge University Press, 1935.

Brumfitt, J. H. *Voltaire, Historian.* London: Oxford University Press, 1958.

Brunner, Otto. *Neue Wege der Sozialgeschichte: Vorträge und Aufsätze.* Göttingen: Vandenhoeck and Ruprecht, 1956.

Butterfield, Herbert. *Man on His Past: The Study of Historical Scholarship.* Cambridge: Cambridge University Press, 1955.

Cassirer, Ernst. *Freiheit und Form: Studien zur deutschen Geistesgeschichte.* 3d ed. Berlin: Bruno Cassirer, 1916.

————. *The Philosophy of the Enlightenment.* Trans. Fritz C. A. Koelln and James P. Pettegrove. Princeton: Princeton University Press, 1951.

Christern, Hermann. *Deutscher Ständestaat und englischer Parlamentarismus am Ende des achtzehnten Jahrhunderts.* Munich: C. H. Beck, 1939.

Dilthey, Wilhelm. *Studien zur Geschichte des deutsches Geistes.* Vol. 3 of *Gesammelte Schriften.* Ed. Paul Ritter. Stuttgart: B. G. Teubner, 1962.

————. *Weltanschauung und Analyse des Menschen seit Renaissance und Reformation.* 9th ed. Göttingen: Vandenhoeck and Ruprecht, 1970.

Eliade, Mircea. *The Quest: History and Meaning in Religion*. Chicago: Chicago University Press, 1969.

———. *The Sacred and the Profane*. Trans. Willard R. Trask. New York: Harper and Row, 1961.

Epstein, Klaus. *The Genesis of German Conservatism*. Princeton: Princeton University Press, 1966.

Ermatinger, Emil. *Deutsche Kultur im Zeitalter der Aufklärung*. Ed. Heinz Kindermann. Potsdam: Akademische Verlagsgesellschaft Athenaion, 1935.

Faber, Karl-Georg. *Theorie der Geschichtswissenschaft*. Munich: C. H. Beck, 1971.

Foerster, Donald M. *Homer in English Criticism: The Historical Approach in the Eighteenth Century*. Yale Studies in English. Vol. 105. New Haven: Yale University Press, 1947.

Fueter, Eduard. *Geschichte der neueren Historiographie*. 3d ed. Vol. 3, sec. 1 of Handbuch der mittelälterlichen und neueren Geschichte. Ed. Georg von Below, Friedrich Meinecke, and Albert Brackmann. Berlin: Oldenbourg, 1936.

Fürst, Friederike. *August Ludwig von Schlözer: Ein deutscher Aufklärer im achtzehnten Jahrhundert*. Heidelberger Abhandlungen zur mittleren und neueren Geschichte. No. 56. Heidelberg: C. Winter, 1928.

Gadamer, Hans-Georg. *Wahrheit und Methode: Grundzüge einer philosophischen Hermeneutik*. 2d ed. Tübingen: J. C. B. Mohr (Paul Siebeck), 1965.

Gay, Peter. *The Enlightenment: An Interpretation*. 2 vols. New York: Knopf, 1967, 1969.

Geldsetzer, Lutz. *Die Ideenlehre Jakob Wegelins: Ein Beitrag zum philosophisch-politischen Denker der deutschen Aufklärung*. Monographen zur philosophischen Forschung. Vol. 33. Meisenheim am Glan: Anton Hain. 1963.

Gilbert, Felix. *To the Farewell Address: Ideas of Early American Foreign Policy*. Princeton: Princeton University Press, 1961.

Gillispie, Charles Coulston. *The Edge of Objectivity: An Essay in the History of Scientific Ideas*. Princeton: Princeton University Press, 1960.

Gollwitzer, Heinz. *Europabild und Europagedanke: Beiträge zur deutschen Geistesgeschichte des achzehnten und neunzehnten Jahrhunderts*. Munich: C. H. Beck, 1964.

Goodwin, Albert, ed. *The European Nobility in the Eighteenth Century*. London: A & C Black, 1953.

Gossman, Lionel. *Medievalism and the Ideologies of the Enlightenment: The World and Work of La Curne de Sainte-Palaye*. Baltimore: Johns Hopkins Press, 1968.

Gurvitch, Georges. *The Spectrum of Social Time*. Trans. Myrtle Korenbaum. Dordrecht: Reidel, 1964.

Harnack, Adolf von. *Geschichte der Königliche Preussischen Akademie der Wissenschaften zu Berlin*. 4 vols. Berlin: Reichsdruckerei, 1900.

———. *History of Dogma*. Trans. Neil Buchanan. 7 vols. in 4. New York: Dover Press, 1961.

Hazard, Paul. *The European Mind, 1680-1715*. Trans. J. Lewis May. London: Hollis and Carter, 1952.

―――――. *European Thought in the Eighteenth Century: From Montesquieu to Lessing*. Trans. J. Lewis May. London: Hollis and Carter, 1952.

Hettner, Hermann. *Geschichte der deutschen Literatur im achtzehnten Jahrhundert*. Ed. George Witkawski. 3 vols. Leipzig: P. List, 1928.

Heussi, Karl. *Johann Lorenz Mosheim: Ein Beitrag zur Kirchengeschichte des achtzehnten Jahrhunderts*. Tübingen: J. C. B. Mohr, 1906.

Hofer, Walter. *Geschichtschreibung und Weltanschauung: Betrachtungen zum Werk Friedrich Meineckes*. Munich: Oldenbourg, 1950.

Horkheimer, Max, and Adorno, Theodor W. *Dialektik der Aufklärung: Philosophische Fragmente*. 1944. Reprint ed. Frankfurt: Fischer, 1969.

Huizinga, Johann. *Im Bann der Geschichte: Betrachtungen und Gestaltungen*. Basel: Pantheon, 1943.

Hunger, Kurt. *Die Bedeutung der Universität Göttingen für die Geschichtsforschung am Ausgang des achtzehnten Jahrhunderts*. Berlin: Emil Ebering, 1933.

Iggers, Georg C. *The German Conception of History: The National Tradition of Historical Thought from Herder to the Present*. Middletown, Conn.: Wesleyan University Press, 1968.

John, Vincenz. *Geschichte der Statistik: Ein quellenmäßiges Handbuck für den akademischen Gebrauch wie für den Selbstunterricht*. Stuttgart, 1884.

Justi, Carl. *Winckelmann und seine Zeitgenossen*. 5th ed. Reprint ed. 3 vols. Cologne: Phaidon, 1956.

Kelly, George Armstrong. *Idealism, Politics and History: Sources of Hegelian Thought*. Cambridge: Cambridge University Press, 1969.

Klempt, Adalbert. *Die Säkularisierung der universalhistorischen Auffassung*. Göttingen: Musterschmidt, 1960.

Krieger, Leonard. *The Politics of Discretion: Pufendorf and the Acceptance of Natural Law*. Chicago: University of Chicago Press, 1965.

Landsberg, Ernst. *Geschichte der deutschen Rechtswissenschaft*. Munich, 1898.

Lovejoy, Arthur O. *The Great Chain of Being: A Study of the History of an Idea*. Cambridge, Mass.: Harvard University Press, 1936.

Lukács, Georg. *Goethe and His Age*. Trans. Robert Anchor. London: Merlin Press, 1968.

Manuel, Frank E. *The Eighteenth Century Confronts the Gods*. Cambridge, Mass.: Harvard University Press, 1959.

―――――. *Utopias and Utopian Thought*. Boston: Houghton Mifflin, 1966.

Meinecke, Friedrich. *Die Entstehung des Historismus*. Vol. 3 of *Werke*. Ed. Carl Hinrichs. Munich: Oldenbourg, 1953.

―――――. *Die Idee der Staatsräson in der neueren Geschichte*. 1924. Vol. 1 of *Werke*. 3d ed. Ed. Walter Hofer. Munich: Oldenbourg, 1963.

―――――. *Zur Theorie und Philosophie der Geschichte*. Vol. 4 of *Werke*. Ed. Eberhard Kessel. Stuttgart: Koehler, 1965.

Neff, Emery. *The Poetry of History: The Contribution of Literature and Literary Scholarship to the Writing of History since Voltaire*. New York: Columbia University Press, 1947.

Nisbet, Robert. *Social Change and History: Aspects of the Western Theory of Development.* London: Oxford University Press, 1969.

Paulsen, Friedrich. *Geschichte des gelehrten Unterrichts, auf den deutschen Schulen und Universitäten vom Ausgang des Mittelalters bis zur Gegenwart.* 3d ed. 2 vols. Berlin: Walter de Gruyter, 1919-1921.

Philipp, Wolfgang. *Das Werden der Aufklärung in theologiegeschichtlicher Sicht.* Forschungen zur systematischen Theologie und Religionsphilosophie. Vol. 3. Göttingen: Vandenhoeck and Ruprecht, 1957.

Polak, Fred L. *The Image of the Future: Enlightening the Past, Orientating the Present, Forecasting the Future.* Trans. Elise Boulding. 2 vols. Leyden: Sythoff, 1961.

Roscher, Wilhelm. *Geschichte der National-Oekonomik in Deutschland.* Geschichte der Wissenschaften in Deutschland: Neuere Zeit. Vol. 14. Munich, 1874.

Seeberg, Erich. *Gottfried Arnold: Die Wissenschaft und die Mystik seiner Zeit.* Reprint ed. Darmstadt: Wissenschaftliche Buchgesellschaft, 1964.

Srbik, Heinrich Ritter von. *Geist und Geschichte: Vom deutschen Humanismus bis zur Gegenwart.* 2 vols. Salzburg: Müller, 1950.

Strauss, Leo. *Natural Right and History.* Chicago: University of Chicago Press, 1953.

Tagliacozzo, Giorgio, and White, Hayden V., eds. *Giambattista Vico: An International Symposium.* Baltimore: Johns Hopkins Press, 1969.

Toulmin, Stephen, and Goodfield, June. *The Discovery of Time.* New York: Harper and Row, 1965.

Unger, Rudolf. *Hamann und die Aufklärung: Studien zur Vorgeschichte des romantischen Geistes im achtzehnten Jahrhundert.* 2d ed. 2 vols. Halle: M. Niemeyer, 1925.

Venturi, Franco. *Italy and the Enlightenment: Studies in a Cosmopolitan Century.* Ed. Stuart Woolf. Trans. Susan Corsi. London: Longman, 1972.

—————. *Utopia and Reform in the Enlightenment.* Cambridge: Cambridge University Press, 1971.

Völker, Karl. *Die Kirchengeschichtsschreibung der Aufklärung.* Tübingen: J. C. B. Mohr, 1921.

Vyverberg, Henry. *Historical Pessimism in the French Enlightenment.* Cambridge, Mass.: Harvard University Press, 1958.

Wach, Joachim. *Das Verstehen: Grundzüge einer Geschichte der hermeneutischen Theorie im neunzehnten Jahrhundert.* 3 vols. in 1. Reprint ed. Hildesheim: Georg Olms, 1966.

Wegele, Franz Xaver. *Geschichte der deutschen Historiographie seit dem Auftreten des Humanismus.* Munich, 1885.

Wehrli, Max. *Johann Jakob Bodmer und die Geschichte der Literatur.* Frauenfeld: Huber, 1936.

Weis, Eberhard. *Geschichtsschreibung und Staatsauffasung in der französischen Enzyklopädie.* Wiesbaden: Steiner, 1956.

Welzel, Hans. *Die Naturrechtslehre Samuel Pufendorfs.* Berlin: Walter de Gruyter, 1958.

Wesendonck, Hermann. *Die Begründung der neueren deutschen Geschichtsschreibung durch Gatterer und Schlözer: Nebst Einleitung über Gang und Stand derselben vor diesen.* Leipzig, 1876.

Wittram, Reinhard. *Das Interesse an der Geschichte.* Göttingen: Vandenhoeck and Ruprecht, 1958.

Wolf, Eric. *Grotius, Pufendorf, Thomasius: Drei Kapitel zur Gestaltgeschichte der Rechtswissenschaft.* Heidelberger Abhandlungen zur Philosophie und ihrer Geschichte, Vol. 11. Tübingen: J. C. B. Mohr, 1927.

Wundt, Max. *Die deutsche Schulphilosophie im Zeitalter der Aufklärung.* Heidelberger Abhandlungen zur Philosophie und ihrer Geschichte. Vol. 32. Tübingen: J. C. B. Mohr, 1945.

Zscharnack, Leopold. *Lessing und Semler: Ein Beitrag zur Entstehungsgeschichte des Rationalismus und der kritischen Theologie.* Giessen: Alfred Töpelmann, 1905.

Articles

Arendt, Hannah. "The Concept of History: Ancient and Modern." In *Between Past and Present: Six Exercises in Political Thought.* Pp. 41-90. New York: Viking Press, 1961.

Barnard, F. M. "The 'Practical Philosophy' of Christian Thomasius," *Journal of the History of Ideas,* 32 (1971): 221-246.

Berlin, Isaiah. "Herder and the Enlightenment." In *Aspects of the Eighteenth Century.* Ed. Earl R. Wasserman. Pp. 47-104. Baltimore: Johns Hopkins Press, 1965.

Berney, Arnold. "August Ludwig von Schlözers Staatsauffassung," *Historische Zeitschrift,* 132 (1925): 43-68.

Caemmerer, Hermann von. "Rankes 'Große Mächte' und die Geschichtschreibung des achtzehnten Jahrhunderts." In *Studien und Versuche zur neueren Geschichte: Max Lenz zum sechzigsten Geburtstage gewidmet von Freunden und Schülern.* Pp. 263-312. Berlin, 1910.

Dilthey, Wilhelm. "Die Entstehung der Hermeneutik." In vol. 5 of *Gesammelte Schriften.* Pp. 317-338. Stuttgart: B. G. Teubner, 1962.

Dorn, Walter, "Prussian Bureaucracy in the Eighteenth Century," *Political Science Quarterly,* 46 (1931): 403-423; 47 (1932): 75-94.

Engel, Josef. "Die deutschen Universitäten und die Geschichtswissenschaften," *Historische Zeitschrift,* 189 (1959): 223-378.

Engel-Jánosi, Friedrich. "Politics and History in the Age of the Enlightenment." *Journal of Politics,* 5 (1943): 363-390.

Gadamer, Hans-Georg. "Rhetorik, Hermeneutik und Ideologiekritik." In *Kleine Schriften I: Philosophie, Hermeneutik.* Pp. 113-130. Tübingen: J. C. B. Mohr (Paul Siebeck), 1967.

————. "Die Universalität des hermeneutischen Problems." In *Kleine Schriften I: Philosophie, Hermeneutik.* Pp. 101-112. Tübingen: J. C. B. Mohr (Paul Siebeck), 1967.

Gay, Peter. "The Enlightenment in the History of Political Theory," *Political Science Quarterly,* 69 (1954): 374-389.

Gerhard, Dietrich. "Assemblies of Estates and the Corporate Order." In *Studies Presented to the International Commission for the History of Representative and Parliamentary Institutions.* Vol. 38, pp. 285-308. 1970.

————. "Probleme ständischer Vertretungen im früheren achtzehnten Jahrhundert und ihre Behandlung in der gegenwärtigen internationale Forschung." In *Ständische Vertretungen in Europa im siebzehnten und achtzehnten Jahrhundert.* Ed. Dietrich Gerhard. Veröffentlichungen des Max-Planck-Instituts für Geschichte, no. 27, pp. 9-31. Göttingen: Vandenhoeck and Ruprecht, 1969.

————. "Regionalismus und ständisches Wesen als ein Grundthema europäischer Geschichte." In *Alte und neue Welt in vergleichender Geschichtsbetrachtung.* Veröffentlichungen des Max-Planck-Instituts für Geschichte, no. 10, pp. 13-39, Göttingen: Vandenhoeck and Ruprecht, 1962.

Holborn, Hajo. "Der deutsche Idealismus in sozialgeschichtlicher Beleuchtung." *Historische Zeitschrift,* 174 (1952): 359-384.

Kaerst, Julius. "Studien zur Entwicklung und Bedeutung der universalgeschichtlichen Anschauung," *Historische Zeitschrift,* 106 (1911): 473-534.

Martin, Alfred von. "Motiven und Tendenzen in Voltaires Geschichtsschreibung," *Historische Zeitschrift,* 118 (1917): 1-45.

Momigliano, Arnaldo D. "Ancient History and the Antiquarian." In *Studies in Historiography.* Pp. 1-39. London: Weidenfeld and Nicolson, 1966.

————. "Gibbon's Contribution to Historical Method." In *Studies in Historiography.* Pp. 40-55. London: Weidenfeld and Nicolson, 1966.

————. "Time in Ancient Historiography." In *History and the Concept of Time: History and Theory.* Beiheft 6, pp. 1-23. Middletown, Conn.: Wesleyan University Press, 1966.

Neumann, Franz. "Types of Natural Law." In *The Democratic and the Authoritarian State: Essays in Political and Legal Theory.* Pp. 69-95. Glencoe: Free Press, 1957.

Tonelli, Giorgio. "Der Streit über die mathematische Methode in der Philosophie in der ersten Hälfte des achtzehnten Jahrhunderts und die Entstehung von Kants Schrift über die 'Deutlichkeit,'" *Archiv für Philosophie,* 9/12 (1959): 37-66.

Unger, Rudolf von. "Zur Entwicklung des Problems der historischen Objectivität bis Hegel," *Deutsche Vierteljahrsschrift für Literaturwissenschaft und Geistesgeschichte,* 1 (1923): 104-138.

Venturi, Franco. "History and Reform in the Middle of the Eighteenth Century." In *The Diversity of History: Essays in Honour of Sir Herbert Butterfield.* Ed. John Huxtable Elliott and Helmut George Koenigsberger. Pp. 223-244. London: Routledge and Kegan Paul, 1970.

Vierhaus, Rudolf. "Ständewesen und Staatsverwaltung in Deutschland im späten achtzehnten Jahrhundert." In *Dauer und Wandel: Aspekte europäischer Vergangenheit: Festgabe für Kurt von Raumer.* Ed. Rudolf Vierhaus and Manfred Botzenhart. Pp. 337-360. Munich: Aschendorff, 1966.

Index

Abbt, Thomas, 82, 87, 246 n. 42
Achenwall, Gottfried: on contracts in natural law, 92-93; educational goals of, 52, 239 n. 87; on religion, 168; on state as a moral body, 146, 253 n. 13; and statistics, 40, 152-154; on wealth, 153, 155; mentioned, 45; *Geschichte der allgemeineren europäischen Staatshändel des vorigen und jetzigen Jahrhunderts im Grundriße*, 40; Nachlasse, 258 n. 77; *Die Staatsklugheit nach ihren ersten Grundsätzen*, 146, 153; *Staatsverfassung der heutigen vornehmsten europäischen Reiche und Völker im Grundriße*, 153
Addison, Joseph: *Spectator*, 200-202
Aesthetics: and creation, 61, 62, 264 n. 45; development of, 59-62, 200; and *Erkenntnis*, 98, 113-114, 121, 275 n. 8; and genius, 61-62, 64-65, 125; and history, 59-60, 61, 62, 64-65, 69-70, 161, 218, 235 n. 38; and Holy Scripture, 82, 241 n. 14; and positive norms, 59, 61, 137; and psychology, 41, 59, 62-64, 66, 198; Wolffian, 59, 60, 61, 137, 236 n. 41 and 46. *See also* Metaphor: of harmony; Perfectibility; Spirit
Alexander the Great, 191
Altdorf, University of, 6
American Revolution, 143
Anabaptists, 18
Ancients and Moderns, 18, 59, 116, 259 n. 93
Antiquarians, 11-12, 202, 222 n. 7
Antoni, Carlo, 62, 63, 237 n. 48, 244 n. 2, 274 n. 5
Apostles, 170-171
Arendt, Hannah, 86
Aristocracy: British, 159, 260 n. 102; as constitutional form, 137, 138, 144-145; critiques of, 144-145, 158, 159, 257 n. 58; education for, 73, 144, 159; German, 5, 73; as oligarchy, 143-144
Arnold, Gottfried: background of, 14, 22-23; on church, 23-26, 28; critiques of, 35, 111, 163; on dogma, 23, 24-25, 26; on heresy, 25-26;

hermeneutics of, 225 n. 55; on history, 27, 28, 29; on Luther, 28; present-mindedness of, 25-26; on reason, 27; and Semler, 44, 50, 166-167, 168, 171; significance of, 22, 23, 24; on society, 28-29; as *unparteiisch*, 26-27; on witnesses of truth, 24-25, 27, 28; *Unparteyische Kirchen- und Ketzer-Historie*, 23, 28, 35, 111
Aufklärers, politics of. *See* Politics
Aufklärers, religiosity of: as Christians, 5, 6, 7, 51, 77, 108, 162, 174; and historical understanding, 8, 43, 76, 92, 105, 108-109, 130, 161, 190; and nature, 33, 97. *See also* Christianity
Aufklärers, social world of, 4-5, 8, 50, 55, 70, 72-73, 144
Autonomous development. *See* Comparative analysis

Baden, Karl Friedrich von, 150
Baeumler, Alfred, 61, 235 n. 38, 236 n. 40 and 41, 237 n. 48, 244 n. 2
Balance of power, 95, 151-152
Barth, Karl, 23, 24
Baumgarten, Alexander: aesthetics of, 60-61, 236 n. 46, 237 n. 48; background of, 236 n. 42; on perception, 62, 236 n. 46, 246 n. 20; mentioned, 66, 116, 170, 200; *Aesthetica*, 62, 236 n. 46
Baumgarten, Sigmund, 43, 165, 166, 228 n. 16, 232 n. 47 and 51, 236 n. 42
Baur, Christian, 166
Bayle, Pierre: on Christianity, 14, 163, 223 n. 17; on evident truth, 13-14, 41, 81; on history, 14, 30; on impartiality, 12; on reason, 13-14, 23
Beaumarchais, Pierre Augustin, 159
Beck, Lewis White, 22
Becker, Carl, 233 n. 1
Beckman, Johann, 157; *Beyträge zur Geschichte der Erfindungen*, 157
Berlin, Academy of, 226 n. 4, 238 n. 65, 250 n. 78
Berlin, University of, 5
Berlin Prize Question of 1763, 248 n. 62
Bernstorff, Johann H. E. von, 73, 195
Blackwell, Thomas: and Bodmer, 203,

207, 208, 210, 211, 273 n. 63; on heroic age, 205-206, 207, 272 n. 51 and 58; on Homer, 203, 205-206, 207, 273 n. 62; on language, 203-204, 206, 207, 272 n. 58; on poetry, 204-207, 211, 219, 273 n. 62; on progression of manners, 204-206; and Vico, 203, 204, 271-272 n. 39; *An Enquiry into the Life and Writings of Homer*, 203, 207, 208, 273 n. 63

Bloch, Marc, 186

Bochart, Samuel, 81

Bodin, Jean, 16, 135, 181, 222 n. 2

Bodmer, Johann Jacob: aesthetics of, 61-62, 200, 203, 236 n. 46 and 47; background of, 119, 199-200; and Blackwell, 203, 207, 208, 210, 211, 273 n. 63; on Dante, 211-212, 249 n. 71; on genius, 61-62, 64; influence of, 63, 200, 248 n. 62, 248-249 n. 66, 249 n. 71; on Middle Ages, 208-211, 212; on Milton, 202-203; on poetry, 64, 202-203, 207, 208, 211-212, 219, 249 n. 71; and *Spectator*, 200-202; and Switzerland, 200-201, 203; mentioned, 214, 226 n. 7, 237 n. 48, 238 n. 65; *Beobachtung der National-Charakter*, 249 n. 66; *Discours der Maler*, 201-202; *Fabeln aus der Zeiten der Minnesinger*, 209; *Helvetische Bibliothek*, 203; *Nibelungenlied*, 209, 210, 211; *Der Parzival*, 209, 210; *Proben der alten schwäbischen Poesie des dreyzehnten Jahrhunderts*, 209; *Sammlung von Minnesingern aus dem schwäbischen Zeitpuncte*, 209; "Von den vortrefflichen Umständen für die Poesie unter den Kaisern aus dem schwäbischen Hause," 208

Böhme, Jakob, 22, 97

Bolingbroke, Henry St. John, 34, 45, 81, 231 n. 42

Bolle, Kees, 89

Bossuet, Jacques-Bénigne, 127, 128; *Discours sur l'histoire universelle*, 127

Boulainvilliers, Henri de, 129

Bourgeosie. See *Bürgerlich* class

Brandes, Ernst, 74, 268 n. 108

Braudel, Fernand, 180

Breitinger, Johann, 119, 201, 203, 226 n. 7, 238 n. 65; *Helvetische Bibliothek*, 203

Britain: Parliament of, 4, 159, 260 n. 102; thinkers of, 4, 31, 34, 35, 36, 133, 147, 159

Brumfitt, J. H., 253-254 n. 15

Brunner, Otto, 147, 148, 180, 257 n. 66

Buffon, Georges Louis Leclerc, Conte de, 85, 98, 241 n. 21

Bürgerlich class: and bourgeosie, 4, 7, 159; definition of, 4-5, 22; development of, 157-158, 159, 160, 260 n. 99; influence of, on Aufkläres, 4, 72, 144

Bury, J. B., 40

Büsch, Johann George, 155

Calvin, John, 164-165, 168, 177, 262 n. 15

Cameralism, 139

Campanella, Tommaso, 18

Canon law, 71, 185, 186, 187

Carlyle, Thomas, 156

Cassirer, Ernst, 31-32, 38, 90, 237 n. 48, 244 n. 2, 264 n. 45

Catholicism, German, 6, 8, 222 n. 8

Change, accidental, 29, 130, 155

Change, catastrophe theory of: definition of, 37, 128-129, 229 n. 24; denials of, 37, 38, 129-130, 133, 134, 155, 176, 252 n. 5

Charlemagne, 182

Charles V, 106-107, 258 n. 83

Chladenius, Johann Martin: background of, 105, 112, 230 n. 34; on Bible, 43, 105; on causal laws, 106-107, 109-112; on conjunctions, 109-110, 111; on diachronic and synchronic studies, 39; on historical understanding, 52, 106-107, 109-112, 132-133, 134, 245 n. 13 and 15; on intuitive knowledge, 110-111, 114; on natural law, 81; on perception, 110, 163, 246 n. 20, 261 n. 8; and rhetoric, 107-109; on state as moral body, 106, 132-133, 134, 245 n. 15, 253 n. 12 and 14; on will, 106, 108, 245 n. 16, 253 n. 11; mentioned, 113, 118, 119, 120, 248 n. 62; *Allgemeine Geschichtswissenschaft*, 43, 52, 106, 108; *Einleitung zur richtigen Auslegung vernünfftiger Reden und Schriften*, 105-106

Christianity: Arnold on, 23-28; Bayle on, 14, 163, 223 n. 17; history of, 28, 162-163, 169-171; and natural law, 75-76, 81, 88-93; Neologists on, 82, 98, 162, 169; Semler on, 51-52, 98, 166-171, 262 n. 18 and 21, 263 n. 25 and 29, 263-264 n. 37, 264 n. 43; and universal history, 9-10, 11. *See also* Aufklärers, religiosity of; Chronology, Christian; Church; Dogma; Holy Scripture

Church: definition of, 23-26, 162-164;

in Middle Ages, 158, 173-174, 191, 267 n. 98; and state, 19, 28, 174, 267 n. 98

Chronology, Christian, 75, 77-87, 92

Cincinnati, Society of, 143

Cities, rise of, 71-72, 157-158, 160, 173, 260 n. 99

Claproth, Johann, 38

Climate, as causal category, 56, 67, 121, 134-136, 153, 159, 254 n. 23

Coherent truth: and Berlin Prize Question of 1763, 248 n. 62; dissatisfaction with, 13-14, 27, 30, 35, 41, 71, 82, 104, 106-109, 115, 118-120, 125-126, 168, 188-190, 192, 215-216, 248 n. 65; in history, 13, 15, 22, 29, 41, 75-76, 117-118; and natural law, 90-91, 95. See also Objectivity; Spirit

Commerce: appreciation of, 46, 149, 150, 151, 153, 154-155, 159; as causal factor, 124, 159, 250 n. 77, 260 n. 99 and 104; and cities, 157-158, 160, 260 n. 99; revolutions of, 157, 259-260 n. 94; in whole house economics, 148

Common sense (sensus communis), 107, 108, 168

Comparative analysis, 193, 198-199, 203, 207, 208, 270 n. 20

Conjunction: apprehension of, 109-110, 111, 120, 170; and causation, 106, 117, 118, 126, 155, 230-231 n. 39; definition of, 37-38, 258 n. 87; in diachronic and synchronic studies, 229 n. 31; and holism, 122; in pragmatic history, 40, 42-43, 230 n. 39; and state, 103-104, 137, 145, 146. See also Metaphor: of harmony

Conring, Hermann, 152, 222 n. 2

Constitution, state's: and causation, 153, 160, 260 n. 104; classical forms of, 136-145, 146-147; Pufendorf on, 16, 18, 20; and Staatsrecht, 93

Constitutional history, German: and canon law, 71, 185, 186, 187; and Empire as historical problem, 14, 20, 55, 93-94, 140, 145; and Faustrecht, 55, 186, 267 n. 99; and feudal law, 20, 71-72, 185; and four world monarchies, 9-10, 19, 75, 182; and Fürstenrecht, 186, 267 n. 102; and Gewohnheitsrecht (common law), 44, 72, 94, 184-186, 250 n. 78; Roman law in, 20, 71-72, 124, 173, 181-188, 250 n. 78, 266 n. 88, 267 n. 102; and theory of two swords, 71, 182-183; and translation theory, 71, 181-183, 222 n. 2, 266 n. 79 and 80, 267 n. 98 and 102

Corsican Rebellion, 144, 256 n. 55

Croce, Benedetto, 31, 237 n. 48

Crusades: and catastrophe theory, 129-130, 252 n. 5; effects of, 158, 173, 208, 260 n. 99; as heroic age, 158, 199; as Völkerwanderung, 173, 198

Crusius, Christian, 226 n. 8

Cudworth, Ralph, 161, 261 n. 7

Dante, 200, 207, 211-212, 249 n. 71

Deism, 262 n. 18

Democracy, 137, 138, 141-144, 256-257 n. 56, 257 n. 58

Descartes, René: and Cartesian method, 7, 15, 33, 113; on history, 11, 17-18; mentioned, 30

Diachronic approaches, 38-40, 199, 229 n. 31, 229-230 n. 32

Diderot, Denis, 4, 53, 98, 104, 235 n. 36; Supplément au voyage de Bougainville, 53, 235 n. 36

Dilthey, Wilhelm, 106, 111, 156, 217, 244 n. 2, 259 n. 90

Dogma: Arnold on, 23-26; and declining importance of, 77, 105, 108, 137; time-bound nature of, 43-44, 51-52, 82, 98, 162-164, 166-169, 190

Droysen, Johann Gustav, 106, 245 n. 15

Dubos, Abbé Jean, 61, 249 n. 66

Economics: as causal factor, 70, 149, 150-152, 153, 154-160, 196; and national wealth, 70, 149-153 passim, 155, 159; science of, 147, 149-150; whole house theory of, 147-149, 150, 257 n. 63 and 66. See also Commerce

Education: of aristocracy, 73, 144, 159; and Bildung, 143, 217, 239 n. 88; goals of, 43, 72, 238-239 n. 79, 239 n. 87; of humanity, 70, 72, 143, 217, 238 n. 71; as ideal, 5, 45, 46-47, 73, 238-239 n. 79; and progress, 68, 70, 71, 122, 239 n. 87, 240 n. 89

Eichhorn, Johann Gottfried, 149, 154, 254 n. 25, 269-270 n. 15

Eichhorn, Karl Friedrich, 228 n. 20, 268 n. 108

Einem, Charlotte von, 77

Eliade, Mircea, 89

Encyclopedists, French, 31, 97

Enlightened Absolutism, 4, 7, 73, 139, 141, 216, 239 n. 80

Enlightened Bureaucracy, 4, 73, 145

Enlightenment: attainment of in Europe, 46, 68, 122, 249 n. 72; Aufklärung's relation to, 1-3, 7, 8, 31-32, 34, 36-37, 46, 217; and Christianity, 233 n. 6, 233-234 n. 9; and economics,

147-149; and history, 45, 191-193, 220, 231 n. 42, 233 n. 1; and Middle Ages, 210, 213, 274 n. 1; and natural law, 242 n. 30; and Renaissance, 174; and republican ideal, 138; and rhetoric, 108; and utopian thought, 48-50, 51-54, 68

Erasmus, Desiderius, 165, 177

Erfurt, University of, 6

Erkenntnis. See Intuitive knowledge

Erlangen, University of, 109

Ernesti, Johann August, 44, 82, 162, 166, 171

Ernst, Fritz, 200

Eschenbach, Wolfram von, 208, 210, 211

Eusebius of Caesarea, 86

Exemplar history, 10, 27, 29, 42

Family, concept of, 93, 148-149, 257 n. 66

Ferguson, Adam, 149, 161, 271 n. 39

Feudal law, 20, 71-72, 185, 186. *See also* Constitutional history, German

Fisch, Max H., 271 n. 39

Fischer, Friedrick Christoph Jonathan, 154-155; *Geschichte des teutschen Handels*, 154

Foerster, Donald M., 273 n. 63

Fontenelle, Bernard le Bovier de, 34

France, 73, 153, 154, 258 n. 83. *See also* Philosophes

Franck, Sebastian, 22, 27

Francke, August Hermann, 111, 166

Franckenstein, Jacob August, 254 n. 23

Franklin, Benjamin, 195

Frederick the Great, 81, 119, 125, 151; *Anti-Machiavel*, 151

Freedom. *See* Spirit

French Revolution, 8, 73, 142, 255 n. 36, 265 n. 61

Fueter, Eduard, 37, 128, 229 n. 24, 231 n. 42

Füssli, Johann Heinrich, 200

Gatterer, Johann Christoph: background of, 77, 112-113, 228 n. 23; on causal analysis, 102, 113, 115, 116, 117-118, 172; on contemporary Germany, 54; and Crusades as *Völkerwanderung*, 173, 198; on diachronic and synchronic approaches, 39-40; on French historiography, 36; on Greek democracy, 142-143; on historical understanding, 113-118, 119; on intuitive knowledge, 114, 116-117; on man as *Nimmersatt*, 69-70, 120; on periodization, 78-81, 87, 115, 247 n. 45; on philosophic

spirit, 113, 115, 117-118; on polyhistorians, 233 n. 59, 252-253 n. 10; on pragmatic history, 40, 42, 108, 230 n. 39; on Renaissance, 175-176; on *Seelenkräfte*, 114, 116; on spirit of events, 117, 180-181; mentioned, 83, 89, 154, 214, 247 n. 46, 248 n. 62; *Abriß der Universalhistorie*, 115; *Einleitung in die synchronistische Universalhistorie*, 78; *Handbuch der Universalhistorie*, 78

Gay, Peter, 49-50, 51, 91, 174, 233 n. 6, 233-234 n. 9

Gelahrtheit, 108

Genius: and causation, 45, 62, 65, 69, 124-125, 161, 162, 219; definition of, 8, 61-62, 64-65, 68, 124-125, 170, 176-177, 179, 250 n. 79, 250-251 n. 81; and *Erkenntnis*, 64-65, 125, 275 n. 8; in heroic age, 272 n. 51. *See also* Great historical figure

Geography, 16, 56, 67, 121, 136, 153, 160, 254 n. 29, 260 n. 104

German Empire. *See* Constitutional history, German

Germany: aristocracy in, 5, 73; Aufklärers' view of, 54, 143, 234 n. 24; in eighteenth century, 4-5, 6, 8. See also *Bürgerlich* class

Gesner, Johann Matthias, 194, 247 n. 46

Geßner, Salomon, 200, 238 n. 65

Gibbon, Edward, 36, 100

Goethe, Johann Wolfgang von, 63, 221 n. 2

Gossman, Lionel, 2-3, 213

Göttingen, University of, 5, 8, 38, 109, 159, 171, 246 n. 26, 266 n. 86

Göttingen-Gelehrten Anzeigen, 194, 269 n. 6

Gottsched, Johann Christoph, 61, 137, 200, 202, 203, 207

Gratian, 185

Great historical figure: Aufklärers on, 45, 53-54, 164-165, 177-180, 191, 262 n. 15; in pre-Aufklärung histories, 29, 128-130. *See also* Genius

Greece, ancient: 19, 142-143, 206, 256 n. 51. *See also* Homer

Gregory VII (pope), 173-174, 176-177, 179, 261 n. 10, 265 n. 56

Grotius, Hugo, 15, 27, 89

Guicciardini, Francesco, 42, 100

Gundling, Nicholas, 229 n. 30, 254 n. 23

Gurvitch, Georges, 17, 224 n. 30, 233 n. 8

Habsburg Empire, 152, 153, 154, 258 n. 83

Halle, University of, 5, 109, 111, 171, 222 n. 9
Haller, Albrecht von, 63, 97, 119, 145, 194, 200, 226 n. 7, 238 n. 65, 284 n. 59
Haller, Karl Ludwig von, 145
Hamann, Johann Georg, 197
Hanau, legal academy of, 181
Hardenberg, Karl August von, 73, 268 n. 108
Harmony. *See* Metaphor: of harmony
Harnack, Adolf von, 77, 162, 261 n. 10
Hazard, Paul, 9; *La crise de la conscience européene*, 9
Heeren, Arnold Hermann Ludwig: on *Bürgerstand*, 158, 260 n. 99; on Crusades, 158, 173, 198-199, 260 n. 99; on Gregory VII, 173-174, 179, 265 n. 56; political analysis of, 45, 137-138, 141, 142, 146-147, 159, 260 n. 102, 264-265 n. 49, 265 n. 61; and pragmatic history, 42, 45; on Reformation, 174, 176, 179; on Renaissance, 159, 174; on revolutions, 158, 172-173, 179-180, 264-265 n. 49; on trade, 158-159, 259-260 n. 94, 260 n. 99; on universal history, 230-231 n. 39; mentioned, 154, 188, 269 n. 6
Hegel, Goerg Wilhelm, 2, 3, 100, 227 n. 10, 245 n. 15
Helmstedt, University of, 6
Herbert of Cherbury, 27
Herder, Johann Gottfried: on Bible, 262 n. 17; on Michaelis, 197, 270 n. 18; and Schlözer, 47, 85, 179, 232 n. 59; mentioned, 34, 106, 161, 177, 191, 200, 219, 269 n. 6
Heresy, 25-26, 162-164, 165, 262 n. 15
Hermeneutics, 41, 82, 106, 166, 171, 225 n. 55, 241 n. 14, 245 n. 13
Herodutus, 100
Heroic age: and Dante, 207, 211-212; description of: 205-206, 207, 272 n. 51 and 58; and Homer, 205-206, 207; in Middle Ages, 158, 198-199, 208-211
Hettner, Hermann, 178
Heyne, Christian Gottlob, 154, 156, 195, 247 n. 46, 269 n. 6
Hintze, Otto, 156
Historicism, 2, 190, 210, 213-214, 217, 219, 220, 274 n. 2
Hobbes, Thomas: and history, 13, 114; and natural law, 15, 89, 90-91, 94, 95, 97, 98, 242 n. 30
Hohenstaufen period, 208-211
Holbach, Baron d', 198
Holism, 121-122, 133

Holy Roman Empire. *See* Constitutional history, German
Holy Scripture: Arnold on, 27, 28; historical analysis of, 6, 44, 105, 135, 153, 169-171, 197, 232 n. 55; as moral truth, 76, 77, 82-83; as reliable history, 9, 43, 75-76, 78-81, 93; as sacred poetry, 86, 87, 194, 241 n. 14; temporal nature of, 82-83, 98, 262 n. 17, 264 n. 42. *See also* Chronology, Christian; Mosaic law; Revelation
Home, Henry, Lord, 66
Homer, 200, 203, 205-207, 208, 272 n. 39, 273 n. 62
Hooker, Richard, 132
Hübner, Johann, 77, 127-128, 131, 240 n. 2, 251-252 n. 1; *Kurtze Fragen aus der politischen Historie*, 127, 252 n. 1; *Zweymahl zwey und fünffzig auserlesene biblische Historien*, 77, 240 n. 1
Hugo, Gustav, 188, 228 n. 20, 268 n. 107 and 108
Huizinga, Johann, 223-224 n. 18
Hüllman, Carl Dietrich, 154
Humanists, 175-176, 177, 210
Human nature: and climate, 134-135, 254 n. 23; definition of, 58, 69-70, 106, 120-121, 124, 243 n. 50, 249 n. 67, 253 n. 11; in natural law, 15, 57, 76, 91, 92; Promethean view of, 51, 65, 69-70; and reason, 95-96; religious drive in, 163-164, 197-198; and sociability, 15, 66, 92-93, 99, 235 n. 28; and "society man," 123-124, 141-142, 249-250 n. 75, 250 n. 76
Humboldt, Wilhelm Freiherr von, 106
Hume, David: influence of, 56, 120, 149, 161, 248-249 n. 66; on religion, 261 n. 7; mentioned, 31, 63, 95, 104, 108, 163, 271 n. 39; *History of Great Britain*, 56; *Natural History of Religion*, 163
Hussites, 178-179
Hutcheson, Francis, 108
Hyperta, Basilius [Samuel von Pufendorf], 9

Idealism, German, 1-2, 70, 221 n. 2, 268 n. 109
Idealism, modern, 56
Ideenwirkung, 120, 162, 172, 176
Iggers, Georg, 217
Innenpolitik, 52, 146, 151-152, 154, 156, 258 n. 83
Intuitive knowledge (*Erkenntnis*): definition of, 63, 69, 117, 214, 275 n. 8; and genius, 64-65, 125, 275 n. 8; and

historical understanding, 98,
110-111, 114, 116, 117, 118, 121,
214, 218, 246-247 n. 42; and humanists, 176
Irrationality. *See* Spirit: and irrationalism
Iselin, Isaak: on ages of man, 67-69, 196;
background of, 65, 87, 238 n. 71,
248 n. 59; on contemporary Europe,
54, 68, 234 n. 22; and education, 68,
238 n. 71 and 79; on genius, 170; on
human nature, 66; and Montesquieu,
66, 135; on progress, 52, 68, 69; on
Seelenkräfte, 66-67; and Wegelin,
119, 120-121; and Wolff, 35; on
women, 68, 238 n. 71; mentioned,
150, 159, 176, 238 n. 65; *Über die
Geschichte der Menschheit*, 52, 54,
65-66, 69, 249 n. 66

Jacobi, Friedrich Heinrich, 97, 197
Jerusalem, Abbt, 82, 98
Jesus, 166, 170, 171, 177, 262 n. 18,
264 n. 43
Jewish history, 82-83, 92, 153, 169,
196-197, 213, 264 n. 43. *See also*
Mosaic law
Joachim of Flora, 18
John of Salisbury, 132
Justi, Johann Heinrich Gottlob von: on
abstract sciences, 41, 115; background of, 150; on conceit of nations, 190-191; and economics,
150-152, 155; on Habsburgs, 152,
154; importance of, 139, 150,
257-258 n. 72; and *Innenpolitik*,
151, 152; on monarchy, 139; on
reason, 95; mentioned, 108; *Staatswirthschaft*, 150; *System des Finanzwesens*, 150

Kant, Immanuel: relation to Aufklärung,
1, 46, 188, 237 n. 62; mentioned, 44,
45, 52, 66, 68, 237 n. 48, 248 n. 62;
*History Written from a Cosmopolitan
Point of View*, 51
Kelly, George Armstrong, 234 n. 12, 268
n. 109
Klopstock, Friedrich Gottlieb, 200
Koch, Christian, 45
Köhler, Johann David, 34, 42, 78, 227 n.
11

Landsberg, Ernst, 186, 188, 268 n. 107
Language: German, 32-33, 108, 208,
211; in heroic age, 67, 206, 208, 211,
272 n. 58; and national consciousness, 82, 121, 161, 194-195, 203,
204-205; and politics, 207; of symbols, 7; written, 84
Lavater, Johann Casper, 200
Lavoisier, Antoine Laurent, 105
Law: as causal category, 56, 134, 161;
and climate, 134-135; and history,
14, 44, 98, 153, 186, 188, 268 n.
107; and national character, 94, 184,
267 n. 92; and tradition, 71-72, 94,
187, 239 n. 82, 267 n. 102. *See also*
Constitutional history, German
Leibniz, Gottfried Wilhelm: and catastrophe theory, 38, 130, 155; on
change and perfectibility, 38-39, 56,
62, 65, 168, 192; general influence
of, 6-7, 31-32, 34, 38-39, 105, 161,
170, 198, 226 n. 4; and harmonic
conjunction, 7, 37-38, 103-104,
109-110, 120, 155, 236 n. 47; on
history, 13, 22; and metaphor of
seeing, 110; and monad theory, 55,
60, 214-215; and Wolff, 32-33, 34,
60, 226 n. 5; mentioned, 108, 119;
Nouveaux Essais, 32, 119
Lessing, Gotthold Ephraim, 1, 34, 46,
51, 67, 97, 98, 125, 159, 200;
Education of the Human Race, 51,
67
Librum feudorum, 185
Liebel, Helen, 73
Linnaeus, 85, 97, 116
Livy, 115
Locke, John, 31, 92, 242 n. 30
Lokalvernunft, 125, 214, 216
Louis XIV, 139
Louis XV, 141
Lowth, Robert, 194, 204, 219, 241 n.
14, 271 n. 39
Ludewig, Johann Peter, 181   *l*
Lukács, Georg, 1-2, 220, 221 n. 2
Luther, Martin, 28, 168, 174, 176-177,
179
Lutheranism, 6, 77, 81

Machiavelli, Niccolò, 11, 100
Madison, James, 44, 256-257 n. 56;
Federalist Papers, 144, 256-257 n. 56
Mannheim, Karl, 110
Manuel, Frank E., 193, 269 n. 6
Marcuse, Herbert, 18
Marsham, John, 81
Mascov, Johann, 44
Mathematical model: limitations of, 7,
30, 41, 61, 97-98, 104-105, 113-114,
188, 218; and natural law, 57, 95; as
universal knowledge, 7, 33

Maupertius, Pierre Louis Moreau de, 226
n. 4
Meinecke, Friedrich, 220, 229-230 n. 32,
242 n. 30, 244 n. 2
Melanchthon, Philipp, 165, 177, 222 n.
4
Mendelssohn, Moses, 62, 63, 64, 66, 97,
98, 117, 226 n. 7, 248 n. 62, 258 n.
87
Metaphors: of growth, 67-69, 97-98,
104, 192-193, 195, 196-197, 198,
204; of harmony, 7, 38, 56, 62, 64,
68, 70, 72, 227 n. 10, 235 n. 28, 236
n. 47, 238-239 n. 79; in language, 67,
200, 202, 204, 206; mechanical,
102-105, 112, 149, 244 n. 8; Newtonian, 123, 124; of seeing, 63, 110,
121, 122, 201, 249 n. 71 and 72
Metternich, Clemens, Fürst von, 8
Michaelis, Johann David: background of,
84, 193-194, 240 n. 2; and biblical
exegesis, 44, 82, 83-84, 135, 153,
194, 197, 264 n. 42; on Divine
Providence, 128; evaluations of, 197,
254 n. 25, 269-270 n. 15; on French
scholarship, 228 n. 23; on language,
84, 194-195; on Lebensart, 168, 263
n. 28; on morality, 58; on Mosaic
law, 135, 184, 188, 195, 196, 197,
239 n. 82, 263 n. 28; on myth,
194-195, 196; as Neologist, 44, 82,
162, 171; on poetry, 170, 194-195,
196, 197, 219, 241 n. 14; on primitive peoples, 194-197; and Schlözer,
84-85, 88, 198; mentioned, 42, 97,
110, 125, 213, 269 n. 6; Mosaisches
Recht, 135, 195, 196, 197, 254 n.
25, 269-270 n. 15
Middle Ages: and Bürgerstand, 157-158,
266 n. 99; church in, 128-130, 158,
173-174, 191, 252 n. 5, 267 n. 98;
cities in, 71-72, 157-158, 160, 173,
260 n. 99; economic analysis of, 155,
156-157, 158; as heoric age, 158,
198-199, 208-211; and Hohenstaufen
period, 208-211; interest in, 44, 46,
199, 210-211, 213, 274 n. 1; political
analysis of, 18-19, 129-130, 140,
144, 191, 216, 267 n. 98; universities
in, 72, 173, 183, 185. See also
Constitutional history, German; Crusades
Miller, Johann Peter, 246-247 n. 42
Milton, John, 200, 202-203; Paradise
Lost, 202-203, 207
Minnesinger manuscripts, 209, 210, 211
Molière, Jean Baptiste Poquelin, 159
Monad, 55, 60, 214-215
Monarchy, 4, 7, 139-141, 216, 255 n.
38, 257 n. 58

Montesquieu, Charles de Secondat: and
catastrophe theory, 37, 130; causal
analysis of, 37, 56, 71, 134-135, 235
n. 27 and 28; evaluations of, 66, 151,
248-249 n. 66, 254 n. 15; and harmonic metaphor, 38, 235 n. 28;
influence of, 4, 31, 37, 56, 71, 87,
120, 130, 133-136, 137; on polyhistorians, 34; Considerations on the
Causes of the Greatness of the Romans and Their Decline, 37, 71; The
Spirit of the Laws, 71, 133-135, 137,
254 n. 15
Montgelas, Maximilian Joseph, 73
Monzambano, Severinus von [Samuel
von Pufendorf], 19
Morality: in Bible, 76, 77, 82-83; as
instinctual drive, 58, 66, 108,
166-167, 262 n. 21; and moral impulse in revolutions, 172-173, 174,
179-180, 264-265 n. 49; and natural
aversions, 58, 235 n. 36; and poetry,
202; and positive law, 58, 96; and
religion, 44, 168-169, 262 n. 21,
264-265 n. 49
Mosaic law, 82, 135, 184, 188, 195, 196,
197, 239 n. 82, 251 n. 83, 263 n. 28
Moser, Johann Jakob, 181
Möser, Justus J., 44, 187, 196, 250 n. 78
Moser, Karl Friedrich von, 44, 244 n. 8
Moses, 83, 84, 125, 196, 263 n. 28, 251
n. 83, 263 n. 28
Mosheim, Johann Lorenz von: on Calvin
and Servetus, 164-165, 177, 262 n.
15; and causal analysis, 102,
129-130, 135, 164, 165; and church
history, 44, 129-130, 162-164, 171,
261 n. 10; on French scholarship,
228 n. 23; on heresy, 162-164, 165,
262 n. 15; influence of, 87, 165, 194;
on the masses, 142; as Neologist, 44,
82, 162-163; on religious drive, 163,
261 n. 7; An Ecclesiastical History
Ancient and Modern, 102, 129, 163,
244 n. 4; Historical Commentaries on
the State of Christianity during the
First Three Hundred and Twenty
Five Years, 163
Müller, Johannes von, 42, 87, 119, 200,
238 n. 65, 248 n. 59; History of the
Swiss Confederation, 87; Vier und
zwanzig Bücher allgemeiner Geschichten besonders der europäischen
Menschheit, 87
Münchhausen, Gerlach Adolf von, 246 n.
26
Mysticism, 178, 263 n. 22
Myth: analysis of, 193, 194-195, 196,
202, 206; Christian, in Aufklärung,
75-76, 78-79, 87-92 passim

National character: as causal category, 56, 122, 162, 180, 260 n. 104; definition of, 121, 140, 249 n. 69; in historical analysis, 16, 117, 124, 136, 197, 219, 229 n. 30; and law, 94, 184, 267 n. 92; and *Lebensart*, 168, 263 n. 28; and national consciousness, 203, 204; and religion, 163, 168, 263 n. 25

Natural law: and Christianity, 75-76, 81, 88-93, 96-97; and coherence theory of truth, 90-91, 95; definition of, 66, 94, 242-243 n. 41; and human nature, 57, 66, 76, 91, 92, 95-96; and nature, 90-91; opposition to, 95, 98-99, 132, 151, 188; and political analysis, 137, 143; and positive law, 57, 58, 93, 94, 96, 143; and secularization, 88-89, 91, 242 n. 30; and social contract, 16, 75, 81, 91, 92-93, 151, 242-243 n. 41; and social origins, 75-76, 91, 120

Nature: as emanation of God, 33, 97, 227 n. 10; as object to be overcome, 66, 69-70; organic conception of, 95, 97-98; and pantheism, 97-98; and social contract, 81, 90-93; and spirit, 56-57, 95, 97, 101-102

Neologists: Aufklärers as, 44, 82, 83, 98, 162, 171; on church, 162; on dogma, 44, 82, 162, 169; goals of, 43, 82, 94, 162, 169, 171; on Holy Scripture, 82-83, 86, 95, 98, 241 n. 55; influence of, 86, 87, 113, 232 n. 55; on natural law, 95; and pragmatic history, 43-44; mentioned, 125, 137, 148

Neo-Rankean school, 48, 101-102, 190, 244 n. 2

Newton, Sir Issac, 30, 50, 104, 105, 123, 124, 149

Nibelungenlied, 209, 210, 211

Nicolai, Friedrich, 63, 226 n. 7

Niebuhr, Carsten, 195

Nietzsche, Friedrich Wilhelm, 202

Objectivity: belief in possibility of, 17, 24, 41, 75-76; and conceit of nations, 45, 88, 190-191, 232 n. 57; as impartiality, 12, 26-27, 41, 45; limited possibility of, 110, 112, 113, 218, 251 n. 87; and points of view, 113, 134, 214-215, 218; and value judgments 251 n. 86 and 87

Ortega y Gasset, José, 180

Otto I (Holy Roman emperor), 182, 267 n. 98

Paoli, Pasquale, 144

Papacy, 19-20, 129-130, 158, 173-174, 185, 186, 252 n. 5, 261 n. 10. *See also* Gregory VII

Paracelsus, Philippus Aureolus, 97, 104

Parzival, 208, 209, 210

Pascal, Blaise, 130, 132

Pelagius, 25

Perception: and aesthetics, 7, 59, 61, 62, 64, 66, 124-125, 264 n. 45; and "confused ideas," 60, 61, 106-107, 145, 236 n. 46, 246 n. 20; and experience, 163, 261 n. 8; and metaphor of seeing, 63, 110, 249 n. 71; and *Seelenkräfte*, 62, 63, 64, 67, 110, 120-121, 163; and sensation, 31, 55-56, 61, 163, 178, 190, 197-198, 261 n. 8. *See also* Aesthetics; Objectivity; Spirit

Perfectibility, 38-39, 58, 60-66 *passim*, 95, 168-169, 192, 214-215, 216

Periodization, 9-10, 19, 75, 79-80, 115, 182, 259-260 n. 94, 263 n. 32

Pestalozzi, Heinrich, 200

Petavius, Denis, 81

Peter the Great, 140

Philosophes: compared to Aufklärers, 43, 54, 55, 73, 122, 146, 215; critiques of, 36, 70-71, 141, 228 n. 23, 239 n. 80; influence of, 4, 34-35, 38, 55, 133, 157, 161, 250 n. 78; program of, 51, 127, 129-130, 156, 159, 163, 193

Physiocrats, 4, 73, 149, 150

Pietism: influence of, 5, 6, 7, 57, 66, 77, 81, 108, 111, 162, 215-216, 240 n. 2; and religious understanding, 6, 44, 162, 225 n. 55

Poetry: in aesthetics, 61; of Dante, 207, 211-212, 249 n. 71; and genius, 170, 197, 219; in Hohenstaufen period, 208-211; of Homer, 203, 205-207, 208, 272 n. 39, 273 n. 62; of Milton, 202-203, 207; and poet, 64, 104-105, 202-203; as sacred, 86, 87, 194, 241 n. 14; and social ages of man, 67, 194-195, 204-207

Polak, Fred, 49

Policierung, 68-69, 122, 249 n. 73

Politics: analysis of, 15-23 *passim*, 44-45, 68, 129-130, 132, 136-147, 151-154, 191, 207; of Aufklärers, 4, 7, 8, 50, 72-73, 121-122, 139-146, 154, 216-217, 239 n. 80, 250 n. 78, 255 n. 38; and balance of power, 95, 151-152; as causal category, 235 n. 28, 264-265 n. 49, 265 n. 61; and education, 47, 70, 71, 122, 143, 239 n. 87, 240 n. 89; and German freedoms, 54, 121, 216, 239 n. 89; and reform, 4, 8, 52, 54-55, 70-73, 91-92, 122, 143, 145-146, 151-152, 216-217, 239 n. 87, 240 n. 89; and women's rights, 68, 148, 238 n. 71. *See also* State

Polyhistory, 31, 34-35, 36-37, 41, 126, 232 n. 47, 233 n. 59, 247 n. 45, 252-253 n. 10

Pombal, Sebastião José de, 141

Pope, Alexander, 139

Positive law, 57, 58, 93, 94, 96, 143

Pragmatic history, 40, 41-45, 125, 230 n. 39, 231 n. 42, 231 n. 44

Primitive peoples, 67-68, 82-83, 88, 92, 136, 193-197 *passim*, 204-205

Providence in history, 9-10, 19, 29, 30, 43, 127-128

Pufendorf, Samuel von: background of, 14, 17, 22, 32; on church and state, 19, 20; coherent analysis of, 15, 17, 22; compared to Arnold, 22-27 *passim*; on constitutional form, 16, 18, 20, 137, 139; on German constitutional history, 20, 35, 94, 145, 181; on Middle Ages, 18-19; natural law of, 15-16, 57, 91, 94, 96, 97; political analysis of, 15-23 *passim*, 29; present-mindedness of, 17-18, 19, 21; and *raison d'état*, 16, 21, 23; on social contract, 16; on sovereignty, 16, 19, 20; on state's interests, 16-17, 19, 21, 148; *The Constitution of the German Empire*, 19, 20, 35, 137; *De rebus a Carolo Gustavo Sueciae rege gestis*, 20-21; *De rebus gestis Frederici III*, 21; *De rebus Wilhelmi Magni electoris Brandenburici*, 20-21; *De rebus succicis ab expeditione Gustavi Adolphi in Germaniam ad abdicationem usque Christianae*, 20-21; *Einleitung zu der Historie der vornehmsten Reiche und Staaten*, 18, 19; *A Historical-Political Description of the Spiritual Monarchy of Rome*, 19

Pütter, Johann Stephan: background of, 181, 187, 228 n. 20, 268 n. 108; causal analysis of, 156-157, 183, 188, 189, 259 n. 93; on deduction, critique of, 35, 94, 186, 189, 214; on German constitutional history, 71-72, 93, 104, 181-187, 188, 266 n. 79 and 80 and 88, 267 n. 98 and 99; on German freedoms, 239-240 n. 89; on *Gewohnheitsrecht*, 44, 184-186, 187, 267 n. 102; on history, 39, 42-43, 153; influence of, 74, 186, 188, 228 n. 20, 266 n. 84, 268 n. 108; on natural law, 93, 94, 242-243 n. 41; on Roman law, 187-188, 266 n. 88, 267 n. 92; on translation

theory, 181-183, 266 n. 80, 267 n. 98; on universities, 266 n. 86; mentioned, 180, 196, 250 n. 78

Pyrrhonism, 12, 30, 223-224 n. 18

Quesnay, François, 149

Raison d'état, 11, 16, 21, 23

Ranke, Leopold von, 2, 3, 39, 48, 100, 156, 199

Reason: abuses of, 13-14, 23, 27; and historical development, 58, 62; limitations of, 94, 95, 107, 108, 111, 113-115, 116, 118, 172, 215-216, 218; and natural law, 57, 95-96, 98; powers of, 67, 68, 95; and will, 57, 95-96, 161, 218

Reformation, 157, 174, 176, 179, 186

Rehberg, August Wilhelm, 74, 268 n. 108

Reimarus, Hermann Samuel, 62, 162, 232 n. 55, 240 n. 2

Religion: Arnold on, 23-27; Bayle on, 14, 163, 223 n. 17; and causation, 56, 134, 161, 166-172, 217, 264-265 n. 49; defense of, 36, 43, 46, 215-216, 248 n. 60; of early peoples, 193, 195, 196, 205-206, 261 n. 7; and history, 6, 14, 43-44, 60; as a human drive, 44, 163-164, 197-198, 261 n. 7; in Middle Ages, 182-183; and moral impulse, 44, 166-167, 168-169, 262 n. 21, 264-265 n. 49; for Neologists, 43-44, 50, 82, 94, 137, 148, 162; in Reformation, 176; in Renaissance, 175; and spirit of the times, 163, 168, 263 n. 25 and 29; and theology, 27, 44, 108, 166-167, 171, 227 n. 10; time-bound nature of, 43-44, 51-52, 82, 98, 162-164, 166-169, 190. *See also* Aufklärers, religiosity of; Christianity; Revelation

Renaissance, 159, 174-176, 210

Republic, ideal of, 138, 139, 142

Resewitz, Friedrich Gabriel, 64-65, 116; *Versuch über das Genie*, 64

Revelation, 75-76, 82, 91-96 *passim*, 193-194, 215, 263 n. 32, 263-264 n. 37. *See also* Christianity; Dogma; Religion

Revolution: definition of, 45, 155-156, 170-171, 176, 179-180; effects of, 68, 158, 204; examples of, 70, 158, 170-175 *passim*; moral impulse in, 172-173, 174, 264-265 n. 49; and nonrevolutionaries, 177, 178-179; and reform, 72, 146, 216; and revolutionaries, 162, 170, 177-178; of trade, 157, 259-260 n. 94

Rhetoric, 105, 107-109, 113
Riehl, Wilhelm Heinrich, 156, 257 n. 63
Ritterakademie, 119, 159
Robertson, William, 149, 161
Roman law: appreciation of, 124, 187-188, 267 n. 92; in German Empire, 20, 71-72, 124, 173, 181-188, 250 n. 78, 266 n. 88, 267 n. 102
Roscher, Wilhelm, 155, 156, 157, 199, 259 n. 90
Rousseau, Jean Jacques, 4, 31, 52, 66, 69, 87, 119, 161, 200, 248 n. 60; *Emile*, 69; *Second Discourse*, 66, 69; *Social Contract*, 66, 69

Sabund, Raymond, 97
Sachsenspiegel, 184
Saint-Pierre, Abbé de, 52
Sartorius, Georg F., 154
Savigny, Karl Friedrich von, 228 n. 20
Scaliger, Julius Caesar, 81
Schleiermacher, Friedrich Daniel Ernst von, 166
Schlosser, Friedrich Christain, 73
Schlözer, August Ludwig von: on ancient Greeks, 143, 256 n. 51; background of, 84, 139, 198, 227 n. 15, 238 n. 71; and Bible, 85-87, 93; and causal analysis, 136, 155-156, 175, 180, 260 n. 104; and comparative analysis, 198, 199, 270 n. 20; and conjunction, 103, 229 n. 31; on conquerors, 53, 175, 179, 191; on Corsican Rebellion, 144, 265 n. 55; and education, 46-47, 238 n. 71, 240 n. 89; and geography, 136, 254 n. 29, 260 n. 104; and Herder, 47, 85, 232 n. 59; and historical understanding, 35, 37, 52, 53-54, 128, 188, 229 n. 31, 245 n. 11; on history's value, 45, 49; on human nature, 69, 99; importance of, 46-47, 228 n. 23, 255 n. 36, 259 n. 90; and mechanical metaphors, 102-104, 244 n. 48; political analysis of, 54, 139-141, 142, 143-144, 239 n. 80, 240 n. 89, 255 n. 38; on revolutions, 45, 155-156, 175; on social origins, 85, 88, 93, 99, 120; on Swiss, 54, 143-144, 238 n. 71; and universal history, 46, 47, 85-86, 232-233 n. 59; and Voltaire, 37, 84, 241 n. 21; mentioned, 83, 87, 110, 151, 153, 154, 158, 159, 213; *Briefwechsel*, 47, 139, 140; Nestor's chronicles, 46; *Staatsanzeigen*, 47, 54, 139, 140, 255 n. 36; *Vorstellung seiner Universal-Historie*, 85
Schlözer, Dorothea, 47, 238 n. 71
Schmauβ, Johann Jacob: background of,

57, 228 n. 17, 243 n. 49; on commerce and *Primat der Innenpolitik*, 150, 154, 258 n. 83; on historical development, 57-58, 62, 106; on history, 42, 45, 102, 150, 232 n. 47; on human nature, 57-58, 95-97, 108 243 n. 50; influence of, 65, 66; on natural law, 57-58, 66, 95-97; on Pufendorf, 57, 96; on Wolff, 35, 57, 95, 96, 125, 151, 235 n. 31; *Einleitung zu der Staatswissenschaft*, 150, 154; *Recht der Natur*, 97
Scholasticism, 7, 27, 33, 35, 57, 125, 176, 191, 223 n. 11, 251 n. 82
Schröck, Johann Matthias, 42; *Abbildungen und Lebensbeschreibung berühmter Gelehrten*, 42
Schwabenspiegel, 184
Secularization, 88-89, 91
Seeberg, Erich, 21, 23
Seelenkräfte (faculties of soul). *See* Spirit
Semler, Johann Salomo: background of, 165-166, 171, 181, 227-228 n. 16, 234 n. 24; on causation, 50, 168-172, 188, 189, 197, 263 n. 25; on deism, 262 n. 18; on dogma, 44, 51-52, 82, 98, 166, 169; on genius, 125, 170, 172; hermeneutics of, 98, 117, 166-167, 170, 171, 214; as Neologist, 82, 98, 162, 171; and New Testament exegesis, 82, 98, 167-168, 169-171, 264 n. 43; on Pietism, 240 n. 2; on rationalism, 35, 172; on religion, definition of, 44, 51-52, 166-167, 262 n. 21, 263 n. 22 and 25, 263-264 n. 37; on religion and spirit of the times, 168, 170, 263 n. 25 and 29; on religious development, 51-52, 166-172, 188-189, 197, 263 n. 32, 263-264 n. 37; mentioned, 76, 112, 154, 178, 193, 232 n. 51
Servetus, Michael, 164-165, 177, 262 n. 15
Shaftesbury, Antony Ashley Cooper, Earl of, 31, 57, 58, 97, 108, 161, 200
Simon, Richard, 81, 165
Skepticism, historical, 12, 30, 223-224 n. 18
Smith, Adam, 150; *Wealth of Nations*, 150
Social class, uniqueness of, 122-123, 140, 249 n. 74
Social contract, 16, 75, 81, 91, 92-93, 151, 242-243 n. 41
Sonnenfels, Joseph von, 73, 150, 151, 154, 255 n. 36, 257-258 n. 72
Sovereignty, 16, 19, 20, 23, 93, 137. *See also* Constitution, state's

Spectator (Joseph Addison), 200-202
Spener, Philipp Jakob, 22, 23
Spenser, Edmund, 200
Spinoza, Baruch, 13, 27, 81, 97, 197, 232 n. 55
Spirit (*Geist, Seele, Gemüt*): as causal category, 62, 106-107, 117, 120, 132-133, 170-173, 177, 180-181, 188-189, 217; and form, 6, 8, 64, 119, 133, 137, 166-171, 178, 192, 197, 217-219, 274 n. 5; and freedom, 8, 68, 70, 106-107, 122, 190, 216-218, 245 n. 16, 253 n. 11; and historical change, 54-56, 58-59, 68-70, 166-171, 172, 189, 197, 219; and historical understanding, 62, 64, 66-67, 114, 116, 118, 170, 173, 214, 216, 217-218; and idealism, modern, 56, 101; and irrationalism, 57-61 *passim*, 64, 66, 95-96, 106, 118, 170, 172-173, 176, 186, 188, 218-219, 236 n. 40; and nature, 8, 56-57, 64, 95, 97, 215; and perfectibility, 55, 58, 62-64, 66, 70, 168-169, 192, 214-216; phenomonology of (logic of), 41, 104, 118, 172, 236 n. 40, 264 n. 45; and religion, 166-172, 197-198, 215-216, 262 n. 21; and *Seelenkräfte* (faculties of soul), 62-64, 66-68, 120-121, 161-163, 237 n. 56 and 62, 242 n. 50, 261 n. 8; as will, 55-59, 60, 95-96, 106-107, 110-111, 161-163, 172, 218, 243 n. 50, 253 n. 11
Spirit of the times: as causal category, 56, 107, 162, 180; definition of, 161; and genius, 62, 168; and religion, 163, 168, 263 n. 29
Spittler, Ludwig Timothy, 154, 159, 173-174, 175-176, 177-179, 181, 183, 252 n. 5, 266 n. 86; *Entwurf der Geschichte der europäischen Staaten*, 159; *Geschichte der Hierarchie von Gregor VII bis auf die Zeiten der Reformation*, 177
Srbik, Heinrich Ritter von, 183, 266 n. 84
Ständestaat: definition of, 207, 221 n. 6; and historical change, 54-55, 72-73, 104, 105; and political outlook of Aufklärers, 146, 154, 216; support of, 4, 7, 50, 121, 133, 141
State: and church, 19, 28, 174, 267 n. 98; as a conjunction, 103-104; creation of, 75, 92-93, 99; and *Innenpolitik*, 146, 151-152; interests of, 16-17, 19, 21, 149, 151-152, 153, 155; as a machine, 102-103, 149; as a moral body, 106, 132-133, 134, 146,

245 n. 15, 253 n. 12 and 13 and 14; and statistics, 40, 152-153; in universal history, 11, 19, 75. *See also* Comparative analysis; Constitution, state's; Metaphors: of growth
Statistics, 40, 46, 152-154
Stein, Baron vom, 73, 268 n. 108
Strasbourg, University of, 8
Strauss, Leo, 13, 90
Stubbs, Bishop, 244 n. 4
Sturm und Drang, 2, 178, 200, 221 n. 3
Sulzer, Johann Georg: background, of, 33, 63, 226 n. 7, 248 n. 59; and Bodmer, 63, 64, 200, 209; on faculties of soul, 63-64, 67, 237 n. 56; on nature, 33, 227 n. 10; and Wegelin, 119, 248 n. 62 and 66; mentioned, 66, 98, 116, 238 n. 65; *Moralische Betrachtungen über die Werke der Natur*, 33
Süßmilch, Johann, 79
Swiss, Aufklärung and, 8, 119, 238 n. 65, 248 n. 59
Swiss Formula of Consensus of 1675, 82, 87
Switzerland, 68, 143-144, 200-201
Synchronic approaches, 38-40, 199, 229 n. 31, 229-230 n. 32

Tacitus, 115
Tanucci, Bernado, Marchese, 71, 141
Tetens, Johann, 64
Theresianum, 159
Thirty Years War, 14, 50, 55, 122
Theology. *See* Religion
Thomasius, Christian, 7, 23, 32, 57, 96, 105, 108, 222 n. 9, 246 n. 26
Thucydides, 100, 115
Tocqueville, Alexis de, 161
Trade. *See* Commerce
Tradition: as causal category, 56, 58, 62, 136, 161; and law, 71, 72, 94, 187, 239 n. 82, 267 n. 102; in primitive societies, 195, 196, 202; as social force, 121, 123, 162, 163, 167, 217
Translation theory. *See* Constitutional history, German
Troeltsch, Ernst, 6
Turgot, Anne Robert Jacques, 70-71, 141

Universal history: critiques of, 10-11, 29, 81; redefinition of, 40, 78, 230-231 n. 39; and Schlözer, 46, 47, 85-86, 232-233 n. 59; traditional forms of, 9-11, 19, 75
Universities, in eighteenth century: Catholic, 6, 222 n. 8; as center of Aufklärung, 5-6, 7, 46, 47, 73, 146, 266

n. 86; cirriculum of, 43, 108-109; in
Enlightenment, 221-222 n. 8; independence of, 4, 141, 146, 255 n. 46,
266 n. 86; reform of, 32, 105, 108,
222 n. 4, 246 n. 26
Universities, medieval, 72, 173, 183, 185
Usher, James, 81, 87
Utopian thought, 48-54 *passim*, 234 n.
12

Venel, Gabriel François, 97
Venturi, Franco, 138, 146, 274 n. 1
Vertot, Rene, Abbé, 129
Vico, Giambattista, 45, 108, 197, 203,
204, 207, 232 n. 57, 271-272 n. 39
Virgil, 205, 207
Vogelweide, Walther von der, 208
Voltaire, François Marie Arouet de: Auf-
klärung's relation to, 7, 31, 81, 161;
and historical writing, 37, 130; on
Holy Roman Empire, 145, 181, 182;
and Schlözer, 37, 84, 241 n. 21;
mentioned, 87, 100, 174, 226 n. 4,
253-254 n. 15; *Dialogue entre un
Brachmane et un Jésuite*, 130; *Essay
on Manners*, 37

Wach, Joachim, 106, 111, 248 n. 66
Wegelin, Jakob: causal explanation of,
120-121, 122-126, 176, 188; and
colorit metaphor, 121, 122, 249 n.
71; on commerce, 124, 158, 159,
250 n. 77; on dead and living forces,
121, 123-124, 217; on genius,
124-125, 250 n. 79, 250-251 n. 81,
251 n. 83; on human nature,
120-121, 249 n. 67; influences on,
118-119, 200, 238 n. 65, 248 n. 62
and 66, 249 n. 71; on national
character, 121, 122-123, 124, 249 n.
69; on *Policierung* 122, 249 n. 73;
and religion, 248 n. 60; on Roman
law in Germany, 124, 250 n. 78; on

scholasticism, 125, 251 n. 82; on
social classes, 122-123, 249 n. 74; on
society man, 123-124, 141, 249-250
n. 75, 250 n. 76; on universal laws in
history, 119-120, 126, 248 n. 65; on
value judgments, 251 n. 86 and 87;
Dialogues par un ministre Suisse, 248
n. 60; *Religiose Gespräche der Toten*,
248 n. 60
Wehrli, Max, 209
Wellek, René, 271 n. 39
Westphalia, Treaty of, 14, 50, 216
White, Haydenv, 274 n. 2
Wieland, Christoph, 200, 255 n. 36
Will. *See* Spirit
Winckelmann, Johann Joachim, 35, 116,
143, 151, 172, 213, 247 n. 46 and
48, 273 n. 63
Wittenberg, University of, 109
Wolf, Friedrich August, 166
Wolff, Christian: and aesthetics, 59-60,
65, 70, 246 n. 20; and German
language, 32-33; and Halle University, 111, 222 n. 9; and history,
definition of, 13, 114, 115, 119, 245
n. 15; and Leibniz, 32-33, 34, 60,
226 n. 5; mathematical ideal of, 7,
33, 55, 56-57, 61, 95, 113-114, 226
n. 8; and monad theory, 60, 115; and
natural law, 57, 91, 95-96, 97; as
neo-scholastic, 7, 33, 35, 57, 95, 125,
143, 151, 166, 172, 235 n. 31;
mentioned, 30, 105, 240 n. 2;
*Anfangs-Grunden aller mathe-
matischen Wissenschaften*, 33; *German Logic*, 32-33; *German Metaphysics*, 32-33; *Latin Logic*, 33; *Latin
Metaphysics*, 33
Wöllner Edict of 1788, 171
Women's rights, 68, 148, 238 n. 71
Wood, Robert, 269 n. 6, 271-272 n. 39;
*Essay on the Original Genius of
Homer*, 269 n. 6
Wundt, Max, 1